NEW CENTURY BIBLE COMMENTARY

General Editors

RONALD E. CLEMENTS
(Old Testament)

MATTHEW BLACK
(New Testament)

The Gospel of MARK

D0803035

THE NEW CENTURY BIBLE COMMENTARIES

EXODUS (J. P. Hyatt)
LEVITICUS AND NUMBERS (N. H. Snaith)*
DEUTERONOMY (A. D. H. Mayes)
JOSHUA, JUDGES, AND RUTH (John Gray)*
EZRA, NEHEMIAH, AND ESTHER (L. H. Brockington)*
JOB (H. H. Rowley)
PSALMS Volumes 1 and 2 (A. A. Anderson)
ISAIAH 1-39 (R. E. Clements)
ISAIAH 40-66 (R. N. Whybray)
EZEKIEL (John W. Wevers)*
THE GOSPEL OF MATTHEW (David Hill)
THE GOSPEL OF MARK (Hugh Anderson)
THE GOSPEL OF LUKE (E. Earle Ellis)
THE GOSPEL OF JOHN (Barnabas Lindars)
THE ACTS OF THE APOSTLES (William Neil)*
ROMANS (Matthew Black)*
1 and 2 CORINTHIANS (F. F. Bruce)
GALATIANS (Donald Guthrie)*
EPHESIANS (C. Leslie Mitton)*
PHILIPPIANS (Ralph P. Martin)
COLOSSIANS AND PHILEMON (Ralph P. Martin)*
1 PETER (Ernest Best)*
THE BOOK OF REVELATION (G. R. Beasley-Murray)

*Not yet available in paperback
 Other titles are in preparation

NEW CENTURY BIBLE COMMENTARY

Based on the Revised Standard Version

The Gospel
of
MARK

HUGH ANDERSON

WM. B. EERDMANS PUBL. CO., GRAND RAPIDS

MARSHALL, MORGAN & SCOTT PUBL. LTD., LONDON

Copyright © Marshall, Morgan & Scott 1976
First published 1976 by Marshall, Morgan & Scott, England
Softback edition published 1981

Wm. B. Eerdmans Publishing Company
255 Jefferson Ave. S.E., Grand Rapids, Mich. 49503
and
Marshall, Morgan & Scott
A Pentos company
1 Bath Street, London ECIV 9LB
ISBN 0 551 00900 4

¡ *Reprinted, November 1987*

Library of Congress Cataloging in Publication Data
Anderson, Hugh, 1920-
The Gospel of Mark.

(New century Bible commentaries)
Originally published: London, Oliphants, 1976.
Bibliography: p. xii
Includes Indexes.
1. Bible. N.T. Mark — Commentaries. I. Bible. N.T. Mark.
English. Revised Standard. 1981. II. Title. III. Series.
BS2585.3.A52 1981 226'.3 81-5106
ISBN 0-8028-1887-0 AACR2

DEDICATION

To the memory of
our son, GORDON TORBIT,
who died very suddenly
on the eve of his twenty-first birthday, 19/12/68.
In Faith and Hope

CONTENTS

PREFACE

The literature on Mark is very extensive, not only in the form of commentaries dealing with the Gospel as a whole or of books and articles dealing with many varied features of it, but also of more general works devoted to christology or the Jesus of history or the Gospels at large. Far from abating, the production of essays on Mark has in the last several years actually increased, scholarly research having lately been given fresh impetus with the shift of interest from the question of the historical reliability of Mark, as providing materials for reconstruction of the earthly ministry and message of Jesus, to the question of the theological aim, intention, and proclamation of the Evangelist in his total witness to Jesus Christ.

In this situation the task facing the commentator is an intimidating one. Unable to acquaint himself with *all* the literature on the Gospel, he is haunted by the thought that he may have missed something of importance affecting smaller or larger details of interpretation. On the other hand, where so many have contributed in so many ways to a fuller understanding of his subject, he has the uneasy feeling that he may unwittingly have passed on, as his own, suggestions that came to him initially from his reading of others, and may therefore have made quite inadequate recognition of his indebtedness.

Among standard commentaries on Mark, those of V. Taylor and C. E. B. Cranfield are indispensable storehouses of information on different facets of the Gospel. As contributions to a specifically religious understanding of Mark's Gospel in its entirety, the works of A. E. J. Rawlinson and more recently D. E. Nineham and E. Schweizer provide invaluable insights into the Evangelist's theological purpose, and the reader familiar with them will readily discern their influence on the following pages.

I am pleased to record my gratitude to the Editor of this series, Principal Matthew Black, for his unfailing kindness and courtesy, to my colleague at New College, Edinburgh, Dr Ian Moir, for his ready help with proof-reading, and to my secretary, Mrs Linda Stupart, for her generous assistance in typing the manuscript.

Finally, I pay tribute to my wife for her continual support and encouragement during the preparation of this commentary.

H. A.

ABBREVIATIONS

BIBLICAL

OLD TESTAMENT (*OT*)

Gen.	Jg.	1 Chr.	Ps.	Lam.	Ob.	Hag.
Exod.	Ru.	2 Chr.	Prov.	Ezek.	Jon.	Zech.
Lev.	1 Sam.	Ezr.	Ec.	Dan.	Mic.	Mal.
Num.	2 Sam.	Neh.	Ca.	Hos.	Nah.	
Dt.	1 Kg.	Est.	Isa.	Jl	Hab.	
Jos.	2 Kg.	Job	Jer.	Am.	Zeph.	

APOCRYPHA (*Apoc.*)

1 Esd.	Tob.	Ad. Est.	Sir.	S 3 Ch.	Bel	1 Mac.
2 Esd.	Jdt.	Wis.	Bar.	Sus.	Man.	2 Mac.

NEW TESTAMENT (*NT*)

Mt.	Ac.	Gal.	1 Th.	Tit.	1 Pet.	3 Jn
Mk	Rom.	Eph.	2 Th.	Phm.	2 Pet.	Jude
Lk.	1 C.	Phil.	1 Tim.	Heb.	1 Jn	Rev.
Jn	2 C.	Col.	2 Tim.	Jas	2 Jn	

DEAD SEA SCROLLS (DSS)

1QpHab (formerly DSH)	Habakkuk Commentary
1QS	Rule of the Community (Manual of Discipline)
1QM	War of the Sons of Light against the Sons of Darkness
1QH	Hymns of Thanksgiving
CD	Fragments of a Zadokite Work (Damascus Document)

PSEUDEPIGRAPHA

2 Bar.	*2 Baruch or Syriac Apocalypse of Baruch*
1 En.	*1 Enoch*
Jub.	*Jubilees*
Ps. Sol.	*Psalms of Solomon*

Sib. Or.	*Sibylline Oracles*
Test.	*Testaments of the Twelve Patriarchs*
Test. Dan	*Testament of Dan*
Test. Issach.	*Testament of Issachar*

JEWISH WRITINGS
Mishnah Tractates

Ab.	*Aboth*	*Qid.*	*Qiddushim*
Ket.	*Ketuboth*	*San.*	*Sanhedrin*
Ned.	*Nedarim*		

OTHER ABBREVIATIONS

B.	Babylonian Talmud
Did.	*Didache*
LXX	Septuagint
M.	Mishnah

SELECT BIBLIOGRAPHY

Abrahams   I. Abrahams, *Studies in Pharisaism and the Gospels*, 2 vols., Cambridge, 1917.

AJT   *American Journal of Theology*

Anderson   H. Anderson, *Jesus and Christian Origins: A Commentary on Modern Viewpoints*, New York, 1964.

Anderson, *UOTN*   H. Anderson, 'The Old Testament in Mark's Gospel', in *The Use of the Old Testament in the New and Other Essays*, edited by J. M. Efird, Duke University, 1972.

Bacon   B. W. Bacon, *The Gospel of Mark*, London/New Haven, 1925.

Bacon, *BGS*   B. W. Bacon, *The Beginnings of Gospel Story*, New Haven, 1909; third printing 1925.

Bacon, *MRG*   B. W. Bacon, *Is Mark a Roman Gospel?* Cambridge, Mass., 1919.

Barrett, *JGT*   C. K. Barrett, *Jesus and the Gospel Tradition*, London, 1967.

Barrett, *HSGT*   C. K. Barrett, *The Holy Spirit and the Gospel Tradition*, London, 1947.

Bartlet   J. V. Bartlet, *St. Mark*, Edinburgh, 1922.

BBH   G. Bornkamm, G. Barth, and H. J. Held, *Tradition and Interpretation in Matthew's Gospel*, translated by P. Scott, London, 1963.

Beasley-Murray, *JF*   G. R. Beasley-Murray, *Jesus and the Future*, London, 1956.

Best   E. Best, *The Temptation and the Passion*, Cambridge, 1965.

Betz   H. D. Betz, *Jesus and the Historian*, Philadelphia, 1970.

BJRL   *Bulletin of the John Rylands Library*

Black, *ARA*   M. Black, *An Aramaic Approach to the Gospels and Acts*, 3rd edition, Oxford, 1967.

Bornkamm   G. Bornkamm, *Jesus of Nazareth*, translated by I. and F. McLuskey, with J. M. Robinson, London, 1960.

Bowker   J. Bowker, *Jesus and the Pharisees*, Cambridge, 1973.

Bowman   J. Bowman, *The Gospel of Mark: A Jewish Christian Passover Haggadah*, Leiden, 1965.

BR   *Biblical Research*

Brandon   S. G. F. Brandon, *Jesus and the Zealots*, Manchester, 1967.

Bultmann, *HST*   R. Bultmann, *The History of the Synoptic Tradition*, translated by J. Marsh, Oxford, 1963.

Burkill   T. A. Burkill, *Mysterious Revelation: An Examination of the Philosophy of St. Mark's Gospel*, Ithaca, New York, 1963.

Butler   B. C. Butler, *The Originality of St. Matthew: A Critique of the Two-Document Hypothesis*, London, 1951.

Carmichael   J. Carmichael, *The Death of Jesus*, London, 1963.

Carrington   P. Carrington, *The Primitive Christian Calendar*, Cambridge, 1940.

CFH   *Christ, Faith and History*, edited by S. W. Sykes and J. P. Clayton, Cambridge, 1972.

Cranfield   C. E. B. Cranfield, *The Gospel According to St. Mark*, Cambridge, 1959.

Crum   J. M. C. Crum, *St. Mark's Gospel. Two Stages of its Making*, Cambridge, 1936.

Davies, *COJ*   W. D. Davies, *Christian Origins and Judaism*, London, 1962.

Davies, *SSM*   W. D. Davies, *The Setting of the Sermon on the Mount*, Cambridge, 1964.

Derrett   J. D. M. Derrett, *Law in the New Testament*, London, 1970.

Dibelius   M. Dibelius, *From Tradition to Gospel*, translated by B. L. Woolf, London, 1936.

Dodd, *PK*   C. H. Dodd, *The Parables of the Kingdom*, London, 1936.

Downing   F. G. Downing, *The Church and Jesus*, London, 1968.

Ellis   E. E. Ellis, *The Gospel of Luke*, London, 1966.

Ellis and Wilcox, *NS*   E. E. Ellis and M. Wilcox (eds), *Neotestamentica et Semitica: Studies in Honour of Principal Matthew Black*, Edinburgh, 1969.

Eusebius, *HE*   Eusebius, *Historia Ecclesiae*

EvTh   *Evangelische Theologie*

ExpT   *Expository Times*

Farmer   W. R. Farmer, *The Synoptic Problem*, New York/London, 1964.

Farrer   A. Farrer, *A Study in St. Mark*, Westminster, 1951.

Fawcett   T. Fawcett, *Hebrew Myth and Christian Gospel*, London, 1973.

FBK   P. Feine, J. Behm, and W. G. Kümmel, *Introduction to the New Testament*, translated by A. J. Mattill, London, 1966.

FGD   *Festschrift für Günter Dehn*, edited by W. Schneemelcher, Neukirchen, 1975.

Fiebig   P. Fiebig, *Die Gleichnisreden Jesu im Lichte der Rabbinischen Gleichnisse des Neutestamentlichen Zeitalters*, Tübingen, 1912.

Fitzmyer   J. A. Fitzmyer, *Essays on the Semitic Background of the New Testament*, London, 1971.

Fuller   R. H. Fuller, *A Critical Introduction to the New Testament*, London, 1966.

Georgi   D. Georgi, *Die Gegner des Paulus im 2. Korintherbrief*, Neukirchen, 1964.

Gerhardsson   B. Gerhardsson, *Memory and Manuscript. Oral Tradition and Written Transmission in Rabbinic Judaism and Early Christianity*, Uppsala, 1961.

Goguel   M. Goguel, *Jesus and the Origins of Christianity.* Vol. II: *The Life of Jesus*, translated by O. Wyon, New York/London, 1960.

Grant   F. C. Grant, *The Gospels: Their Origin and Their Growth*, New York, 1957.

Grässer   E. Grässer, *Das Problem der Parousieverzögerung in den synoptischen Evangelien*, Berlin, 1960.

Haenchen   E. Haenchen, *Der Weg Jesu*, Berlin, 1966.

Hahn   F. Hahn, *Christologische Hoheitstitel*, Göttingen, 1963.

Harvey   V. A. Harvey, *The Historian and the Believer*, New York, 1966.

Higgins, *LSNT*   A. J. B. Higgins, *The Lord's Supper in the New Testament*, London, 1952.

Hill   D. Hill, *The Gospel of Matthew*, London, 1972.

Hooker, *JS*   M. D. Hooker, *Jesus and the Servant*, London, 1959.

Hooker, *SMM*   M. D. Hooker, *The Son of Man in Mark*, London, 1967.

HTR   *Harvard Theological Review*

Jaubert   A. Jaubert, *The Date of the Last Supper*, translated by I. Rafferty, New York, 1965.

JBL   *Journal of Biblical Literature*

JBR   *Journal of Bible and Religion*

Jeremias   J. Jeremias, *The Parables of Jesus*, translated by S. H. Hooke, 2nd edition, London, 1963.

Jeremias, *JPN*   J. Jeremias, *Jesus' Promise to the Nations*, translated by S. H. Hooke, London, 1958.

Jeremias, *EW*   J. Jeremias, *The Eucharistic Words of Jesus*, translated by A. Ehrhardt, 2nd edition, London, 1966.

Jeremias and   J. Jeremias and W. Zimmerli, *The Servant of God*,
  Zimmerli, *SG*   London, 1957, 2nd edition, London, 1965.

JMH   *Jesus and Man's Hope*, Pittsburgh (Perspective Book II), 1971.

Johnson   S. E. Johnson, *The Gospel according to St. Mark*, London, 1960.

Josephus, *Ant.*	Flavius Josephus, *Antiquities*.
JTS	*Journal of Theological Studies*
Jülicher	A. Jülicher, *Die Gleichnisreden Jesu*, 2 vols., 1st edition 1888; reprinted in one volume, Darmstadt, 1963.
Kähler	M. Kähler, *The So-called Historical Jesus and the Historic Biblical Christ*, translated by C. E. Braaten, Philadelphia, 1964.
Käsemann	E. Käsemann, *Essays on New Testament Themes*, translated by W. J. Montague, London, 1964.
Käsemann, *NTQ*	E. Käsemann, *New Testament Questions of Today*, translated by W. J. Montague, London, 1969.
Keck	L. E. Keck, *A Future for the Historical Jesus*, Nashville, 1971.
Kertelege	K. Kertelege, *Die Wunder Jesu im Markusevangelium*, Munich, 1970.
KJV	*King James Version*
Klostermann	E. Klostermann, *Das Markusevangelium*, 2nd edition, Tübingen, 1926.
Lightfoot	R. H. Lightfoot, *Locality and Doctrine in the Gospels*, London, 1938.
Lightfoot, *HIG*	R. H. Lightfoot, *History and Interpretation in the Gospels*, London, 1935.
Lightfoot, *GMM*	R. H. Lightfoot, *The Gospel Message of St. Mark*, Oxford, 1950.
Lindars	B. Lindars, *New Testament Apologetic*, London, 1961.
Lohmeyer	E. Lohmeyer, *Das Evangelium des Markus*, Göttingen, 1937.
Lohmeyer, *GJ*	E. Lohmeyer, *Galiläa und Jerusalem*, Göttingen, 1936.
Lohse	E. Lohse, *Mark's Witness to Jesus Christ*, London, 1955.
Loisy	A. Loisy, *L'Evangile selon Marc*, Paris, 1912.
Manson, *TSM*	T. W. Manson, *The Servant Messiah*, Cambridge, 1953.
Manson, *Sayings*	T. W. Manson, *The Sayings of Jesus*, London, 1949.
Manson	W. Manson, *Jesus the Messiah*, London, 1943.
Martin	R. P. Martin, *Mark: Evangelist and Theologian*, Exeter, 1972.
Marxsen	W. Marxsen, *Introduction to the New Testament*, translated by G. Buswell, Oxford, 1968.
Marxsen, *ME*	W. Marxsen, *Mark the Evangelist*, translated by R. A. Harrisville, Nashville/New York, 1969.
Mauser	U. Mauser, *Christ in the Wilderness*, London, 1963.
Meyer	E. Meyer, *Ursprung und Anfange des Christentums I*, Berlin, 1921.

Minette de Tillesse	G. Minette de Tillesse, *Le secret messianique dans l'évangile de Marc*, Paris, 1968.
Montefiore	C. G. Montefiore, *The Synoptic Gospels*, 2 vols., London, 1927.
Nineham	D. E. Nineham, *St. Mark*, London, 1963.
Nineham, *SG*	D. E. Nineham, editor, *Studies in the Gospels*, Oxford, 1957.
Nock	A. D. Nock, *Early Gentile Christianity and its Hellenistic Background*, New York, 1964.
NovT	*Novum Testamentum*
NT Apocrypha	E. Hennecke, *New Testament Apocrypha*, 2 vols., English translation edited by R. M. Wilson, London, 1963–5.
NTS	*New Testament Studies*
Parker	P. Parker, *The Gospel before Mark*, Chicago, 1953.
Perowne	S. Perowne, *The Later Herods*, London, 1958.
Perrin	N. Perrin, *Rediscovering the Teaching of Jesus*, London, 1967.
Philo, *De Spec. Leg.*	Philo, *De Specialibus Legibus*.
Rawlinson	A. E. J. Rawlinson, *The Gospel According to St. Mark*, 2nd edition, London, 1927.
RB	*Revue Biblique*
RHR	*Revue de l'histoire des religions*
Riesenfeld	H. Riesenfeld, *The Gospel Tradition and its Beginnings: A Study in the Limits of 'Formgeschichte'*, London, 1957.
Robinson, *PHM*	J. M. Robinson, *The Problem of History in Mark*, London, 1957.
Rohde	J. Rohde, *Rediscovering the Teaching of the Evangelists*, translated by D. M. Barton, London, 1968.
RSV	*Revised Standard Version*
Sanders	E. P. Sanders, *The Tendencies of the Synoptic Tradition*, Cambridge, 1969.
SB	H. L. Strack and P. Billerbeck, *Kommentar zum Neuen Testament aus Talmud und Midrasch*, 6 vols., Munich, 1922–8.
Schmidt	K. L. Schmidt, *Die Rahmen der Geschichte Jesu*, Berlin, 1919.
Schmithals	W. Schmithals, *The Office of Apostle in the Early Church*, translated by J. E. Steely, Nashville/New York, 1969.
Schniewind	J. Schniewind, *Das Evangelium nach Markus*, 4th edition, Göttingen, 1947.

Schweitzer, *MKG*   A. Schweitzer, *The Mystery of the Kingdom of God*, translated by W. Lowrie, London, 1925.

Schweitzer, *QHJ*   A. Schweitzer, *The Quest of the Historical Jesus*, translated by W. Montgomery, London, 1911.

Schweizer   E. Schweizer, *Jesus*, translated by D. E. Green, London, 1971.

Schweizer, *GNM*   E. Schweizer, *The Good News According to Mark*, translated by D. H. Madvig, London, 1971.

SG   *Studies in the Gospels*, edited by D. E. Nineham, Oxford, 1957.

Sherwin-White   A. N. Sherwin-White, *Roman Society and Roman Law in the New Testament*, Oxford, 1963.

SJT   *Scottish Journal of Theology*

Stendahl   K. Stendahl, *The School of St. Matthew and its Use of the Old Testament*, Uppsala, 1954. American edition, Philadelphia, 1968.

Streeter   B. H. Streeter, *The Four Gospels*, London, 1926.

Suhl   A. Suhl, *Die Funktion der alttestamentlichen Zitate und Anspielungen im Markusevangelium*, Guterslöh, 1965.

Taylor   V. Taylor, *The Gospel According to St. Mark*, London, 1953.

Tiede   D. L. Tiede, *The Charismatic Figure as Miracle Worker*, Society of Biblical Literature Dissertation Series 1, Missoula–Montana, 1972.

Tödt   H. E. Tödt, *The Son of Man in the Synoptic Tradition*, translated by D. M. Barton, London, 1965.

Trocmé   E. Trocmé, *La Formation de l'Evangile selon Marc*, Paris, 1963.

Trocmé, *JC*   E. Trocmé, *Jesus and His Contemporaries*, translated by R. A. Wilson, London, 1973.

Turner   C. H. Turner, *The Gospel according to St. Mark*, London, 1928.

Turner, *SNT*   C. H. Turner, *The Study of the New Testament, 1883 and 1920*, Oxford, 1920.

USQR   *Union Seminary Quarterly Review*

Vaganay   L. Vaganay, *Le Problème Synoptique*, Paris, 1954.

Vermes   G. Vermes, *Scripture and Tradition in Judaism*, Leiden, 1961.

Weeden   T. J. Weeden, *Traditions in Conflict*, Philadelphia, 1971.

Werner   M. Werner, *Der Einfluss Paulinischer Theologie im Markusevangelium*, Giessen, 1923.

Winter   P. Winter, *On the Trial of Jesus*, Berlin, 1961.

Wrede   W. Wrede, *Das Messiasgeheimnis in den Evangelien*,

Göttingen, 1901, 2nd edition 1913, reprinted 1962.
English translation by J. C. G. Greig, *The Messianic Secret*, Cambridge, 1971.

Zeitlin S. Zeitlin, *Who Crucified Jesus?* New York/London, 1942.

ZNW *Zeitschrift für die neutestamentliche Wissenschaft*
ZThK *Zeitschrift für Theologie und Kirche*

INTRODUCTION

to

The Gospel of Mark

INTRODUCTION

1. CHANGING ATTITUDES TO THE GOSPEL

For the better part of two centuries now the Gospels have been subjected to searching critical scrutiny. Before this period, interest in the Gospels, as in the *NT* literature generally, was largely pre-scientific, devotional, and doctrinal. But the Church was not, at least according to her lights, greatly disadvantaged, and the Gospels contributed handsomely to the edifying of piety.

We may not therefore claim that such illumination on the origin and character of the Gospels as has come to us from continual research necessarily renders us more devoted and faithful disciples than our ancestors. What I think we can justly claim is that for us there is no turning back to the posture of a pre-critical age. If the contemporary biblical fundamentalist were to respond to the question of Mark's status by saying quite simply that the Gospel is 'holy Scripture' since it belongs to the *NT* canon, we could scarcely leave the matter there. The present-day reader of the Gospels can hardly escape from thinking historically or scientifically, not at any rate if he would avoid the charge of being terribly out of tune with his own time and place. In any case it certainly does not follow that Christian nurture and critical, scientific study of the Gospels cannot walk together as friends. Apposite here, as in other contexts, is F. R. Barry's challenging observation that what we need today are believers who dare to enquire and enquirers who dare to believe.

The word 'enquirer' is especially appropriate to the Gospels and Gospel-study. In its nearly two hundred years Gospel-research has instigated far more enquiries than it has been able definitively to answer. Whereas anyone familiar with the story of Gospel-criticism would by no means wish it to be deemed a story of failure, it remains true even at the present time that nearly all major issues remain open-ended and unresolved. Only on one or two relatively fixed points affecting Mark's Gospel particularly is there anything like widespread scholarly agreement. First, Mark's Gospel, it is generally held, is the earliest of the four in the *NT*. Second, although it may be very disappointing to all who recognise that the endless significance and attraction of the Gospels lies in what may be gleaned from them about the person of Jesus, the earliest Gospel is no longer thought to be in any normal sense of the words a biography, life, or history of Jesus. We have now to consider the circumstances leading up to and surrounding the contemporary consensus of opinion on these matters.

The Gospels do not of course, like modern books, carry publication dates. Nor does any of them so clearly refer to any known historical landmark as to be readily datable from it. The case for the priority of Mark depends in fact on a particular reading or understanding of the obvious interrelationships of the Gospels of Matthew, Mark, and Luke. That they are interrelated was clear even to the early Church. Latterly they have come to be known as the Synoptic Gospels. When placed in parallel columns and looked at alongside each other they reveal a common or synoptic view or perspective. And the Synoptic Problem, as it is called, is quite simply the problem of how their striking resemblances as well as their differences in literary form and content are to be explained.

As a proposed solution to the Synoptic Problem the Two-Document Hypothesis has largely held the field for some fifty years now. Behind the Two-Document theory lies the insight that where Matthew and Luke, in their arrangement of materials, follow the same sequence of narratives, they appear to be following the order given in Mark. Not only so, they each reproduce over 50 per cent of Mark's actual words (e.g. compare Mk 8:34b–37 with Mt. 16: 24b–26 and Lk. 9:23b–25). The most plausible explanation is that Matthew and Luke were already familiar with Mark. Also, so the theory runs, together with Mark as a source, Matthew and Luke employed a document containing mainly sayings of Jesus—known in modern Gospel study as Q (from the German *Quelle* = source). No such document has indeed survived to us. Its existence is inferred from the fact that there are about 200 verses common to Matthew and Luke, but not in Mark, in which there is a sufficiently close verbal similarity to suggest a single written collection.

Can we then forthwith simply take our stand on this now 'classical' solution to the Synoptic Problem? The answer must be that we cannot, not at any rate without taking notice of the fact that the theory is in no wise allowed to go unchallenged today. In fact a few scholars have been appealing for a reopening of the whole subject (e.g. Farmer, p. vii; Sanders, pp. 276ff.). The supposed sayings source in particular has lately been the target of some very sharp criticism (see e.g. Farrer, *SG*, pp. 55–88; Farmer, p. 209). The criticism is in part at least well grounded. While we must almost certainly assume that Matthew and Luke had access to common materials beyond Mark, the contours of the hypothetical Q document are so indistinct, and so extremely difficult has it proven to set objective limits to its scope and extent (see C. E. Carlston and D. Norlin, *HTR* 64:1 (1971), pp. 59ff.), that a more fluid picture of Q would seem to be desirable and would leave room for the fact that in the approximately 200 verses of non-Marcan tradition where Matthew and Luke overlap there are, as well as numerous cases of exact or partial verbal correspondence, some cases of only very slight verbal correspondence (e.g. Mt. 18:15, 21f. = Lk. 17:3f.). Whether or not the varied phenomena of correspondence are held to rest on the fact that Matthew and Luke had recourse to a common *oral* tradition (Jeremias, *ZNW* 29 (1930), pp. 147ff.; FBK, p. 60; Fuller, p. 72; Ellis, pp. 23f.), the view has been gaining ground that a more 'plastic' conception of Q is in order.

Of more immediate concern to us, however, is recent opposition to the priority of Mark (see e.g. Butler, Vaganay, Farmer). The notion that Matthew's Gospel was the earliest and that Mark subsequently copied from it and abridged it goes back in ancient Church tradition as far as Augustine. But modern defences of the priority of Matthew are based not on dogmatic acceptance of Church tradition, but rather on critical grounds. An assault has been made, for instance, on the long-standing argument from order (namely, that Mark must constitute common ground for Matthew and Luke) because, in regard to sequence of narratives, Mark is never the odd man out against them both, but rather they diverge in sequence from each other only where they each diverge from Mark. The argument, it is claimed, is fallacious and does not logically prove the Marcan priority it is supposed to prove—we might equally well explain the difference in order between Mark and either of the other Synoptic Gospels if we took it that he decided to follow the order of one rather than the other when they depart in sequence from each other (Farmer, pp. 63ff.; also *BR* 6 (1961), pp. 18–42). It may be that a few dents have been made in the armour of the 'classical' case for the priority of Mark. But without entering into detail on this complex issue, and looking at it broadly, we can say that just to try to imagine what Mark's procedure must have been like if he copied from Matthew tells heavily against the possibility that he actually did so. We should then have to picture Mark not merely omitting but in fact taking pains to cut out cleanly just those most significant materials common to Matthew and Luke that have given rise to the Q hypothesis. We would have to think of Mark excising the Sermon on the Mount, the parables of Mt. 13:24-30, 33, 36-50; 18:23-35; 20: 1-16; 21:28-32; 22:1-14; 24:42-51, the whole of chapter 25 as well as the exhortations to the community in Mt. 18:10-22, disrupting the arrangement of Matthew and cutting off its beginning and end, suppressing almost all the Matthean references to *OT* 'proof-texts' and neglecting such decisive christological texts as Mt. 11:25-30; 14:33; 16:16ff. Even if it be conceded that abridgement or condensation of earlier documents was by no means impossible in the situation of the early Church (witness Tatian's *Diatessaron* as a harmony of all four Gospels), is there not weight in the contention that a Mark based on Matthew or on some earlier form of Matthew would have ended up by being much more like the canonical Matthew than the canonical Mark (Trocmé, p. 8; FBK, p. 45)?

At a time when, as we shall see frequently in the following pages, the predominant interest in Gospel study is in the peculiarities of each Gospel, in the individual outlook and intention of each Evangelist, it is worth noting that supporters of the theory that Mark copied from and abbreviated Matthew have not as yet produced any persuasive exposition of Mark's aim and purpose on the basis of that assumption (J. M. Robinson, *JMH*, p. 102). On the other hand fair progress has been made in explicating the theological standpoint of both Matthew and Luke on the assumption that they used Mark (see especially BBH and Conzelmann).

If, therefore, Mark's Gospel actually *was* the oldest (as still seems most likely), we have to look upon him as a quite outstanding innovator in early Christianity. By telling the 'good news' in story form, and 'good news' is what the word 'gospel' meant for Mark, he had created for the Church a new type of literature. But what was the nature of Mark's achievement? How are we to characterise his version of the good news? Is it an accurate record of past events in the life of Jesus?

In the latter part of the nineteenth century, when the Life-of-Jesus movement among the liberal theologians was in its heyday, Mark's Gospel appeared to serve the interests of the quest of the historical Jesus very well. Coupled with the growing conviction that it was the earliest of the four Gospels was the obvious fact that it was the shortest. Unlike Matthew and Luke it contained no perplexing birth stories and only a very terse and reserved report of the resurrection (see pp. 351ff.). Consequently Mark's Gospel was eagerly embraced as a reliable account of happenings in the life of Jesus. However, early in the present century the old confidence in Mark's historical reliability was very seriously shaken (see Anderson, pp. 3ff.). W. Wrede contended that Mark's record was determined not by historical but by dogmatic or doctrinal considerations belonging to the theology of the early Church. Jesus issues recurrent injunctions to silence, to the demons (Mk 1:25, 34; 3:11f.), after miraculous works (1:44; 5:43; 7:36; 8:26), after Peter's confession (8:30) and during the descent from the Mount of Transfiguration (9:9) (see Taylor, pp. 122ff., Rawlinson, pp. 258ff.). These injunctions to secrecy, the so-called 'Messianic secret', Wrede regarded as a dogmatic literary device on Mark's part to explain why Jesus was not recognised and confessed as Messiah during his life on earth (even his disciples found his 'secret' unintelligible, 9:32), but only after his resurrection. So the vantage-point from which Mark proceeds is the faith of the Church and his account is *theologically* orientated (Wrede, p. 114).

In his monumental critique of the nineteenth-century Lives of Jesus as highly subjective modernisations founded less on the Gospel data than on the several writers' own imaginative filling out of the gaps in the Gospel record, A. Schweitzer demonstrated that none of the Gospels provides materials for a Life of Jesus in any biographical sense (Schweitzer, *QHJ*, pp. 1–12, 328ff.).

Finally, K. L. Schmidt sharpened and sustained the insights of Wrede and Schweitzer, maintaining that all Mark had at his disposal for the writing of his Gospel was isolated fragments, disconnected sayings and stories. These he assembled and around them built his own little opening and closing connecting links and occasionally also inserted brief summary statements of Jesus' activity (e.g. 1:14f.; 2:1f.; 3:6, 7–12; 4:1f.; 6; 7, 12f.; etc.). The Evangelist could thus be likened to a child threading pearls on a string (Schmidt, pp. 6ff.).

Now although the view that Mark presents a fairly straight report of Jesus' life still dies hard, the onus of proof today falls squarely on its supporters, so compelling is the main thrust of the arguments we have just outlined. Wrede, it is true, almost certainly miscalculated in representing Mark as the 'inventor' of the 'messianic secret': the traditions that Mark took up and used in his Gospel were already messianic. Nevertheless the 'secret' is an essential ingredient of Mark's Gospel and its very presence indicates that Mark is no straight story-teller, content to narrate a collection of Jesus' miraculous acts which would have blinded all bystanders with God's revealed glory. That would have been merely spectacular news (see L. E. Keck, *NTS* 12 (1965–6), p. 368). Rather the 'secret' allows Mark to proclaim the good news that God has acted in 'hiddenness' in his Son, whose way is the lowly way of the cross. In short, the Marcan witness *is* impregnated with theological ideas.

The stuff of biography, as Schweitzer showed, is really lacking in the Gospels. Of the birth, infancy, and early years of Jesus, Mark tells us nothing. In fact we are simply left to gauge the duration of the public ministry of Jesus as around a year (just over three years in the Gospel of John). There is no playing of the 'personality game' with Jesus in Mark; nothing is said overtly about his self-consciousness, how he thought about himself; only veiled hints are given. Nor is any estimate made of the part played by Jesus in the history of the Jewish people, of the Roman empire or the wider conflicts of world politics (Bornkamm, pp. 27ff.).

As to the view that Mark pieced many separate items of tradition together with almost no concern for chronological sequence, it should be noted how the 'plot' of the Gospel is kept moving by the frequent insertion of vague linking words like 'immediately', 'again', or simply 'and'. Often no indication whatever is given of the point of time in Jesus' ministry or of the location at which an incident occurred, as with the dispute with the scribes and Pharisees about ritual hand-washing (7:1–23). Again it is difficult to suppose that the events related from Mk 1:21 to 1:34 could have taken place in one day. Rather these verses appear to compress events that took place over several days into what Mark construes as a typical day in Jesus' ministry. The same applies to Mk 3:9 to 5:43. At 3:9 Jesus asks his disciples to have a boat ready for him, and between the request and the eventual appearance of a boat (4:1) there occur healing miracles, the appointment of the Twelve, a visit of Jesus to his home, a dispute with the scribes, and an encounter with his mother and brothers. From the boat Jesus then teaches the people publicly in parables and the disciples privately. In the late afternoon of the same day (4:35) he sets out with his disciples, encountering a storm during the crossing to the far side of the lake of Genessaret, a distance of some five to eight miles. Still beyond that there is room for the cure of the Gadarene demoniac (5:1–20), a journey back to the western shore of the lake, and two further healing miracles. Since in this whole section there is but a solitary denotation of time (4:35) the impression we get is that everything was crammed into one day (Lohse, pp. 27f.). We might surely have expected from a writer with some interest in chronology a more exact time-tabling. It would seem that whatever else Mark had in mind it was not his ambition to set things down with anything like the accuracy of a modern police report.

The arguments presented above for the view that Mark's Gospel is not a chronicle are not the only ones. Others will appear in the next section when we discuss the problem of the Evangelist's sources. Meantime the point to be made is that when once the conception of Mark as a chronicler is abandoned, the question of what his aim or purpose really was is left wide open. It is the intention or theological perspective of the Evangelist understood as an 'author' in his own right that has become the major preoccupation of recent Gospel study. If the sequence of the Gospel is not historical, we have next to ask whether by his selection, ordering, and arrangement of materials into the total framework of his Gospel, the Evangelist is seeking to express his own particular message. This is in fact the line of enquiry pursued by the relatively new method of Gospel research commonly called redaction criticism, because it investigates the Evangelist's editorial activity as the clue to his own theological understanding and purpose. The subject of Mark's aim and purpose will be very much in the forefront of our interest. But first we have to consider the preliminary but related problems of the sources, date, location, and authorship of the Gospel.

2. MARK'S SOURCES

According to the Two-Document Hypothesis, as we saw, Matthew and Luke had behind them as source materials Mark and Q. When, however, we try to penetrate behind Mark into what is sometimes called the 'twilight period' between the death of Jesus and the writing of the earliest Gospel around AD 70 (see pp. 6ff.), we are in very misty terrain indeed with scarcely a landmark to guide us. It is not surprising then that theories about written

sources behind Mark are somewhat bewildering in their complexity and variety. Broadly speaking such theories have fallen
into two categories: either Mark is regarded as an abbreviation
of a longer 'original gospel' or as the end-result of a process of expansion and embellishment of a rudimentary Palestinian 'gospel'.

Eusebius, historian of the early Church, cites a statement of
Papias from the early second century concerning Matthew's Gospel, that Matthew put together the *logia* ('sayings', 'oracles') in
the Hebrew language (Aramaic?) and each person 'translated'
(*hermēneusen*) them as best he could (*HE* III., 39, 15). Some modern
critics have taken Papias' notice to refer to an early form of
Matthew or an Aramaic Proto-Matthew that must have constituted a common base for all three Synoptic Gospels, and have then
propounded different theories of how this 'original gospel' was
employed by each of the Evangelists (see Vaganay; cf. Parker, pp.
141ff.). But the criticisms levelled earlier (see above, p. 4) against
the notion that Mark abbreviated Matthew or an earlier form of
Matthew apply also to such theories. If Mark (and Luke) followed
an Aramaic 'original gospel' that would have comprised five
booklets each consisting of a group of narratives succeeded by a
discourse (Vaganay), why then should Jesus' discourses in Mark
conform so little to a plan like this and why especially should Mark
have nothing equivalent to the first two discourses in Matthew, the
Sermon on the Mount and the missionary discourse? The difficulty is hardly overcome by holding that Mark could quite naturally have suppressed the Sermon on the Mount because his chief
interest lay in narratives (Vaganay, *RB* 58 (1951), pp. 5–46).
Mark *does* stress the teaching activity of Jesus and *does* include
some of its content (e.g. chapter 4). Nor need we suppose that the
obvious break between Mk 3:19 and 3:20 is caused by his ex-
cision of the Sermon; it could just as well have arisen from his inclusion at 3:16–19 of an already existing list of the Twelve
(Trocmé, p. 15, note 38).

From another angle it may be claimed that in any case Papias'
statement scarcely secures the existence of an Aramaic 'original
gospel', so uncertain is what he means by the *logia* and 'in the
Hebrew dialect' and 'each one translated or interpreted (*hermēneusen*) them as best he could'. The Semitic flavour of Mark's
Greek could be due not to an underlying Aramaic document but
to the utilisation by the Septuagint translators and *NT* writers
like Mark of 'a living dialect of Jewish Greek' (N. Turner, *ExpT*

76 (1964–5), p. 45). Or it could be due to a process of 're-Judaising' through which bilingual Gentile Christians, say in centres like Syrian Antioch, introduced Aramaisms into a basically Greek tradition (see Black, *ARA*, p. 17; also M. Smith, *JBR* 24 (1956), pp. 92, 95). Sanders (pp. 209ff.), on the basis of extensive comparative lists, finds some little evidence for the *later* introduction of *Semitisms*). In this connexion it is also worth noting the increasing tendency of late to ask whether in fact the inhabitants of Palestine in Jesus' day may not to some extent have spoken Hebrew and Greek as well as Aramaic (see R. Gundry, *JBL* 83 (1964), pp. 404–8), or whether Jesus himself may not occasionally have taught in Greek as well as in the Galilean Aramaic that was his mother tongue (A. W. Argyle, *ExpT* 67 (1955–6), pp. 92f., 383; cf. M. Black, *NTS* 3 (1956–7), pp. 305f. For a useful summary of the debate in this area, see Sanders, pp. 190ff. See also J. Barr, *BJRL* 53 (1970), pp. 9ff.).

If Mark was not dependent on a longer Aramaic 'original gospel', is it any more likely that there lay behind the canonical Gospel a shorter 'primitive Mark' (*Urmarkus*)? In the light of Luke's omission of Mk 6:45–8:26 and the several agreements in wording between Matthew and Luke together over against Mark, it has often been supposed that Matthew and Luke must have been using not the Mark we know but an earlier form of it. However, there may be hints elsewhere in Luke's Gospel of his acquaintance with the section Mk 6:45–8:26 (H. Schürmann, *NTS* 6 (1959–60), pp. 193ff.), and more importantly we have to make due allowance for the fact that Luke was no slavish copyist but made his sources subservient to his own purposes (Ellis, p. 27). As to the agreements between Matthew and Luke against Mark, some are simply stylistic improvements of Mark that Matthew and Luke may both have hit upon by coincidence, and further we have to leave room for the assimilations that crept into the text of the Gospels in the long course of the copying of manuscripts by scribes (Streeter, pp. 295–321), as well as for the possible influence of oral tradition on Matthew and Luke (FBK, pp. 49f.).

Turning now to the other type of 'primitive Mark' hypothesis that relates to the intrinsic process by which Mark's Gospel was built up, we encounter numerous compilation theories postulating a fairly wide variety of different sources. Among such compilation theories two recurring features stand out and call for brief comment. First, some scholars have been attracted by the idea of a special 'Twelve-source' (Meyer, pp. 121ff.; Johnson, p. 28). Passages relating specifically to the Twelve occur spasmodically in Mark at 3:13–19; 6:7–13; 9:33–7; 10:32; 11:11; 14:1–2, 10–11, 17–25, 43–46. But 'source' is hardly the right word to apply to these somewhat fugitive pieces. Mark, it seems, lacking more precise information and having to hand only one or two fragmentary traditional units like the list in 3:16–19, has constructed these sections himself in a generalising way. The vagueness of 3:13–15, for example, is noteworthy (Taylor, p. 83; see also p. 74 and p. 229).

A second source often thought to lie at the base of Mark is a literary composition consisting of reminiscences of Peter. But there is no notice in early Christian literature of anything bequeathed *in writing* from Peter to Mark, nor is it easy to see what purpose, if any, a mere recital of events written down by Peter would have served for the early Christian movement (Trocmé, pp. 20f.).

The trouble with compilation theories is that their very number and variety show how hard it is to set up objective criteria for determining written sources. The character of the source or sources envisaged is very much at the mercy of the principles of selection adopted by each individual critic. Moreover, no matter how the Gospel is broken up, the several parts still bear a close linguistic affinity with one another. 'The manifest unity of the Markan style constitutes a formidable objection to all forms of the Urmarkus hypothesis' (Taylor, p. 68). Finally, where awkwardness or disjointedness occurs in Mark's narrative, as at 3:13, we are not inevitably faced with the intrusion of a written source. The disjointedness may be due rather to the discrepancy existing between the material the Evangelist has to hand and the framework he has created (Marxsen, pp. 26f., note 6).

If source-hypotheses of this kind have carried but little acceptance, that is not of course to say Mark had nothing whatever before him in writing. The principal threads of the passion narrative, it is commonly agreed, had been woven together considerably before Mark's time. Nothing less than a continuous record of the last days and hours of Jesus' life would have helped the first Christians to overcome the scandal of the cross. Although Mark and the other Evangelists adapted and extended the story each in his own way, the striking agreements in all four Gospels confirm the existence of an original *Grundstock* reporting the passion (Taylor, pp. 524ff.). In addition a few other collections had most likely been formed already before they reached their present position in Mark, like the group of conflict-stories or debates of Jesus with his opponents in Mk 2:1–3:6 or like the sayings of Mk 9:33ff., which would have been gathered around catchwords like 'name', 'fire', 'salt' for catechetical purposes in the early Church. Beyond these few complexes (the view recently advanced that Mark also took over a written cycle of miracle-stories requires much further investigation: see Robinson, *JMH*, p. 103), Mark had to rely upon traditions relating to Jesus that circulated *orally* among the first Christians.

Aside from the Gospels and considerably before the time of their appearance, the letters of the *NT* reveal quite clearly that sayings of Jesus were cited by way of precept in the oral preaching and teaching of the Church. To comfort the Christians at Thessalonica, disconsolate because some of their number had died before the expected final coming of Christ, Paul for instance reports as a 'word of the Lord' concerning the ultimate fate of the departed the gist of a saying or sayings that has no counterpart in the Gospels (1 Th. 4:15–17). Addressing married members of the Christian community at Corinth, Paul is at pains to point out that on the issue of divorce he appeals not to his own personal opinion but to the Lord's pronouncement: 'To the married I give charge, not I but the Lord, that the wife should not separate from her husband —and that the husband should not divorce his wife' (1 C. 7:10–11). The saying has its echo in Mk 10:11–12 and Mt. 5:32). Later in the same context, and on the subject of intermarriage between Christian believers and unbelievers, Paul is equally at pains to say that the decision he gives he has reached by his own judgment, presumably in the absence of a definitive guiding word of Christ on the matter: 'To the rest I say, not the Lord' (1 C. 7:12). Then in 1 C. 11:23–25 Paul passes on his account of the last supper of Jesus with his disciples as something he has received 'from the Lord'. The hotly debated phrase 'from the Lord' possibly points back to the Lord Jesus in his actual history as the source of the tradition, but even more so does it hold up the living Lord in his contemporary commands to the Corinthian congregation regarding its existing eucharistic practice.

While such references to the Lord's sayings and deeds are anything but frequent in Paul's letters, there are enough to show that appeal could be made to them as illustrative material in preaching or as paraenesis, the guidance of Christians in conduct and liturgi-

cal practice. That in these cases 'the Lord' seems to have been
equivalent to the traditions of the apostolic Church handed on as
the voice of the living Christ (O. Cullmann, *SJT* 3 (1950), pp.
180–97) is of vital importance: it suggests that the words of Jesus
were passed on as the words of a living Lord, and were cherished
more for their present power and relevance in the lives of Christ's
disciples than for their value as purely historical reminiscences. In
the early Christian communities, in short, 'old words' of the earthly
Jesus were not separated or differentiated from words that continued to be spoken to them in the Spirit by the living Christ.
Since the Spirit spelt freedom ('Where the Spirit of the Lord is,
there is freedom', 2 C. 3:17), the 'old words' could in fact be
freely brought to life for them in the new pronouncements of the
Spirit within the ongoing activity of the congregations. So without
restraint the Seer is able to put words on the lips of the heavenly
Christ (Rev. 2:1 and 7): 'He who has an ear let him hear what the
Spirit says to the churches' (Schweizer, p. 7).

   The dynamic process by which individual sayings and stories or
Jesus were transmitted, adapted and developed orally before they
were incorporated in written collections has been greatly illumined
for us by the method of Gospel study known as form criticism,
initiated in Germany around 1920 (Bultmann, Dibelius, Schmidt).
Form criticism's primary aim is to sift out and classify the many
different units of tradition according to their own particular *form*.
From investigation of the form of single segments of tradition the
form critics concluded that the particular shape each had taken
went hand in hand with a particular function or need in the life
of the early Christian communities. In other words, community
function or need determined and gave rise to a relatively small
number of stereotyped forms, sayings of Jesus, pronouncement-
stories (designated 'paradigms' by Dibelius), miracle-stories or
tales and legends.

   Pronouncement-stories, for example (e.g. Mk 2:16f., 23–26; 7:
1–8; 11:27–33), consist of a short narrative framework designed
to give prominence to a statement of Jesus embedded within it and
related to a community requirement or problem. Now perusal of
the Marcan pronouncement-stories listed by Vincent Taylor (pp.
78f.) does show that it is unwise to limit a specific form too narrowly to a single 'life-situation' in the early community like the
activity of preaching, as Dibelius does. Rather, numerous and
varied interests of the community in mission, preaching, teaching,

liturgy and worship, education, polemical debate, and ecclesiastical organisation affected the formation of the traditions of Jesus' sayings and deeds. Consequently the matching of a particular form with a particular 'life-situation' in the Church has not always proven easy for the form critics themselves. Nor has the end of the road been reached so far as the decipherment of forms hitherto undetected is concerned: witness E. Käsemann's recent attempt to isolate a highly stylised type of utterance in the *NT* which he describes as 'sentences of holy law', stemming from the activity of Christian prophets or Spirit-filled men who in Christ's name declare God's recompensing action on the last day, as probably in Mk 8:38: 'Whoever is ashamed of me and of my words . . . of him will the Son of man also be ashamed' (Käsemann, *NTQ*, pp. 66ff.).

Despite difficulties and disagreements about forms and corresponding 'life-situations', however, the broad lines of the picture form criticism presents of the circumstances surrounding the transmission of the traditions of Jesus stand forth clearly enough. The concrete conditions and urgent practical requirements of the Christian community, and not any straight historical interest as such, determined not only what traditions were preserved but also how they were preserved, modified and renewed. Also these traditions initially circulated orally as isolated fragments, each complete in itself and without any fixed context and usually without any reference to time or place. What was at stake was not the location of traditions at fixed points in the ministry of Jesus, but their relevance and applicability to specific situations in the Church.

Such a view of things, if accepted, has a direct bearing on the way Mark's work is to be understood. The traditions of Jesus the Evangelist had at his disposal would not have come to him direct, intact or untouched from the time of Jesus either as straightforward reports of separate past events or as integral pieces in a continuous life story. They would have passed through the crucible of the Church's communal existence and would have been developed under the banner of its Easter faith in Christ as the risen Lord who was still on his way with his Church every day.

The stance of form criticism has of course met with stiff and even passionate opposition. What are we to make, it is asked, of a method that dares to find in the Gospels a clear graph of the collective consciousness of the early Church, and yet with excessive scepticism finds nothing or next to nothing in the way of reliable information about that Jesus whose life and ministry were after all the most vital element in evangelism? The case against form criticism has usually revolved around three main points:

(i) Gospel stories contain numerous circumstantial details. Such details could not possibly have had theological significance or practical applicability for the Church, and so must have been preserved simply because they were true to what actually happened.

(ii) In the Church's first age eye-witnesses of Jesus' ministry aplenty were around to keep a check on reports and guard against distortion.

(iii) The transmission of the tradition was in fact tightly bridled and did not take place in the free and volatile fashion associated with folklore, as the form critics maintained.

According to Vincent Taylor, the wealth of graphic detail in numerous Marcan stories is evidence of their historical trustworthiness (see the long list for the first six chapters of Mark in Taylor, pp. 135ff.). 'What point is there in mentioning "the hired servants" (Mk 1:20), the fact that the paralytic was "borne of four" (2:3), the description of the breaking up of the roof (2:4) . . . "companies", "green-grass", and "ranks" (6:39f.), his passing by the disciples (6:48), mooring (6:53), and other details unless these things were known and remembered?' (Taylor, pp. 139f.). However, Taylor himself concedes that such graphic touches may be products of fancy (as the form critics have always insisted), and that it is speculative to decide what is imaginative expansion (Taylor, pp. 135, 139). Accordingly the presence of vivid, incidental descriptive items is not in itself a 'sure criterion' (Taylor, p. 135) for establishing the historical authenticity of a story. The whole question of details, names of people, places, colourful pieces of information, as well as explicitness through the specifying of the subject or object of a verb, etc. has recently been investigated in depth through a comparison of the Synoptic Gospels themselves and more broadly through a comparison of the Gospels with the evidence from the post-canonical tradition, texts of MSS, *NT* Apocrypha and certain patristic sources. The conclusion reached is that no universal tendency either of addition or omission can be discerned and that great caution is necessary in the application of the criterion of detail. But even so the major drift is toward more popular forms of speech, with the details lending colour and verisimilitude and so enhancing popular interest (Sanders, pp. 88ff.; 188f.; 282ff.).

More crucial is the argument that behind Mark's Gospel stood the testimony of eye-witnesses of Jesus' ministry, and especially Peter. It has been maintained, for example, that the Form Critics proceed as if the original eye-witnesses were all caught up to heaven at the Ascension and the Church were banished to a desert island. Or again, 'it is quite impossible to rule out the influence over the community of commanding personalities who had a share in its life' (W. Manson, p. 27). At first glance these contentions make good sense. But the matter is not so simple. Even if, against the notion of a free community transmission and development of the tradition, it could be proven that an élite of historically minded eye-witnesses kept a constant and vigilant check on adaptation, that would not automatically guarantee the veracity of traditions (Downing, p. 110). That reporters' eye-witness accounts of one and the same event can be notoriously dissimilar is a well-known fact even today. But in any case the *NT* did not necessarily understand 'eye-witness' as we do now. There is little or no evidence that in the first age of the Church the credentials of the eye-witness resided in his ability faithfully to preserve things as they actually happened rather than simply in the fact that he had been with Jesus through the climactic events of his ministry. There is indeed some evidence to the contrary. Luke speaks about appeal to eye-witnesses (Lk. 1:2) and yet proceeds, using Mark as a source, to leave out circumstantial detail that is supposed to be connected with eye-witness testimony in Mark (D. E. Nineham, *JTS* ns 9 (1958), pp. 13ff., 243ff., and *JTS*, ns 11 (1960), pp. 253ff.).

The most ancient authority connecting Mark with direct eye-witness testimony, and the nub of most modern arguments for the historicity of the Marcan traditions, is the statement of Papias, bishop of Hierapolis in Asia Minor around AD 130, quoted by Eusebius: 'And the Elder said this also: Mark, having become the interpreter of Peter, wrote down accurately all that he remembered of the things said and done by the Lord, but not however in order. For neither did he hear the Lord, nor did he follow him, but afterwards, as I said, Peter, who adapted his teaching to the needs (of the hearers), but not as though he were drawing up a connected account of the Lord's oracles. So then Mark made no mistake in thus recording some things just as he remembered them, for he made it his one care to omit nothing that he had heard and to make no false statement therein' (*HE* III.39, 15).

The Elder here is possibly John, the Elder. Probably only the first sentence of the quotation is his. The remainder represents Papias' own interpretation, and it has become the subject of protracted controversy. Overlooking the implausibility of Papias' suggestion that Peter would have employed an 'interpreter' for his missionary preaching and his no less implausible characterisation of Peter's preaching as 'teachings' or of Mark's work as 'memoirs' or 'reminiscences', modern critics frequently use his words as a springboard for tracing a considerable quantity of Marcan materials directly back to Peter, 'eye-witness'-in-chief. Was he not the only one present on certain occasions (e.g. Mk 1:29–39; 9:2–13; 14:32ff., 66–72)? Or alternatively, is he not often presented in such a sinister light that only he himself could have told it so (e.g. Mk 8:32f.; 14:66–72)? But on the contrary the pre-eminence of the 'prince of apostles' in Mark should not be over-emphasised. In chapters 1–13 Mark seems just as concerned to stress the existence of a little group of intimate disciples as to underline the supremacy of Peter (e.g. Mk 1:16–20; 5:37; 9:2; 13:3). In fact Peter is more notably singled out from all the rest of the disciples in Matthew and Luke (Mt. 16:17ff. and Lk. 5:1–11). By the same token, stories of Peter's reprehensible conduct in Mark serve the Evangelist well as exemplars of a typical theme of his Gospel, the obtuseness of *all* the disciples. Finally, and perhaps most decisively, the narratives commonly supposed to be Petrine are not so distinct from other narratives in Mark as to convince us that they particularly came straight from an eye-witness and did not pass through the alembic of the Christian community (FBK, p. 68; Nineham, pp. 26f.; Schweizer, p. 25).

Conceivably then the Papias claim that Peter stood immediately behind the Marcan materials was derived from the fleeting reference to 'my son Mark' in 1 Pet. 5:13 or from the traditional association of both Peter and Mark with Rome. And whereas there may be one or two residual but somewhat fugitive Petrine elements in Mark (Mk 1:29–31), it is open to serious doubt whether modern scholars would ever have claimed Peter as authority for the materials of the Marcan record without Papias' observations.

Over against the form critics' picture of the volatile communal development of the Jesus-traditions, the Scandinavian scholars H. Riesenfeld and B. Gerhardsson have lately brought forward their own special defence of the historical trustworthiness of these traditions. The heart of their case is that the process of transmission was in fact quite narrowly restricted to a fixed channel. The first apostles formed a college in Jerusalem not unlike the Jewish rabbinical schools. Their own teaching in Jerusalem stood in unbroken continuity with the teaching of Jesus. Like the Jewish teachers of his day, Jesus himself 'must have made his disciples learn certain sayings by heart; if he taught, he must have required his disciples to memorise' (Gerhardsson, p. 13). As devoted custodians of the words of Jesus they would have handed them on strictly as they received them, and so eventually they would have found their way into the written Gospels in materially unchanged form.

Now in the Semitic cultural context the remarkable power of memory has to be reckoned with. So also has the fact that Jesus couched some at least of his teaching in easily memorised form. Nevertheless the Scandinavian case has not on the whole been well received. Why, if the words of Jesus were transmitted in such closed and deterministic fashion, should there be so many variant reports of single sayings of Jesus in the Gospels? (e.g. at Mk 10:18 Jesus says: 'Why do you call me good? No one is good but God alone. You know the commandments.' At Mt. 19:17 (parallel to Mk 10:18) Jesus says: 'Why do you ask me about what is good. One there is who is good. If you would enter life keep the commandments.') Again, while the Twelve most probably figured largely in the emergence of Christianity, they scarcely constituted a central council intent chiefly on transmitting Jesus' teachings as a tightly preserved 'holy word'. As W. D. Davies has remarked, the process of transmission culminating in the Gospels is different from that operative in the mother faith. Judaism always distinguished between its Mishnah, its authoritative 'holy word', and its Talmud, its *gemara* or comment on the 'holy word'. But in the Gospels no distinction is drawn between *ipsissima verba* of Jesus and the materials which arose from the use of his words in the Christian community and became fused with them. What counted most for primitive Christianity was not a fixed code of the sacred words of the Lord, but the person of Jesus Christ himself (Davies, *SSM*, pp. 464ff.).

We are back, therefore, at the idea we have already stressed that the traditions of Jesus had been absorbed into the earliest Christian congregations' own witness to the crucified and risen Christ as the living Lord. The freedom they enjoyed under the promptings of the Spirit would have tended less to the preservation of a static 'holy word' than to flexibility and the readiness to adapt the traditions in the face of ever-changing needs and challenges. So deeply imprinted were the materials Mark took up for his Gospel with the stamp of the community of faith that, even had he so desired, he could not have become simply a purveyor of the facts of Jesus' history. The Evangelist was in a tough spot if, as is often proposed, the call of the second-generation Christians of his day was for a permanent record of the 'old' words and deeds of Jesus before they should pass into oblivion. But there is really precious little likelihood that the people Mark addresses will have wanted merely a prosaically accurate account of what Jesus had said and done *in the past*. Their conditions will have been too pressing and the demands of discipleship too stringent for that: 'they will have had little leisure, even had they had the aptitude, for antiquarian research into Christ's earthly life; nor would they have thought it worth while (expecting as they did the imminent coming of Christ to set up his kingdom), seeing that they did not look forward to any posterity who might be expected to profit from the result of it' (Nineham, p. 18).

In the light of the preceding arguments is it to be assumed that the exponents of form criticism have the very last word? To assume so much would be to overestimate its scope. The discussion of form criticism has in fact been included here under the heading 'Sources' because, although its focus is on the pre-literary stage of the tradition, it may logically be regarded as but one branch of *Quellenkritik* or source criticism (Moule, *JMH*, Vol. II, p. 31). It does not displace investigation of written sources. Nor does it displace tradition criticism, that is the study of the history of items of tradition in regard to their *content* rather than merely their form. By itself the 'form' of a unit of tradition may not be a satisfactory criterion for a judgment on its historical authenticity. The classification of the accounts of exorcisms and healings on the part of Jesus as miracle-stories (Bultmann, *HST*, pp. 209ff.) should not preclude the possibility that Jesus was in reality exorcist and healer (Hill, p. 57). Where leading form critics seem to have allowed considerations of 'form' alone to prejudge the issue of historicity they have come under heavy fire from their opponents, and most of all where, by interlocking Christian community-life and 'form' so closely, they have conveyed the impression that the Church not only modified, adapted, and developed Jesus-traditions but freely invented them *ex nihilo*. The response that there are Gospel 'moments' when the Church is not so much completely master of the tradition as mastered and controlled by the primary data of traditions emanating from Jesus himself is not unjustified. It is, for instance, hard to envisage a Church that was ever more ready to confess Christ as the 'sinless' one contradicting its confession by creating and putting on the lips of Jesus a saying like the one alluded to earlier in Mk 10:18: '*Why do you call me good?* No one is good but God alone.'

Nevertheless in certain important respects form criticism has been a most fruitful method of Gospel study:

(i) Form criticism has engendered and encouraged a mood of scepticism about the recovery of the facts of Jesus' life from the Gospels. Such a mood of scepticism, if not of complete negativism, has in the long run been arguably a healthy thing. It has led to resistance to the confusion of statements of faith with conclusions of historical research or to the substitution of the former for the latter. It has also helped toward the conviction that the Gospels should not be fenced off as a reserved area to which the normal checks and warrants of historiography do not apply or to which the secular historian is denied access (Harvey, pp. 84ff., 113ff., 158f.). To be sure the historian of Jesus should not prematurely foreclose his mind to the possibility of the 'strange' or the 'extraordinary'. But neither should he allow the commitment of faith to suspend his critical judgment. The matter is stated acidly but challengingly by H. R. Trevor-Roper: 'If a secular historian told us that an army of five thousand men had gorged themselves on five loaves and two fishes, and that twelve hampers were needed to carry away the scraps, we should be very sceptical about anything else that he told us even if he insisted that he had been there at the time' ('The Gospels according to . . .', *The Spectator*, 27 Feb. 1971, p. 280).

The sceptical attitude, which is 'to be not merely tolerated but nurtured because it is essential to historical work' (Keck, p. 21), has informed recent attempts to go beyond

form critical principles and enunciate fresh scientific criteria for getting back through the Gospel materials to the
actual words and deeds of Jesus. According to the criterion
of dissimilarity, wherever a saying of Jesus does not have
the ring of contemporary Judaism on the one hand or of
the Church's proclamation on the other, there we are hearing the authentic Galilean accent (Käsemann, p. 37; Perrin,
pp. 39ff.). The criterion of consistency means that when
by application of the rule of dissimilarity a residual minimum
of authentic Jesus material has been sifted out, there may
also be allowed to enter the historical picture additional
teachings of Jesus that cohere with this 'torso'. According
to the criterion of multiple attestation, motifs occurring in
multiple strands of the Gospel tradition like Mark and Q
possibly represent genuine historical traits. Each of these
criteria singly is disputed, particularly the criterion of dissimilarity whose rigorous use it is commonly agreed would
give us a Jesus in such radical discontinuity with both
Judaism and Christianity as to appear just like a bolt from
the blue. But it is their application cumulatively to the
Gospel materials, together with other standard tests, literary, linguistic, historical, and theological, that not only
satisfies the scientific demands of the historian's craft but
also holds the promise of securing for us the main linea-
ments of Jesus' history. Paradoxically then, today scepticism is on the way to overcoming scepticism.

(ii) Redaction criticism, a more recent method of Gospel research, is an extension and in a sense a correction of form
critical analysis. Whereas form criticism centred on individual units of the tradition and on the way these units
have been shaped up by the postures, procedures, and
theologising processes of the early Church, redaction study
takes a further step and asks about the theology of each
whole Gospel as a unit. It sees each Evangelist not as a
mere collector of fragments but as an individual theologian
and interpreter (see above, p. 8). Each has his own special
message and that message can be gauged from the way he
selects, structures, and collects his material into the total
framework of the Gospel.

(iii) If the Church selected, preserved, and adapted only such
materials as were directly relevant to its daily life, and if

in turn the Evangelists selected, adapted, and assembled only what served their own theological interpretation, the question of the *truth* of the Gospels clearly forces itself upon us. How true are these documents if they are so theologically loaded? How much, if at all, does their truthfulness depend on the accepted norms of modern scientific historical research?

In paragraph (i) above we ventured the opinion that scepticism has had a constructive role to play in the historical study of Jesus. The scientific and sceptical spirit of our age impels us to the quest of the historical Jesus. 'As men of the twentieth century', says E. Schweizer, 'we cannot help asking historical questions when we read the Gospels' (Schweizer, *Jesus*, p. 11). The commentator, therefore, will not altogether neglect the question of the historicity of the traditions lying behind Mark. Although, as we have seen, the Evangelist offers neither a 'history' nor a 'biography', such historical interest is by no means necessarily in contradiction with the Gospel, since 'it is beyond all doubt that Mark wants to emphasise that God's revelation happened in the historical life and death of Jesus, that is, in a real man' (Schweizer, *NTS* 10 (1963–1964), p. 431).

But secondly and more importantly, it is the function of the commentator to concentrate heavily upon what Mark himself has written, to elucidate the theology of the Evangelist as a believing witness to what on his view has really happened in Jesus Christ.

Thirdly, if the present-day reader of Mark is properly to appreciate Mark's work as a religious document of compelling force with its own powerful message to convey, it is essential to come to terms with the problem of the truth of the Gospel. Certainly its truth does not hinge on whether the Evangelist has presented all the facts about Jesus with the exactitude of a modern scientific report. Just as it is commonplace today to acknowledge that even the most scientific historian is not just a neutral observer and collector of facts of the past but an interpreter of materials that reflect the conceptual horizons of those who first furnished them, so Mark is an interpreter and one who belongs to a period and environment very remote from our own. It is both helpful and liberating to think of Mark as writing two-dimensionally or as telling two stories. The one is natural and descriptive and may very well convey solid information about Jesus. The other, woven into the same narrative, is supernatural and interpretative (J. A. T. Robinson).

For example, Mark's story of Jesus' submission to baptism by John (Mk 1:9–11) is deeply impregnated with the interpretative element of Christian faith. But that the story contains a substratum of fact is clear. The early Church did not invent this story (see commentary, pp. 74f.): so scandalous was the fact for it that Luke only fleetingly glances at it in a participial clause (Lk. 3:21), Matthew inserts a brief explanatory conversation, the writer of the Fourth Gospel omits it, and the later apocryphal *Gospel according to the Hebrews* actually puts on the lips of Jesus the direct challenge, *Quid peccavi?* 'Wherein have I sinned?' (Barrett, p. 5). But what of the opening of the heavens, the descent of the Spirit, and the voice from heaven that says to Jesus: 'Thou art my beloved Son; with thee I am well pleased' (Mk 1:11)? Surely the truthfulness of the Gospel at this juncture does not depend on whether the modern historian could substantiate the actuality of that heavenly voice. The voice in fact echoes *OT* texts (see commentary, pp. 78ff.) and by it Mark wishes to show that the Jesus whose story he is telling is given the divine imprimatur or that this Jesus, to be fully understood, must be spoken of not only in man-language but in God-language.

Similarly Mark's account of Jesus' calling of disciples (Mk 1:16–20) probably contains a nucleus of historical fact, no more than a bare nucleus to be sure since it tells nothing of the disciples' previous preparation nor of Jesus' strategy. But the significant thing for Mark, as for earlier preachers who used the story, is its other dimension, namely that it clarifies that in this Jesus who summons men to follow him everything decisive has happened and God's own grace and call have gone forth. Then again, at the close, in the passion story the Evangelist has interwoven with the narrative so many *OT* reminiscences that it is difficult to work with it purely historically. He might instead have communicated to us a hundred factual details, offering what E. Schweizer calls 'a sound film of the crucifixion of Jesus' (Schweizer, p. 22). But then, even if it means making a Roman army officer utter what is a statement of faith rather than a bare statement of historical fact, 'Truly this man was the Son of God' (Mk 15:39; see commentary, p. 347), he would rather expound for us what the suffering and death of Jesus have come to mean for him as a believer.

In sum, Mark's message or the truth of the Gospel he proclaims, though not unrelated to historical reality, does not depend on historical verification. The Evangelist's challenge to his reader is to share with him the response of faith's 'Yes' to all that God has done in Jesus.

3. DATE, LOCATION, AND AUTHORSHIP OF THE GOSPEL

Date

In the past a minority of scholars proposed a very early date for Mark, as early as AD 40. C. C. Torrey, for instance, argued for AD 39–40, maintaining that the words in Mk 13:14 about 'the abomination of desolation standing where it ought not' must have been written just prior to the assassination of the emperor Caligula on 24 January AD 41 (Taylor, p. 31). Caligula, it is true, planned an outrage against the Jerusalem Temple when he commanded his statue to be set up in the sacred precincts. But the prophecy of Mk 13:14 might equally belong to a considerably later time when the seer was expecting another imminent sacrilege no less sinister than Caligula's (see commentary, p. 295).

Very recently and on completely different and somewhat spectacular grounds a date of around AD 40–50 has again been advanced for Mark. Working on fragments from Qumran Cave 7 (the materials from which in contrast to the other caves, are all in Greek) the Spanish papyrologist, Father José O'Callaghan, became convinced that among other small segments of the *NT*, he had found two tiny pieces of Mark's Gospel. The application of scientific techniques to these fragments, notably the study of the characteristics of the script, has led to the assignment of a date not later than AD 50. Fragment 5 consists of a large part of Mk 6:52f., and fragment 7 of the tribute-money saying of Mk 12:17. It is fragment 5 that has caused a stir since it is conjectured to belong to a narrative part of Mark and so to demonstrate the existence of a complete manuscript of the Gospel sometime before AD 50. O'Callaghan's findings have been enthusiastically embraced by some conservatives eager to seize upon something that seems to them (albeit mistakenly, see above, p. 19) to corroborate the 'truth' of the Gospel by validating its historicity. It has even been asked whether one small fragment like this could shake the world (see the reprint from *Eternity*, published by the Evangelical Foun-

dation, Philadelphia, 1972). The question assuredly arises mcre
from the first flush of rapture and romance than from sober appraisal. Fragment 5 is not in fact well preserved and contains no
more than fifteen definable Greek letters. Even at that, in identifying it with Mk 6:52f. ('. . . (they had not) understood about the
loaves, but their minds were closed. And they finished the crossing
and came to Gennesaret where they made fast'), O'Callaghan has
to allow for the omission of three words that are included in all
known mss of Mark as well as to accept the letter *t* where we should
expect a *d*, there being no evidence of such a transposition of letters
in extant Palestinian Greek texts.

Consequently, aside from the broader difficulty of accounting
satisfactorily for the presence of Christian fragments at Qumran,
when so eminent a palaeographer as Father Benoit has access
to the papyrus in question at the Rockefeller Museum, is not dependent merely on a facsimile, and declares himself not in the
least persuaded about the equation of fragment 5 with Mk
6:52f. (Benoit, *RB* 79 (1972), pp. 321ff.), extreme caution on
the whole subject is obviously the order of the day. In short,
at this stage, the identification with Mk 6:52f. is at best highly
conjectural.

As things stand, the majority view that Mark was written within
the period AD 65–70 has still much to commend it. The fairly advanced theological development of the traditions Mark drew on
for his Gospel, envisaged in our section on 'Sources', indicates a
time for the writing of Mark at least a full generation after the
death of Jesus. From another angle we should also take into con-
sideration the statement of Irenaeus at the beginning of Book III
of his work *Against Heresies*: 'And after their deaths (the deaths of
St Peter and St Paul) Mark, the disciple and interpreter of Peter,
himself also handed down to us in writing the things which Peter
had proclaimed.' Irenaeus' accuracy is of course by no means
guaranteed, especially when we remember he also says that
Matthew was written while Peter and Paul were still active in
preaching. Nevertheless some weight should be given to A. E. J.
Rawlinson's interesting argument: the utter frankness with which
Peter is depicted in his blindness and humiliation in Mark's Gospel
would make sense at a time after his martyrdom when his final
loyalty unto death after previous failures would bring great encouragement to ordinary Christians that in Christ sacrificial
strength could ultimately come out of weakness (Rawlinson,

p. xxix). Since the persecution under the emperor Nero broke out in AD 64, the likeliest *terminus a quo* suggested for Mark's work would be AD 65.

On the other side no modern scholar has argued more vigorously or ingeniously for dating Mark's Gospel toward the close of of the year AD 71, after the destruction of Jerusalem in AD 70, than S. G. F. Brandon. For Brandon the Gospel is an Apology to Roman Christians. Indeed it was addressed to Christians in the specific circumstances obtaining for them in Rome late in AD 71, when before their very eyes the Flavian triumphal procession made its way through the city's streets displaying the spoils brought back from the ravaged Jewish capital and Temple of Jerusalem (Brandon, pp. 227ff.). But if Mark's Gospel is not the kind of apology Brandon supposes it is, and it scarcely looks like such (see below, p. 41), then his proposed dating becomes very suspect.

Internal evidence, especially Mk chapter 13, suggests on the contrary not that Jerusalem has already been destroyed or that, as another critic maintains, only the conclusion of hostilities with the impending fall of the fortress of Masada in April AD 73 is awaited (Johnson, p. 20), but rather that the sack of the city is still to come. Mark makes no explicit reference to the siege of Jerusalem. Luke does: 'But when you see Jerusalem surrounded by armies, then know that its desolation has come near' (Lk. 21: 20). According to Mk 13:9, 14–20, the clouds of war appear just to be rolling in on the horizon. Indications are, therefore, that the Gospel should be dated between AD 65 and 70 and possibly earlier in that period than later, just around the outbreak of the Jewish War.

Location

Ancient testimony almost entirely supports a Roman provenance for Mark, and most modern critics have adopted this view and buttressed it with critical arguments. In antiquity, however, Chrysostom at least did say that Mark wrote in Egypt (*Hom. in Matt.* 1). Chrysostom was no doubt drawing on Eusebius who in one passage remarks: 'They say that Mark set out for Egypt and was the first to preach there the Gospel which he had composed' (*HE* 11.16.1). But Eusebius' information is ambiguous and certainly does not clearly state that Mark composed his Gospel in Egypt. Chrysostom probably picked him up wrongly. In any case, inasmuch as Alexandrian Christianity appears to have stayed remote from the mainstream of the Church's life in its earliest history, it is unlikely that so epochal and formative a work as Mark should have originated there.

Ancient testimony to Rome as the place of composition is manifold. Irenaeus, Clement of Alexandria (around AD 200) as quoted in Eusebius (*HE* VI.14.6), and the Anti-Marcionite Prologue which states that 'after the departure of Peter himself, he (Mark) wrote down this same gospel in the regions of Italy'. Such testimony is invariably closely linked with Mark's association with Peter, for which the evidence of Papias is fundamental. Though Papias does not himself mention Rome, other traditions do connect the apostle Peter with that city. Our estimate of the value of the ancient testimony linking the Gospel with Rome will be proportionate then to our estimate of the value of Papias' evidence linking Mark with Peter, an association we found reason to question (see above, pp. 16f.).

If the ancient traditions are essentially inconclusive, what about the modern critics' defences of the Roman origin of Mark? A good deal has been made of the occurrence in Mark of numerous Latin loan-words, e.g. *modius* (4:21), *legio* (5:9, 15), *speculator* (6:27), *denarius* (6:37), *sextarius* (7:4), *census* (12:14), *flagellare* (15:15), *centurio* (15:39, 44ff.). Mark has for the most part simply transliterated these Latin words into Greek letters (FBK, p. 70). Latin forms of expression also occur, e.g. *verberibus eum acceperunt* (14:65), *satisfacere* (15:15). But the presence of such Latinisms is by itself no proof that Mark was explaining Greek words by Latin ones for the benefit of a Roman audience (Bacon, pp. 54–8). The Latin terms in Mark are largely military and would have been familiarly used in many parts of the Roman empire wherever Roman soldiers had gone. Luke–Acts, unconnected with Rome, has a number of Latinisms. There is the added factor that if the Marcan Latinisms were already embedded in the traditions he took over, they would give no indication of the place where Mark himself finished his work.

The point made in Mark about the right of the wife to dissolve a marriage (Mk 10:12) is sometimes held to be an accommodation to Roman marriage law, but it might just as well apply to the Hellenistic situation. Of possibly greater validity is the observation that the many hints in the Gospel of the necessity of suffering and persecution for the disciples of Christ (e.g. Mk 8:34ff.; 10:30; 10:33; 10:45; 13:8, 10) are consonant with the desperate situation of the church in Rome at the time of the Neronic persecutions. But even this does not point only to Rome, for in the empire persecution could be widespread, and the most we can say is that the Marcan church seems to be going through a time of great hardship. The contention that Mark, in direct competition with Matthew, could have gained official recognition from the Church at large only if it had enjoyed the sanction of a supremely influential congregation like that in Rome, is very dubious. The sanction of any great centre of Gentile Christianity in an age when Rome's supremacy still lay in the future would have served the same purpose. Incidentally, since on his own testimony Papias was patently eager to uphold the integrity and worth of Mark, possibly in competition with another Gospel, he and the other ancient authorities who followed him in associating Mark with Peter, and so with Rome, could well have been motivated by the desire to 'canonise' Mark, at a time when Rome's influence was definitely on the increase. It remains to add that S. G. F. Brandon's highly individualistic arguments for locating Mark in Rome under the conditions prevailing there in AD 71 are so integrally related to his overall characterisation of the Gospel as an *Apologia ad Christianos Romanos* that they stand or fall with that (see pp. 40ff.).

A case has been made for other locations. J. V. Bartlet proposed Antioch. John the Elder cited by Papias lived in the East; Peter was connected with Antioch; Mark employed Aramaic words; Antioch was a centre of Roman culture (Bartlet, pp. 26f.). But the uncertainties of Papias' evidence we have already noted (see pp. 16f.). Mark's use of Aramaic words may reveal no more than his indebtedness to materials with a strong Semitic cast, and the fact that he translates Aramaic terms into Greek (e.g. 15:35) suggests only that he was addressing Gentile readers. Other cities than Antioch were centres of Roman culture, and in any case we have noticed how Mark's Latinisms tell us nothing definite about the provenance of the Gospel.

More recently W. Marxsen has maintained that Mark was located in the region of Galilee and that the Gospel was composed with the specific intent of exhorting the church in Jerusalem to move out there to await the return of the Lord in his parousia (see especially Mk 16:7. Marxsen, p. 142; and Marxsen, *ME*, p. 107). As with Brandon's Rome hypothesis, Marxsen's Galilee hypothesis is inseparably tied up with his whole understanding of the Gospel as in essence a summons to flee to Galilee to meet the Lord who was coming soon. Once discredit the theory of Mark's purpose, and few if any have subscribed to it (see below, pp. 42f.), and the argument for Galilee is dissipated.

Marxsen's individual perspective aside, if Mark belonged to a Galilee–Jerusalem axis, it is very surprising indeed that he should feel constrained to inform his readers, as if they were non-Jews, about Jewish customs (Mk 7:3f.), the coinage of Palestine (12:42), the climate of the Levant (11:13), or to translate for them Aramaic words and phrases, even the word *Abba*, Father (14:36). Finally, there is a growing tendency to think of Mark as dependent on a cycle of miracle stories for the earlier part of his Gospel (Robinson, *JMH*, vol. I, pp. 102ff.). Now it may be that such a cycle had its first home in Galilean territory, which is in fact the scene of most of these stories. But even if their place of origin was Galilee, it does not follow that the Evangelist was in Galilee when he incorporated them in the final draft of his Gospel.

Ultimately the safest conclusion about the provenance of Mark is that it was composed for Gentile readers in some unspecified part of the Roman empire. Our inability to be more definite about the location of the Marcan community does not mean, however, that we cannot glean further knowledge about its attitudes and problems from the internal evidence of the Gospel itself.

Authorship

Nowhere in the Gospel does the author divulge his own identity. A number of commentators have none-the-less detected a signature of sorts in the work, thinking of that strange and faintly humorous note about the young man fleeing naked from the scene of Jesus' arrest in the garden (Mk 14:51f.) as a brief autobiographical reminiscence of the author's. Reconstructions suggesting that the youth followed Jesus from his home, 'the house of Mary the mother of John whose surname was Mark' (Ac. 12:12), where the Last Supper was held (Mk 14:15) (e.g. J. M. C. Crum, pp. 42f.) go much too far. The notice of Mk 14:51f. is very terse. If the Gospel writer wished to intrude himself in his narrative, he chose an extremely condensed and cryptic way of doing so. It is not even necessary to assume that the Evangelist would only have inserted the memorandum about the youth if it had come to him directly from an eye-witness. Possibly he had to hand an old piece of information about a youth who after the death of Jesus joined

the Christian community and told his story there. The incident
is loosely appended to the preceding statement about the flight of
all the disciples (Mk 14:50), and the young man's abrupt departure serves to heighten the loneliness of Jesus.

The only truly independent witness to the authorship of the
Gospel by one Mark is, as we have seen, that of Papias (the observations of other ancient authorities after him are founded upon
his). When we recall that Mark (*Marcus*) was just about the com-
monest Latin name in the Roman empire, the question that arises
is whether the Mark of Papias' testimony is none other than the
John Mark mentioned several times in the *NT*. He was the son
of that Mary whose house was a meeting-place for the early Christian congregation (Ac. 12:12). John Mark accompanied Barnabas
and Saul on their return to Antioch after they had brought the
famine relief to Jerusalem (Ac. 12:25), and appeared again as
their assistant in Cyprus (Ac. 13:5). Thereafter he left the entourage of Paul (Ac. 13:13), and subsequently as the result of dis-
sension, and out of loyalty to John Mark, Barnabas broke with
Paul and took John Mark with him, independently this time, to
Cyprus (Ac. 15:39). The way Mark is commended in Col. 4:10
as the cousin of Barnabas ('if he comes to you, receive him'), suggests his eventual restoration as a servant of the Pauline mission,
and finally in 2 Tim. 4:11 he is lauded as a faithful Christian
worker.

It is noteworthy that, although it does not preclude any possible
connexion of John Mark with Peter, all these passages picture him
in contact with Paul rather than Peter. In Ac. 12:12 Luke does
not go beyond simply mentioning Peter's visit on his release from
prison to John Mark's mother's house, so that we are left only to
guess that the two then formed a close association. The remaining
NT reference to the name Mark is 1 Pet. 5:13: 'She who is at
Babylon, who is likewise chosen, sends you greetings; and so does
my son Mark.' Whether this is a word of the apostle Peter himself
(the problem of the authorship of 1 Pet. is unresolved—by the
apostle or later and pseudonymous?), or whether the man here
called Mark must perforce be John Mark, it is impossible to say
with complete assurance.

Whatever the source of Papias' information then (he clearly far
outruns the minimal evidence to be gleaned from the *NT*!), it is
virtually certain that the Mark whom he attests as the interpreter
of Peter and the author of the Gospel he intended to be identified

with John Mark, the servant of the apostles. In view of the apparent early tendency to assign the Gospels to the personal disciples of Jesus (FBK, pp. 70, 84ff.) it is quite unlikely that Papias would have ascribed the Gospel he was obviously keen to have accredited to an unknown Mark who had no connexion with the disciple or apostle group.

Many leading scholars (e.g. Rawlinson, pp. xxxf., Taylor, pp. 26ff., Cranfield, pp. 5f., Martin, pp. 53ff.) consider the identification of the Evangelist with John Mark to be a thoroughly established fact of criticism. Nevertheless it bristles with difficulties that cannot be overlooked (Johnson, pp. 17ff., FBK, p. 70, Schweizer, pp. 24f.). The author of the Gospel is not well versed in the geography of Palestine. That the country of the Gerasenes stretched to the Sea of Galilee is by no means certain (Mk 5:1). The topography described in Mk 7:31 is obscure. Nothing is known of the Dalmanutha referred to in 8:10. The geographical connotations in 10:1 and 11:1 are quite vague. Moreover the report of the Baptist's death the Evangelist transmits in Mk 6:17ff. reflects some insensitivity on his part to inaccuracies regarding the members of Herod's family and Palestinian practices. Again, when he explains Jewish customs in 7:1-23 (for the benefit of his Gentile readers), he evinces a good deal of hostility toward them.

Ironically enough, scholars who are most concerned to defend the historical trustworthiness of Mark's record by attributing it to John Mark, and connecting it with Petrine eye-witness, are generally quite happy to explain away the topographical difficulties in the Gospel by saying that John Mark, with his home in Jerusalem, would have been satisfied to give broad general descriptions of areas with which he was personally unfamiliar (e.g. Martin, p. 60); or again to explain away his polemic against Jewish customs by saying that he intentionally occupies the stance of his non-Jewish readers at this point (e.g. Cranfield, p. 232). But in fact we could barely expect the features listed in the previous paragraph in a work from the hand of the Jerusalemite John Mark, 'cousin of Barnabas'.

Certainty eludes us in this matter. We do not know for sure who the author was. That of course in no way detracts from the magnitude of his achievement in writing the earliest Gospel. The power of the Gospel does not reside in the credentials of its writer either as preacher-teacher in the Pauline mission or as sound historian, as judged by twentieth-century standards. The Gospel carries its own authority as Gospel, as the Evangelist, hiding himself behind his witness to Jesus Christ, surely wanted it to do.

4. STRUCTURE, OCCASION, AND PURPOSE OR MESSAGE OF THE GOSPEL

Structure

The way Mark built up his Gospel, the forces which precipitated the writing of it and the theological message he wanted to express are clearly all intermeshed. The conception or conceptions that guided him and the aim or aims he had in view have everything to do with the manner in which he has combined individual units of tradition, just as the content of what he has to say relates to the circumstances, secular, or ecclesiastical and religious, that impelled him to his task. However, for the sake of presenting the main theories concerning each of these factors as clearly as possible we here deal with them severally.

First, the question of structure. We have already suggested that Mark's work is not to be classed as a chronicle (see above, pp. 6ff.). However, many critics still consider biography-chronology to be a concern of Mark's structure. One cannot help feeling they are unduly influenced by Papias' statements about Mark and Peter. Recoiling from any thought that Papias might have been motivated less by historical than by apologetic or dogmatic interests (perhaps in polemic against the claims of gnostic gospels, as K. Niederwimmer has recently argued, *ZNW* 58 (1967), pp. 172–88), and evaluating his evidence positively, they see in Mark a writer who 'had considerable opportunities of gathering knowledge of the kind that would later be useful in the composition of the Gospel' (T. W. Manson, p. 37). But even if it were proven that Mark enjoyed and used these opportunities and so had access to historically reputable items of tradition, *it would not follow that when he strung these together in his final composition he did so with a historian's or chronicler's intent.* Indeed Papias himself acknowledges the 'disorder' of Mark's arrangement. And the Evangelist joins the various units of tradition together quite loosely with vague linking words like 'and', 'and immediately', 'again', 'then', 'in those days', etc.

In regard to the Marcan structure, more influential even than the ancient testimony has been the thesis of C. H. Dodd. Avail-

able to the Evangelist as a sort of *aide-mémoire* was an outline of
Jesus' earthly ministry preserved in the early Church and consisting of a fuller version of the scheme represented in Ac. 10:37–
41 and 13:23–31. Such an outline would have become standard
and would have served as an introduction to the passion story.
The 'summaries' of the first six chapters of Mark (e.g. 1:15;
3:16–19), when read consecutively, reflect a minimal sketch
of this kind (C. H. Dodd, *ExpT* 43 (1931–2) pp. 396–400).
But the hypothesis is very shaky. Summaries like Mk 1:15 and
3:16–19 no doubt contain early materials. But they are in the
same key as later summaries accompanying detached sayings of
Jesus (9:30; 10:1; 10:32; 12:38), which Mark has composed to
cement his narrative, and are therefore most probably due to the
Evangelist's editorial activity. Also the continuity Dodd finds in
the summaries of chapters 1–6 certainly does not stretch through
these later summaries. If Mark was using the conjectured outline,
he might reasonably have been expected to follow its order
throughout. The fact that he has not done so points to an alternative explanation: no such outline existed (Nineham, *SG*, pp. 223–
239; Trocmé, p. 24; Robinson, *Quest*, p. 58).

The feeling that Mark's order is not after all determined by a
biographical-chronological interest has given rise to different
literary theories of the Gospel's construction; or to 'patternistic
analyses', as a recent commentator has described them (Martin,
p. 91). According to A. M. Farrer, Mark's arrangement conforms
to the most intricate architectonic designs, involving a complicated
pattern of cycles and sub-cycles, all conjured up out of the
Evangelist's preoccupation with *OT* prototypes and their fulfilment in Christ (Farrer). On this view the Marcan text becomes
a remarkable series of cryptograms and the task of interpreting
Mark's theology is a matter of decoding their symbolism. But
such a reading of the Gospel is altogether too subtle and ingenious. It runs counter to the Evangelist's crudely simple style and
even more to the realism with which he witnesses to wh. actually
happened in Jesus. He is no poet bemused by fanciful typological
correspondences.

P. Carrington considers that the sequence in Mark is determined by a Christian liturgical calendar, based on that of the
Jewish synagogue, and intended to be read piece by piece in
worship from the New Year in September to the season of Tabernacles. He also thinks that the chapter divisions of the oldest

Gospel manuscripts bear traces of the lectionary arrangement according to which Mark structured his work with great care (Carrington, pp. 15ff.). But the lectionary hypothesis has been strongly opposed. If Mark was drawing up a liturgical calendar, there are gaps and omissions that are hard to explain. Evidence that primitive Christianity borrowed the lectionary practice of the Jewish synagogue is lacking (Davies, *COJ*, pp. 67ff.). There is no indication that, aside perhaps from the passion narrative, the chapter divisions of the oldest manuscripts have a liturgical significance (R. P. Casey, *Theol.* 55 (1952), pp. 362–70). No doubt the Gospel of Mark came eventually to figure in the worship practices of the Church. But it is one thing to say that and quite another to say that Mark composed it with that very purpose in view.

J. Bowman has recently maintained that Mark is far too compressed and too much of a unity to think of it as a spread of lectionary materials for use over an entire liturgical year. He therefore traces its overall pattern to the one great Jewish festival of Passover, and characterises it as a Jewish Christian Passover Haggadah for Jews in Rome (Bowman, especially pp. 90ff.). Just as in their Passover celebration Jews narrated how God had redeemed his people of old and how what he had done embodied the promise also of their future deliverance, so Mark re-tells episodically the new Christian Passover story consisting not only of the passion and death of Jesus but of events in his life. Now it is not surprising that, with its emphasis on the passion, Mark's Gospel should seem to have strong paschal overtones. But it is quite another matter to describe it *in toto* as a new Christian Passover narration. Bowman has not taken anything like adequate account of the complex problem of the purpose of the Marcan redaction. If he had done so, he would have noticed that Mark addresses himself to Gentile readers for whom he has to explain Jewish customs and translate Aramaic terms (see above, p. 28). For such a Gentile constituency a Christian Passover pattern would surely have been an extraordinary and unlikely design to aim at (L. E. Keck, *NTS* 12 (1965–6), p. 356; Martin, pp. 85f.).

It is no more likely that Mark wanted to provide for the Church through his Gospel a complete framework of catechesis, with the course of Jesus' life presenting a normative pattern of the progressive experiences of Christian converts in baptism, in instruction and nurture in the faith, in the Lord's Supper, and in the testing of persecution with the crowning glory of martyrdom at the end (G. Schille, *NTS* 4 (1957–8), pp. 1–24). That Mark contains groupings of material collected for catechetical purposes is scarcely in doubt (e.g. 9:48–50; 10; 11:48–50). But the Gospel as a whole does not look like an instruction-book for catechumens. Unlike Matthew, Mark reports but little of the content of Jesus' teachings. What he tells us about Jesus appears to function not as a model for the behaviour of believers but as an invitation to join the one in whose presence God's grace and God's demands are decisively encountered.

It is a feature of the various 'patternistic analyses' we have looked at that they try to project on to Mark from outside ground-plans on which the Gospel itself is conspicuously silent. Consequently one can readily subscribe to the verdict of R. P. Martin: 'Patternism as a method of gospel study must be pronounced a brilliant, but unachieved, endeavour to read into Mark what is not there' (Martin, p. 91).

Literary theories of another kind seek to listen more attentively to the way the Gospel unfolds itself internally, to what the Evangelist himself is about. It has of late been claimed, for example, that the form the Gospel takes emerges from the fact that the Evangelist had to hand and took the initiative in bringing together two great written collections, on the one side the passion story and on the other a cycle of miracle-stories analogous to the clusters of wonder-working tales that occur in the semi-official biographies of heroes in the Hellenistic world. Between the two there stands as a watershed the episode of Caesarea Philippi (Mk 8:27–33). Thus J. M. Robinson states: 'The drastic operations evident here (in the Caesarea Philippi tradition) seem to be in the function of forcing into some kind of ecumenical working relationship two ancient cycles, the passion narrative on the one hand and the *Novellen* cycle [the cycle of miracle-tales] on the other' (J. M. Robinson, *JMH*, p. 106). But such a theory would not really move us very far toward a fuller understanding of the Marcan structure. It gives a novel slant to truths long recognised, namely, the cruciality of the Caesarea Philippi episode, the bringing together of the passion story in its main lines considerably before Mark's time, and the prominence of miracle-stories in the Gospel. As to miracle-stories, there are some twenty such in Mark as well as three further references to healings achieved by Jesus (1:32–34, 3:7–12; 6:53–55). They occupy slightly over one fifth of the whole Gospel, about the same space as the passion story. Now it may be that some miracle-stories had been collocated prior to Mark, like those in Mk 5:21–43. But there is no solid evidence of the existence of a much larger cycle of miracle-stories, and the impression one has is that in the main Mark himself has brought them together and combined them with other materials, e.g. with the teaching activity of Jesus in the synagogue (1:21–27), or with the controversy about what is lawful on the sabbath (3:1–6). Even if the Gospel form did in fact arise from the juxtaposition of two great written cycles, that would represent only the broad landscape of the Evangelist's structural canvas. The foreground detail would remain to be filled in.

To sum up, exposure of an overarching principle of design for the Marcan construction has proven exceedingly difficult. Suffice it here then to draw attention to what appear to be salient characteristics of Mark's structuring procedures:

(i) As we noted already, the main threads of the passion story had been drawn together into a connected whole a good while before the Gospels were compiled in their final form. General acceptance of this insight of form criticism has caused widespread publicity for an earlier dictum of Martin Kähler, who had Mark particularly in mind when he described the Gospels as 'passion narratives with extended introductions' (Kähler, p. 80, note 11). Following Kähler's designation, W. Marxsen considers that Mark 'composed backward' so to speak (Marxsen, pp. 132ff.). Beginning from the passion story, which probably opens at 14:1, the Evangelist moves back through three complexes, the events in and around Jerusalem (from 11:1 on,) the ministry of Jesus in Galilee and up to his stay in Jerusalem (1:16–10:52), and behind that introductory materials (1:1–15), including the reports of John the Baptist and the baptism and temptation of Jesus. Such a procedure would be consonant with the direction taken by the early Church's process of theological reflection. The concrete Easter stories told in the Gospels affirm much more than merely the isolated fact of the resurrection. As vehicles of the Church's theology, by their very concreteness, they communicate, among other things, the conviction of the earliest followers

of Jesus that the one who had made a fresh start with them
at Easter was no other than that same Jesus who had been
crucified on the cross. Easter is, in other words, inextricably
linked with Jesus' passion and death. In turn, concentration on his passion and death prompts questions about
who this one was in his earthly ministry, culminating in
his death in Jerusalem. Then out of interest in who he
was in his ministry there arises the question of whence he
came, a question each Evangelist answers in his own way:
John in a hymnic prologue to the *Logos*, Matthew and
Luke in their infancy stories, and Mark in his undoubted
emphasis on the verb of motion, 'comes', applied to
Jesus in the early part of his Gospel (1:9, 14, 24, 38).
When Mark is approached from this perspective, it helps
to clarify that his structure is in the first instance theological rather than biographical-chronological, a fact confirmed by his opening description of his work as *euangelion*
('good news', Mk 1:1).

(ii) 'Passion narrative with extended introduction' is not,
however, an entirely satisfactory definition of the Gospel.
It too greatly de-emphasises the importance to Mark
of his so-called 'introduction': he wants to locate God's
activity with its challenge to faith decisively not only in
the 'moment' of Jesus' death, but in the 'moments' of
his earthly ministry, in his words and deeds leading up
to his Passion. Accordingly Marxsen correctly recognises
an interest on Mark's part in a *history* that from John the
Baptist thrusts forward inexorably and with a sort of
breathless rush to Jesus' crucifixion (Marxsen, p. 134).
A large part of the genius of Mark's structure is the way
it conveys restless *movement* from beginning to end—by
a relatively simple and artless and even crude literary style;
by the repeated use of linking words like 'and', 'immediately', 'then', 'again'; by the inclusion of very many
verbs of motion (e.g. 1:9, 14, 21, 24, 29, 35f., 38f.; 2:1,
13; 3:1; also 8:31; 9:30; 10:32ff., etc.); by the threefold
prediction of the passion (8:31; 9:31; 10:32ff.).

In view of the focus on movement all the way in the
Gospel it is not surprising that it should contain certain
indications of a rudimentary geographical construction:
Galilee; Galilee and surrounding regions; journey to

Jerusalem; Jerusalem. Is this geographical framework theologically motivated or not? According to E. Lohmeyer, Mark just has to attach an excessive weight to Galilee as the land of Jesus because in the Evangelist's own time Jesus is active there in and through the preaching of a distinct Christian community, and in Mk 14:28 and 16:7 this Jesus foretells his parousia in Galilee (Lohmeyer, pp. 26ff., 58, 96f. See also Lightfoot, pp. 52–65, 73–7). But the argument is scarcely supported by the evidence. There is no direct information in the *NT* about the existence of a separate early community with its own particular brand of Christology in Galilee; the terminology of Mk 16:1–7 and especially the promise of Mk 16:7 ('But go tell his disciples and Peter that he is going before you to Galilee; there you will see him, as he told you') most probably alludes not to the parousia but to the appearances of the risen one in Galilee. Consequently it is not necessary to suppose that Galilee and Jerusalem are both theologically loaded terms for Mark; that he draws a contrast between Galilee as the scene of Jesus' final work of victoriously consummating God's purpose and Jerusalem as the city of sin and death (3:22; 7:1; 10:33; 11:18; chapters 14–15); or that he intends by the contrast to show how God is withdrawing his saving grace from the Jews who have rejected Jesus and is turning instead toward believing Gentiles.

Doubtless the dominance of the Galilean tradition is a fact of the Gospel. Witness Mark's fondness for miracle-stories which may well have emanated from the Galilean territory. Doubtless also the tradition clearly attests Jerusalem as the place of Jesus' death. So from his tradition Mark has already a rough geographical outline that offers him great scope for a proclamation in story form of the movement of Jesus on the way of the cross, whose shadow casts itself back, on his very first steps.

(iii) One structural device stands out prominently in Mark. Even where he is creating a sequence that may be very questionable historically, he has a way of fitting one report into the midst of another. In 3:19–21 Jesus goes home, the crowd gathers, and his friends accuse him of being beside himself. Then there is interpolated a report of an encounter and controversy of Jesus with the scribes who come down from Jerusalem (3:22–30). Only after that is the little drama of the 'home', mother, family, and friends picked up again and concluded (3:31–35). Conspicuous in this insertion procedure are the frequent verbs of motion, 'went' (3:19), 'came together' (3:20), 'went out' (3:21); 'came down' (3:22), 'came' (3:31). In 5:21–24 Jairus comes and entreats Jesus to heal his daughter and Jesus goes with him. Then comes an account in 5:24–34 of how a woman with a flow of blood accompanies the crowd following Jesus, touches his garment out of belief in him, and is healed through her faith. Only after that is the account of the healing of Jairus' daughter taken up again and brought to a conclusion (5:35–43). Conspicuous here also are the verbs of motion. Compression of two incidents by insertion after this fashion does not arrest but accentuates the *movement* Mark desiderates. But it does more. The two accounts brought together illumine each other, serve to bring out what is really going on in Jesus, as a believer might perceive it, or highlight a particular facet of his person and its challenge to faith (see also Mk 6:14–29 inserted in 6:6–13, 30f.; 11:15–19 inserted in 11:12–14, 20–25; 14:3–9 inserted in 14:1f., 10f. FBK, p. 64).

Another feature of Mark's design are the vivid scenarios that occur at intervals. The generalising summaries of Jesus' healing activity in 1:32–34, 3:7–12 and 6:53–56 enhance the impression of the busy movement on the way of Jesus.

(iv) The outstanding phenomenon of Mark's structure is of course quite simply that he *narrates* the 'good news'. Wishing to proclaim the gospel, he yet tells a continuous story. What models, if any, did he possess for his pioneering enterprise? We cannot arbitrarily exclude the possibility of dependence on the current literary products of the Hellenistic world, whether semi-official or popular biographies, or tales of 'divine men', wonder-working heroes (see H. D. Betz, 'Jesus as Divine Man', *Jesus and the Historian*, Philadelphia, 1970, p. 116; also Nock, pp. 45f., Votaw, *AJT* 19 (1915), pp. 45–73). But it is not necessary to have recourse to pagan parallels to explain Mark's achievement. The Jesus Mark tells about is more than a thaumaturge whose miracles startle or a wise man whose sayings are worth preserving. The Marcan narrative is at one and the same time both historical-descriptive and theological-interpretative, and for that there was a distant precedent in sections of historical books of the *OT* or possibly the book of Jonah (Schweizer, *Jesus*, p. 129). In other words, Mark's narrative is an amalgam of two stories he really wants to tell: the story of Jesus' way with the world of his time and place from start to finish of his ministry, and the story of God's ongoing way with the world in this Jesus.

Occasion of the Gospel

What is meant by 'occasion' in this context is not the fixing of an exact date for the Gospel. We have in mind rather the question of whether we can identify specific conditioning circumstances that induced Mark to write as he did. Recent theories on the subject fall into two different kinds. Either they connect the composition of the Gospel with a particular set of external historical facts, or with internal religious or churchly factors prevailing in the community to which Mark belonged. Among the former the theories of S. G. F. Brandon and W. Marxsen merit special mention.

Brandon believes the life-setting of the Gospel as a whole to 'correspond exactly to that of the Christian community at Rome in the years immediately following the Flavian triumph in AD 71 over insurgent Judaea' (Brandon, p. 242). Addressed to the Christians in Rome at this precise juncture, the Gospel is an apology designed to divest Jesus of his true historical garb as a Zealot sympathiser and political dissident bent on liberating his people from the Roman yoke, and to move toward an un-Jewish, a-political and 'transcendental conception of Christ' (Brandon, p. 281) that would be inoffensive to Gentiles in the Roman empire. Brandon's thesis is presented with an impressive wealth of detail. Here we restrict ourselves to the main lines of his argumentation. Jesus' saying about the tribute-money (Mk 12:13–17) was, when first uttered, an absolute injunction against the payment of the tax to Rome, but Mark has subsequently editorialised it and transformed it into a quiescent counsel to pay it. Despite the fact that the Romans executed Jesus in the customary Roman way, obviously persuaded that he constituted a political threat, Mark the apologist in his account of the passion is at pains to exculpate the Romans and shift the blame for Jesus' death on to the Jews (15:6–15). It is again Mark the apologist who puts on the lips of a Roman centurion the sublimest confession in the Gospel: 'Truly this man was the Son of God!' (15:39). The rending of the Temple veil leading up to this confession is, according to Brandon, a Marcan *theologoumenon* that would have been made not only understandable but graphically real to Christians in the streets of Rome when in the Flavian procession the spoils brought back from the Temple, including the torn curtain itself, were paraded before their very eyes.

Without here entering into full discussion, we may register broadly the chief grounds of our opposition to Brandon's hypothesis. The less firmly established we take the Roman provenance of Mark and a post-AD 70 date for it to be, and we have seen good reason to question both (pp. 26ff.), the more distinctly shaky does Brandon's whole case of course become. But more pertinently, a segment of Mark's passion story (15:6–15) may contain some trace (not all that clearly defined) of anti-Jewish polemic: there may indeed be traces of anti-Jewish polemic elsewhere in the Gospel (3:6; 7:6,8; 8:31; 9:31; 10:33; 12:12; 13:2); yet the Gospel as a whole does not read like the pro-Roman apology written for pagans envisaged by Brandon, but rather like a version of the good news addressed to the Christian community. In discovering in Mark an apologist through and through, who for the sake of the Romans overturns the true historical understanding of Jesus as a very Jewish 'fellow-traveller' of the Zealots with their revolutionary aspirations, Brandon may simply be confusing two things. He may be 'confusing Mark's *Gentilization* of the Gospel tradition with what he alleges to be Mark's *de-politicization* of that tradition. When Mark generalizes the tribute saying into an injunction to all Christians to pay taxes, is he disarming a volatile political bombshell, or is he simply adapting the Gospel to changed (i.e. Gentile) circumstances? For the question of tribute is not one for which Roman Christians would have needed guidance, especially after the destruction of the Jewish temple and nation' (W. Wink, *USQR* 25 (1969), pp. 48f.).

But it is in fact not at all clear either that Jesus originally forbade the payment of taxes to Rome or that Mark has de-fused this political bomb into a supine command to all Christians to pay taxes. When Jesus was proffered a coin bearing Caesar's image and superscription, it would not have been mere sophistry but a natural reaction on his part to say that the coinage was a basic datum of the daily traffic of Jewish life and that it would as a matter of course find its way back to the imperial treasury—'render to Caesar what belongs to Caesar'. 'This means that the question concerning the Caesar tax, taken so seriously and put so provocatively by his opponents (with their supposedly so pious sentiments and religious scruples) is put in the margin' (Bornkamm, pp. 120ff.). Then Jesus adds what really matters, 'render to God the things that are God's': as men who bear the image of God we owe God our complete allegiance. When Mark takes up the tribute-money incident he places it immediately after the parable of the wicked husbandmen (Mk 12:1–12), with its theme of the father's final sending of the beloved son. In his editorial preface to the story he then illustrates the mounting Jewish hostility toward this Jesus, who is the one sent of God, in the desire of the Pharisees and Herodians to entrap him in his talk (Mk 12:13). Later on Jesus discerns their hypocrisy (12:15). From Mark's standpoint what is at stake is not a burning problem of Jewish politics but the nature of those opponents of Jesus who by their trickery want to have him rejected before giving him a hearing. For Mark 'the story is a warning against the kind of discussion in which a person does not seek to learn but already has a closed mind toward Jesus' (Schweizer, p. 244). Once more then, Mark is not Brandon's kind of apologist to outsiders. On the contrary he is concerned to challenge the Church of his time to genuine openness toward Jesus.

W. Marxsen follows Lohmeyer (p. 38 above) in thinking that the concept 'Galilee' has profound theological significance for Mark (Marxsen, pp. 136ff.; also *ME*, pp. 102ff.). He posits a close connexion between Mk 14:28 and 16:7, which contain the promise that the risen one will go ahead into Galilee and appear to his disciples there, and a statement in Eusebius (*HE* iii.5, 3): 'Moreover, the people of the church in Jerusalem were commanded by an oracle given by revelation to men worthy of it, before the war, to depart from the city and to dwell in a certain city of Perea, named Pella.' The outbreak of the Jewish War in AD 66 kindled a mood of apocalyptic fervour among Jerusalem Christians, whereupon they fled in obedience to the oracle (mentioned by Eusebius) to the region of Galilee. It is to this emigrant community Mark belongs and to which the final redaction of his Gospel is directly addressed in the period AD 67–69. By inserting Mk 16:7 into the context of 16:1–6, 8, the Evangelist reveals his own situation: he is there and then in Galilee expecting the parousia. The solitary message of the entire Gospel is that Jesus is coming soon to make a final rendezvous with his people in Galilee. In Marxsen's view Mark placed the designation 'gospel' at the head of his work (1:1) and highlighted the concept 'gospel' throughout, in order to show that his work is purely an intimation and a summons and not in any sense a report about the past of Jesus of Nazareth. It is the risen one who speaks throughout the Gospel. The fact that Mark tells stories of Jesus is quite incidental. They serve only to announce the one theme, the imminent parousia of the risen Jesus.

Marxsen's daring reconstruction of the Marcan situation is at once too imaginative and too narrow. To say that the whole message of the whole Gospel is that Jesus is coming very shortly to greet his people in Galilee is about as restrictive as saying that the whole of *Hamlet* is the fearful dilemma of a Danish prince. If that is all Mark wanted to say, he surely has dragged in a lot of redundant material (Martin, p. 74; L. E. Keck, *NTS* 12 (1965–6), pp. 358). As we indicated earlier, the very fact that he does *narrate* shows that he is interested not only in the risen one and his words but in the way of the earthly Jesus, which is for Mark a necessary constituent element of 'gospel'. Moreover the Eusebius tradition about the flight of Jerusalem Christians to Pella has lately been much controverted (Martin, pp. 71f.; Rohde, pp. 122ff.). The notices that exist about the flight (they may or may not derive from questionable second-century sources) belong to the fourth century, and interestingly enough Brandon rejects the report of an oracularly inspired emigration as a Church legend devoid of historical value (Brandon, pp. 208ff. Contrast W. Wink, *USQR* 25 (1969), pp. 41ff.). The tradition of the flight to Pella must be deemed a sandy foundation on which to build. Nor finally is there in any case independent testimony to the sort of Galilean church Marxsen supposes: it emerges out of the mists of silence only by way of inference from the concept 'Galilee' in Mark, as Marxsen understands it.

Perhaps the most striking fact about the theses of Brandon and Marxsen is that, taking off from the same evidence, they reach such radically divergent conclusions. It is a very far cry from an apocalyptically excited community in Galilee awaiting the imminent return of Jesus in AD 67 to a group of Roman Christians awaiting only an apologist like Mark to rid them of the embarrassment of owing allegiance to a Lord who in his days on earth had been a political agitator with Zealot leanings. The polarities of viewpoint clearly suggest that each has selected and magnified different parts of Mark's Gospel as though they were the totality. It is a fair deduction that in our present state of knowledge it is proving virtually impossible to fix precisely the historical locale and circumstances within which Mark carried through his task.

However, it is not the *method* of either Brandon or Marxsen that is at fault, but the absolute precision of their results which seem to arise from a too great fascination with and too subtle interpretation of only certain ingredients of the Marcan record. The truth remains that the Gospel does possess a 'quality of the moment' (Rohde, p. 127); it is addressed to a community, we know not exactly where or which, but a community within the context of whose theological or religious understandings and ecclesiastical needs Mark's witness to Jesus Christ takes the shape it does. That is what, in its more sober vein, redaction criticism is all about in fact. It seeks to determine, at least approximately, the nature of the association or the mutual interaction between the Evangelist as individual theologian in his own right and the community in its theological beliefs and thoughts. But now that we have begun to define 'occasion', not as the external historical forces that precipitated the Gospels, but as the intra-community concerns and problems that elicited the Evangelist's response in the form of his Gospel, we cannot any longer hold separate the question of 'occasion' and the question of the author's theological aim and purpose. They coalesce.

Purpose or Message

Long before the recent wave of redaction studies in the Gospels, W. Wrede, as we saw (p. 6), put forward in his epochal work on the 'messianic secret' a comprehensive theory of the Evangelist's theological intention that was to become a springboard for similar later theories. The four principal points in Wrede's analysis of Mark are as follows (Wrede, pp. 9ff., 81ff., 209ff.):

(i) Jesus refuses to divulge the secret of his Messiahship so long as he is on earth.

(ii) He does in fact reveal himself to the disciples but not to the crowd generally. Even the disciples, however, persistently fail to understand him in his revelations. Not until the resurrection is the 'preternatural stupidity' with which they appear to be credited overcome: only with the resurrection does the real knowledge of who Jesus is commence (see Rawlinson, p. 261).

(iii) The secret notwithstanding, the demons recognise Jesus and promulgate their knowledge. They are rebuked and ordered to stay silent (1:25, 34; 3:12; 5:6f.; 9:20).

(iv) The mighty acts of Jesus as a healer also reveal his divine character and mission to those who have discernment, but the healed persons are enjoined not to publicise it (1: 43 –45; 5:43; 7:36; 8:26).

The oscillation of concealment and revelation of the secret, according to Wrede, adds up to a picture of Jesus that is not really intelligible as history. It is the Evangelist as theologian from the vantage-point of Easter faith who has imported into Jesus' earthly life a messianic character that did not actually dawn on any one before the resurrection. The following observations may be made on Wrede's thesis:

(i) Beyond question it is correct to emphasise the pivotal nature of Easter (see above, p. 14). The scales do fall from hitherto blind eyes after the resurrection. But, on the other hand, the *NT* does not construe the event of Easter as an isolated miracle by which God first bestows on the disciples the light of divine knowledge and power through the risen one, nor as the birth of faith or the emergence of the message of Christ. Rather does it see Easter as an event inseparable from that Jesus whose life of supreme trust in God led up to his death on the cross. And in his earthly career, Jesus' life of trust contains within itself already a challenge to bystanders to surrender to the God in whom he trusted and who had therefore chosen him, a challenge not declared openly from the housetops but hidden in veiled hints and allusions.

(ii) As H. Conzelmann has pointed out, Mark was not responsible for impregnating the traditions about Jesus that came to him with the category of Messiahship. The mass of materials Mark employed already contained the secret of his status as the Christ (Conzelmann, pp. 42ff.). Since Mark knew retrospectively that the secret of who Jesus was *from the very beginning of his career* was only finally disclosed in his passion and death, his problem in witnessing to Jesus in story form, with only such traditions at his disposal, was how to preserve the integrity of the historic earthly way of Jesus (with the secret still intact) as a movement toward the denouement of the cross (de Tillesse, pp. 321ff.). In sum, as Conzelmann notes, the secret is not a dogmatic invention of Mark's to explain why faith arose only after Easter, but it belongs to the pre-Marcan traditions and is an indispensable prerequisite of the Gospel form.

(iii) The commands to keep silent in the healing stories hardly relate to the concealment of Jesus' status *as Messiah*. In the healing miracles Jesus figures more as a 'divine man', the type of wonder-working hero familiar in the literature of the Hellenistic world. In any event, in these stories the secret is not only poorly kept, it is promulgated: 'And he charged them to tell no one, but the more he charged them, the more zealously they proclaimed it. And they were astonished beyond all measure, saying, "He has done all things well" ' (Mk 7:36f.).

(iv) In the course of his record Mark constantly portrays Jesus in the company of his disciples. He does not treat the person of Jesus or his status as an isolable phenomenon, but testifies to him as the one who brings a summons to follow him in discipleship, a discipleship that inescapably involves cross-bearing (L. E. Keck, *NTS* 12 (1965–6), p. 364).

All in all Wrede's comprehensive theory of Mark's theological intention is to be judged too narrow and too rigid. The messianic secret is a feature of the Gospel. But it does not embrace the whole purpose of the Evangelist. Hence other scholars have subsequently sought to modify or extend it. Bultmann agrees with Wrede that the secret is a Marcan construct to account for the fact that Jesus was not recognised for who he really was during his lifetime. But he says further that the Evangelist's aim has been to unite the Hellenistic preaching of Christ, which consists essentially of the myth of Christ as heavenly redeemer as we gather it from Paul

(Phil. 2:6ff.; Rom. 3:24) with the traditions of the story of Jesus. In and with this union the mystery of the heavenly redeemer must be kept in hiddenness during the ministry of Jesus on earth (Bultmann, pp. 347f.). Of the same order is Dibelius' stress on the powerful Hellenistic influences operative in the Marcan tradition, leading him to characterise the Gospel as a 'Book of the secret Epiphanies of the Son of God, the "divine man" of Hellenism' (Dibelius, pp. 93ff. and 266ff.).

More recently J. Schreiber has taken up and developed this viewpoint. The Evangelist draws upon gnostic ideas of the heavenly redeemer, who descends as a divine being, touches the earth for a moment and returns triumphant to heaven (as in Phil. 2:6–11.) But he then Christianises these ideas by accommodating them to the death of Jesus on the cross. Mark's Jesus journeys through the earth as a divine Saviour incognito and finally engages the cosmic powers of evil, who fail to recognise him, on the cross. They are thereupon vanquished by him, and being now saved himself, the Saviour is exalted to Lordship over the whole cosmos (J. Schreiber, *ZThK* 58 (1961), pp. 154–83). In particular, Schreiber is quick to detect typical gnostic motifs at crucial points in the Gospel. The rending of the Temple veil (15:38) signifies the eradication of the barrier between earth and heaven; the centurion's confession of Jesus as the Son of God (15:39) is an acknowledgement of his revelation as the victorious redeemer of gnostic mythology; Mk 16:7 alludes to the heavenly glorification of Christ. But far more plausible alternative interpretations of these passages suggest themselves. The rending of the veil signifies not a cosmic wonder but the end of Jewish worship in the Temple; the Gentile centurion's confession of Jesus as the Son of God relates not to a miraculous gnostic redeemer-figure, but to the decisiveness, for Mark, of Jesus' way of suffering and death; the language of Mk 16:7 points more naturally to an appearance of the risen one in Galilee than to the heavenly glorification of Christ.

To say that Hellenistic ideas are imprinted on the Gospel, however, is one thing. That would be quite consonant with Mark's efforts toward a certain Gentilising of the Palestinian traditions of Jesus' life and death. It is quite another thing to claim that the Evangelist is actually working with full-blown gnostic ideas. In fact the normal ingredients of the gnostic redeemer-myth are altogether lacking from the Gospel. Mark's Jesus, it is true, 'comes' (the verb is used frequently of him in the early part of the Gospel) with mysterious suddenness, but there is simply no explanation of the manner of his coming. Mark says nothing of his pre-existence, birth, or incarnation. Nor is there any indication, at the close, of the ascension of Jesus from the cross to enthronement as heavenly cosmocrator (FBK, p. 67).

If a clear explanation of the goal of the Evangelist does not yet follow from the suggestions of Bultmann, Dibelius, or Schreiber, they do serve to show that, since Wrede, discussions of the theology of Mark have mostly revolved around the christological question. The heart of the problem lies in the duality of Mark's witness to Jesus Christ. On the one side, Jesus appears as the strong Son of God, healing, exorcising, working miracles, and teaching with unprecedented authority. The so-called messianic secret notwithstanding, Jesus' transcendent glory keeps shining through. At 1:11 Jesus is given the divine accreditation: 'And a voice came from heaven, "Thou art my beloved Son; with thee I am well pleased".' At 1:12f., as the bearer of the same kingly power possessed by Adam in Paradise, Jesus emerges victorious over Satan. The demons know who he is (e.g. 1:34). At Caesarea Philippi (8:27–33, long held to be a crux for understanding the Gospel), Peter confesses Jesus as Messiah or Christ. But what is highlighted here is the ignorance on the part of even the leading disciple of the true status or function of the Son of man. At the close the highest confession breaks from the lips of a Roman centurion: 'Truly this man was the Son of God' (15:39). On the basis of such episodes E. Lohmeyer was able to say of Mark's Jesus: 'The Son of God is not primarily a human but a divine figure . . . he is not merely endowed with the power of God, but is himself divine as to his nature; not only are his word and work divine but his essence also' (Lohmeyer, p. 10).

But, on the other side, Jesus appears in Mark as a distinctively human figure, who resolutely refuses the Pharisees' demand that he should authenticate his claim with an overwhelmingly miraculous sign from heaven (8:11–13) and travels the lowly and obscure way of the cross.

In the light of the two-sidedness of Mark's presentation, it is inappropriate and does violence to the Gospel as a whole to say that his chief concern is with the human Jesus, whose earthly life he supremely wishes to document in a series of accurate historical reminiscences. It is no less inappropriate on the other hand to say that the Evangelist's chief concern is with the sovereign Christ or heavenly Son of God who, in so far as he touches history at all, touches it only in the sense that it becomes the stage-setting for the God-man's mythical conflict with his enemies (Käsemann, *NTQ*, p. 22).

The question that has come to the forefront in recent debate then is this: What *does* the Evangelist intend by the diverse emphasis in his work and how do they relate to the circumstances prevailing in the community he addresses?

Much of the debate has centred on Mark's handling of the miracle-stories transmitted in considerable volume in the earlier part of his work. Is the witness to Christ enshrined in these miracle-tales a constituent element of Mark's own christology? Or rather, seeing that the Evangelist attaches to them stringent checks and restraints (e.g. the injunctions to silence or the 'secret' so-called) are they, from Mark's standpoint, the stock-in-trade of opponents in his environment who have fallen victim to a false theology by surrendering to the notion of Jesus as a legendary wonder-working hero of the Hellenistic 'divine man' type, and against whom he wishes to polemicise?

Now whether or not Mark drew upon an already written cycle of miracle tales (Robinson, *JMH*, pp. 104ff.), there is no doubt that in the circles from which such tales emanated they would have stood as propaganda for a Jesus who manifested himself as a divine being in the healings and wonderful works he performed. 'The content of faith in such a connexion,' writes Dibelius (p. 79), 'is not the conviction that through Christ God's call has gone out to all mankind, but the confidence that Jesus, the great miracle-worker, excelled all other thaumaturges' (of whom there were any number in the cities of Greece, Asia Minor, and Syria).

If at the pre-Marcan stage the miracle tales reflect allegiance to Jesus as a divine man, are they also, within the context of the Gospel, intended by the Evangelist to be open windows on the erroneous and indeed heretical beliefs of dangerous foes in the Church of his day, who think of Jesus as the greatest miracle performer and mightiest healer of them all? And does Mark set out to negate or correct them by his own theology of the cross? In an article entitled 'The Heresy that necessitated Mark's Gospel' (*ZNW* 59 (1968), pp. 145–58), T. J. Weeden has made a daring attempt to show that this is in fact the case with Mark. He has subsequently developed his ideas further in a full-scale work, *Mark—Traditions in Conflict*.

According to Weeden, the different emphases in Mark's presentation issue from the conditions of struggle and tension existing between Mark and his heretical opponents in the community. The interaction between the disciples and Jesus lies in the foreground of the Gospel. In his portrayal of the disciples as men whose lack of perception of who Jesus is (1 : 16–8 : 26) gives way to misconception (8 : 27–14 : 10) and finally to utter rejection (14 : 10–16 : 8), Mark is actually dramatising the spurious beliefs of the deviationists in his congregation. Like them the disciples view Jesus as a divine man, whose wonder-working prowess fascinates them. Peter's confession at Caesarea Philippi is really a confession to just such a divine man, and for it he is sternly rebuked and aligned with Satan (8 : 33). Over against all this Mark's Jesus speaks of the divine necessity of messianic suffering, and of a discipleship that consists of cross-bearing, and herein resides Mark's own viewpoint.

Chapter 13 is the most 'seminal and transparent passage' (Weeden, p. 71), mirroring the ecclesiastical circumstances of Mark's time. In it he puts out two stern warnings against messianic impostors (13:5–6, 21–23). These impostors are 'pneumatic' and 'enthusiastic' or 'exalted' Christians. Occupying the same stance as the opponents of Paul in 2 Corinthians (described by D. Georgi, pp. 210–18 and 220ff.), they claim that the powers of the resurrected Lord are present with them, subscribe to a theology of glory, and perform miracles, signs, and wonders to prove the truth of their theology. Accordingly, Mark repeatedly takes up the material most prized by such opponents and turns it against them. He plays down the miracles by means of the secret and so furls the flag of the divine man christology to which his heretical enemies, typified in the Gospel by the disciples, have succumbed. The account of the transfiguration which represents for his opponents the post-Easter story of an epiphany, is located by Mark in the earthly ministry of Jesus, and is followed immediately by a command not to divulge the event until after the resurrection (Mk 9:9) and by talk of the coming suffering of the Son of man. The opponents' use of the story as a picture of their dependence on the risen Lord's appearance to them for their powers is thus effectively demolished. Finally, the disciples and their latter-day counterparts, the 'pneumatics', are not truly directed by the Holy Spirit at all (Mk 14:38). The Spirit who informs the Christians (13:11) is not representative of the resurrected Lord, but is rather that same Spirit who impels Jesus to his vocation of messianic suffering (1:10) and must also impel his faithful followers along the same way.

Weeden's imaginative reconstruction of the Marcan situation is more ingenious than convincing. The thesis, that Mark's characterisation of the *dramatis personae*, and particularly of the disciples in the Gospels, is controlled or determined entirely by the ecclesiastical struggle raging in his surroundings, is something of a *tour de force*. It is more natural to suppose that he was influenced by the content of the traditions he had at his disposal. These traditions in their complexity cannot be reduced to 'ad hoc appropriations which can be explained by the conflict situation' (Tiede, p. 259). For instance, the blindness of the disciples, which is unquestionably a dominant motif in the Gospel, may well have been a feature of the tradition that came to Mark, rather than a purely polemical construct of the Evangelist's, and reflect historical reality (Martin, pp. 152f.). Any supposed thread of connexion between the disciples of Jesus, blind though they may have been, and the messianic impostors of Mk 13, the 'pneumatics' of the Marcan community, would be tenuous in the extreme. Moreover, in view of the great diversity of early Christianity (Koester, *HTR* 61 (1968), pp. 203–47) and the varied range of functions and activities that might be denoted by terms like 'pneumatic' and 'exalted', is it justifiable procedure to do as Weeden does and foist directly on the Marcan 'enthusiasts' the characteristics of the opponents of Paul in 2 Corinthians?

Again, if we are right in thinking that Mark was significantly influenced one way or another by the traditions that came to him, then the large block of miracle-stories in chapters 1–8 is more than simply a device to document the process by which the disciples were misled (Tiede, p. 260). Rather, despite, or better because of, his editorial unease and reserve about them or about the way they could be employed (in the service of a 'divine man' christology), the miracle-stories do come to possess a positive christological force for Mark himself. They evoke the religious response of awe and wonder as in the presence of the numinous (Mk 4:41; 5:20, 42; 6:51; 7:37). They function not as open and objective proofs of Jesus' wonder-working power, but as indicators for those whose faith can see beyond them of the hidden mystery of Jesus' person. In terms of Mark's Gospel, to give this Jesus just a messianic title is almost to blaspheme (Mk 8:29–33): before him the adequate

posture is one of bewildered amazement (1:27; 4:41; 7:37;
9:32; 10:32; 14:3; 16:8). Accordingly, reports of Jesus' mighty
works appear to have kerygmatic or preaching value for Mark,
attesting as they do the closeness of the kingdom's presence in
him for those, as Mk 8:18 indicates, who have eyes to see and
ears to hear (U. Luz, *ZNW* 56 (1965), pp. 29ff.).

Nevertheless Weeden's thesis contains basic insights that are
fruitful for an understanding of Mark's purpose:

(i) Mark is unhappy about the propagandising use of miracle-
stories.

(ii) The decisive things about Jesus for Mark are his suffering
and death and the summons to a discipleship that also
follows the way of suffering and the cross.

The miracle-tales Mark refuses to accept as unambiguous
demonstrations of Jesus' divine power. Viewed only on their
external side, the mighty works may give rise merely to misunderstanding or non-understanding (Mk 6:3, 6; 8:17, 21; 9:6). But
by his editorial insertion at 8:11–13 of the brief report concerning
the Pharisees' demand for a sign from heaven and Jesus' absolute
rejection of it, the Evangelist shows that Jesus will not and cannot
legitimate his authority by any stupendous miracle to sensation-
seeking outsiders to his mission. The miracle-stories constitute
good news for Mark then only in the sense that, for those possessed
of faith's perception within the true missionary circle, they attest
the *concealed* presence and power of the Son of God on earth
(Kertelege, pp. 89, 170f.). It is the nearness for faith of the
kingdom's blessings in Christ, the salvation-bringer, that by way
of his redaction Mark accentuates in the miracle-tales, as in his
stress on 6:50 ('It is I; have no fear.') in the story of the walking
on the water (6:45–52); in his comment at 8:18 on the feedings
of the multitude (6:34–44 and 8:1–10) and at 7:37 on the healing
of the deaf-mute; or in the way he introduces the healing of the
blind man at Bethsaida (8:22–26) as an indication of how the
blindness of insensitive disciples (8:21 and 33) could yet be overcome. We may then think of Mark transforming the miracle-
stories from their use as vehicles of propaganda for a divine man
wonder-worker into a means of 'preaching Christ in his present
availability. He is Lord of the waves, conqueror of death, con-
troller of evil powers, restorer of human dignity—and dispenser
of true bread' (Martin, p. 176).

Mark's distinctive contribution, however, was to take the message of the hidden presence of God's rule in the Son of God and subject it to and interpret it by the theology of the cross (U. Luz, *ZNW* 56 (1965), pp. 28ff.). The passion of the Son of man is given an axial place in the Gospel (8:27–9:1). Though Jesus' glory shines through momentarily in the transfiguration (9:2–8), it can only be climactically revealed in his coming suffering (9:9–13). Not until the moment of death of the one who refused to come down from the cross (15:29–32), who entered the depths of self-humiliation and felt himself forsaken by God (15:34), can the centurion's ultimate confession to Jesus as Son of God be made (15:39). It is there, in the passion and death of Jesus, according to Mark, that authentic faith discerns the divine compassion.

Now just as in Mark the centre of gravity is occupied by the passion and death of Jesus, so the missionary proclamation of the apostle Paul is focused on the cross (see e.g. 1 C. 2:2; Gal. 3:1). In an earlier period of critical study the 'Paulinism of Mark' was for long a subject of intense debate. To what extent was the Evangelist in his soteriology, and indeed in all his leading ideas, influenced by Paul? Whereas scholars like Loisy and Bacon upheld the Pauline character of Mark, others like Schweitzer and Werner vigorously denied it. In a judicious summary in his commentary (pp. 127–9) Vincent Taylor concluded by pleading for a 'qualified negative' instead of Bacon's 'decided No' (Bacon, p. 271) to the question: 'Can we imagine a gospel such as Mark taking form in a community ignorant of the teaching of Paul?' Lately the question of the relationship between Paul and Mark's Gospel has been given another slant. The new angle of vision on it arises on the basis of two considerations. First, for all his massive concentration on the cross, and for all that he undoubtedly acknowledged the historical reality of the one who surrendered to death on the cross, Paul refers hardly at all to the traditions of Jesus' words and deeds in his earthly ministry. Secondly, Mark for his part is not content to testify to the bare fact of Jesus' death, but draws upon many traditions of the human ministry in order to show how the gospel is rooted and grounded in history and what is the impact upon faith of the actual life that ended on the cross.

In view of the high significance for Mark of his great 'historical addendum' to the kerygma of the cross, it is now suggested that he was in fact responding to the threat posed to the integrity of the gospel in post-Pauline Christianity by reductionist interpretations of a docetic kind (Schweizer, *GNM*, pp. 380–6). At Corinth, for example, Paul had apparently in his own lifetime to combat a tendency among certain 'enthusiasts' to concentrate on the resurrection as though it were already past (1 C. 15:12) and on the heavenly Christ (1 C. 4:8) at the expense of the historical Jesus. Even more so in the situation that obtained in the post-Pauline Church, Mark was faced with the task of ensuring that the kerygma should not altogether be uprooted from history or Christ dissolved into a mere mythical symbol—and this he did by telling the good news in *narrative* form (Schweizer, *EvTh* 24 (1964), p. 338).

Expanding on Schweizer's viewpoint, R. P. Martin has recently described the life-setting within which Mark compiled his Gospel as follows: 'We imagine an over-compensating stress on Paul's kerygmatic theology which placed all emphasis on Christ as a heavenly figure, remote from empirical history and out of touch with earthly reality. The end-result of this attempt to carry Paul's transcendental christology to extreme limits (a trend clearly visible in Ephesians), possibly in the interests of a wisdom theology or by too close an association of a Christ-figure with contemporary saviours and mediators in hellenistic religion, was the gnostic version of Christianity in the second century' (Martin, p. 160). In such a situation of crisis for the true Pauline gospel Mark appeared as one who understood its essence and took the unprecedented step beyond Paul of combining selected Jesus-traditions into a narrative whole 'in order to compensate for what he believed to be a serious distortion of his master's thought as apostle *par excellence*' (Martin, p. 161).

On the face of it this explanation of the life-setting of Mark seems both neat and reasonable. Unfortunately, however, it may exist only in the mind of the modern scholar who has access (unlike Mark's first readers) to the whole Pauline corpus in the *NT* and is able to draw correlations between what he finds in many different letters and what he finds in Mark. It is highly speculative to suppose that the Marcan community was in peril *specifically* from diluted or rarefied interpretations of Paul's gospel or that the Evangelist's chief wish was to reconstitute essential Paulinism.

Overall, therefore, the most we should say is that Mark's

Gospel reflects a community undergoing considerable duress, most probably from incipient persecution (8:34ff.; 8:38; 10:30; 13:8, 10), and agitated by great theological turbulence, particularly over the question of the true nature of Jesus' *authority*. We may regard Mark as doing battle on two fronts in the midst of such turbulence. On the one hand, he campaigns against custodians of the tradition who appear to be truncating the gospel by imagining that Jesus' authority can be guaranteed simply by transmitting and repeating reports of his past words and acts. But Mark will not allow that Jesus can be exhaustively grasped by objective knowledge of the concrete data of his earthly life— rather his unique divine 'authority' discloses itself only to the faith that, in responding to the Church's proclamation of Christ, sees beyond the historical dimension (Schweizer, *NTS* 10 (1963-4), p. 422). In this connexion it is striking how little of the content of Jesus' teaching Mark communicates, although he stresses the fact that Jesus did teach. By collocating the teaching activity of Jesus with a miracle of healing (1:21-27) Mark indicates that Jesus' authority consists not in a body of teaching that can be passed on but in the fact that where he is present God's healing and reconciling power is released (see especially 1:22 and 1:27). Again the so-called messianic secret in Mark, as E. Schweizer observes, may be construed as a 'No-trespassing sign for all handing down of the "historical Jesus", namely for all mere repetition of his sayings or of reports of his deeds which would not be, at the same time, the proclamation of the Christ of faith' (Schweizer, *NTS* 10 (1963-4), p. 431).

On the other hand, Mark campaigns against balcony-type Christians who are too high for the mission and discipleship that in Mark's terms necessarily involves cross-bearing and self-sacrifice. Now they lose themselves in vain recollection and contemplation of the mighty works and glorious heavenly status of Christ (see e.g. Mk 9:5-6). Now captivated by the thrill of living, as they believe, in the last days, they claim a private lien on the divine authority of Jesus and seek to prove their own messianic status by performing outward signs and wonders (Mk 13:5, 21-22). Such exalted ones the Evangelist must bring down to earth and warn that the only authentic Christian way is the way of the suffering Son of man. In this regard it is instructive to compare items in chapter 13 with their immediate sequel in the passion story, e.g. 13:9 with 14:53-15:15; 13:22f. with

14:33–46, 50, 66–72; 13:32f. with 14:35, 37 (Schweizer, *GNM*, pp. 247f.). But Mark has other means of remonstrating with exponents of a 'theology of glory' and of indicating to his readers how genuine Christian faith must express itself. He directs attention, not to the person of Jesus in isolation nor to any messianic titles or dignities or the confession thereof for their own sake (Mk 8:29f.), but to the Master in relation to and in company with his disciples. In insisting on the mission of Jesus in his onward movement to the cross, he emphasises what is common to the Master and his followers (8:31, 34). The gospel for Mark is not just a spectacular record of what Jesus said and did in life and in death as the Son of God, but it carries within itself the necessity of suffering for his sake (8:35; 10:29) and sounds forth the summons to follow him in cross-bearing. Faith is no static acknowledgement of Jesus alone but active discipleship (Schweizer, *NTS* 10 (1963–4), p. 432; Trocmé, pp. 125ff.; especially Keck, *NTS* 12 (1965–6), pp. 364ff.).

Mark therefore is no speculative or reflective theologian who could have fulfilled his task by an expert treatise on christology. The picture of the Evangelist that emerges is of an adventurous Christian passionately concerned to move his community away from inhibiting disputation to active participation in discipleship and mission. If our picture is correct, it is not in the least surprising that modern scholars should have failed to isolate any single purely christological purpose that informs and shapes the whole structure of the Gospel. Leading theories of a christological master-plan not only diverge radically from one another, but each in itself does less than justice to the varied themes of Mark: e.g. the theory that Jesus' mighty works do in fact exhibit his Messiahship (Burkill, p. 41) but Mark has forced on the material the idea of the messianic secret in order to show that the baffling unbelief of the Jews was due to divine predestination (Burkill, *NovT* 3 (1959), p. 41); the theory that Mark depicts Jesus' life as a *cosmic* struggle with Satan and the powers of evil culminating in the crucifixion (Robinson, *PHM*); or the theory that the governing principle of Mark's work is not the cosmic overthrow of Satan but the redemption of men from sin (Best, especially p. 189).

As we shall see in the commentary, a number of striking themes in fact appear in the Gospel that are more or less closely related to Mark's practical concerns, e.g. the coming kingdom of God at the heart of Jesus' message; the pre-determining will of God for

Jesus, the Jews, and the world; the turning of the gospel of God's
grace toward the Gentiles.

A large part of our Introduction has been devoted to the question of the theological-ecclesiastical aim(s) and goal(s) of the
Evangelist as editor or redactor *vis-à-vis* the life-setting in which
he carried through his work. It may be felt that the vital issue
of the extent to which Mark's record preserves accurate historical
reminiscences of Jesus' words and deeds has been unduly neglec-
ted. We therefore conclude with two signally important observations:

(i) Study of the Gospel writer's purpose in relation to the
Church of his time (redaction study) neither prejudges
nor forecloses the problem of the historicity of events
reported. Rather it leaves the problem open. Though
redaction study proceeds from the insight that the Evangelist was not first and foremost a historical reporter, it by
no means follows that the traditional materials he employed
are devoid of historical data from the life of Jesus which
had not yet been disturbed or distorted in the process of
transmission up to the Evangelist's time. To take but one
example: we noted that Mark appears to be in conflict with
different views of the 'authority' of Jesus Christ held in his
own community, and that by his own selection and organisation of Jesus-traditions he offers his own response. But
those traditions which allude to the question of Jesus'
authority probably reflect the actual circumstances of his
ministry in which the Jewish quarrel with him was in part
at least that in various ways he claimed and manifested
direct 'authority' and power from God (e.g. Mk 1:21–28).

(ii) It should not be forgotten that investigation of a Gospel
writer's distinctive message is an exercise in historical study
of great significance in its own right and in so far as we are
then attempting to elucidate a particular example of early
Christian preaching within a concrete context. As J. Rohde
puts it: 'The individual Gospels are canonical examples
of the way in which the problem of how the message of
Christ is to be interpreted was answered in a new situation.
To this extent, redaction criticism is of supreme importance
for practical theology today, and especially for homiletics,
for the more successful it is in determining the setting of a

gospel in the life and history of the earliest church, the more contemporary practical theology can learn how the message of Christ is to be presented in a new situation' (Rohde, pp. 257f.).

AN ANALYSIS OF THE GOSPEL

THE GOSPEL ACCORDING TO
MARK

PREFACE: THE GROUND OF THE GOSPEL
1:1–15

Like most other ancient writings, the Gospels contain introductory and concluding materials that furnish or might be expected to furnish important clues as to the author's overall meaning and purpose. In the infancy stories of Matthew, for example, there is a considerable stress on the theme of Emmanuel, 'God with us' (Mt. 1:23). Consonant with this is the fact that Matthew inserts the great body of teaching of the Sermon on the Mount (Mt. 5–7) between the brief report of many mighty works performed by Jesus (Mt. 4:23–25) and the healing of a leper (Mt. 8:1–4). Thereby it is made clear that the Jesus to whom Matthew bears witness is more, much more, than the teacher of a heroic ethic: he is the bearer and exerciser of the very power of God for all who believe, 'God with us'. Again at the end, the exalted Christ reiterates the assurance and consolation of Emmanuel: 'Lo, I am with you always to the close of the age' (Mt. 28:20); and further the Church's own missionary movement into the future is to be controlled and governed by the way Jesus has already gone and the message he has already proclaimed ('Go therefore and make disciples of all nations . . . teaching them to observe all that I have commanded you' Mt. 28:19f.).

In John's Gospel there is a statement at the close which is decisive in relation to the dialectic of 'seeing' and 'believing' which is a feature of the Gospel as a whole: 'Blessed are those who have not seen and yet believe' (Jn 20:29). There is also a firm declaration of the writer's goal: 'These are written that you may believe that Jesus in the Christ, the Son of God, and that believing you may have life in his name' (Jn 20:31). The Prologue of John's Gospel (1:1–18) is a hymn to the *Logos* or Word, couched in theological or confessional language and bearing upon a matter crucial for John, the question of Jesus' origin. Not only does the specific term *Logos* recur through the work (5:37f.; 8:31–37; 14:23f.; 17:16–17), but themes introduced in the Prologue are picked up and developed later (e.g. 'light', 3:19–21; 'life', 3:15, 36; 5:17f.; 'truth', 3:33; 18:37f.).

Mark's Introduction and Conclusion (see commentary, pp. 64ff., 351ff.) are also key passages. Like John's Prologue, the

Marcan Preface raises the curtain on a number of themes subsequently spelled out by the Evangelist. But unlike John, Mark gives
us an Introduction in *narrative* form. The narration has such an
air of realism that it might seem as though the writer were leading us into a straight account of the historical words and acts of
Jesus. But while the Jesus of Mark's Gospel is most assuredly a
figure of real history, we would miss the point if we imagined that
the life of this one could be comprehended by historical enquiry
and research, or depicted by a natural and descriptive report.
The Marcan Introduction is in fact 'theologically loaded'. The
credentials of Jesus are not human at all; they are divine. At the
Baptism he is designated the Son of God (Mk 1:11). He is driven
by the Spirit into the wilderness and conflict with Satan (1:12f.).
He 'comes', and 'comes' abruptly and mysteriously, into Galilee,
'preaching the gospel of God' (1:14). By such indications as these
the Evangelist unlocks for his readers the secret of who this Jesus
is whose story is to be told. There is a transcendent dimension
to his history, without which that history could never be understood. Lacking intelligence of the other dimension, Mark's readers
would be in no better position than the many actors in the story
who are blind to the truth about Jesus. But in arming them with
such intelligence, Mark is also challenging his readers and putting them in the place of decision: to believe (or not believe) that
Jesus both brings and is the *good news of God*.

In respect of what it seeks to do for the reader Mark's Introduction is somewhat reminiscent of the Prologue to the Book of
Job (also in the form of a narrative). In the colloquy in heaven
that takes place there between God and Satan concerning Job,
God is at once connected with the coming ordeal of Job and though
the Job of the poem is unaware of what has occurred in the
heavenly court, *the reader knows* and so is put in the picture about
the real scope and intensity of Job's agonising struggle.

As to the extent of Mark's Preface, most commentators assume
that it consists of 1:1-13 (e.g. Taylor, Cranfield, Schweizer), in
which case the generalising summary of verses 14-15, reporting
Jesus' appearance in Galilee, his preaching of the kingdom of God
and his call to repentance, begins the story proper. But there are
good grounds for holding that the Introduction is in fact comprised of verses 1-15, in which case verses 14-15 round off Mark's
prefatory disclosure of who Jesus really is. (a) The term 'gospel'
is clearly crucial for Mark and is no less prominent in 1:14f. than

it is in the opening statement of 1:1. (b) In the words of verse 14, **Now after John was arrested** (or 'delivered up'), the absolute use of the Greek verb for 'delivered up' carries with it the idea of a destiny decreed *by God's will*. Accordingly, Mark is not here offering in any biographical sense a precise denotation of the very moment at which Jesus' ministry was separated from that of John the Baptist. Rather is he bringing the work of Jesus in preaching within the orbit of the divinely ordained fate of the Baptist, with possibly just a hint of Jesus' coming passion. In 9:11–13 it is again suggested in a thinly veiled way that the Baptist's tragic fate, divinely willed, is the precursor of the sufferings of the Son of man. (c) Mark manifests no historical interest in the Baptist or his career for their own sake in his Introduction. The Baptist simply points to Jesus as the Stronger One (1:7), and verses 14–15 admirably clarify the reason for the Baptist's deference. 'John came baptizing in the wilderness and preaching the baptism of repentance, while Jesus came preaching the gospel of God. In other words, Mark sees the preaching of the gospel as part of the surpassing strength of Jesus *vis-à-vis* John. So regarded verses 14f. are a climactic statement that fulfils the word of John about Jesus, while at the same time it rounds out the overarching interest in the *gospel*' (L. E. Keck, *NTS* 12 (1965–6), p. 361). (d) The account of the testing of Jesus by Satan is extremely bare in Mk 1:12–13, and only if we link verses 14–15 with 12–13 does Jesus' ultimate triumph come into full view. 'Mark's Jesus is the victorious Son of God who returns from the testing-ground with the *gospel*' (Keck, *NTS* 12 (1965–6), p. 362).

The Introduction in 1:1–15 may then be described as a disclosure scene. What is unveiled is that the Gospel has Jesus both as its content *and* initiator. If the Gospel has its beginning in a history that can be narrated, it is none-the-less a history in which faith discerns much more than meets the naked eye, and which challenges to religious belief.

The upshot of taking 1:1–15 to constitute the Marcan Preface is that the story proper then opens with the call of the four disciples (1:16–20). The theme of discipleship thus stands as the frontispiece of Mark's record. For the Evangelist *gospel* and discipleship are inextricably bound together. It is surely striking (and a further argument for the unity of Mk 1:1–15) that not only this first section but the next two in the Marcan structure (see Analysis, pp. 58f.) open with the 'disciple motif': the Commis-

sioning of the Twelve in 3:13-19a and Missionary Marching
Orders to the Twelve in 6:7-13.

THE APPEARANCE OF JOHN THE BAPTIST 1:1-8

For this section Mark clearly had a good deal of traditional
material to draw upon. Before Mark's time the Church had
applied the *OT* prophecy (Mal. 3:1) found in Mk 1:2 to John
the Baptist, perhaps prompted by the fact that Malachi predicts the
return of Elijah (Mal. 4:5). The prophecy of Mal. 3:1 is referred
to the Baptist in Mt. 11:10 amid material drawn from the earlier
Q. Lk. 1:17 and Mk 9:11-13 show how lively in the early Church
was the idea that the Baptist was Elijah *redivivus*.

Mark obviously knew more about the Baptist than he chooses
to record in his Introduction. He is aware that he gathered
disciples about him (2:18; 6:29), that he was executed by Herod
Antipas (6:14-29) and that his veneration by the mass of people
as a prophet was troublesome to the Jewish authorities (11:27-33).
If he was familiar with the longer Q version of the activity and
preaching of the Baptist (Mt. 3:7-12; Lk. 3:7-14, 17), he has
certainly chosen not to use it. He restricts himself to a highly
condensed account of the Baptist's religious acts and his Elijah-
like garb in order to bring into high relief his role as the divinely
appointed Forerunner of the Stronger One, Jesus. The process by
which the Baptist was subordinated to Jesus, drawn into the Gospel fold, so to speak, and located at the turning of the ages, is
plainly discernible in Mark. It culminates in the Gospel of John
where the Baptist openly declares concerning Jesus: 'Behold, the
Lamb of God, who takes away the sin of the world!' (1:29);
'And I have seen and have borne witness that this is the Son of
God' (1:34); 'He must increase, but I must decrease' (3:30).

The NT contains references or allusions to a movement inspired by the Baptist. Aside from Mk 2:18 and 6:29, there is a
mention of 'John's disciples' in Jn 3:25, and Ac. 19:1-5 points to
the existence of a group of Baptist followers at Eph us. Also
scholars have detected in John's Gospel traces of a polemic against
a Baptist sect. There survives, in small numbers, to this day in Iran
the sect of the Mandeans. Their sacred texts (mainly liturgical)
were published by M. Lidzbarski in the 1920's and more recently
by Lady Drouwer, and it is notable that the sect traces its descent
from John the Baptist. From all of this we may infer that the
Baptist was an important figure of history in his own right. But

the Gospels afford us but little opportunity of recovering accurate historical data relating to the Baptist, since their interests in him are primarily theological, that is, he functions, as in the Marcan Introduction, as a signpost to the true identity of Jesus.

1. The beginning of the gospel of Jesus Christ, the Son of God: a superscription or title to the whole work. It is Mark's whole narrative that is *gospel* and the whole Gospel is rooted and grounded in the one from whom and with whom it starts, namely, the Jesus who lived and taught and called men to follow him on the way of the cross. A number of commentators do not insert a full stop after **Son of God** and take the opening words with what follows, **John the baptizer appeared**, in which case Mark would be indicating the exact chronological starting-point of the good news (Rawlinson, p. 6). Others take the opening words to refer to what is related in verses 1–8 or verses 1–13 (e.g. Cranfield, pp. 34f.). But in view of the primacy of Mark's theological concern and of all that the term 'gospel' means for him, it is better to regard verse 1 as an overall title than as a reference to those historical events that Mark considered to be a prelude to the public ministry of Jesus. (No other single section of Mark is introduced with a title.) **The beginning:** echoes the first words of Genesis and of the Gospel of John. But of course there is no speculation in Mark on the question of Jesus' origin or of his pre-existence. Mark's Jesus 'comes' suddenly and unexpectedly (note the repetition of the verb in 1:9 and 1:14), and there is no reflection on whence he came. The gospel starts for Mark with a history, the story of Jesus with his preaching and teaching and call to cross-bearing discipleship, and the term 'beginning', with its echo of Gen. 1:1, signifies a new day of God's creative activity now inaugurated in this very story.

gospel: at the time of Mark's writing not the name of a special literary genre, but a general term for 'good news' that had none-the-less an extensive background of usage long before Mark in the *OT* and Hellenistic circles and in the earliest Christian mission. Not until Justin, around AD 150, did Gospel become the title of a book as applied to the four documents in the *NT* and as designating a particular type of literature. It has for long been widely held that as a form of literature the Gospels were unique in the ancient world, but in view of the contemporary debate about the possible relation of the Gospels to Hellenistic aretalogies, or stories of the miraculous deeds of gods or heroes, the claim that the canonical Gospels are absolutely *sui generis* should not be made too lightly (Robinson, *JMH*, pp. 103f.). Between the fifth century BC and the third century AD words clustering around the term 'gospel' were used in the Hellenistic world to signify victory, and could denote the 'good news' of a Roman emperor's birth or enthronement, or of military or political triumph. In the Greek *OT* (LXX) the word occurs almost entirely in its verbal form, 'to proclaim the good news', especially of victory (e.g. 1 Sam. 31:9). Frequently in Isaiah the good news announced consists of the coming of God's rule or salvation or vindication (Isa. 40:9; 41:27; 52:7; 60:6; 61:1). In the context of the Pauline mission, the word 'gospel' is frequently used by the apostle to denote either the act of preaching or the message of God's victory in the death and resurrection of Jesus Christ, through which God himself summons men to believe in him. For Mark **gospel** refers both to the good news proclaimed by the Church about Jesus Christ and the good news brought by Jesus in everything he is and says and does as narrated by Mark. Hence in the phrase **of Jesus Christ** it is misleading to suggest that the genitive is strictly objective, 'the message about Jesus Christ' (Taylor, p. 152), since Mark does not distinguish between the gospel preached by the Church and the gospel Jesus himself proclaimed (in 1:14 the one who is the content of the Church's preaching also appears as the herald of the *gospel of God*). The name **Jesus** occurs not infrequently in the *OT* and among Jews until the second century AD. According to Luke the name given to our Lord was no accident, but the instruction of an angel (Lk. 1:31; 2:21). The name means *Yahweh is salvation* and Matthew picks this up and in his fondness for proof from prophecy relates it to Ps. 130:8 (LXX) and to Isa. 7:14 (Mt. 1:21–23). **Christ** is of course not a name at all but an honorific title, 'the anointed one' or Messiah. Whether it would still have retained its titular force for Mark's readers is difficult to say. Certainly Mark himself exhibits a good deal of reserve toward the title Christ (Mk 8:29–33; 14:61f.). **the Son of God:** omitted by several MSS and a number of Church fathers. But it is most probably original to Mark: (a) the weight of textual evidence supports its inclusion; (b) the designation **Son of God** is crucial for Mark (3:11; 5:7), most particularly in the centurion's confession (15:39).

  2. As it is written: a common formula of citation. There are several examples of **as** at the beginning of a sentence in the *NT*

(Lk. 11:30; 17:26; Jn 3:14; 1 C. 2:9), but in Mark it occurs only here. Accordingly the presumption is, and it is supported by the fact that this formula always introduces a scriptural confirmation of a *preceding* statement, that Mark intends to apply the scripture(s) he quotes to his opening words in 1:1, and thus to demonstrate that the gospel's 'beginning' (i.e. the whole story of Jesus) is in conformity with the will of God expressed in the *OT*. This is the only place in the gospel where the author introduces an *OT* quotation in his own name. Everywhere else references to the *OT* by citation or by allusion are on the lips of a speaker in the story, most frequently of Jesus himself. By contrast, Matthew is very often profoundly concerned with the letter of the *OT* and its precise fulfilment in detail in the events surrounding Jesus (e.g. Mt. 3:3; 4:12-16). It is enough for Mark to intimate in the broadest sense by an appeal to Scripture at the very outset that God himself was acting and speaking afresh and finally in the good news. Only from the vantage-point of Easter faith could one begin in this way (Schweizer, *GNM*, p. 31). If Mark gives the impression of being much less controlled by the *OT* than Matthew, or if the exact correspondence between *OT* prediction and *NT* fulfilment means much less to him, it is possibly because he has a stronger conviction of the sheer unexpectedness or newness of the event of Jesus Christ who 'came' (Mk 1:9, 14), Mark says not whence (Suhl, p. 137; Anderson, *UOTN*, pp. 285f.).

in Isaiah the prophet: the trouble is that not all of the quotation that follows is from Isaiah, and this has led to the correction found in a number of ancient textual authorities, 'in the prophets'.

2, 3. The first part of the citation agrees with Exod. 23:20a, the second part with Mal. 3:1, except that it reads **thy way** instead of Malachi's 'the way before me' (Yahweh's way), and the third part with Isa. 40:3 (LXX), except that Mark replaces 'of our God' by 'his': *make his paths straight*. Since the whole citation is assigned in Mark to Isaiah, are the words from Mal. 3:1 to be regarded as the gloss or interpolation of an early copyist in the Marcan text (as in the view of Rawlinson, pp. 7f. and Taylor, p. 153)? In favour of such a view is of course the attribution to Isaiah in Mark and the rather puzzling omission of Mal. 3:1 in the parallel contexts of Mt. 3:3 and Lk. 3:4. On the other hand Mark could arguably have taken over the different texts from an oral or written collection of testimonies, in which they had already been combined under the name of one author, perhaps because of the appearance of the same phrase *pinnah derek* ('prepare the way') in each. But the arguments on either side are hardly decisive. A possible explanation is that since the prophecies in the composite quotation have to do with John the Baptist, they may have been taken over into the Gospel from the disciples of John the Baptist *in the form used by them* (Stendahl, pp. 50ff., 215f.). The Qumran sect also used the prophecy of Isa. 40:3, but the sect followed the form of the Hebrew text and so made it apply to the life and activity of its own desert community of the elect in the last days: 'Prepare in the desert Yahweh's way' (1QS 8:14; 9:19). The followers of the Baptist on the other hand adopted the LXX form of the Isa. 40:3 text and applied it to their own 'wilderness-preacher-leader' (conceivably in opposition to Qumran?), **the voice of one crying in the wilderness**. If Mark took up the citation already so adapted within the Baptist circle, it would have served his purpose well. His interest in it would then lie not in offering *his own* biographical notice about the location of the Baptist's activity, or even in making the citation point specifically to the coming of Jesus, since **the way of the Lord** could have meant for him 'the way of Yahweh' and not 'the way of the Messiah' (Mark does not use *Lord* as a christological title). What then is important in Mark's use of the quotation is that the voice of the herald has sounded, the time of the good news, involving the will and plan of God, the time of John and Jesus and the Church, has dawned (Schweizer, p. 32).

4. John the baptizer appeared in the wilderness: the word **appeared** (*egeneto*) is a Semitism, and in its *OT* flavour re-echoes the notion that John's emergence is in accordance with the divine will and purpose. Here John is described by the present participle of the verb *baptizein* (elsewhere by the substantive *baptistēs*, 6:25; 8:28), and this lays emphasis on his repeated action in baptising and is correctly rendered **the baptizer** in *RSV*. Not a word is said about the antecedents of John, and this suggests two things: (a) the name and role of the Baptist was already familiar to the early Church; (b) the Evangelist is not concerned with the Baptist's history in itself but only with John's place *vis-à-vis* Jesus in the salvation-time of the spread of the good news. Consequently the locating of John's activity **in the wilderness** in accord with the adapted form of Isa. 40:3 does not betoken a biographical interest on Mark's part, but rather symbolises the area where God comes to meet his people (Hos. 2:14) and lead them in a new

exodus. **preaching a baptism of repentance for the forgiveness of sins:** preoccupation with the good news and its promulgation leads Mark to stress the preaching activity of the Baptist
in what is at first sight a strange expression, **preaching a baptism**. Not only did John have people baptized (by total immersion presumably, *baptizein* meaning 'to dip' or 'plunge'), he
proclaimed what it was all about. It was a baptism of repentance,
the genitive denoting the essential nature and quality of the whole
religious act, althougl· it is not entirely clear whether repentance
was an indispensable precondition or, on the other hand, a direct
result of admission to baptism. More likely the expectation was
that the act of baptism would be accompanied by a radical
transformation of life in which men were opened up to the grace
of God that liberated from past sins and would sustain them in the
approaching judgment (hence **for** or 'towards the goal of' the
forgiveness of sins.) The Greek word *metanoia* ('repentance') has
its background in the Hebrew root *šûb* ('return'). Whereas in the
OT this word has most often its ordinary secular meaning, it is
also frequently used in a deeply religious sense in contexts where
the primary thought is of God's steadfast covenant-love toward
Israel and his longing for a perverse people to end their alienating
ways and turn back to him. The word *metanoia* means literally
'change of mind', but in light of its *OT* background it denotes in
the *NT*, and certainly here in Mark, not just a change of inward
disposition but a complete turnabout of one's life, with all that
such a re-direction implies of the need for God's help on the one
side and of ethical conduct on man's side. Strikingly enough,
according to Mark, Jesus also comes summoning men to repentance (1:15), and immediately calls disciples to follow him (1:16–
20). In response they have to forsake altogether their customary
mode of living as fishermen and 'turn' and become 'fishers of
men'.

The historical origins of John's baptismal practice are obscure.
Ritual lustrations are required by the Law in the *OT* (e.g. Lev.
15:5, 8, 13, 16), and in Isa. 1:16 'cleansing' is connected with
repentance. But these are at best a distant background. Jewish
sectarian practices about the time of Jesus did include baptismal
rites. Among the Covenanters of Qumran, for example, repentance and entry into the new covenant were associated with
baptismal ceremonials (1QS 3:4–12; 15:13f.), the confession of
sins also being involved in preparation for a coming divine

judgment (1QS 1:24ff.; 5:13). The beginnings of proselyte-baptism within 'official' Judaism are unclear, but even if it were established practice in John's day, it could hardly have been the source of derivation of his baptism, since: (a) John's baptism was administered to Jews, not outsiders, and it came as an invitation to a truly purified and refined Judaism; (b) as we gather from the longer accounts of the content of the Baptist's preaching from Q in Mt. 3:7–12 and Lk. 3:4–9, it was directly connected with the imminent coming of God in judgment. Accordingly, John's closest affinities are with Qumran. Yet, if due account is taken of the NT evidence, it could scarcely be claimed that the Baptist himself was or had been a member of the Qumran community. Traditions respecting John in the Gospels in fact also suggest salient contrasts between him and what we know of the sectarians. (a) At Qumran baptism was an often repeated ritual, not entirely unconnected with the removal of sins, but directed chiefly toward ceremonial cleanliness. With the Baptist it was a once-for-all act in face of the impending judgment of God, tied up inescapably with the forgiveness of sins, which may have come home to John with singular force from his own brooding on prophetic passages (e.g. Isa. 1:16; 33:24; 40:2; 53:5f.; Jer. 31:34; Ezek. 36:25–27; Mic. 7:18). (b) The ritual of baptism at Qumran was monopolised by those members of a separatist group who had withdrawn into a monastic life and regarded themselves as the elect. John's baptism was for *all* and carried the appeal to *all* to be ready against God's day.

5. No doubt the Baptist and his activity did attract a considerable crowd. But Mark puts the attendance figures rather high: **And there went out to him all the country of Judea, and all the people of Jerusalem:** 'A touch of oriental extravagance', says Rawlinson (p. 8); but more than that, a vivid stroke by which the Evangelist illustrates the stir and excitement accompanying the inauguration of the good news and the dawning of the time of salvation. **and they were baptized by him in the river Jordan, confessing their sins:** as Mark has it, the people who came to John were already moved to contrition and, prepared as they were to acknowledge their sins at baptism, the act of baptism itself becomes an expression of their readiness to repent and turn to God and so opens the way to the divine removal of sins. This means that the act of baptism *per se* is no guarantee of forgiveness. **the river Jordan:** had many sacred associations,

e.g. in the prophetic careers of Elijah and Elisha, and especially
in the story of Naaman (2 Kg. 5), and was altogether a suitable
setting for the revival of that spirit of prophecy that ushered in the
new and final day of the good news.

6. No doubt Mark's very brief description of the clothing and
diet of the Baptist was already traditional. The traditional por-
trait, especially the leather girdle, would have conjured up mem-
ories of Elijah (2 Kg. 1:8), and the diet of locusts and wild honey
would have been recognised as the typical food of wandering
tribesmen in the desert. But Mark does not here link the Baptist
specifically with Elijah, nor is there any hint that voluntary
renunciation of normal worldly pleasures was required of those
baptised by John. John's asceticism, as a datum of the tradition
(attested also in Lk. 1:15), is of very small moment to Mark, and
so the Evangelist hastens on forthwith to the Baptist's preaching.
He neither applauds nor denigrates the strange unworldly appearance of the Baptist as a 'holy man'; his interest lies in John's
participation in the *kerygma* or proclamation.

7–8. A relatively full account of the Baptist's preaching is given
in Q (Mt. 3:7–10 = Lk. 3:7–9, 17): his resounding words about
the wrath to come, the axe laid to the root of the trees, the Coming
One with winnowing fan in hand to separate the wheat from the
chaff in the day of fiery judgment. Mark discounts these data and
compresses everything into one theme: the Baptist in his proclamation declares himself the Forerunner of the Stronger One,
whose baptism will supersede his own baptism by water.

After me comes he who is mightier than I: the words
after me strike a note of eschatological urgency. It is the turning
of the ages and the time is short, for even before Mark's Introduction is over we learn that Jesus came at once into Galilee after
John was delivered up. It is God's time rather than man's time
that is in view. **comes:** a graphic present-tense signifying immediacy. On John's lips we find the same verb that Mark himself
employs to denote Jesus' sudden and unexplained but God-
directed (1:1–3) appearance ('came' in 1:9 and 1:14). **he who is
mightier than I:** the Baptist's designation of Jesus as the
Stronger One also carries eschatological overtones, suggesting
that Jesus is the final deliverer, as is implied in Mk 3:27 (compare
Lk. 11:22, where the idea is made explicit). **the thong of whose
sandals I am not worthy to stoop down and untie:** beside
Jesus the Baptist cannot claim even a slave–master relationship.

It was the duty of a slave to carry his master's shoes after him or to take them from his feet (for examples in rabbinic literature see SB vol. 1, p. 121; vol. 2, p. 1). **I have baptized you with water; but he will baptize you with the Holy Spirit:** whereas this statement is kept separate from the statement of verse 7 in Mark, the two are fused together into one in Q (Mt. 3:11 = Lk. 3:16). The fusion of the two strands in Q appears to be a later form than the separation in Mark. Looked at from the historical angle, the form of the Baptist's words regarding the two baptisms in Mark presents grave difficulties. His prophecy of Jesus' coming baptism of men with the Holy Spirit appears to reflect the full-blown Christian type of baptism known in the Church at and after Pentecost, when the Spirit was experienced as God's gift in and through the finished work of Jesus Christ. In Q (Mt. 3:11 = Lk. 3:16) the Baptist's prophecy is reported in a different form: the baptism of the Coming One is described as being 'with the Holy Spirit *and with fire*'. The questions of how to reconcile the divergent forms of the saying, or of whether the Baptist was actually predicting baptism with the Holy Spirit (the specifically Christian mode), have been variously answered: (a) The words 'with fire' in the Q version are the original ones in the Baptist's statement. Baptism with fire would denote, in contrast with his own water-baptism, the final judgment, as the context of the saying in Mt. 3:10-12 clearly indicates. The Baptist's words would then have been Christianised in conformity with the Church's understanding of baptism, either by the insertion of the phrase 'with the Holy Spirit' as in Q, or by the substitution of 'with the Holy Spirit' for 'with fire' as in Mark (Rawlinson, p. 8; Taylor, p. 157). (b) The Baptist originally said 'with wind and fire' (the Greek word *pneuma*, like the Hebrew *rûaḥ*, means 'wind' as well as 'spirit'). Wind, required for threshing, and fire occur together in the picture of the judgment of the Coming One in Mt. 3:12, and they both appear also in Isa. 29:6; 30:27f.; Ezek. 1:4 as well as in an apocalypse of the first century AD, 2 Esd. 13:1, 27 (Barrett, *HSGT*, p. 126; Schweizer, *GNM*, p. 34). The early Church would then have seen in the word *pneuma* in this context a reference to the Spirit and would readily have made it the Holy Spirit. The omission of the words 'and with fire' in Mark could be construed as an accommodation to the Christian idea of the Holy Spirit as a *gracious* endowment. (c) The Q version of the saying is the original one, only the Baptist himself meant it in the sense: 'with the Holy Spirit and with fire'. In that case he would be referring to the twofold work of the judge, refining and cleansing in a redemptive judgment and destroying with fire. For the notion of the Spirit's function in refining and cleansing, there is an interesting parallel at Qumran: 'God will cleanse them by a holy spirit from all evil deeds' (1QS 4:13, 20f.). The prediction of Ezek. 36:25–27 connects the pouring out of the Spirit directly with cleansing and that of Jl 2:28 with the revival of prophecy *and* fiery judgment (Hill, pp. 94f.). But if the Baptist did predict a 'baptism with the Holy Spirit', it is hard to determine whether he contemplated it as the activity of *God* himself, as the prophecies of Ezekiel and Joel and probably 1QS 4:13, 20f. also do, or of a coming messianic figure. Mk 1:8 may be interpreted in the former sense, and the Baptist's followers appear to have thought of him as *himself* a messianic agent (Lk. 1:16f.; Ac. 19:2f.). On the other hand Mk 1:7, with its promise of the Stronger One, clearly points to a messianic figure.

Obviously the historical posture of the Baptist *vis-à-vis* Jesus and the exact form of his saying here are by no means easy to recover. Bearing in mind the early Church's tendency to locate the Baptist within the orbit of the good news of Jesus Christ, we may most reasonably suppose that the Marcan version of his statement (1:8) reveals a shaping up towards the Church's experience and interpretation of baptism. At all events, as Cranfield correctly observes (p. 49), what is at issue here for Mark is not the *contrast* between John's baptism and Christian baptism. That in fact is incidental to Mark's desire to underscore the involvement of the forerunner with Jesus at the opening of the salvation-time of the gospel.

THE BAPTISM OF JESUS 1:9–11

The event of Jesus' baptism is recorded in all four Gospels (Mt. 3:13–17; Lk. 3:21ff.; Jn 1:32–34), and we may take it to be one of the indisputably historical traits of Jesus' ministry. 'Jesus' baptism by John is one of the most certainly verified occurrences of his life' (Bornkamm, p. 54). The Church would have been quite unlikely to invent the story of an event that occasioned for it so much theological difficulty. In the Gospel reports the difficulty is already adumbrated. According to Matthew, the Baptist indeed sought to prevent Jesus from submitting to baptism by him (Mt. 3:14). In Luke Jesus' baptism is placed alongside the baptism of

the multitude, and is passed over apparently with embarrassed
haste in a participial clause (Lk. 3:21). According to John, there
is no explicit statement at all that the Baptist did in fact baptise
Jesus (Jn 1:29, 32–34). In the second-century apocryphal *Gospel
of the Nazarenes* Jesus himself protests: 'Wherein have I sinned that
I should go and be baptized by him?' (*NT Apocrypha*, 1, p. 147).
Mark, for his part, records the baptism in a straightforward but
very condensed fashion.

It can be inferred that the event of the baptism was a hotly
disputed subject in the early Church. That it should have caused
perplexity is quite understandable. Why should he who came to
be recognised and confessed as the 'sinless one' give himself to a
sinner's repentance-baptism? The notion that Jesus, though himself without sin, undertook an act of vicarious repentance is the
product of later theological reflection, and is foreign to the Gospel
texts. Also foreign to the texts is speculation about what the
baptism meant for Jesus, for his own decisions and inward life. In
Mark's account the phenomena occurring at the baptism are
restricted to Jesus' own subjective experience. In Matthew the
opening of the heavens and the heavenly voice are treated as
objective events perceivable to bystanders (Mt. 3:16–17). In
Luke also there is a high degree of objectivity, for the dove appears in 'bodily form' (Lk. 4:22). The texts do not really invite us,
however, into a realm of clinical or psychological investigation
about the miraculous phenomena or about the inner development
of Jesus. Permeated as they are with *OT* allusions (the opening of
the heavens, the Spirit, and the heavenly voice being construed as
signs of the last days), and expressed in the language of *revelation*,
they reveal how the story was transformed into the kind of
testimony to Christ that only the Christian believer could make.
Accordingly, while the far-reaching importance of the fact of
Jesus' baptism for the early Church should not be denied, it is no
longer possible for us to determine with any accuracy the details
of what happened.

9. In those days Jesus came from Nazareth of Galilee:
the opening phrase **in those days** is a connecting link of Mark's.
It is Semitic-sounding, imprecise, and has a biblical ring. It is
a mistake to think that Mark is here envisaging a significant
historical or chronological turning-point—the work of the Baptist
is complete and now the public ministry of Jesus begins! Rather
is it punctually to the hour decreed by God that Jesus appears.

John's 'appearance' and Jesus' 'coming' are merged at the inauguration of the new day of salvation. **Jesus came:** the verb has a theological flavour for Mark (see also 1:14). The whence of his coming is not at all discussed, so it is implied that he came as the divine envoy or in conformity with the will of God. To hold that **came** signifies a belief on Mark's part in the pre-existence of Christ is to transgress the limits of his Gospel's evidence. It is no less a mistake to deduce from this verb, or from the affirmation of the heavenly voice (**'Thou art my beloved son'**), that Mark operated with an adoptionist christology and thought of Jesus as the one adopted by God at a particular moment in his life. For the Evangelist, as we have seen, Jesus 'comes' as the one whose *whole story* is the *archē* or 'beginning' of the Church's gospel. **from Nazareth of Galilee:** just as the verb 'came' in its bareness is in harmony with Mark's subsequent concern over the secret of who Jesus is, so also is this solitary note about his home town. Nothing is said about his age, his physical characteristics, his personality, or his family status; nor indeed does **Nazareth** give anything away, for it was a negligible village that is never mentioned in the *OT*, Josephus, or the Jewish Talmud (see also Jn 1:46).

10. And . . . immediately he saw the heavens opened: 'and immediately' is a favourite joining phrase of Mark's, used by him over forty times; it helps to impart to the narrative a sense of the inexorable forward movement of Jesus' ministry toward his divinely willed death on the cross. **he saw;** the experience of the opened heavens and the Spirit descending (as well as of the voice in 1:11) are confined by Mark to Jesus alone. Nevertheless we should not without more ado maintain that Mark intended to record a vision enjoyed by Jesus, albeit one that communicated a real message from God (for this view, see Cranfield, pp. 52f.). On the contrary, Mark's interest lies not in the mind or *psychē* of Jesus, but in the *reality* of what happened in the baptism, a reality open only to faith's insight, namely, that the way of Jesus is indissolubly bound up with God's own way with the world. That none but Jesus saw could have suggested for Mark not only the unique role of Jesus as the Son but that the natural man (without faith) could not possibly recognise that role. **the heavens opened;** recalls the ancient view of the universe, with the firmament or visible sky above the earth, a number of heavens above that and God's dwelling-place beyond all. The 'rending of the heavens' is a familiar symbol of the late Jewish apocalypses (e.g. Bar. 22:1;

Test. Levi 2:6; 5:1; 18:6; *Test. Judah* 24:2), but it does go back
to the *OT* (Isa. 64:1; Ezek. 1:1) and is found elsewhere in the
NT (Jn 1:51; Ac. 7:56; Rev. 4:1; 11:19; 19:11). This graphic
piece of imagery signifies that God is about to communicate with
or reveal himself to men, and in Mark it is the prelude to the final
and decisive disclosure of God. **and the Spirit descending upon
him like a dove:** does not denote that Jesus was possessed or even
uniquely possessed inwardly of the Spirit. There is no support here
for the view that it was only as the person possessed of the Spirit
that the earliest Christians could persist in designating Jesus as
Messiah, even though the title as normatively understood in
Judaism did not actually suit him (W. C. van Unnik, *NTS* 8
(1961–2), pp. 101–16). As we have remarked, Mark concentrates
on the 'objective' divine reality ('objective' for faith's perception)
of what happened in the baptism. Accordingly the Evangelist
intends the descent of the Spirit upon Jesus to indicate that the
days of Spirit-famine are ended, that the prophetic promises
have now come true, and that the Spirit is potently active in this
new and last epoch of the ministry of Jesus. **like a dove:** the
dove-symbolism has caused a tremendous problem for modern
commentators, and all the indications are that it was problematic
from the very outset. In Mark's report the Greek, no less than the
English, is ambiguous. It is not clear whether it likens the Spirit
to a dove, or describes the dove-like descent of the Spirit. The same
is true of Matthew's report. Luke, however, has quite unambiguously assigned independent, objective existence to the bird—it
descends 'in bodily form'; and John also seems to imply this in the
added comment, 'and it remained on him' (Jn 1:32). In the later
apocryphal *Gospel of the Nazarenes* the dove has vanished altogether and is replaced by 'the whole fount of the Holy Spirit'. The
origin and meaning of the dove-symbolism still remains obscure.
Many of the explanations offered are quite implausible, e.g. (a)
that it goes back to a fairy-story motif that occurred in 'Call to
Kingship Sagas' featuring in oriental cults like that of Ishtar in
Babylon (for an account and dismissal of this kind of explanation,
see Bultmann, *HST*, pp. 248ff.); (b) that it is related to Noah's
dove (Gen. 8:8–11), a connexion supported in some measure by
the Church fathers who, on the basis of the analogy between the
Flood and Christian baptism (1 Pet. 3:20f.), relate the Jordan
dove with Noah's; (c) that the dove is a type of gentleness, or of
divine wisdom. But the trouble with these supposed parallels is

that the dove is nowhere explicitly associated with the Holy Spirit. Nor is it wise to probe for great hidden depths of symbolism in the dove reference, and to hold, for instance, that since the dove is related to Jesus' immersion in the Jordan water, Yahweh's creative activity in conjunction with the primeval ocean is in view (Gen. 1:2), or that, just as Noah's dove brings a message of the ending of the divine wrath and the beginning of mercy, the descent of the dove upon Jesus suggests the coming of God's peace (Fawcett, pp. 132f.).

Probably we do not need to look further than those rabbinic texts that do compare the Holy Spirit to a dove or bird. Ben Zoma speaks of the hovering of the Spirit of God on the waters 'like a dove which hovers over her young without touching them' (*B. Hagig.* 15a). R. Jose talks about 'hearing the divine voice cooing like a dove' (*Berak.* 3a). It has lately been pointed out, however, that the point of comparison in such texts is with the activity or *motion* of the dove. From this starting-point it is argued that in the Marcan version the phrase **like a dove** is nothing more than an adverbial phrase referring to the *dove-like descent* of the Spirit. The tradition of the baptism, full as it is of Semitic data, emanates from Palestinian Aramaic-speaking Christianity, and only later did Hellenistic Christianity transform the simile of movement into a phenomenon, giving the dove an independent form or existence (as in Luke), and so making it a separate object of interpretation. Accordingly, in the most ancient account, this detail should be thought of in a general way as a 'folk-comparison between the gentle flight of a dove and the way in which the Spirit came to Jesus' (L. E. Keck, *NTS* 17 (1970–1), pp. 41ff.; especially pp. 66f.). At any rate this view has the merit of preventing us from being side-tracked into great symbolic subtleties that are not there in Mark, and of allowing us to focus on Mark's chief concern, the divine designation of Jesus as Son, whereby it is revealed to the reader that there is a transcendent dimension in Jesus' life that elicits the response of faith.

11. and a voice came from heaven, "Thou art my beloved Son: with thee I am well pleased": the centre of gravity of the baptism story lies in God's assent to Jesus as Son. The voice from heaven is the *baṭ-ḳôl* ('the daughter of the voice'). In times when the immediacy of the prophetic 'thus says the Lord' had waned, the rabbis taught that when God spoke from highest heaven, what was heard on earth was the *echo* of the divine voice. Among the rabbis also the dove, *baṭ-ḳôl*, and Holy Spirit formed a group of associated ideas, and the *baṭ-ḳôl* could be described as 'moaning or chirping like a dove' (Abrahams, 1, p. 43). Most often, when the *baṭ-ḳôl* did speak, it recited words of Scripture, as here in Mark. The divine voice is heard again in Mk 9:7 (as well as in Jn 12:28 and Ac. 9:3–7). The actual words uttered in Mk 1:11 are not a direct quotation of any one or more *OT* passages, but rather a mosaic of various *OT* elements: possibly Ps. 2:7; Isa. 42:1; Gen. 22:2 (LXX). It is usually assumed that basically we have here a combination of two texts, Isa. 42:1 and Ps. 2:7. The Isaianic passage refers to the Servant of God (possibly Israel) ordained to a mission of redemptive suffering (cf. Isa. 49:1–6; 50:4–9; 52:13–53:12): 'Behold my Servant, whom I uphold, my chosen in whom my soul delights; I have put my spirit upon him' (Isa. 42:1). The Greek word for 'servant' (Hebrew *'eḇeḏ*) is *pais*, and *pais* means either 'servant' or 'son'. Greek-speaking Christians may have changed the original *pais* to the unambiguous Greek word for 'son', *hyios*. There would then be no need to look beyond Isa. 42:1 as the primary determinant of the meaning of the heavenly message in Mk 1:11—Jesus is stamped as the suffering Servant of God (see Cranfield, pp. 54f.). On the other hand the change from *pais* to *hyios* ('son') may have been an assimilation to Ps. 2:7 (which would thus be under recall here also): 'You are my son: today I have begotten you.' This is a coronation or adoption formula (usually associated with God's authorisation of a newly enthroned king) related in the Psalm to Israel's messianic king (for recent evidence of 'Son of God' as a messianic title in the Qumran context, see 4QFlor 10-14). If Ps. 2:7 coupled with Isa. 42:1 is in view at Mk 1:11, then Jesus is designated as the kingly Messiah whose task is radically reinterpreted in terms of the mission of the suffering Servant of God.

But there is need for caution. Mk 1:11 is reminiscent of Isa. 42:1, but the language is not the same. Even if in Mk 1:10 the Evangelist is thinking of Jesus' 'anointing' with the Spirit, that does not necessarily link Mk 1:11 with the Servant, for there are many *OT* passages where the gift of the Spirit is not (as in Isa. 42:1) connected with the Servant, e.g. Isa. 11:2 and 61:1 (Nineham, p. 62). Nor is it by any means certain that the word **beloved** in Mk 1:11 echoes the 'chosen' who is the special recipient of divine favour or love in Isa. 42:1. **Beloved** may denote 'only' or 'only-begotten' (C. H. Turner, *JTS* 27 (1926),

M—D

pp. 113ff.) and this possibly signifies the uniqueness of Jesus' Sonship (I. H. Marshall, *NTS* 15 (1968-9), pp. 326-36). Some interpreters however, have postulated a link with Gen. 22:2 (LXX) and have seen a veiled allusion to Jesus as the second Isaac (described as Abraham's only 'beloved son'). The further thought that, with the 'binding of Isaac' in view, there is a pointer here to the true high priest of the last days who gives himself up sacrificially, is highly speculative (Schweizer, p. 38; cf. G. Vermes, pp. 222f.; J. E. Wood, *NTS* 14 (1967-8), pp. 583-9).

Whatever exactly the case may be, by the very evocative *OT* language of the divine voice here, by the opening citation of Scripture in 1:2-4, by the signs of the opened heavens and the descent of the Spirit, Mark intends to confirm to his readers that in Jesus uniquely God's appointed time for the fulfilment of his purpose has arrived. In Mk 1:11 the emphasis is on *God's* initiative and *God's* act, and it does not invite us to psychologising investigation of Jesus' self-awareness, nor even to regard what is happening here as corroboration of Jesus' own filial consciousness (Cranfield, p. 55). That is not to deny that in his life Jesus actually had an unprecedented sense of the most intimate communion with God: he calls God *Abba*, Father, and says 'my Father', never joining himself with anyone else in saying 'our Father'.

Even if the adoption formula of Ps. 2:7 ('Thou art my Son') is in sight here, Mark is not subscribing to an 'adoptionist christology'. No question is asked or hint given about what or who Jesus may have been before his baptism. Again, in confessional formulae like Phil. 2:6-11, Ac. 2:36, and Rom. 1:3-4, the tendency is to locate Jesus' installation to Lordship or divine Sonship at the resurrection. Mark locates Jesus' entry on Sonship at the baptism, eager as he is to affirm that the gospel begins with the whole story of Jesus. But that does not set him poles apart from these other christological confessions, since for Mark too the 'beginning' can be seen for what it really is only from a resurrection standpoint, and Easter is the final unveiling (see especially Mk 9:9).

THE TESTING OF JESUS 1:12-13

This story appears in much fuller form in Q (Mt. 4:1-11 = Lk. 4:1-13). In Mark it is told with the greatest economy, in very bald and even cryptic language. Presumably Mark's readers either knew the details of a larger account long transmitted orally in the Church, or Mark greatly abridged it to suit his own design.

In neither the longer versions nor the shorter Marcan version is the interest biographical. The question of whether the story would have passed into the tradition through the memory of the disciples with whom Jesus had shared his lonely inner experience, is a modern one, not relevant to the Evangelists. In particular Mark appeals to his readers to look in faith to that Jesus who as the strong Son of God goes to do battle with Satan and is victorious. God's Word in Jesus (the Word of the 'good news') encounters the sternest trials, but to all believers it is the last Word and overcomes all opposition. The judgment that the all-embracing theme of Mark is Jesus' cosmic conflict with Satan, culminating in the crucifixion (J. M. Robinson, *PHM*), is too sweeping and does less than justice to the stress in Mark on God's act in the *historical* life and death of Jesus among men and for men (see E. Best). But by the same token it is clear here also that no historian as historian could grasp the broader and indeed universal scope of Jesus' work.

12, 13. The Spirit immediately drove him out into the wilderness: empowered and impelled (the Greek word for **drove him out** is a forcible one, toned down in Mt. 4:1 and Lk. 4:1), Jesus enters the **wilderness** (1:13): regarded in the ancient Near Eastern milieu as the haunt of demons and evil spirits (SB 4, pp. 515f.). The report of Jesus' sojourn in the wilderness was no doubt a great consolation to Christians in their own 'wilderness' in days of anguish and doubt. It was a graphic reminder in life's hard proving-grounds that the Son of God had travelled that way before at the very behest of God himself under the impulse of his Spirit. By the close proximity of this account to 1:11 in Mark it is made plain that God's way for Jesus is no easy way to glory. **forty days:** a 'sacred' number with strong *OT* associations, recalling Moses' forty days and nights on Mount Sinai (Exod. 34:28) and Elijah's similar experience (1 Kg. 19:8; cf. also the forty days of the resurrection appearances in Ac. 1:3). Whereas, however, Moses and Elijah fasted during that period, Mark says nothing openly about Jesus fasting (cf. Mt. 4:2; Lk. 4:2). Whether he means us to understand that Jesus actually was fasting and was sustained throughout by the supernatural or spiritual food provided by **the angels,** or that their provision made fasting for Jesus quite unnecessary (see Mk 2:19), it is impossible to decide. **tempted by Satan:** the present participle of the verb **tempted** suggests that the struggle was not over in a moment, but was protracted over the whole span of time. The Greek word *peirazein*, like the English 'tempted', may connote moral struggle against the enticement of sin (e.g. Jas. 1:13f., 1. C. 7:5; Gal. 6:1, 1 Th. 3:5), but here it carries the wider meaning that Jesus was 'tested' by Satan in a climactic 'trial of strength'. The realism with which Mark depicts the decisive eschatological contest with Satan should restrict our inclination to construe the data of the story as symbolising only Jesus' own struggle within his own being about the true nature of his being. **Satan:** belief in angels and demons is generally thought to have entered Jewish religious life and thought from Zoroastrianism during and after the Babylonian exile. At an earlier stage of development Satan is not yet the arch-enemy of God, but rather the 'prosecuting attorney' of the heavenly court (e.g. Job 1 and 2). Subsequently he stands absolutely over against God as the adversary supreme, the Prince of the devils, and it is in that guise that he appears in the *NT* and in the *Apoc.* and apocalyptic literature, but under various names like Sammael, Mastema, and Beliar or Belial (frequently in the Qumran writings). **and he was with the wild beasts:** more than just a picturesque image of the utter loneliness of the place. In the old pastoral society of the Hebrews the predatory raids of wild animals led to their being connected with the powers of evil (e.g. Ps. 22:11–21; Ezek. 34:5, 8, 25) and to the further notion that in the new age, when righteousness at last prevailed, they would be completely tamed (e.g. Isa. 11:6ff.; Hos. 2:18). A remarkable parallel to Mk 1:13 is in fact found in *Test. Naphtali* 8:4: 'If you do good, my children, both men and angels shall bless you, and the Devil shall flee from you and the wild beasts shall fear you and the Lord shall love you'. The idea may also be present that Jesus has restored the situation that obtained before the fall when Adam was king of paradise and lord of the wild animals. **and the angels ministered to him:** did this happen after his victory in the 'trial of strength' and is it then 'a special assurance of the divine presence' to Jesus (Cranfield, p. 60)? It is more natural to think of the angelic ministration as continuing throughout the period of the testing. It would then signify not just that the angels were the only witnesses of Jesus' encounter, but that God's power (angels being the representatives of God) and no merely human resources, was engaged and won through in the conflict with Satan.

We cannot be sure what thoughts the several items in the story would have evoked in the early Church's telling of it. But there is no doubt that within the Marcan Introduction the *OT* language and allusions here as well as in the message of the divine voice, together with the opening citation of Scripture, all single out Jesus as the one who has appeared, in accordance with the will of God expressed in the *OT*, to achieve God's final purpose.

THE INITIATION OF THE 'GOOD NEWS' BY JESUS 1:14-15

The 'kingdom of God' was without doubt at the heart of Jesus' historic message. But we should not suppose that on his appearance in Galilee he constantly repeated the fixed formula of these two verses. What we have here is a summary of Mark's own, containing much typically Marcan vocabulary and expressed in the language of the Church of Mark's time, e.g. 'gospel of God'; 'the time is fulfilled' (cf. Gal. 4:4); 'believe in the gospel'; the call to 're-pent' (Ac. 5:31, 11:18; 20:1). By fusing together an essential ingredient of Jesus' teaching and Church terminology, Mark demonstrates what is important for him, namely, that the Church's 'good news' and the 'good news' brought by Jesus overlap: the Church's proclamation and the Proclaimer are at one.

Mark's summary rounds off his Preface (see pp. 63f.). The Stronger One to whom the Baptist had pointed emerges victorious from his contest with Satan and comes as the herald of the 'gospel of God'. The 'good news' thus released in Jesus' preaching is continued in the Church's missionary proclamation, and so is no 'dead fact' of the past, but vital, relevant, and challenging in Mark's own time: such is the import of Mark's précis.

14. after John was arrested: the account of John's incarceration and execution is not given until Mk 6:17-29. Here the Evangelist is not interested in biographical matters relating to John, nor even in *dating* the start of Jesus' Galilean ministry after John's imprisonment. The Greek word for **arrested** is a general one and accordingly is usually defined by the addition of some such phrase as 'into prison'. But there is no defining phrase in Mark, and indications are that the word is to be taken in its general sense of 'delivered up', i.e. delivered up to death in faithfulness to God's will, even as the Son of man himself was delivered up. See Mk 9:31, 10:33, etc.; cf. Isa. 53:6, 12 (LXX). Mark sets 'the preaching and summons of Jesus into the divinely willed deathward work of John' (L. E. Keck, *NTS* 12 (1965-6), p. 360).

Jesus came ... gospel of God: it is as preacher of the **gospel of God** that Jesus proves himself to be the Stronger One indicated by the Baptist. His triumph is that his gospel lives on. **came:** if this is a technical theological term for Mark and suggests that he appeared mysteriously and unexpectedly from the human point of view, albeit in conformity with the will of God, it is idle to ask whether he came straight from the scene of the testing or whether some other activity in Judea preceded the Galilean ministry (Cranfield, p. 62). **the gospel of God:** occurs frequently in the *NT* as a description of the whole Christian message of salvation (1 Th. 2:2, 8, 9; Rom. 1:1; 15:16; 2 C. 11:7). It may mean the 'good news about God' or the 'good news from God', but more probably the latter, i.e. the 'good news' entrusted by God to Jesus that his kingdom was close at hand.

15. the time is fulfilled: not the historical circumstances of the age that prepared for and led up to the moment of Jesus' proclamation. It is **time** seen from the divine side; the space of time decreed by God has now elapsed (see Dan. 7:22 (LXX); Ezek. 7:12; cf. Gal. 4:4; Eph. 1:10), and the 'hour' for the final accomplishment of his purpose has arrived. **the kingdom of God is at hand:** the phrase **kingdom of God** is introduced without explanatory comment. For Jesus' first hearers, as presumably for Mark's readers, it was not the empty or nebulous term it often is today. The concept had a long history and an extensive background in the *OT*, extra-canonical works of the intertestamental period, and in the rabbinic literature (where by a reverential substitution of 'heaven' for the name of God it is described as 'kingdom of heaven', and the use of 'kingdom of heaven' in Matthew reflects the Jewish rabbinic environment of his Gospel). In the Psalms the kingship of Yahweh is lauded (e.g. Ps. 103:19; 145:10–13). Yahweh's sovereign power is celebrated in the enthronement Psalms (e.g. Pss 47, 93, 96): elsewhere too he is praised as the king of Israel (e.g. Isa. 43:15; Jer. 8:19) and of the whole world (e.g. Jer. 10:7; Mal. 1:14). But the acknowledgement of his present kingly power becomes also an expression of hope for the future when the very last enemy of God will be vanquished and he himself will be all in all. In late Judaism this hope took mainly two forms. (a) Apocalypticism expected the coming day of God to be preceded by terrible tribulations and then to be ushered in with the cataclysmic overthrow of the existing world-order. Cosmic expectations are depicted in

bizarre and even grotesque imagery, and there is frenzied preoccupation with calendar calculations of the sequence and order
of events in the last days before the day of God. (b) In circles
where the Law was supremely venerated, diligent and punctilious observance of the Law's commands on the part of the
believer in Israel's God was equivalent to taking upon himself the
yoke of the kingdom of heaven (SB 1, pp. 172ff.), and so of
hastening its advent.

Now while the 'kingdom of God' in Jesus' teaching came out of
an *OT* and late Jewish *milieu*, his own proclamation of it is quite
distinctive. Jesus, too, knows of a day of judgment and of an era
of dire distress previous to the end of the world (Lk. 17:26f.:
21:34f.); he speaks of the coming judgment of the Son of man
(Mk 8:38). Nevertheless, his message is characterised not by the
preoccupations of apocalyptic but by eschatological reticence
(e.g. Mk 13:33; Mt. 24:44—the hour of God's victory is beyond
human calculation). With Jesus everything is subordinated to the
one essential declaration: *God's reign is coming*. It is as direct and
unadorned as that, and Mark has captured its directness in 1:15.
Again, with Jesus, the kingdom cannot be earned even by the
most faithful fulfilment of the Law's demands; it is God's gracious
gift (Lk. 12:32; Mt. 21:43). Therefore men can only receive it
(Mk 10:15 = Lk. 18:17), or open themselves toward it expectantly (Mk 15:43 = Lk. 23:51), or seek it (Mt. 6:23), or enter it
(Mt. 5:20, 7:21, etc.; Lk. 13:24), or sacrifice everything in order
to enter it (Mk 9:47; 10:17ff.), or inherit it (Mt. 25:34).

Even this terminology itself reveals that in Jesus' message it is
now the futurity of the kingdom that is stressed, now its present
possibility. Indeed there are sayings which testify that the rule of
God is happening here and now in Jesus' ministry (Mt. 11:6;
Lk. 10:23f.; 11:20; 17:20f; cf. Mk 3:27), and others again which
testify that it is coming in the future (e.g. Mk 9:47; 14:25; Mt.
13:41ff.; 20:21; Lk. 22:16, 18), sometimes the imminent future
(e.g. Mk 9:1). In regard to the oscillation between present and
future, Mk 1:15 is most significant. Here Jesus calls attention not
first to his own person but calls instead to decision in face of the
coming kingdom of God. Even though it is true that Jesus both
in word and action occasionally fastens on to the present moment
of the reality of God's kingdom, and though the early Church
would not have separated participation in the kingdom's power
from Jesus and all that he had said or done, so far as the Synoptic

Gospels are concerned, and Mark in particular, we can hardly go so far as to say that the kingdom of God *is* Jesus and Jesus *is* the kingdom of God (Cranfield, p. 66; see Origen's notion of the *autobasileia*: Jesus is himself the kingdom). Just as in Mark Jesus makes no direct and open claim to messianic status, so the power of God's kingdom lies hidden in his words and deeds. They are tokens and intimations for faith's discernment of the one assurance faith needs: God *will* reign. **is at hand:** what has just been said is in agreement with the now generally accepted meaning of the Greek verb *engiken*, 'is at hand'. On etymological and exegetical grounds (see J. Y. Campbell, *ExpT* 48 (1836–7), pp. 9f.; K. W. Clark, *JBL* 59 (1940), pp. 367ff.), this is preferable to the view of C. H. Dodd (pp. 43ff.), leading advocate of 'realized eschatology', that the word means 'has come', 'has arrived'. **repent, and believe in the gospel:** the approach of God's kingdom brings its own ineluctable demand for the radical re-direction of men's lives (for 'repentance' in this sense, see p. 70). Though the kingdom cannot be built up or attained even by the most heroic human endeavour alone, and is only God's to give, yet it is not for men to hope for it endlessly in complete passivity. Reckoning with the future, and acknowledging in faith that God will then reign, liberates men for the filling of the present moment with new life. 'Those who wait in the right way are called to fulfil the will of God now with all their might' (Bornkamm, p. 95).

JESUS' WORK IN GALILEE AND ITS CONSEQUENCES
1:16–3:12

THE AUTHORITATIVE CALL TO FOLLOW 1:16–20

With the Preface complete, and Mark's reader aware of the supra-historical dimension that is the key to the events about to be related, the Evangelist starts his story of Jesus proper with a report embodying the discipleship motif. The good news has gone forth and is immediately accompanied by the call to follow. Thus early it is announced that whoever really listens to the good news is at once faced with the decision about whether to take the way of Jesus. (For the integral connexion of the gospel with discipleship on the way of Jesus, see p. 56.)

Accounts of the calling of disciples would have circulated widely

in the Church before Mark and been very meaningful to it in its
first age of missionary expansion. Two accounts are combined
here, the calling of Simon and Andrew and the calling of James
and John, and there is the calling of Levi in Mk 2:14. Bultmann
suggests that Mk 1:16–20 is the description of an 'ideal scene'
spun out of the metaphor 'fishers of men' (*HST*, p. 28). But there
is no good reason to doubt either that Jesus initiated a movement
that brought followers around him, like the movement of John
the Baptist, or that there is at least a historical kernel in Mk
1:16–20. However, the common argument that the existence of
items of colourful detail in the story (**casting a net ... fishermen
... fishers of men ... in their boat mending the nets**)
betokens that we are here in touch with a piece of Petrine eye-
witness, does not in fact prove so much (see above, p. 17). Indeed
the report is remarkable for the bare minimum of information it
provides. It is not told as a historian would tell it. Not a word is
said about any psychological preparation on the part of the disciples nor about their antecedents. Instead the impression given is
that Jesus appears abruptly and just as abruptly the men are up and
off with him, and that is all that needs to be said.

   16. And passing along ... fishermen: the point of placement of this report (which bears no note of time) and the locating
of it by the **Sea of Galilee** (which fits in only very awkwardly in
the Greek) are due to Mark. We should resist the tendency to
manufacture connexions, where there are none in the text, by
imagining either that there must have been a lapse of time for
Jesus and the men called to get to know each other, or that they
must have heard of his preaching. Again, the attempt to explain
the abruptness in Mark by the analogy of the wandering *guru* in
India, for whom people leave home at once (Rawlinson, p. 14),
obscures rather than illumines Mark's standpoint. The abruptness is indeed vital to Mark in order to focus only on the master
who calls and on his decision to call.

   17. Follow me: in this call everything decisive has happened:
God's grace and God's command have come in the sovereignly
authoritative word of Jesus and men must say Yes or No. In Mark
follow is a technical term for discipleship. The Jewish rabbi too
had his *talmîdîm* or pupils who had to learn a stern discipline of
following. But Jesus is more than rabbi. He calls whom he chooses;
the rabbi waits for followers to seek him out. Jesus teaches not only
in synagogues but on his travels in the fields and by the lake shore.

His followers include strange folk: women and children, tax collectors, and sinners, whom no rabbi would countenance. Above all, Jesus' authority is not drawn from any appeal of his to a skilfully interpreted sacred text, but is underived (see Mk 1:22 and 27). The rabbi's pupil might eventually excel his master and become a rabbi himself, but no followers of Jesus could ever overreach him (see e.g. Mk 8:35; 10:39; 14:37). Accordingly, when Jesus says **Follow me**, he speaks a *new* word. **fishers of men:** a metaphor used in the *OT* of searching out men for judgment (Jer. 16:16), but here with special relevance to the Church engaged on mission, of 'catching' men out of the turbulent waters of the world in the net of the company of Christ that expects God's coming reign.

18. And immediately they . . . followed him: Mark's linking phrase underlines the instantaneousness of the response to Jesus' word. Deliberation and discussion are no indispensable precondition of discipleship. Jesus chooses whom he will and out of whatever worldly business they happen to be engaged in. Human questions and judgments on why he chooses this one or that one are beside the point. (Sometimes he rejects the apparently willing one and accepts the reluctant one: see Lk. 9:57–62.) **they left their nets:** by following they exchange their livelihood for *life*.

20. they left their father . . . with the hired servants: by following, in this instance, they exchange their family and family ties for the new family of God. There is an implied contrast between the sons who leave and the **hired servants** who remain in the boat with the father. For a Church that in its mission knew about the renunciation of the means of subsistence and the severance of family bonds, these two brief 'call'-stories would have been a graphic reminder of the cost of Christian discipleship. However, Mark's primary intention is to focus upon the sovereign authority and finality of the call Jesus brings, and not upon the conditions of those called.

JESUS' AUTHORITY IN WORD AND DEED **1:21–28**

The divine authority manifested in Jesus' call is now illustrated in his activity of teaching and healing. There is a gap between Mk 1:16–20 and 1:21ff. It is not said whether any of the disciples went with Jesus; the subject of the verb **went** (1:21) is the indefinite *they*. The events of 1:16–20 could not have taken place

on the sabbath, since mending of nets and fishing were strictly
prohibited by the Law. Accordingly, the words **and immediately** do not signify a chronological connexion but are once
more the 'Marcan particle of transition' (Rawlinson, p. 17).
Mk 1:21 should thus be regarded as a Marcan linking insertion
between two items of tradition. But the bridge for him is christological, the subject of the authority of Jesus.

Mark lays great emphasis on the fact that Jesus **taught**. The
verb is used of him sixteen times in the Gospel, and on eleven
occasions he is described as 'teacher'. In comparison with the
other Gospels, however, Mark records relatively very little of the
actual *content* of Jesus' teaching; in fact, here in 1:21–28 nothing
at all. Possibly he was impatient with those in his congregation
who felt they understood Jesus wholly by simply preserving his
words out of the past, or whose participation in rabbinic-style
casuistical debates about Jesus' teaching obscured the authority
of the living Christ and pegged back the Church's missionary
enterprise. Perhaps above all he wanted to show that when Jesus
taught, things did not stay as they were, but God himself was on the
move against all evil forces of the world. So here he amalgamates
a brief account of the expulsion of a demon in 1:23–26 with
witness to Jesus' teaching and his unprecedented authority
(1:22, 27).

21. Capernaum: introduced earlier at Mt. 4:13 and Lk.
4:31 before the call of the disciples. Mark's insertion of it here,
together with the vague phrase of 1:16 'passing along by the
Sea of Galilee', suggests that topography was by no means his
chief concern. **Capernaum** is normally identified with the
modern *Tell Hûm*, on the lake near the Jordan's entrance. It was
the site of a synagogue going back to the third or second century
AD, possibly replacing an even earlier building. **entered the
synagogue and taught:** nearly all towns and villages of Palestine
had a synagogue. The service on the sabbath consisted of praisings
and blessings, with prayers, and the reading of the Law and the
Prophets, accompanied by an exposition or sermon. There was no
residential ordained ministry of the synagogue. Arrangements for
services were made by synagogue elders or a leading elder or
'ruler', and certain duties were performed by the *hazzan*, a paid
local official. But any adult male Israelite, especially if he enjoyed
the reputation of being skilled in interpretation of the Law and
scribal tradition, could be invited to preach. The Gospel tradition

depicts Jesus as having free access to the synagogue and suggests that he was recognised as a rabbi (Mk 9:5; 10:51; 11:21; 14:45; cf. also Mk 12:14, 32). Whether he was officially trained as such we do not know.

22. they were astonished . . . as the scribes: nothing is divulged of the content of Jesus' **teaching** or of its continuity or discontinuity in substance with rabbinic teaching. It is the **authority** of the teacher that is at stake. **they were astonished:** that Jesus' teaching created this impression in the course of his historical ministry is more than likely. His radical freedom, over against the scribal tradition, would have shocked his Jewish hearers, and led to mounting opposition. But the fact that Mark uses this verb five times, and other words expressing amazement very frequently indeed, indicates that it is not merely a historical reminiscence, but a favourite theological motif of the Evangelist's. As the one in whose teaching God's power is breaking through and new miracles are happening (as in the exorcism of 1:23–26), Jesus must evoke astonishment. **not as the scribes:** the term **scribes** is used here in the broadest sense of the doctors of the Law, professional interpreters whose teaching, mainly conducted and transmitted orally, became known as 'the tradition of the elders'. The aim of the 'tradition' was the implementation of the commands of the Law within the details of every phase of daily life. By contrast, with Jesus it is not prior observance of the prescribed commands of the Law or tradition that counts. Everything hinges on the initiative and action of God, who is not necessarily visible in the letter of the Law but to faith (see Bowker, p. 43). This is what Mark brings out in the exorcism story.

23. And immediately . . . an unclean spirit: ordinarily a demoniac would not have been permitted to attend the synagogue service. But this has not prevented Mark from combining an exorcism story with the teaching of Jesus in the synagogue. **with an unclean spirit:** a spirit that made him ceremonially impure, or possibly that debarred him from worship and fellowship with God. But since disease, particularly mental disease, was attributed to demon-possession at that period, the picture here may only be of someone suffering through an evil spirit. Nevertheless, Mark took the activity of demonic forces very seriously and realistically, and what is in the forefront for him is the contest of the power of God in Jesus with the supernatural power of the demonic.

24. he cried out: the strong emotional outburst of the evil spirit, the dialogue with the exorcist, the method of cure, and the expulsion of the demon to the amazement of bystanders, all these are regular features of this kind of story. **What have you to do with us, Jesus of Nazareth?:** in classical Greek the question would mean 'What have we in common?' But here it probably corresponds to Hebrew usage and means: 'Why are you bothering us?' The plural **us** suggests either that the demoniac is spokesman for the whole world of demons or that he is split in himself. **of Nazareth:** in Greek a single word, *Nazarēne*, the meaning of which is much disputed. It may denote the name of the town from which Jesus came. On the other hand it may mean 'shoot', 'branch', or more likely, 'consecrated', 'holy', in which case it would have been confused with Nazarite (*nāzîr*). The adjacent title 'Holy One of God' could then be the Church's interpretation of *Nazarēne* in this sense. (But the question involves complex philological points and is hardly resolved; see Taylor, pp. 177f.) **Have you come to destroy us? I know . . . God:** The question really amounts to an acknowledgement, and expresses the standpoint of the Gospel that the moment for the overthrow of the powers of evil has arrived. **I know who you are:** the idea was widespread at the time that exact knowledge of the other's name brought mastery or control over him. But here, of course, it does not come off for the demon: against even this stratagem the power of Jesus is irresistible. **the Holy One of God:** a rare title in the *OT* (Jg. 13:7; 16:17 (LXX)). It occurs in the *NT* elsewhere only in Jn 6:69, where it refers to Christ's supernatural origin rather than to his messianic dignity (cf. Jn 10:36). There is, however, some indication of its appropriation as a messianic title in the Church through the connexion of Ps. 16:10 with the resurrection as in Ac. 2:25ff. (although the word for 'holy', from the LXX of Ps. 16:10, in Ac. 2:27 is different from the word for 'holy' here in Mk 1:24).

25. But Jesus rebuked . . . come out of him: in Jewish and Hellenistic exorcism-stories magical manipulations, like extracting the demon from the nose of the demoniac with a ring, feature largely. Here by contrast the *word* of Jesus alone leads to the banishment of the demon. But from the fact that terms like **rebuked** and **Be silent** (literally 'be muzzled') are common formulas of Hellenistic magic it may be inferred that at an earlier stage of transmission this story would have borne witness to one who was recognised as a charismatic person of extraordinary healing power.

26. The fact that the demon, **crying with a loud voice,** leaves the possessed attests the success of the exorcism and authenticates the victory of the exorcist to those standing by.

27. The climax of the report as Mark intends it is now reached in the agitated questioning that follows upon Jesus' success. **What is this? A new teaching!:** having witnessed the power of God operative in the exorcism, the people remarkably revert to the *teaching* of Jesus (described in 1:21f.). The miracle in and for itself passes quickly out of view and kindles only thoughts of the God-given authority of the *teacher*.

28. his fame spread everywhere: the word about Jesus and the power of his word goes forth beyond Capernaum. Probably 'beyond Capernaum' is all we should take out of the somewhat vague phrase **throughout all the surrounding region of Galilee** (which in the Greek might in fact indicate also 'the country surrounding Galilee').

A HEALING IN SIMON'S HOME 1:29–31

This very brief narrative is often taken to be a genuine piece of Petrine tradition. Insignificant features of interest only to the participants are prominent; there is considerable manuscript support for the reading '*they* came out of the synagogue and went straight to...', and if we adopt that reading, the phrase **with James and John** is intelligible only if the statement is directly from the mouth of Peter: 'we came into our house with James and John' (see Turner, p. 16). But even if this little account stemmed from an old Petrine tradition (for arguments against the view, see Nineham, p. 81), there is no indication at all that the Evangelist treasured this particular item above other items that came to him from the general oral tradition and included it here because of its superior historical value as a Petrine reminiscence. Rather, the item signalises once more the authority of Jesus, this time not in exorcism but in a straight act of healing.

30. immediately they told him of her: sometimes taken as simply an apology for her absence. But more likely the disciples defer to the unique authority of Jesus as healer. Conceivably their deferral to him would have reminded leaders in the Church of Mark's day that no charisma of theirs could take the place of the unique power of Jesus.

31. And he came . . . she served them: Jesus takes the
initiative and goes to the room of the sick woman. Without
employing any magical technique, he heals her. None-the-less the
terms employed here, **took her by the hand . . . lifted her up
. . . the fever left her,** are all favourites in Jewish healing
stories in the Talmudic literature. **she served them:** waited
upon them at table. E. Schweizer offers the interesting comment
that this being the mode of discipleship for a woman (Mk 15:41;
cf. Lk. 8:3; Jn 12:2), this story here goes further than the previous
one. There Jesus' exorcism is followed by questioning and amazement (1:27); here his healing is followed by the discipleship of
service (Schweizer, *GNM*, p. 53).

RECOGNITION AND RESERVATION **1:32-39**

This section came to Mark already connected in the tradition
with 1:23-26 and 1:29-31, all of these depicting *specimen* scenes
in our Lord's ministry rather than reproducing accurately Peter's
personal reminiscences of the first day of Jesus' ministry in
Capernaum. Certainly the interest of these traditions even at the
pre-Marcan stage would have lain in their witness to typical
activities of Jesus more than in their *correctness*, as eye-witness
reports. The hand of the Evangelist, in view of his tendency to
stress the extensive impact Jesus made, is most probably to be
detected in the **all** of verses 32, 33 and 39, and almost certainly in
the notice in 34*b* about why the demons were prohibited from
speaking.

32. at sundown: this precise note of time in the tradition safe-
guarded the fact that only with **sundown** when the sabbath was
over would it have been permissible to carry the sick through the
streets.

33. the whole city: the exaggeration, like the 'all' in verse 32,
aids the characteristically Marcan stress on the universal outreach of Jesus' ministry and mission. The verse is lacking in
Matthew and Luke.

**34. and he would not permit the demons to speak,
because they knew him:** the first hint of the 'messianic secret'
in Mark. It is now generally agreed that Wrede's theory of the
'secret' is too monolithic, viz., that it was a dogmatic device on
Mark's part to explain why Jesus was never recognised as Messiah during his lifetime, but only after the resurrection (see above,
p. 6). If, however, one holds (against Wrede) that the 'secret'

belonged to Jesus' history, that he did enjoin silence on demons or person(s) healed (e.g. possibly in 1:44), in order to stifle public acclaim of him as a wonder-working divine agent, one is then forced to account for the evident inconsistency between this and his performance of miracles in public (e.g. 1:23-27: 2:7-11). More to the point is it to notice that the traditions Mark drew upon were already impregnated with the 'secret', and no one could have produced the form of a Gospel, purporting at one and the same time to testify to Christ crucified and risen and to his historical ministry, without recourse to the 'secret'. But one cannot leave the matter there, for the only adequate response to Wrede, if one is dissatisfied with his version of the 'messianic secret', is to press further the question of how the 'secret' *does function* for Mark.

The salient feature in Mark is that silence in regard to Jesus and his work is frequently commanded, but equally it keeps coming into the open with surprising regularity that he is the agent of the divine power. Injunctions to silence are given not only to the demons (1:34; 3:11f.), but to the healed (5:43; 7:36), and to the disciples as well (8:30; 9:9). No less striking is Jesus' remarkable reserve about appropriating for himself any particular messianic dignity (see e.g. 8:29-31; 14:60-62; 15:2-5). He speaks in parables in which is enwrapped the hidden 'secret' of the kingdom's dawn (4:11; cf. 4:33), and on his lips is found the somewhat enigmatic title Son of man. In Mark's presentation, then, Jesus will not say himself or have it said openly who he is. On the other side, however, the 'secret' is very poorly preserved. Jesus' identity repeatedly breaks through. In 1:24-27 the demon knows him and comes out with loud cries, to the astonishment of the people nearby. The healed leper spreads the news (1:45). The healing of the paralytic is a public miracle that stirs excitement all round (2:12). An assembled crowd is present at the miracle recorded in 5:35-42. In a different way, in the story of the transfiguration (9:2-8), Jesus' heavenly glory shines forth before his intimate disciples. If then the secret is so often out, why the reiterated charges to silence in Mark at all?

One can understand why in the Gospel narrative there can be no complete suppression of Jesus' supernatural authority: because it is of God, it must show itself. Mark knows that in his own day the truth about Jesus is plain only to some but obscure to others, and so there is about it also an element of concealment and mystery. The 'secret', the injunctions to silence that accompany

Jesus' mighty works, is the means by which the mystery of God's presence in Jesus is upheld and protected. His real identity cannot be disclosed by the externals of the miracle in itself. Such externals might satisfy the popular craving for the spectacular, but they do not ever constitute the good news. For Mark the good news begins with Jesus and what is decisive about Jesus is his suffering and death and call to men to follow him. So through the 'secret' in Mark all manifestation of divine power in Jesus is subordinated to the lowliness and self-negation of his way to the cross. His historic way is inherently ambiguous. It does not compel everyone's recognition and assent, for the presence of God is *hidden* in it. It therefore always requires faith to be at risk and discipleship to be a costly venture.

35. Jesus' withdrawal to solitude and prayer points up his dependence on God, the only true source of his authority. Mark has taken pains to link this to what precedes with an unusually exact denotation of time (**and in the morning, a great while before day**) and possibly wants to enforce the lesson conveyed by the 'secret' (1:34) that fascination with Jesus' mighty works is not the desired outcome of his ministry.

36–37. Since the Greek word for **followed** here usually has the sense of 'pursuing in hostile fashion', and that for **searching** occurs nine times in Mark in the sense of 'seeking someone out from wrong motives', we have the first suggestion in Mark of the blindness of the disciples.

38. Let us go ... that I may preach there also: at the pre-Marcan stage of the tradition, this might have come as a reminder to itinerant preachers of the Church not to stay too long in one place (cf. Mt. 10:14; Lk. 9:5; and see *Did.* 11:4–5). But for Mark it sets the activity of preaching over against mighty works, and accords with his view that primarily Jesus is the bringer of the good news. **that is why I came out:** the verb may mean either 'came out from Capernaum' or 'came as God's representative in accordance with his will' (cf. Lk. 4:43: 'I was sent into the world'). If the former, the Evangelist will have thought of the road along which the good news had to travel as one of continual movement (toward the culmination of the cross); if the latter, he will have thought again of Jesus' whole mission as one of proclamation.

39. From the style and vocabulary this may be adjudged a summary of Mark's own (supporting the latter more theological interpretation of 'I came out' in 1:38). The mission of Jesus to take the call of the gospel to all people proceeds. **and casting out demons:** sometimes taken to be a redactional addition, at odds with Mark's viewpoint. But it is not necessarily so. It is noteworthy that the **casting out demons** is brought into the closest connexion with Jesus' *preaching* in the Marcan summary.

THE LORD, THE LEPER, AND THE LAW 1:40-45

The story is only very loosely joined to the previous units (with a simple **and**), and no doubt circulated as a separate item in the tradition. The impression we get is that the story contains a sizeable historical nucleus (e.g. Jesus' fidelity to the Law of his own people: **show yourself to the priest, and offer for your cleansing what Moses commanded**), and that Mark was strained to adapt it to a particular theological purpose. He may have included it at this point by way of preface to the ensuing conflict-stories in order to show that Jesus had no iconoclastic or revolutionary disrespect for the Law (Rawlinson, p. 22; Nineham, p. 87; Schweizer, p. 58). Or again, Mark may have regarded this story as a sort of climax to 1:21-39, exemplifying most graphically the divine authority of Jesus, since even the most loathsome of diseases yielded to him. Lepers could neither enter a dwelling nor have any kind of communication with other people, and they were also required by the Law to give warning of their approach by shouting 'Unclean, unclean!' (Lev. 13:45-46), and in the unlikely case of their being cured, to obtain a certificate of ritual cleanliness from the priest and offer the prescribed sacrifices (Lev. 14). The story contains strong emotional overtones (Lightfoot, *GMM*, p. 25), and is unquestionably lifelike in its pictorial detail. However, it does not follow from Mark's realistic narration that he is interested in the story merely as a piece of historical reminiscence. The 'secret' in verse 44*a* and the subsequent promulgation of the healing in verse 45 are most probably Marcan touches.

40. The **leper** breaks all customary regulations in approaching Jesus without warning, and in genuine expectancy of what Jesus' power can accomplish (though his expectancy is still not *faith* in the full Marcan sense), he commits himself unreservedly (there is some MS evidence against the reading **kneeling,** but it should probably be accepted) to him.

41-42. Moved with pity: if only because it is much the more difficult reading, it is likely that 'moved to anger' (attested in a few MSS) was the original Marcan term. There is, therefore, here

at least no support for the view that the healing miracles were
motivated by human feelings of compassion on Jesus' part. But
why was Jesus angry? Was he outraged by the foul disease of
leprosy? Was he annoyed at the leper's interruption of his preaching ministry? Or was he indignant at the leper's breach of the
Law? It is preferable to regard Jesus' anger as due to his conviction that, whereas God's will is to cross customary religious
boundaries to reach out to the outcast, the religious people, the
custodians of the Law and even the Law itself are quite incapable
of doing anything to help the leper. **stretched out his hand and
touched him:** thereby not violating the Law, but making himself ceremonially unclean, and so doing something *humanly* inconceivable within the religious pale. **I will; be clean:** once again
the magical practices of the Hellenistic wonder-worker are
conspicuous by their absence. A word from Jesus is enough.

43-44. In an earlier stage of its transmission, this aspect of the
story may have been construed as an impressive reinforcement of
Jesus' healing power—the priestly certification guaranteeing that
even the priests were altogether satisfied a cure had been effected.
But by the intrusion of the 'secret', **See that you say nothing to
anyone,** Mark completely shifts the focus. The command to
silence once more diverts attention from the miracle in itself, but
it is also here given very special weight by the strong language that
accompanies it. **he sternly charged him, and sent him away
at once:** the verb translated **sternly charged** means rather
'roaring at' or 'snorting' (like a horse). Inasmuch as the healing was
well-nigh incredible (among the rabbis the healing of leprosy
was as difficult as the raising of the dead), the temptation to
fascination with the mighty work for its own sake needs to be the
more strongly and even vehemently warded off by the 'secret'.

45: The word about Jesus is quickly promulgated by the leper,
and once again Jesus moves on (cf. 1:38), this time into the
country, drawing people to him from all around (the Marcan
refrain of the universal outreach of Jesus' mission).

This short story provides an excellent example of the dialectic
of disclosure and non-disclosure that characterises Mark's Gospel.
The spectacular miracle that could so easily be used as propaganda
merely for Jesus' wonder-working prowess is checked by a particularly stringent injunction to secrecy. On the other hand the
divine authority here manifested in Jesus is irrepressibly great.
Not only does he heal the worst of diseases, but in so doing he

eradicates the barriers between those within and those outside respectable Jewish society (Montefiore, 1, p. 39). To that extent this story is both a fitting climax to the series dealing with Jesus' authority over demons and disease in 1:21–39, and a suitable introduction to the reports of his controversies with Jewish authorities in 2:1–3:6.

THE BRINGER OF DIVINE FORGIVENESS 2:1-12

Mk 2:1 clearly opens a new section of the Gospel. There is a distinct break between 1:45 and 2:1. At 1:45 Jesus is in the country, unable to enter the town openly. Now at 2:1 he is back in the city of Capernaum again. The section from 2:1–3:5 contains five conflict-stories (the call of Levi report in 2:13f. thematically leads very well into the dispute about table fellowhip with sinners). The complex in whole or in part is most likely pre-Marcan, arranged not according to historical sequence but topics dealt with. Certainly the interrelatedness of the topics in 2:18–3:5 suggests a collection suited to the catechetical interests of the Church. The conflict-stories may have had a background in the debates and controversies of the rabbinic schools. But as they have been taken over into the Gospel the focus of interest is no longer the process of debate but the kerygmatic significance or the way they witness to Jesus. From the standpoint of form criticism they are labelled 'paradigms' (Dibelius, pp. 42f.) or 'pronouncement-stories' (Taylor, pp. 91f.), i.e. they each provide the setting for an important saying of Jesus as in 2:9f.; 2:17; 2:19; 2:25–26 (27?); 3:4. In each case the sayings here bear significantly on the person and work of Jesus.

The subjects dealt with in the conflict-stories, forgiveness (2:5–11); table fellowship (2:18–20); working on the sabbath (2:23–26); healing on the sabbath (3:1–5), no doubt in the process of their transmission at the pre-Marcan stage, corresponded to disputed problems in the early Church, to pardon sins or not (at baptism); whom to receive to table fellowship (in the Eucharist); the pros and cons of fasting in the new Christian community; whether to observe the Jewish sabbath or the Lord's day; how far the observance should go (M. de Tillesse, pp. 157ff.). But there is no need to suppose that all of these were still matters of debate in Mark's congregation in his time. By then, for instance, the Church's keeping of Sunday was already well under way (see 1 C. 16:2; Ac. 20:7; and for the actual designation

'Lord's day' see Rev. 1:10). In fact the main value of the conflict-stories for Mark lies elsewhere. The Evangelist's 'pragmatic
concluding sentence' (Dibelius, p. 219), with its notice of a con-
spiracy to destroy Jesus (Mk 3:6), shows that for him the passion
is in view and that the shadow of the cross already falls across this
segment of the Gospel. Hence the mounting hostility of the Jewish
authorities to Jesus.

The account in 2:1–12 is usually entitled 'The Healing of the
Paralytic'; but from the standpoint of the Gospel our heading
above is more suitable, since what appears to be decisive for Mark
is that new aspect of the divine authority in Jesus by which he
forgives sins. The report as it stands is extremely awkward and can
scarcely have been a unity originally. The large central section in
verses 5*b*–10*a* is entirely devoted to the question of forgiveness.
It is formulated in theological terms that are in marked contrast
to the graphic concrete details in the narrative about the paralytic
in verses 3–5*a* and 11f. Moreover, verses 11f. form a conclusion
only to the healing miracle and do not allude at all to the discussion about forgiveness. Finally, the words of verse 5*a* **he said to
the paralytic** are repeated in a cumbersome parenthesis in 10*b*
where it may be an insertion, the omission of which together with
the whole section 5*b*–10*a* leaves us with a straight report of the
healing of a paralytic in 3–5*a* and 11f. Amid a great deal that is
uncertain about exactly how these two initially separate units
came to be combined, this much is virtually certain that the
Evangelist himself was not responsible. In view of the importance
of the 'secret' for him, would he have formulated matters so
ambiguously as to suggest that the miracle of outward healing was
convincing *proof* of Jesus' authority (2:10–11)? The composite
narrative of 2:1–12 is due then to the moulding of traditions in the
Church before Mark. A reasonable explanation of the factors at
work in the compilation is advanced by Rawlinson: 'We may
suppose that the episode of the paralytic came to be expanded in
Christian preaching in such a way as to convey the lesson that
bodily healing is but a sacrament of the more important healing
of the soul, and that the controversial element came in as an echo
of early Christian controversy with the synagogue' (p. 25).
Whether such a lesson is the significant thing from the standpoint
of the Evangelist himself, however, is a question (see comments on
2:10–11).

2. preaching the word: possibly an editorial modification.

Certainly it agrees with the Marcan stress on Jesus as the bearer of the good news, and brings the whole section 2:1–3:6 under the rubric of proclamation. The expression means 'preaching the gospel' (see 4:14ff., 33; cf. Ac. 4:29, 31; 8:25; 11:19; 13:46).

4. Access to the **roof** would have been by an outside stairway. The roof would consist of cross-beams overlaid with a matting of branches and hardened mud. The picture of a hole being dug in the roof while the one-storey house was crowded is a little strange, but it does underline the tremendous eagerness of the pallet-bearers to reach Jesus and makes way for the statement that follows.

5. when Jesus saw their faith: the **faith** of the pallet-bearers alone, or of the paralytic as well? Possibly the paralytic is included, but since the faith of his friends is very much involved, this passage offers no springboard for a general theory about a believing attitude on the part of the sufferer being a necessary precondition of healing. Faith is here for Mark not yet the full and final recognition of who Jesus really is. But it is obviously more than a nod in the direction of the great miracle-worker. It is the openness and expectancy toward Jesus that is well on the way to learning of him, and so even now can experience God's forgiveness through him. **My son, your sins are forgiven:** the endearing form of address might indicate Jesus' recognition of the readiness to enter into a relationship with himself. Jesus is not arrogating to himself the sole right to dispense forgiveness. He does so only as the one who stands in God's stead or as God's representative (a point fully developed and articulated in the later affirmations of the Chuch that sin could be forgiven *by, and in the name of Jesus*).

The declaration of forgiveness comes suddenly and surprisingly before any word of healing. But it is not that Jesus sees this man as particularly sinful. Nor does he think, in accordance with the old Deuteronomic orthodoxy so acidly questioned in the Book of Job, that a man's suffering is proportionate to his sin (a view flatly contradicted in Lk. 13:1–5 and Jn 9:2f.). The horizons here are broader. The insight is that there is indeed a close and age-old connexion between man's fallen estate and everything that afflicts him, with the further implication that God's will is for man's wholeness, or completeness in every aspect of his being.

6–8. The account of the disputation with the **scribes** is some-what stylised. The scribes do not say anything, simply question

in their hearts. Jesus perceives their complaint in his spirit.
Only a very rigorist attitude to this report as an eye-witness
record of history could allow one to say: 'No doubt their faces
expressed it' (Cranfield, p. 98). Rather do we have here the
Church's formulation of the essential or typical scribal complaint
against the Christian association of forgiveness with the name or
person of Jesus, although that is not to deny that the formulation
accurately reflects the historical posture of the scribes toward
Jesus during his earthly ministry. **It is blasphemy! Who can
forgive sins but God alone?:** both sides in the dispute would
have answered: no one but God (see comments on 2:5). The real
heart of the scribes' quarrel is *the right of Jesus* to act in God's
stead in bestowing forgiveness. And what from the Gospel perspective, elicits the accusation of blasphemy is the blindness of the
Jewish lawyers that prohibits them from seeing that the signs of
the kingdom of God are present in, with, and around Jesus, and
therefore a new and unprecedented authority accrues to him.

9. The one questioned does not in the first place divulge anything but answers with a perplexing and provocative question.
The logic of the passage suggests that the opponents would have
responded that to declare the forgiveness of sins is easier, since
forgiveness, unlike the miracle of healing, is not subject to verification. From the standpoint of the Evangelist, however, the forgiveness of sins is both prior and more difficult. The thrust of the
question, then, may simply be to prompt the reflection that since
Jesus can say either **Your sins are forgiven** or **take up your
pallet and walk,** and since in fact he began by saying the
former (2:5), his authority is more than and different from that of
the wonder-worker.

10-11. In view of the prominence of the secrecy motif in the
Gospel, the Evangelist could hardly have thought of the miracle
of healing as an outward visible demonstration to convince
opponents. **that you may know:** the pronoun here need not
refer only to the scribal opponents but may include the crowd of
verse 4, and so mean 'all'. Or possibly these words are a Marcan
editorial comment addressed to the readers of the Gospel (Cranfield, p. 100). For Mark the miracle points away from itself to
what is the ultimately significant thing for all men, the authority
of the Son of man, which is beyond empirical verification and is
perceptible only to faith (see verse 5, 'and when Jesus saw their
faith'). This is the first time 'Son of man' is used in Mark (for com-

ment on the wider issues raised by the designation, see on 8:31).
The term is a literal translation of the Aramaic *bar-nāsh(ā)*, which
can mean simply 'man'. Accordingly, it is sometimes suggested
that Jesus is here only teaching that man on earth (as well as God
in heaven) can forgive sins. But the subject of dispute in the
passage is not (as we noted in regard to 2:6-8) whether man on
earth can forgive sins as well as God, but *Jesus'* right to do so.
Here, therefore, 'Son of man' is descriptive of Jesus. Now in some
sayings the designation looks like a circumlocution for 'I', just as
in Aramaic the expression *hāhū gabrā* ('that man') can denote 'I,
the speaker' (see G. Vermes in Black, *ARA*, 1967, pp. 320-7).
It is frequently argued that this is how it is used here, especially
on the ground that not until after Caesarea Philippi (Mk 8:27ff.)
does it carry its full titular force for Mark as referring to the
heavenly figure of the end-time who would play a decisive role in
the last judgment. One suspects, however, that even this early
in the Gospel, the title carries for Mark at least something of its
transcendent colouring and points to Jesus as the bearer and representative on earth of the power of God in heaven. Even so, the
way the title is used here is no breach of the 'secret'. Jesus is not
publicly revealing his own identity. It is, as Rawlinson observes,
'a question not of the mere use of the title Son of man, but of the
exercise of a divine prerogative' (p. 25).

12. they were all amazed and glorified God: we noted that
properly this is only the conclusion of the miracle-story (and not
of 5b-10a). The **all** can scarcely include the scribes, for their
hostility continued, witness the plot to kill Jesus (3:6). By the fact
that the praises of *God* are sung in response to the miracle and by
the exclamation **'We never saw anything like this!',** the
challenge presented by Jesus to faith has now been greatly
sharpened. Can men accept that in him the new day of God has
come and the powers of the kingdom, even to the forgiveness of
sins, are hiddenly at work?

TABLE FELLOWSHIP WITH OUTCASTS **2:13-17**

The conflict story in 2:15-17 is here preceded by the story of the
call of Levi, which has the same stark features as the call story in
1:16-20. Here too everything hinges on the one who calls and the
decisiveness and finality of the call. That it is inserted here and not
combined with the earlier report is due to the fact that here the
call is issued to one who as a customs official stood outside the

boundaries of Jewish religious respectability and was *persona non grata* with the Jewish religious authorities. In this respect the story provides an eminently suitable introduction to the dispute about Jesus' table fellowship with religious outcasts in 2:15-17. At a time when the two stories circulated separately in the tradition, the phrase **in his house** in 2:15 could only have meant 'in Jesus' own house' (the one provided by Peter as a base for Jesus in 1:29). But with the locking together of these two narratives **in his house** may equally refer to the house of Levi, and presumably that is how Mark himself took it, especially if he were responsible for the combination. Certainly the passage shows clear signs of Marcan editorial activity. Verse 13 contains typically Marcan traits, the broad outreach of Jesus' mission and message, and the reference to Jesus' teaching activity, and is most probably a Marcan transition.

14. Levi the son of Alphaeus: not mentioned under this name in the list of the Twelve in Mk 3:14-19. Jesus' followers were not of course restricted to the Twelve (see 2:15 'there were many who followed him'). But the similarity in form of this story to that of 1:16-20 rather tends to suggest that, like the four mentioned there, Levi belonged to the group of the Twelve 'apostles'. A James who is also son of Alphaeus is included in Mark's list of the Twelve (Mk 3:18), but notice is given of Matthew the taxgatherer in Mt. 9:9 and 10:3. Possibly then this Matthew and Levi are one and the same person. But of any such identification Mark says nothing, either because he could assume that Levi's identity was well known, or perhaps because his sole interest lay in the implications for the gospel of the call to a despised outsider. **sitting at the tax office:** Levi would be a 'civil servant' in the government of Herod Antipas and not, strictly speaking, one of the *publicani* or provincial contractors who farmed out the public taxes under the empire. But that would barely diminish Jewish hatred for him or his office, which brought him into constant contact with Gentiles and rendered him legally 'unclean' in Jewish eyes, and also had a notorious reputation for corruption and 'fleecing' the people. That Jesus should select such a person for his band of followers could only have caused the most grievous offence.

No doubt the story of Levi's call would have brought a vivid reminder to the Church that in the following of Jesus there was room for all-comers, and that her mission in the name of Jesus broke through all fences of Law and custom and status. It is in fact the Law and its restrictiveness that is the underlying subject of dispute in the conflict story of verses 15–17.

15. sat at table: more correctly 'reclined'. The usual practice at feasts and banquets was for the guests to recline on the left elbow on divans arranged around the table. The offence to the ardent devotees of the Law is all the greater because this strange fellowship-meal is a festive occasion for the participants. **tax collectors:** the *KJV* rendering 'publicans' is based on the Vulgate *publicani* (see above on 2:14), but customs-officials like Levi were 'merely the small fry of the bureaucracy' (Rawlinson, p. 28). **sinners:** in the Jewish context 'the people of the land', who either through contact with Gentiles, or through their sitting loose to the commands of the Law, put themselves outside the limits of official Judaism and were shunned by the Pharisees. For Mark, however, as for the Church of his time (when the term 'tax collector' in itself was no longer a term of reprobation), the word 'sinners' would have borne the more general sense of 'people of questionable morality'. **there were many who followed him:** an awkward expression in Greek, literally 'there were many and they followed him'. But it is in the style of Mark, and is probably an explanatory notice, linking the attendance at the banquet with Levi's 'following' of Jesus (1:14).

16. the scribes of the Pharisees, when they saw: we are not told how the **scribes** came to be there. To be sure they would not have contaminated themselves by getting close to such a disreputable company at such a banquet, and the statement **they saw** is appropriately vague. We infer that what is described here is the prevailing and typical conflict situation of Jesus' ministry. In so far as it was a ministry to outcasts, it sorely wounded scribal susceptibilities. The term **scribes of the Pharisees** is found only here. The description may reflect with remarkable accuracy the circumstances of Judaism in the period of Jesus. Indications are that the party of the **Pharisees,** by no means illiberal according to the Jewish historian Josephus, were in process of transition, of taking the harsh, extremist line of the *perûshim* ('separatists') roundly condemned in the rabbinic sources for their eagerness to subjugate the whole of life to every single detail of the Law. Likewise the **scribes,** the professional teachers of the Law associated with the Pharisees, were in process of dividing into dissident groups, the more liberal supporting the more broadly tolerant

Pharisean position, the more extreme adopting the more rigid
orthodoxy toward the Law of the school of Shammai, particularly
in their attitude to the 'outcast' (see Bowker, pp. 29ff.). At any
rate what is involved for the Evangelist here is the staggering contrast between a hard legalism that writes certain people off as
'outsiders' (to the true religious circle and so to God as well),
and the forgiving grace of God that in Jesus reaches out to all men,
even the most unlikely, without imposing any prior conditions or
requirements. **said to his disciples:** the scribal question (as
much an exclamation as a question) is put to the disciples and then
Jesus answers. The disciple-Church relied not on its own inven-
tiveness or cleverness, but on its Master's word and guidance. In
Mark the scribal wrangle is not over a complex point of theology
but simply over the *action* of Jesus ('Why does he eat with such
people?').

17. Taken as actual words of Jesus, the saying about the
physician, coupled with the terse statement **I came not to call
the righteous, but sinners,** has caused the commentators
considerable difficulty. What is the correspondence, if any,
between **those who are well** and the **righteous**? Is Jesus
simply taking over the terminology of his opponents? Why is his
call not for the righteous? Does he think there are righteous who
do not need it? It is hard to resist the conclusion that in this
Gospel Jesus' reply to the scribes reflects the standpoint and
experience of the Church. The proverb concerning the **physician**
has parallels in Hellenistic literature, and for the Gentile or
Greek Church would have summed up very well the whole spirit
of Jesus' mission. In the declaration attached to the proverb
(somewhat loosely), the verb **I came** appears to carry the Marcan
connotation of the whole mission of Jesus in accordance with the
will of God. Members of the early Christian communities knew
that they were the beneficiaries of that mission to outcasts. They
knew themselves to be outsiders, astonishingly admitted to the
fellowship of Christ, and they in turn in their continuing mission
admitted other outsiders. By contrast the **righteous** had allowed
the Gospel to pass them by because they felt that religiously they
had arrived already. For Mark at any rate the story evokes a
decision about the character of the God who acts in Jesus. Can
men accept a God who accepts them prior to or without their
fulfilment of legal or religious scruples and across every boundary?

The Church by no means *created* such a report as this. Jesus did as a matter of historical fact go to the outcasts and admit them to the company of his followers. But we may see the Church working out and shaping up the report in the light of its growing experience of everything Christ meant to it.

OLD RITUAL FORM AND NEW FREEDOM 2:18–22

The third in the series of conflict-stories consists of two segments (2:18–20 and 2:21–22). The sayings of Jesus reported in verse 19a and verses 21–22 (possibly drawn from a sayings collection) may be regarded as authentic. In the former Jesus is suggesting in parabolic fashion that mourning or fasting are as out of place at the time of the approach of the kingdom of God as at a wedding feast. In the latter he is speaking more generally to the theme of the relation of the old and the new. But verses 21–22 say nothing specifically about fasting, and either Mark, or more probably the Church before him, has linked them to the unit on fasting, since they deal broadly with the incapacity of the ancient ritual forms of Judaism to embrace the new life of the Church, or at least the Gentile Church. Verse 20 appears to reflect the concern of the early Church about fasting and contains a veiled allusion to the death of the 'bridegroom' Jesus. The impression that it is an addition of the Church is heightened by the fact that it is out of harmony with the figure of speech employed by Jesus in 19a. The departure of the bridegroom at a wedding feast would still be no cause for mourning or fasting. Again the omission of 19b from Mt. 9:14–15 and Lk. 5:33–35 prompts the question as to whether it may not have stood in the tradition but be an addition of Mark's to lead into verse 20, or perhaps a later gloss (it is missing from a number of mss). If verse 20 is a word of the Church, it would appear to offer some justification for the practice of fasting. That the Church did practise fasting is evidenced in *Did.* 8:1 where the contrast is drawn between fasts of the 'hypocrites' (Jews) on Tuesdays and Thursdays, and Christian fasts on Wednesdays and Fridays. However, even if Mark knew of fasting in the Church, what he would have in mind here, in view of verses 21–22, would be the radical difference between the old Jewish forms and the new practices of the new community.

18. This episode is not linked to what precedes by any note of time or place. An independent item of tradition has therefore been located here by Mark, or possibly by the Church at an earlier stage, because its subject-matter is in accord with the

other conflict stories. Rawlinson suggests (pp. 3of.) that the phrases
and the Pharisees and **the disciples of the Pharisees** are
later editorial insertions—the episode belongs to a period of time
just after John's death and originally the reference was quite
specifically to his disciples' mourning of their master. But **disciples of the Pharisees** may mean those scribal adherents of the
more extremist *perûshim* among the Pharisean party who would
have had a great deal in common with the austere outlook of the
disciples of the Baptist (Bowker, p. 40). Accordingly, the verse may
reflect quite accurately the conditions of Jesus' time and may
have been framed at an early stage by the Church as typifying
the overall situation during Jesus' ministry and as a suitable
generalising introduction to what follows here. The question put to
Jesus concerns no profound theological or christological point of
debate but quite simply the action or non-action of his disciples.

19a. The question is about the conduct of disciples. Jesus' reply
in the form of a question is expressed in the imagery of a wedding
feast that would have had special point for Jewish hearers who
regarded the wedding as a not-to-be-missed celebration. The
intention of Jesus' question is to show that just as glad celebration
is the hallmark of the wedding feast, so joy is the hallmark of his
disciples. The melancholy of the disciples of the Baptist and of
the Pharisees is the melancholy of those whose pathway to God is
hedged about by the requirements of fastidious religious observances. The rejoicing of the followers of Jesus is the rejoicing of
those who in faith discern the signs that God's kingdom is coming
toward them as his free gift.

19b–20. It is often held that in the image of the **bridegroom**
Jesus is alluding allegorically to himself either as Messiah (with
whose coming the rabbis associated wedding imagery; see Taylor,
pp. 21of.) or as Son of God (cf. the imagery of Isa. 54:5; 62:4f;
Jer. 2:2, 32f.; 3:1, 14; Ezek. 16:8; see Cranfield, pp. 11of.), and is
pointing forward to his death and to the fasting and mourning
that will be in order after it (Cranfield, p. 111). But it is more
natural to suppose that if Jesus employed the word **bridegroom**
initially in a metaphor intended only to underscore the contrast
between his own disciples and others, the Church would quickly
have fastened on to it and taken it as an allegorical representation
of his person. Verses 19*b* and 20 would then be framed as a plea
of the Church for the propriety of fasting in the situation after the
death of Jesus. Certainly it would have been quite uncharacter-

istic of Jesus to offer any prophecy about the ritual practices of the later Church (**they will fast in that day.** See Nineham, p. 102).

The practice of fasting in the Church, implied in verse 20, is neither defended nor criticised by Mark. His principal interest lies in the glad liberation that discipleship to Jesus brings from all attempts to reach God by the prior accomplishment of religious rules or duties. But the demeanour of seriousness and sobriety encouraged by fasting would not have been incongruous for a Church like Mark's that watched and waited for the *parousia* of Christ and God's last great victory over sin and evil (Mk 14:33, 37; see Schweizer, p. 69).

21-22. Placed in this context, these originally independent sayings of Jesus pick up and amplify the question about the particular custom of fasting and apply it to the larger issue of the radical incompatibility between the new message, faith, and life of the Church, and the old institutions and practices of Judaism. Taken on their own, as words of Jesus, they are consonant with his message of the kingdom of God and his call to the new future of God. They contain no suggestion that the old (either the **old garment** or the **old wineskins**) is to be discarded. Jesus was no abolitionist in respect of Jewish Law or custom (see Mk 7:8ff.; Mt. 5:17ff.). But as the Church repeated these sayings in their contemporary situation they no doubt reminded themselves that there could be no compromise between their new life-situation and the old limiting religious ordinances.

The point of the metaphors of patching and the use of wineskins is reasonably clear. The patch of **unshrunk** ('uncarded') cloth shrinks as it dries out and presumably stretches the threads of the garment. **Old wineskins** would be too brittle to withstand the fermenting process of **new wine** or 'must'.

THE NEW FREEDOM CORROBORATED AND EXTENDED 2:23-28

This narrative contains no note of time or place and is a composite of items of tradition that originally circulated independently. The considerably expanded versions of Mt. 12:1-8 and Lk. 6:1-5 suggest that Mark has been content to pass on the story without filling it out or embroidering it.

By the time of Mark the **sabbath** was no longer observed by Gentile Christians. In narrating this episode the Church was no doubt justifying its freedom. It is the behaviour not of Jesus but of the **disciples** (the disciple-Church) that is in question, and *Jesus'* *reply* provides the source or ground of their liberty (Bultmann, *HST*, p. 16). But in itself the episode still presupposes the existence of sabbath obligations and the dispute is over how far these are binding. The plucking of **ears of grain** by the disciples would be construed, at least from the stricter perspective of Jewish legalism, as tantamount to reaping, and reaping was one of the thirty-nine activities forbidden on the sabbath (cf. Exod. 34:21). The case made by Jesus on the basis of the old Scripture (1 Sam. 21:1–6) is that the sabbath regulations have on occasion to be suspended in the interest of a human need or emergency (in the case of David's men, and presumably of Jesus' disciples, the need of bodily sustenance). Jesus' ensuing words about the sabbath being made for man (2:27) are preceded by a formula (**and he said to them**) that introduces an originally independent saying. The saying in itself furnishes a satisfactory answer to the question of verse 24, **Why are they doing what is not lawful on the sabbath?** Consequently one may suppose that Mark or the Church brought in the scriptural argument of verses 25–26 as a concrete illustration or proof of the broad principle enunciated in verse 27. The closing declaration of verse 28 brings in a factor that is not at all related either to the argument from Scripture that the Law may have to be suspended in specific cases or to the general principle that the Law of the sabbath is always subordinate to human needs (2:27). In its own affirmation that the **Son of man is lord** of all things, including the sabbath (an affirmation that had its roots in Jesus' historic freedom in regard to the sabbath), the Church finds the all sufficient answer to the question of verse 24 and the ultimate vindication of its liberty.

23. as they made their way: the Greek here may be translated 'began to make a way, plucking ears of grain', and this has led to the suggestion that the breach of the Law involved was 'walking' or 'making a road' on the sabbath (Bacon, *BGS*, pp. 30f.). But as the episode develops, it is 'reaping' and eating corn on the sabbath that constitutes the disciples' offence; *RSV*, therefore, correctly renders Mark's meaning.

24. the Pharisees said: they crop up here somewhat startlingly in the most unexpected place—among the cornfields on the sabbath! Once more the account is stylised, reflecting the prevailing situation of Jesus' ministry during which Pharisean opponents were evidently scandalised by his lack of scrupulosity about the sabbath.

25–26. and he said to them: a Marcan connecting-link leading into an originally independent item of tradition. **Have you never read?:** the familiar mode of rabbinic counter-question introducing an argument from Scripture. **the house of God:** used in Jg. 18:31 (LXX) of the tent containing the sacred ark. **when Abiathar was high priest:** the story does not keep close to 1 Sam. 21:1–6 in detail, and notably deviates here in naming Abiathar instead of Ahimelech his father as high priest. Either it is a copyist's gloss, or quotation is being made from memory, or the account in Mark is based on a midrashic exposition of 1 Sam. 21:1–6. It is a mistake to think that the changes from the details in 1 Sam. are due to Christian assimilation of the passage to the Messiah who dispenses the eucharistic bread. The purpose in the present context is only to stress that **David** was prepared to use the consecrated bread to satisfy human need. **bread of the Presence:** represents the Hebrew *lehem hapanîm*, 'bread of the face' or 'presence-bread', and describes the twelve newly baked loaves that were laid in two rows on a table before God in the tabernacle every sabbath, and were later eaten by the priests (Lev. 24:5–9). On the face of it, the scriptural argument of verses 25–27 on its own relates only to the priority of human need over the ceremonial law, and not to the sabbath. Accordingly, only through the Church's collocation of it with the question of verse 24 and the statement of verse 27 is it made to apply explicitly to the sabbath. Perhaps, however, the connexion was initially possible because of the known fact that the showbread was laid out **on the sabbath.**

Whether this scriptural argument is a product of the Church or goes back to Jesus himself is difficult to determine. It is true that there is no hint here of the new situation (in respect to the kingdom of God and the signs of its approach) that has arrived with Jesus. It is true also that the Church may have debated in this way after the manner of its opponents where and as it became unmindful of the new state of affairs brought by Jesus (see Schweizer, pp. 70f.). But by the same token the very absence of a christological element from the scriptural argument may point to Jesus himself as its originator—provided one is prepared to concede that Jesus was not so distinctive from everything in his environment that he could not sometimes reason like a rabbi (see Keck, pp. 33f.).

27. The liberal spirit of Jesus' statement (for an interesting

modern story illustrating how hard it is for 'legalists' to swallow it,
see Käsemann, *JMF*, p. 16), was not entirely alien to the more
liberal tendency within Pharisaism (see above on 2:16). One or
two rabbis were able in fact to say: 'The sabbath is delivered unto
you, and you are not delivered to the sabbath.' But it is one thing
to hold that men should rejoice in keeping the sabbath. It is
another to hold that true joy lies in the freedom to transcend the
prescribed duties of the Law for the sake of direct obedience to
God's will and of immediate response to human need.

28. the Son of man is lord even of the sabbath: nowhere
else does Jesus make such a claim. The difficulty is not resolved by
supposing that here **Son of man** = 'man', and that Jesus is
simply driving home the point of verse 27 by affirming that man is
in control of the sabbath. On the contrary, Jesus would have
acknowledged the divine institution of the sabbath. It is best to
regard this statement as the comment with which the Church
crowned the logic of verse 27 and concluded the story, and in
which it found the vindication of its break from the sabbath to
Sunday observance. As God's representative Jesus has himself
replaced the codified prescriptions of the Law for the community
of Christians and has himself become the embodiment of the divine
will.

The Church, and not Mark, has been responsible for this
formulation. It is hardly in line with the 'secret' in the Gospel.
Here Mark has allowed his tradition to stand without controlling
it.

PHARISEAN NARROWNESS AND THE BREADTH OF JESUS' MISSION
3:1–12

The fifth in the series of conflict-stories (3:1–6) is set in the
synagogue. The variety of settings of these reports is noteworthy:
Jesus' home in 2:1–12; the home of Levi (probably) in 2:15–17;
location unspecified in 2:18–22; the cornfields in 2:23–28; finally
here the synagogue. This variety of setting was probably significant for Mark as indicative of the mobility of Jesus' mission and
of the fact that the good news brought by him must reach into
every corner.

We have noticed how the first four conflict-stories depict typical
crisis situations of Jesus' ministry. This last story, however, gives a
stronger impression of recalling a *particular* historical incident.
The impression is supported not so much by the presence in

verses 2-3 of vivid details (see Taylor, p. 220; Cranfield, p. 119), which in themselves are no guarantee of authenticity (see Sanders, pp. 88ff., 282ff.), but by the probably original radical saying of Jesus in verse 4, which presupposes a specific act of healing like the one described here.

At all events the centre of interest in the narrative is not the healing itself but the religious issue affecting the Law. There is no indication of any response to the miracle after verse 5. Instead, rather surprisingly, since at this juncture Jesus has as yet done nothing worthy of death in Jewish judicial terms, what is reported is the outcome of the dispute, a plot to destroy him. Verse 6 is inserted here by Mark to conclude the section 2:1-3:5. Jewish hostility has reached its zenith. The breach with Judaism that will eventually encompass Jesus' death is now irreparable.

Verses 7-12 may be construed as a bridging summary between 2:1-3:6 and the new section of the Gospel that opens in 3:13. In a few typical scenes, these verses portray the outstanding success of Jesus' mission on a broad front, so broad that it touches even the unclean spirits who acknowledge his divine authority and have to be commanded to silence—in marked contrast to the narrowness of Pharisean vision which is unable to perceive the signs of the new state of affairs inaugurated by him.

1. again: this report is only very loosely linked to the immediately preceding conflict-story. The **again** is simply a narrative connexion formula (Bultmann, *HST*, p. 33a). Or less probably it may hark back to or denote a regular action of Jesus (cf. 1:21). **entered the synagogue:** Jesus goes to the synagogue and to that extent identifies himself with Jewish custom. But it gains him nothing. Only once more in the Gospel does Jesus appear in a synagogue, in his own country, and the upshot is his rejection by his own people (6:1-6). Elsewhere in Mark Jesus himself speaks only in derogatory terms of the synagogue (12:38f.; 13:9). Mark regards the synagogue negatively. It is the seat of opposition and misunderstanding. It is by the *lake* Jesus wins a response and finds a following (1:16; 2:13; 3:7). **a withered hand:** probably from some form of paralysis. In the *Gospel of the Nazarenes* we find an interesting embellishment: 'I was a mason seeking a livelihood with my hands: I pray thee, Jesu, to restore me mine health, that I may not beg meanly for food.'

2. It is not here specified who **watched** Jesus (cf. Lk. 6:7). The subject is the vague **they.** Only the redactional verse 6

implies that the Pharisees have been involved. One wonders
whether the tradition referred initially only to the curious watching of the crowd, among whom Jesus enjoyed a reputation as
healer. The insertion of verse 6 might then lead to the adaptation
of verse 2 to a hostile watching with the intent to accuse Jesus. As
it stands verse 2 prepares for the sabbath question and its final
outcome (verse 6) rather than for the miracle of healing.

3. Come here: in the first place Jesus calls for action (cf. Mt.
12:10ff.). The Greek means literally 'arise into the midst'. The
man's being stationed in full view of the assembly lends a very
dramatic touch to the question that follows.

4. To heal **on the sabbath** was regarded as doing a work,
expressly forbidden by the Law. The only exception was that a
physician might be allowed to heal where it was a matter of life or
death. Against this background the question, by which Jesus
vindicates his own action in healing on the sabbath, is variously
interpreted. One argument is that Jesus is drawing a sharp distinction between right doing and wrong doing, and not just in a
general way but with particular reference to the goodness of the
act of healing over against the evil desire of his enemies to get rid
of him (to **kill** him) (Rawlinson, p. 36; Taylor, p. 222). But the
argument is unconvincing. On the highly questionable assumption
that verse 6 is original, it reads into verse 4 Jesus' own presenti-
ment of his opponents' murderous intent, and obscures the fact
that the primary concern is the sabbath and the Law. Another
view is that Jesus is defending an *occasional* breach of the sabbath
Law when a special need demands it. If the Pharisees object, as
they might, that the man with the withered hand is no case of
special need since he could very well wait a day or two, then the
point is that Jesus must be urgently about the work of the kingdom
which must go forward on any and every day (Nineham, pp.
109f.). But casuistry about *exceptions* to the sabbath Law hardly
accounts for the sinister outcome of the murder plot. The Pharisean rabbis were well accustomed to debating about exceptions
and would hardly have faulted Jesus for taking them on at their
own game.

As the narrative stands, it is preferable to hold that the whole
principle of the Law or legal observance is at stake. The force of
Jesus' question is that to tolerate evil whenever or wherever it is
found, to do nothing about it, is to opt for evil rather than good,
for death rather than life. Inaction in the facing of glaring human

need or helplessness, sabbath or no sabbath, stands condemned before God. **they were silent:** not because they were aware that Jesus had sensed their foul intention toward him. Their silence expresses their disagreement with any principle that would undermine the sovereignty of the Law.

5. their hardness of heart: the Greek word *pōrōsis* in the *NT* means not so much 'insensitivity' as 'lack of comprehension' or 'obtuseness'. What angers and vexes Jesus is not just their complacency about suffering, but their blindness to the new dispensation, now unfolding, that frees men from legal theorisings and calculations. In the new dispensation (of which Jesus' act of healing on the sabbath is a sign) obedience expresses itself as a merciful self-giving which is a joyous response to God's own giving and takes precedence over all dutiful fulfilment of written commandments of the Law.

6. with the Herodians: it is not easy to say whether the collusion could only have belonged to a later period of recorded Pharisean support for Herod the Great (see Josephus, *Ant.* 14:15:10), or whether it might refer to Pharisean alliance with members of the entourage of Herod Antipas, tetrarch of Galilee, in the time of Jesus. At any rate the **Herodians** were not a religious sect or party, and would have represented a different system of authority from the Pharisean. Most probably their appearance here signifies for Mark the comprehensiveness of the opposition to Jesus—the authorities religious and secular are all ranged against him and his authority. The passion is already in view.

7a. Jesus withdrew ... to the sea: only the zeal to discover *biographical* connexions in the Marcan structure would lead one to ask here about the motives of Jesus. Did he retire to avoid the pressing danger from the Herodian government or further controversy with his opponents? For Mark the **sea** denotes the place where Jesus' mission is successful and disciples are recruited, and his intention in the summary of 3:7–12 is to set the positive response to Jesus of the crowd of ordinary folk (and the 'unclean spirits') against the bitter enmity of the leaders of the people in the towns and villages. Perhaps he intended a warning to the leaders of the Christian congregation of his own time that they had no monopoly of understanding the gospel just by being leaders.

7b–10. a great multitude ... touch him: the textual tradition reveals one or two variant readings in verses 7b–8.

There is MS evidence for the omission of **followed** (7*b*) and **a great multitude** (8). If, however, we accept the reading and punctuation adopted by *RSV*, it appears that Mark wishes to distinguish between the initial Galilean followers of Jesus (**Galilee** having a special significance in the Gospel: see 14:28 and 16:7), and those visitors who came to him from more distant places. **Jerusalem** is singled out as the capital city from the province of Judea generally. **Idumea** (the *OT* Edom) lies to the south, **beyond the Jordan** is the region of Perea to the east, and **Tyre and Sidon** in Gentile territory to the north-west but with strong associations with north Galilee. No doubt Mark wants to stress the universal appeal of Jesus' ministry and message. Jesus neither encourages nor invites this vast concourse. They gather to him of their own accord, drawn by his fame principally as a healer (see verse 10). Mark accentuates the fact that the soil of official Judaism has proven quite inhospitable, but despite the sternest opposition the good news is not hindered from travelling on its way with Jesus.

11. whenever . . . Son of God: the demons' declaration **"You are the Son of God"** is not to be understood as a dogmatic or doctrinal confession. It denotes that the demons bow before the power of God actually at work in Jesus. Ironically, what the supernatural forces of evil experience as a reality, the earthly representatives of religion have failed to acknowledge even as a possibility. The statement that **the unclean spirits fell down . . . and cried out** indicates that the demons so overwhelmingly possessed and controlled the actions of the sick that they could be said to act in their place.

12. Once more in the injunction to silence the Evangelist gives notice that the time for the full promulgation of Jesus' identity has not yet come. The healings, given as signs to faith, cannot in themselves reveal the final truth about him.

THE DISCIPLE FAMILY OF JESUS AND 'OUTSIDERS'
3:13-6:6
THE COMMISSIONING OF THE TWELVE 3:13-19a

The Evangelists place the appointment of the Twelve at different points in their composition (cf. Mt. 10:2-4; Lk. 6:12-16). That Mark locates it here at the opening of a new section of his Gospel reminds us how important the discipleship theme is for him. The report highlights the sovereign decision of Jesus in selecting and appointing certain individuals from among the crowd, and in turn the decision required of them to follow him. It is, therefore, a suitable preface to a section which testifies in various ways to the signs of the divine authority exercised by Jesus. Before his sovereign authority it is quite simply a matter of understanding or not understanding. The opportunity of understanding is given especially to his followers or disciples, who occupy a privileged position in respect of his teaching (4:11f., 33f.). They are his very own or are **with him** (3:14) in a way that his natural kinsfolk who reject him (6:1-6) can never be.

Verses 13-15 have all the appearance of a Marcan summary providing the *mise en scène* for the list of the Twelve which has come to Mark from the tradition.

13. went up into the hills: the Greek reads 'into the mountain', and unless we adopt the suggestion that the term reflects the Aramaic *tura*, meaning 'open country' (Black, *ARA*, p. 96), we should think of 'the mountain' not as a specific place, but in the biblical sense the place where God reveals himself and gives out his commandments (cf. Exod. 19:20; 1 Kg. 19:8). **called to him those whom he desired:** no doubt a contrast is intended between the crowd of visitors who come to Jesus of their own initiative (3:7f.), and those who respond here to *his own prior choice and call*. Not everyone who moves toward Jesus with the crowd that seeks his healing touch, is selected to be a disciple.

14-15. he appointed . . . demons: the literal meaning of the word **appointed** in Greek is 'made'. It is used in LXX, representing the Hebrew verb 'made' or 'do', of the appointment of priests (e.g. 2 Chr. 2:18). The number **twelve** symbolises the twelve tribes of Israel (cf. Mt. 19:28; Lk. 22:30), and shows how the disciples were conceived as the new people of God in the last days with a mission to the whole of Israel. There is little if any reliable evidence of councils with *twelve* members in Judaism (1QS 8:1ff. probably presupposes fifteen officials rather than twelve, according to recent textual evidence). Mark's brief account of the reasons for the appointment of the Twelve is perhaps based on information that he had from the tradition about what the disciples of Jesus actually did (cf. 6:7-13). However, the Evangelist's own interest here is theological. He wants to clarify what it means to be a disciple, and does so under the influence of

his own conception. The first thing in discipleship is to be with
Jesus. Drawn into his company, the disciples enjoy the shared
experience of the powers of the kingdom already present in his
word and deed. But they are not thereby constituted a closed
circle, aloof and apart from the world. The kingdom's privileges
go hand in hand with the kingdom's responsibilities, to perpetuate
the good news and do battle in Jesus' name and strength against
the hosts of evil.

16-19a. The way the list of the Twelve is linked to the preceding
summary is awkward in the Greek, and the MSS show a number of
variants. Some repeat **he appointed twelve** (from verse 14) at
the beginning of verse 16, possibly by dittography. There is also
some evidence for the insertion of the words 'first Simon' before
the clause 'and he gave Simon the surname of Peter', and this
helps to relieve the grammatical awkwardness. However, the
general sense is not affected and is well enough conveyed by *RSV*,
which also correctly omits the reading found in some MSS after the
words **he appointed twelve:** 'whom he also called apostles',
most probably an assimilation to Lk. 6:13.

The list of the Twelve Mark obtained from the tradition. That
the tradition knew also of variations is clear from the different
order of listing in Mt. 10:2-4; Lk. 6:14-16; Ac. 1:13; as well as
from the confusion over **Thaddaeus** (Mk 3:18). The MSS alternate
between Thaddaeus and Lebbaeus at Mk 3:18 and Mt. 10:3, no
doubt through assimilation, in which case two different individuals are involved. Luke does not mention either Thaddaeus or
Lebbaeus and has instead another Judas, son of James (6:14-16;
Ac. 1:13). John also includes this second Judas and also one
Nathanael (1:44ff.; 21:2) (whose identification with Bartholomew is sometimes conjectured but on no good grounds). At a time
when later legend had obviously taken a hand, entirely different
lists appear in both Greek and Jewish sources. But such fluidity as
does exist in the traditional listings, even at the earlier stage, suggests that most of these men were anything but well known and
had in the main become mere names.

Two of the names listed (**Andrew** and **Philip**) are distinctively
Greek. Others (**Thomas, Bartholomew, Thaddaeus, Matthew**
are Greek in form, although Semitic in origin. While the vast
majority of scholars are still agreed that the mother tongue of
Jesus and his disciples was Galilean Aramaic, the presence of
Greek names or forms of names among the Twelve should not

surprise us in view of the now commonly recognised fact that Greek was also widely spoken in the Galilee of the period.

Simon whom he surnamed Peter: the name **Simon** (= Hebrew, Symeon) is no longer used in Mark, except once at 14:37. The name **Peter** comes from the Greek word for 'stone' or 'rock' which in turn has behind it the Aramaic *kephas* (see e.g. Jn 1:42; 1 C. 1:12; Gal. 1:18). Whatever else might have evoked the name of Peter (his status as the 'rock' on which the Lord would choose to build the Church, Mt. 16:18f.?), it was surely not his *vacillating* character. Mark for his part offers no enlightening comment. **Boanerges:** presumably represents an obscure Hebrew or Aramaic form which is represented in the Gospel as **sons of thunder,** possibly = 'men of thundery temperament' (see Lk. 9:54) or 'fiery apocalyptic preachers'. But the designation has never been satisfactorily explained, either in respect of its derivation or its meaning. Some MSS (Western) apply the term to all the disciples, and it has been supposed that, since it may relate to 'twins', it alludes to the calling of the disciples in pairs and their being sent out two by two. But this is only guesswork. **Matthew:** if Mark thought of him as identical with Levi, he certainly has not said so. **Simon the Cananaean:** derived not from Canaan or Cana, geographical terms, but from the Hebrew *ḳanā* meaning 'man of zeal', rendered *ho zēlōtēs* in Lk. 6:15 (= Zealot?). It is unlikely that the Zealots became a *distinct party* dedicated to revolutionary action against the Roman occupying power until about the time of the Jewish War in AD 66. Earlier the word 'zealous' was possibly a general epithet describing anyone fanatically devoted to his ancestral religion. In his attempt to show that Mark's chief aim was to rid the Gospel of all traces of the revolutionary political sympathies of Jesus and his movement, Brandon makes the special point that Mark changed Zealot into the obscure **Cananaean** (obscure to Gentile readers) to conceal that Simon was in fact a Zealot insurrectionist (pp. 243ff.). But it is much more likely that having taken over terms like Boanerges and Cananaean from his tradition, Mark made what he could of the former and attached no special significance to the latter. Besides, if he really were out to placate the Romans, he might at this point have identified Matthew with Levi, and indicated that he was an official of the Roman, or pro-Roman, Herodian tax administration. **Judas Iscariot:** the latter word is left unexplained by the Evangelist. Modern attempts to explain it as meaning 'man of Kerioth' (*iš keriyyot*), or 'assassin' (Latin *sicarius*), or 'man of falsehood' (*seḳarya*) remain doubtful.

The Twelve

The idea of the Twelve is sometimes held to be an invention of the Church in the situation after Easter. While resisting such a negative judgment, we may concede that the circle of Jesus' followers was by no means restricted to the Twelve and that the Gospel tradition reveals a tendency to assign to the Twelve a representative significance and to have them everywhere as the constant companions of Jesus (e.g. Mk 2:15f.; 3:7; 4:10, 34; 6:1, 53f.; 8:27; 10:46; 11:12, 19, 27*a*; see Bultmann, *HST*, pp. 343ff.). Such a tendency of the tradition, however, by no means stamps the Twelve as a fiction of the Church. That Jesus in fact instituted the Twelve can hardly be doubted. How else would the Church have included Judas Iscariot in their number? Moreover the very old tradition cited by Paul in 1 C. 15:3ff. testifies to an appearance of the risen Christ to twelve disciples, who must therefore have existed as a group before Easter. Again, most of the Twelve listed in the Gospels had become no more than names, as we noted, and as a group they do not appear to have played any special role as leaders of the early Church: so they are scarcely a post-Easter Church circle.

Confronted with the list of those named, the Church was no doubt reminded that, without prior requirements of background, status, prestige, or religious leanings, different individuals uniquely experienced the sovereign call of Jesus. Also, in so far as the later Church saw itself in the disciples, the fact that all the lists begin with Peter, who disavowed Jesus, and end with Judas, who betrayed him, brought no doubt a timely warning that discipleship did not mean immediate 'perfection' but left open the hard road of temptation and trial.

THE 'BLINDNESS' THAT EXCLUDES JESUS' OWN PEOPLE 3:19b-35.

Following upon the appointment of the Twelve as the nucleus of the new Israel of God, the theme of how the wider family of the new Israel is constituted is taken up. Those who enter into such a relationship with Jesus that they are able to share with him in spontaneous obedience to the will of God are a quite unexpected company. The expected ones, the religious leaders of the day and Jesus' own natural kinsfolk, in fact disavow Jesus out of their

blind prejudice. From the standpoint of its post-Easter faith
in Jesus, the Church could barely credit that Jesus should
not be received by his own people. And in verses 21–29 we see
mirrored not only the Church's incredulity but its attempted explanation of this paradoxical rejection of Jesus by his own. Only
their own stony-heartedness (already foreseen in the plan of
God himself, according to Mk 10:11–12) made them incapable of realising that God was at work in the words and acts of
Jesus.

In this long section Mark's editorial activity is very much in
evidence. In Luke the parallel subject-matter is introduced by a
brief report of the casting out of a devil from a dumb man (Lk.
11:14). Mark by contrast sets the scene with a typical description
of the overwhelming response of the crowd to Jesus, thus providing
a foil to the sinister repudiations that follow. It is also characteristic
of Mark to interpolate one episode into another (see above, pp.
38f.). Here the departure of Jesus' own people is reported in verse
21, but their arrival only in verse 31. As Mark's explanatory editorial insertion in verse 30 shows, verse 29 is a reply to the charge
of the scribes in verse 22, and verses 33–35 a response to the grievous misunderstanding of the relatives of Jesus in verse 21. The
rather sudden introduction of the scribes from Jerusalem in verse
22 and the intercalated materials of verses 22–30 allow Mark to
set the more reserved accusation of Jesus' relatives and the more
explicit accusation of the scribes alongside each other, and to offer
a fairly comprehensive theological commentary on both. Verse 23
occurs in neither Mt. 12:22–32 nor Lk. 11:14–23. We infer that
it is a Marcan construction, which offers the first hint of a subject
to be developed fully in chapter 4, that Jesus answers his blind
and uncomprehending critics in *parables*.

19b. home: probably once more the house (of Peter?) in
Capernaum (See 2:1 and 1:29–33).

20. again: not necessarily referring back to 3:7 or 2:2 but
simply a Marcan connective.

21. his friends: the phrase so translated is in Greek not very
precise, and may mean 'agents', 'neighbours', 'friends', 'relatives'.
Here it probably denotes 'the members of his own household or
family'. **they went out to seize him, for they said:** it has been
suggested that **they said** is to be taken impersonally, like the
French *on disait*, 'people were saying', in which case the family of
Jesus are thought to be responding to a charge actually levelled

by the crowd. While such an interpretation may offer some sort of apologia for the family of Jesus, it is much more natural to suppose that it is in fact they who have come out to seize him and affirm **He is beside himself**: the Greek verb means 'has gone out of his mind', 'has become mad or insane', and since madness was attributed to demon-possession, this is tantamount to saying that Jesus was under the control of devils. Mark's sharp contrast between the natural and the true family of Jesus in verses 31–35, and his story of the rejection in 6:1–6, as well as his positive estimate of the crowd, all of this should prevent us from trying to soften or tone down or even explain away the harshness of his portrayal of the relatives here.

22. the scribes ... from Jerusalem: a Marcan redactional specification (cf. Mt. 12:24—'Pharisees', and Lk. 11:15—the crowds; see also Mk 7:1 and cf. Mt. 15:1 and Lk. 11:37). That the official leaders of Judaism should come from such a distance from the very headquarters of their religion is with Mark a sign of how widespread the fame of Jesus has become and of how **Jerusalem** (where his death will be encompassed) is the principal seat of opposition to Jesus. **he is possessed ... demons**: their malicious accusation implies that they have sensed in Jesus a destructive threat to everything they stand for, and that they take for granted that **he is possessed** *of supernatural power*—only they claim it is the power of evil and not of good. At this point in the Gospel the level of engagement, theologically speaking, is deeper and more crucial than in the earlier conflict-stories. It is a question now not just of religious practice or observance on the part of Jesus or his disciples, but of the very nature and origin of his authority. **Beelzebul**: understood by Matthew and Luke to be synonymous with the prince of the demons, Satan (Mt. 12:24; Lk. 11:15) and most probably also by Mark (although elsewhere, e.g. in the Qumran literature, this name, as opposed to others like Beliar, is not used of Satan). The Syriac version and the Vulgate read 'Beelzebub', the name of a Philistine god mentioned in 2 Kg. 1:2 meaning 'Lord of the flies'. **Beelzebul** may be a contemptuous alteration, employing a form of the Hebrew word *zebel* = dung. More likely it means 'Lord of the house or dwelling' (see Mt. 10:25). **by the prince of demons**: exercising the same power or operating in the same sphere as Satan, Jesus is like him, according to the charge, supremely an agent of evil.

23. This verse is peculiar to Mark and contains typically

Marcan vocabulary, e.g. the verb **called** (cf. 3:13; 6:7; 7:14; 8:1, 34; 10:42; 12:43). Once more Jesus takes the initiative and manifests his authority by summoning the accusers. His reply is given in parables. The Greek word *parabolē* is found in the *NT* only in the Synoptic Gospels and has behind it the Hebrew *mashal* = 'proverb', 'wise saying', 'illustrative story'. Mark lays a great deal of stress on Jesus' teaching *activity* (note the incidence of the words 'taught' and 'teaching' in the seams of the Gospel narrative). This does not necessarily mean, however, that he wishes to elevate Jesus' teaching above his healing or exorcism (see Best, p. 72). The fact is no less striking that Mark conveys relatively very little of the content of Jesus' teaching (virtually nothing up to this point in the Gospel). We may infer that he desires to focus on the person and deed of Jesus: by putting the speaker and his actions (whether teaching or healing or exorcism) before his spoken words, he militates against any mere preservation and transmission of the sayings of Jesus as an interesting contribution to the history of religious ideas, as if their value or validity would be the same *no matter who had uttered them.* Even here in 3:23 Mark's first concern is with the *mode* of Jesus' teaching. He teaches parabolically, in a veiled sort of way, or as one might say, by indirection. Just as in his person and deed Jesus does not proclaim himself from the house-tops (note the 'secret' in relation to his healing and exorcism), neither does his teaching disclose everything openly to all listeners. Its manner is secret and mysterious. For Mark this corresponds to what was certainly still a fact of Christian existence in his own time, that there are those outsiders, as the rather shattering conclusion in 3:28 shows, who are so incredibly hard and perverted in their attitude to Jesus that the secret or mystery of his teaching might remain for ever impenetrable to them. Mk 3:23, with its mention of Jesus' parabolic mode of teaching, prepares the way for the Evangelist's fuller treatment of the subject in chapter 4.

How can Satan cast out Satan?: not 'How can one devil cast out another?' but 'How can Satan cast out himself?' Jesus does not question the reality of Satan's power as chief of the demons. His question implies that demons are in fact being expelled through his own ministry and that it is quite inconceivable that it could be Satan who was taking up arms against himself or his own. The parabolic sayings that follow (verse 27 probably initially circulated independently but was combined with the

preceding sayings in the tradition before Mark. Notice the catchword 'house' in verses 25 and 27 and the related idea of the
'kingdom' in verse 24) drive home this logic.

24–26. The scribes' accusation had clearly acknowledged the
continuing power of Satan (3:22). Jesus also accepts the fact and
now turns it back upon themselves. Civil strife in any realm or
house is inevitably disruptive and ultimately destructive. Therefore, since by the scribes' own confession Satan's empire is not
destroyed but still holds out, he obviously cannot be at war with
himself within his own domain. If things are happening and
demons are being cast out, *another power* must be at work.

27. One should not press the details of the parable by regarding
his goods as Satan's unfortunate victims or the binding of **the
strong man** as the tying up described in 1:21f. (Schweizer,
GNM, p. 86). In its present context the parabolic saying comes as
a challenge to faith to recognise the hidden power of God at work
in the ministry of the 'stronger one' (see 1:7; cf. Isa. 49:25;
53:12).

28–30. Truly ... eternal sin: the composition and placement
of these verses is almost certainly due to Mark. Possibly verses
22*b*–27 and verses 31–35 lay alongside each other in the tradition
received by Mark. He then added verses 21–22*a* as introduction,
and by inserting verses 28–30 brought both the family of Jesus and
the scribes from Jerusalem under the indictment contained there
(for detailed argument in support of this see J. D. Crossan, *NovT*
15 (1973), pp. 81ff. and especially pp. 94ff.)

The word *amēn* (= 'truly') is a Hebrew expression (from a root
meaning 'to be faithful'), commonly used after a wish or a prayer
= 'so be it'. Its usage at the beginning of a sentence is characteristic of Jesus, and the force of the usage in his sayings is: 'I am
faithful to the word I speak, and the promise contained in it will
be fulfilled.' The saying reported in verses 28–29 has a different
form in Q (cf. Mt. 12:31–32; Lk. 12:10), where a contrast is
drawn between speaking slanderously against the Son of man
(in Q = Jesus in his earthly ministry), which is pardonable, and
speaking slanderously **against the Holy Spirit,** which is un-
pardonable. In the Marcan form of the saying, the horizons are
widened and a contrast is drawn between the lavishness of God's
grace that freely forgives all, and the incredible hardness of those
who by their wilful spurning of that grace shut themselves off
from its blessing.

There is hardly any reference to the Holy Spirit in other sayings of Jesus, and verse 29 as it stands appears to have been shaped within a Church that had come to equate slander against the Son of man with slander against the Holy Spirit, and to see in this the ultimate diabolical opposition to the good news of God. (Probably the Evangelist himself radically reworked the Q *logion* into the form of verse 29, which contains characteristically Marcan terminology (see J. D. Crossan, *NovT* 15 (1973), pp. 93f.). By his editorial comment in verse 30, **for they had said 'He has an unclean spirit'**, Mark links up the sin against the Holy Spirit specifically with the charge that Jesus is possessed by the devil. There is certainly no word of condemnation here for honest doubt or questioning, and accordingly no justification whatever for the fanaticism that would try to expand the statement of verse 29 into a universal theology of the dire fate in store for those who interrogate God's claim in Jesus. The accusers come not as questioners but as the official guardians of religion who have known God and his Spirit already (Cranfield, p. 143; Schweizer, *GNM*, p. 87.) Yet knowing God, they vehemently resist him when he seeks to confront them. By declaring that Jesus' works are of the devil, they in effect set themselves up as lordly judges of the work of God himself. That is their sin and it is eternal inasmuch as their own consummate lordliness presents an impregnable barrier to the mercy of God.

31–32. As we have noted, Mark's insertion of verses 28–30 between 22*b*–27 and 31–35 exposes both the scribes and the family of Jesus to the ominous warning of verse 29. The relatives are certainly not spared. Here they are placed as 'outsiders' in regard not to any inner circle of the disciples but to *the crowd* (there is no parallel to 3:32 in Mt. 12:46 or Lk. 8:19). There is no mention of the supposed father of Jesus, Joseph, in 3:31–35. Was he dead by this time? Or is the omission intentional on Mark's part—either for dogmatic reasons to protect the Virgin Birth (see further on 6:1–6), or because Jesus reserved the name of Father for God (Rawlinson, p. 46; Robinson, *PHM*, p. 81, note 1), or because Mark is here polemicising against the Jerusalem community for which Joseph held no interest (J. D. Crossan, *NovT* 15 (1973), p. 112)? On the question of a Marcan polemic against the relatives = mother-church in Jerusalem, see on 6:1–6.

33–34. There is no need to read into the question of verse 33 great doctrinal depths or difficulties in regard to the parentage or lineage of Jesus. The point of the question of verse 33 and the statement of verse 34 is that natural ties of kinship do not confer any special privilege or right of entry into the company of Jesus. Wherever Jesus is present he offers himself as gift to all people irrespective of their background or descent. Consequently the reader of Mark, whoever or wherever he is, is here placed before Jesus' invitation and is asked to accept fellowship with him.

35. Over against the fourfold **mother** and **brothers** of verses 31–34, the addition of the words **and sister** here is noteworthy. It is scarcely a gesture toward the presence of women in *Jesus'* audience (Rawlinson, p. 46), for then we might have expected the occurrence of the word 'sister' in the question of verse 33 and the statement of verse 34. It may in fact reflect the Church's recognition of women disciples. Verse 35 offers a qualifying comment on the remarkable breadth of the offer and invitation of verse 34, and may have been added by the Church to accentuate its own response to that offer (Schweizer, p. 84.) Or possibly it is due to Mark. The phrase, **the will of God,** is Pauline (e.g. Rom. 1:10; 12:2; etc.), but occurs nowhere else in the synoptic tradition (where it is always the Father's will that is in question, e.g. Mt. 6:19; 7:21; 12:50; 18:14; 21:31; 26:42; Lk. 11:2; 22:42). Certainly for Mark, just as Jesus himself surrenders to God's will (14:36), so discipleship consists of unreserved obedience on the part of his followers (cf. 1:16–20, 2:14; 6:7–13; 8:34f.; 10:17–31).

THE PARABLE OF THE SOWER AND THE SEED **4:1-9**

The Evangelist has been careful to try to preserve the ambiguity inherent in Jesus' ministry. Not everyone around can see and understand in it the signs of the presence of the kingdom of God. In fact some can even accuse Jesus of being possessed by the demon (3:21–22). It is thus made clear that the actualisation of the reign of God in Jesus' word and deed is certainly not a matter that everyone can immediately grasp. Rather is the kingdom of God *hidden* in him. 'Not in the way the apocalypticists thought, beyond the heavens, in the bosom of a mysterious future, but here, hidden in the everyday world of the present time, where no one is aware of what is already taking place. Of this Jesus speaks in his parables of the kingdom of God' (Bornkamm, p. 69).

For the better part of nineteen centuries, however, the Gospel

parables were understood as profound theological treatises which
expressed symbolically all the mysteries of Christ and the Church
and the Christian faith. At the earliest stage, when the parables
were transmitted from their setting in the life of Jesus to their
setting in the life of the early Church, the Church itself treated
them as allegories and sought to uncover in every item and word
deep new spiritual meanings. Now in an allegory the story itself is
unimportant and does not ring true. So in one of Aesop's characteristic fables, when the fox cannot reach the grapes he wants and
convinces himself that they are sour grapes, we are dealing not
with a real fox at all, since foxes do not eat grapes, but with
hidden allusions to man's situation. The allegory ties up numerous
strands of meaning in its deliberately puzzling details and a very
special insight is required to unravel them (see the allegorising
equations in the interpretation of the parable of the sower, e.g.
the birds = Satan, Mk 4:14-20).

Not until the close of the nineteenth century was the allegorical
understanding of the parables decisively challenged, by Adolf
Jülicher in his famous book, *Die Gleichnisreden Jesu*. Jülicher argued
that the intention of any given parable of Jesus was to make its
meaning perfectly lucid, that it offered essentially only *one* point
of comparison to which all details were subservient, and that it
belonged to a particular concrete situation in the public ministry
of Jesus. Although in its broad lines this thesis has been widely
accepted in recent parable-research, many different viewpoints
have arisen regarding the actual life-setting of the parables in the
ministry of Jesus, e.g. that Mark is right in considering them to be
popular stories addressed to the crowds (see below, on 4:33-34);
that they belong to conflict situations in Jesus' ministry (C. H.
Dodd, J. Jeremias); that their original context was always a sermon
based on particular scriptural texts (C. H. Cave, *NTS* 11 (1964-5),
pp. 374-87); that they were told in the social *milieu* in which
Jesus moved, especially when he was a guest at table (e.g. Lk. 7:36;
10:38ff.; 11:37ff.; 14:1ff.; 19:1ff. see E. Trocmé, *JC*, pp. 81ff.).
If there is disagreement about the difficult question of the actual
life-setting of Jesus' parables (the difficulty arising partly of
course from the fact that they were often handed down without
any exact note of the occasion on which they were given), there is
also considerable disagreement about the *one point per parable*
theory, which has frequently been held to be excessively rigid.
Even if one does not accept the contention that Jesus himself told

certain parables as allegorical tales embodying numerous symbolic features (e.g. the parable of the sower, the tares, and the
wicked tenants (see M. Black, *BJRL* 42 (1960), pp. 273-87;
R. E. Brown, *NovT* 5 (1962), pp. 36-45), one should concede
that, for Jesus' first listeners, around the several items in a story
would cluster constellations of images, giving rise to various
trains of thought in accordance with the customs and traditions
of their time and place (see Derrett, pp. xxiff. and 100ff.).

Nevertheless the view has hardly been shaken that Jesus uses
the language of the parables to carry the hearer along toward
this *one* certainty, 'the one pearl of great price'. For anyone willing
to see or listen, God's reign is already discernible in the everyday
world men inhabit. Whereas with the Jewish rabbis, who also
extensively taught in parables, the parable was intended to
illustrate a lesson or truth that was already contained in a written
text or could be grasped independently of the story told, Jesus'
parables do not point to an ideal or truth that exists outside of
themselves. They are in fact the direct and indispensable com-
municators of the truth Jesus means to affirm. He addresses his
hearers in the commonplace language of the ordinary life of
nature or man, of fields and fishing, sheep and goats, workmen
and bosses, savings and debts. And this common language becomes the vehicle conveying his message of the mysterious action
of God in his ministry and putting men on the spot where they
have to decide for or against. In the parables of the sower and
the harvest, for instance (Mk 4:3-9; 4:26-29), in these so
humdrum facts men are confronted through Jesus with the
unspectacular, insignificant, and obscure beginnings of the
kingdom of God, beginnings all the same which contain within
themselves the hope of the coming glory of the kingdom to be
bestowed by God alone.

1-2. Again . . . said to them: the word **again** is simply a
Marcan connecting link, and does not necessarily point back to
any previous passage. The form and language of these verses is
definitely Marcan (although the notice about the boat, already
mentioned in 3:9, is most probably from the tradition), and the
Evangelist is here clearly setting the scene for a typical collection
of parables. Is Mark historically correct in picturing Jesus as
teaching in parables in the midst of a very great throng of people?
The vividness and simplicity of Jesus' parabolic speech, with its
seemingly popular appeal, suggest he might be. But on the other

hand the endless hustle and bustle of the crowds, which Mark himself records most graphically (1:31–45; 2:1ff.), hardly provides a suitable setting for parabolic discourse. Accordingly, Mark's view that the parables were related popularly to the crowd (cf. 4:33f.) is possibly part of his wider conception of how the good news travelled with Jesus in a great rush and reached out rapidly far and wide. The parables that are told in verses 3–30 were not originally spoken in a continuous series, as the familiar connective **and he said** shows (see 4:11, 21, 30).

3. Listen! A sower went out to sow: The opening command (cf. Dt. 6:4, etc.), together with the closing statement of verse 9, not only calls attention to the seriousness and solemnity of the utterance but summons to a total attention to and involvement in the words of Jesus. The first sentence of the parable is extremely matter of fact. The focus is on a trivial enough sight in the real world of everyday, a **sower** and his action. Therefore, of the one who would **listen,** no previous theoretical knowledge or philosophical or theological training is demanded.

4–8. In Palestine the sowing of seed preceded ploughing, and terrain being what it was, it was inevitable that some parts of a field, where a pathway was trodden or where limestone lay just under the soil's surface or where weeds remained rooted in the ground and impoverished it, should be inhospitable and unproductive. There is accordingly no criticism, overt or implied, of the husbandry in the story. By contrast with the barren spots, the yield where the soil is fertile, is as described in verse 8, quite enormous, a one-hundredfold crop being very rare indeed. The impression of amazing productivity is further enhanced by the imperfect of the Greek verb = **brought forth,** and the present participles **growing up** and **increasing.**

Since we owe the present location of the parable to Mark, we do not know the situation or context in which it was first told, and so it is difficult to recapture its original meaning. Various suggestions have been made: e.g. (a) the message is that despite an unpromising reception in many quarters Jesus' work would produce an amazingly rich harvest—the final coming of the kingdom of God in power; (b) the parable indicates that despite all obstacles the kingdom of God *is here already*, with the full harvest just waiting to be reaped; (c) the point is that every preacher and teacher must face discouragements and failures, but enough success is assured to make their labour worth while;

(d) the crucial feature is the differences of soil, corresponding to the different ways of hearing and responding to the Word of God.

To the mind of Mark, however (if one recalls his first notice of Jesus' parabolic mode of teaching in the context of the Beelzebul controversy, 3:22ff.), the parable illustrates the ambiguity to which the word and act of God in Jesus is inevitably exposed in the world. Hostility, misunderstanding, and rejection are facts that will not hide. Since God chooses to speak and act *in concealment* (as the seed is covered in the earth), there *will* be the blindness of unfaith and opposition. But even in the midst of all opposition there is assurance—'a sower goes out to sow: nothing more; that is what God's new world means' (Schniewind, p. 75). And just because the sower goes out, the future is bright with promise, beyond what men normally or naturally expect (4:8).

9. He who has ears to hear, let him hear: always on the lips of Christ in the *NT* (cf. Mk 4:23; Mt. 11:15; 13:9, 43; Lk. 8:8; 14:35; Rev. 2:7, 11, 17, 29, etc.). Here it implies the recognition that not all will understand or do understand, since understanding is God's gift to faith.

THE 'HEARING' OF THE PARABLES AS THE GIFT OF GOD **4:10–12**

At verse 10, **And when he was alone,** there occurs a rather abrupt change of scene that interrupts the unity of 4:1–36— although there is no indication of any shift of audience between verse 11 and 33, verses 33f. still imply that the preceding parables have been spoken to the crowd, and verses 35f. find Jesus still in the boat mentioned in verse 1. It is, therefore, fairly certain that verses 10–12 (together with the interpretation of the parable of the sower in verses 13–20) have been inserted into their present context. This impression is strengthened by the somewhat awkward and curious expression in verse 10, **those who were about him with the twelve,** which introduces the change of scene. Possibly at an earlier stage in the transmission of the tradition, verse 13 with its question first of all about t parable of the sower followed immediately upon verse 10, which originally read the singular, 'asked him concerning *the parable*' (i.e. the parable of the sower). The singular would have been altered to the plural, **concerning the parables,** meaning 'concerning his parabolic mode of teaching in general', in order to lead into the particular view of it expressed in verses 11–12, when these verses were finally inserted.

However one estimates the stages by which the composite materials of 4:1–35 were built up, one thing seems clear enough. The words of verses 11–12 in their present form are not words of Jesus, for with their understanding of his parabolic teaching as a deliberate veiling of the truth, they in fact contradict his parables which, with consummate artistry to be sure, address men in plain, simple, and 'earthy' language, just where they are amid the realities of their own world.

The question then arises whether the so-called 'parable theory' of verses 11–12 is Mark's own or represents his own standpoint. In fact the theory of the parables here presented as an esoteric teaching designed only for a select inner group, breaks down against clear and contrary indications of the Evangelist's conception elsewhere in 3:23 where the crowd is involved, in 4:3 and 9 where all are invited to 'listen', in 4:13 where it is implied that the inner group themselves do not understand, and above all in 4:21–25 and 4:33. Accordingly we are led to the conclusion that verses 10–11 represent the viewpoint of the early Church, which drew a sharp distinction between itself as receptive to God's bestowal of the 'secret' of his kingdom and those outsiders who by their own wilful repudiation of Jesus and his claim showed that God had not destined them for such 'seeing' and 'hearing' as bring salvation. The reason why Mark could here have incorporated a Church statement that appears at first sight to be at odds with his own ideas will be discussed below.

10. those who were about him with the twelve: the phrase **with the twelve** is awkwardly tagged on and is probably a Marcan addition (Bultmann, *HST*, p. 325, note 1). He wishes to specify that, like the larger group around them, even the innermost circle of the disciples were short on understanding and had to seek an explanation of Jesus' parabolic teaching. For Mark of course the very frailty of the select group itself makes God's gift of the 'secret' of the kingdom to them (11a) all the more miraculous. In view of the pervasive motif of the blindness of the disciples in the Gospel (see below), it seems preferable to take verse 10 this way than to think (with Nineham, pp. 137f.) of a *specifically Marcan stress* on the exclusive right of a small, select inner band to have the parables explained to them.

11–12. That this statement is a Church formulation is supported by a fair weight of evidence—the terms **secret** and **those outside** occur, the former in Paul and the Apocalypse, the latter in Paul but nowhere else in the Gospels except here. But certain features in the statement suggest that it goes back to the Jewish-Christian, Aramaic-speaking Church in Palestine. The phrase **everything is in parables** is peculiar in Greek = 'all things happen or are done in parables', and makes sense here only because the Hebrew or Aramaic word for 'parable' has various shades of meaning and may be synonymous with the word for 'riddle'. In Palestine **those outside** designated Gentile unbelievers. The form of the quotation from Isa. 6:9f. in verse 12 is much closer to the Aramaic Targum than to either the *OT* or LXX. Again, there may underlie the Greek conjunctions for **so that** and **lest** in verse 12 Aramaic terms meaning 'with the result that' and 'unless'. Possibly then in its primary setting the saying stated only that to unbelievers everything must remain enigmatic, since for all their seeing and listening they had no chance of understanding unless they repented (Jeremias, pp. 14ff.; Schweizer, *GNM*, pp. 92f.) The severity of the saying can also be mitigated in another way if one recalls that in the Apocalyptic literature, Qumran, and Paul the word 'secret' (Greek *mystērion* = 'mystery') denotes not a mystery held back from the uninitiated, but one that has hitherto been concealed and is now revealed by God (Taylor, p. 255; Cranfield, p. 152).

Nevertheless the statement as it stands in the Greek of Mark can hardly be freed of its extreme stringency. In the later apocryphal books of the Greek *OT* (e.g. Wis. 14:15, 23) the term 'secret' relates to the pagan 'mysteries' and here in Mark it would have suggested for his Gentile readers an analogy with the pagan mystery-cults, in which only the initiates were privileged to possess esoteric knowledge of the divine 'mystery' of salvation (Rawlinson, pp. 51f.). At any rate the Church that lived under the guidance of the Marcan form of this saying certainly worked with a theory of blinding or hardening, implied in the way the citation from Isa. 6:9f. is used. The gap between insiders who were honoured with esoteric instruction and explanation and hardened outsiders to whom Jesus' teaching must remain baffling was divinely willed or providentially decreed.

However, Mark himself, as we noted above (p. 126), thinks of the parables as intended for all the people (3:23; 4:3 and 9, 33). He is apparently at pains to counter any claim that the parables (or some of them) were meant only for an elect few like the Twelve. In the later part of the Gospel particularly, the terms

'the disciples' (Greek *mathētai*) and **the twelve** seem to be inter-
changeable (C. H. Turner, *JTS* (1926–7), pp. 22–30), and as the
Evangelist develops the motif of the disciples' blindness, the
select inner band is assuredly not spared. Despite *private* instruction and *open* pronouncement (see especially 8:31f.) they never
really learn but remain uncomprehending (see 7:17f.; 8:14–21,
27–33; 9:9–13, 30–32; 10:23–31; 32–45; 11:20–25; for their
blindness in the midst of their experience with Jesus, see 4:35–41;
6:45–52; 9:2–8; 14:17–25, 32–42). All the way through to the
cross and resurrection the 'secret' is still a 'secret' for them. Mark
for his part is accordingly scarcely operating with the doctrine of
a divinely decreed election of the few who surely know everything
already (Schweizer, *GNM*, p. 94). Why then has he included the
severe saying of verses 11–12 at this point in his Gospel? He is
aware that it protects a basic truth. Jesus' teaching does contain a
mystery, and it is a mystery that cannot be seen in this world by
human eyes. The fact that it is not seen even by the disciples (who
stay blind to the end) only makes God's gracious desire to impart
and unfold it to them through Jesus' word all the more wonderful.
In Mark's view the mystery the parables enclose is the hidden
dawn of the kingdom of God, and it is hidden *not only from outsiders but from the community of disciples as well.* Since it is so veiled, it
places *all men* in their freedom, whatever is their position in their
actual world, in a crisis of decision, for God's will that some
should not see or hear does not extinguish human responsibility.
The mystery can only be listened to, appropriated as God's gift,
and believed. Conceivably the Evangelist, by his radicalising of
the statement of verses 11–12, wished to convey to leaders of the
Christian congregation in his own day that the gift of understanding the mystery is only from God and not from their own
privileged situation or special ability (for a similar type of interpretation of verses 10–11, see Schweizer, *GNM*, pp. 94f.)

AN EXPLANATION OF THE SOWER AND THE SEED **4:13–20**

It is not impossible that on occasion Jesus may have offered an
explanation of a parable or even that some of his parables, like
some of those of the rabbis, as Fiebig argued (see especially pp.
31–5), could have contained allegorical features. Nevertheless
there are very strong grounds for thinking that the explanation
of the parable of the sower originated not with Jesus but with the
Church. Aside from linguistic considerations (e.g. the lack of

Semitic flavour and the frequency of words that occur elsewhere
in the *NT* only in the Epistles; see further Jeremias, pp. 61f.), the
passage seems to assume a long period during which the missionary
work of the Church has been under way (4:17, 19). Interest is
transferred from the mystery of the kingdom's dawning in the
ministry and message of Jesus to studied appraisal of the various
states of mind of those who are confronted with the Church's
missionary proclamation. Whereas the parable of Jesus (4:3-8) is
marked by eschatological confidence that in the midst of the
everyday world with all its difficulties and obstacles there lies
concealed the promise of the coming great harvest, there is
scarcely a trace of that left here. In Jesus' story the variations of
soil denote quite simply that, for the farmer, sowing is always a
risky business. Here the seed falling on different spots represents
various categories of men in their different responses to the
Christian message (verses 15*a*, 16-20). But inconsistently, in
verses 14 and 15*b*, **seed** = the Christian message. Compared
with the natural, commonplace situation depicted by Jesus
(4:3-8), the interpretation here is forced and probably arises
from confusion of two separate ideas, that the Word of God is
seed sown in man (2 Esd. 9:31) and that men are themselves seed
sown by God (2 Esd. 8:41).

13. The first question refers back to verse 10, which originally
read the singular, 'parable' = the parable of the sower. The
second question broadens the perspective and puts even the
disciples on the spot. They too have no secure or perfect knowledge of the mystery enshrined in the parables. For them too, as
for all men, further intent listening to Jesus' word is necessary. In
fact with Mark fuller understanding demands a long apprenticeship in following Jesus all the way to the cross and through
Easter.

14-20. The interpretation of the parable picks up and offers
a brief commentary upon the various phrases used in 4:3-8;
**sower, along the path, rocky ground, among thorns, good
soil.** Taylor rightly suggests that they could with advantage be
put in inverted commas in translation of the explanation in
verses 14-20 (p. 259). The sower is not defined; he could be any
Christian preacher or missionary, in the light of what follows.
Sows the word: the term **the word** (Greek *ho logos*) is noticeably
not used in the parable of Jesus (4:3-8). In Mark it may carry its
ordinary sense of 'word', 'report', 'account' (e.g. 1:45, 5:36,

7:29; 10:22, 11:29; 14:39. See Best, pp. 69f.), but here, as in
2:2; 4:33, 8:32, it denotes the Christian message, the Word of
the Church's proclamation. It is significant for Mark that the
Word preached by the Church (4:14) is in continuity with the
Word spoken by Jesus (8:32). **Satan . . . comes:** clearly the
Church did not think that the menace of Satan had been completely overcome through the work of Jesus; they awaited his
final overthrow when God's reign would be established. But
meanwhile he remained active as the great enemy, impeding the
Church's mission and blocking its message (**takes away the
word**). Verses 16–20 reflect the experiences the Church has
already had with converts in the course of its mission. There are
those who at first welcome the Word, but shortly defect when
faithfulness to the Word involves hardship or tribulation; there
are those who temporarily respond to the Word, but their growth
in it is stunted by the vicissitudes of life, by the allure of material
possessions, and by the tyranny of their own fleshly appetites;
lastly, there are on the contrary those who hear the Word and
welcome it and bear fruit. The present participle (**are being
sown**) in verses 16 and 18 stresses the Church's repeated attempts
to implant the Word. In verse 20 the past participle (**were once
sown**), followed by the present tenses of the verbs **hear** and
accept, serves to emphasise the continual faithful and fruitful
service of those who have truly responded to a sowing of the Word
successfully completed in the past.

The explanatory parable proceeds in a very matter-of-fact
way: this is just how things really are. There being no explicit
word either of warning or encouragement, it is usually assumed
that the parable offers to preachers the consolation that despite
setbacks they will also enjoy their successes. However, the description of those who receive the Word into their lives is least of
all developed (verse 20: **bear fruit** may suggest either their own
ever-deepening loyalty to the Word or their spreading of the
Word to others through the example of their own obedience).
Consequently Mark possibly thinks of the parables as a warning
against those who refuse to open themselves completely to all
that God desires to offer in the gift of his Word.

The significance of the fact that side by side within a single
chapter of the Gospel there occur a parable told by Jesus himself
and a Church interpretation of it should not be overlooked. It
shows that even at the very earliest stage the words of Jesus were

not regarded as a static Holy Word that simply had to be repeated in order to make their point. Rather from the beginning
the Church felt free to adapt Jesus' words to its own practical
situations and problems in the present. It implies also of course
that the ancient Church's interpretation should not pre-empt the
meaning the parable of Jesus might have for us if we expose ourselves to it in our own new circumstances (see Schweizer, p. 98).

GOD'S WORD INTENDED FOR ALL WHO LISTEN **4:21–25**

Five or six originally independent sayings of Jesus have been
combined into this short catena. Verses 21 and 22 both contain
the idea that the light is meant to shine. Verses 24 and 25 have in
common the notion of what is about to **be given.** The latter two
verses may have been connected with the former two because
'measuring' is related to the word 'bushel', which in Greek is a
transliteration of the Latin word *modius* = 'two-gallon measure'.
Whether the tradition before Mark, or Mark himself, made the
combination is very hard to say. But verse 23, **If any man has
ears to hear, let him hear,** and verse 24*a*, **take heed what you
hear,** are almost certainly Marcan redactional elements designed
to link up these sayings with his view of the parables, and to show
that the hearing that leads to understanding is dependent not on
men's cleverness but on God's gracious initiative.

The sayings collected here are scattered in Matthew and Luke
in different contexts, although Luke also reproduces them *en bloc*
in 8:16–18. Since their sense would be largely determined by
their original context, and we do not know what that context
was, we can now only conjecture their meaning as independent
sayings. Verses 21–22 could have suggested that God wants to
reveal himself in the words and deeds of Jesus and to enlighten
men, and will in the end do so. Verses 24–25 are more obscure.
Verse 24 may initially have referred to the judgment of God. As
men judge others, so will they be judged by God, only more
rigorously (this is the construction put upon the saying in Q,
Mt. 7:1f. = Lk. 6:38). Verse 25 may be based on a popular
proverb relating to prevailing social conditions in oriental
society, where the rich get richer at the expense of the poor, who
become more and more downtrodden (Rawlinson, p. 55; Taylor,
p. 265). Within the ministry of Jesus it would apply to the gift
of discernment of the mystery of the kingdom. But it is more

important to ask what Mark makes of these sayings by locating
them at this point in his Gospel.

21-25. Is a lamp brought in?: the Greek reads literally
'Does the lamp come?' and the awkward Marcan expression is refined in Mt. 5:15 and Lk. 8:16. In view of the significance of the
verb 'come' for Mark in regard to the historic appearance of Jesus
(see above, pp. 76, 84), it is just possible that there is an allusion
here to the coming of Jesus. Thinking of verse 22 as the explanation of verse 21, the Evangelist has in mind that the secret dawning of the kingdom of God that lies concealed in Jesus' parables it
is God's will finally to make fully manifest. That the promise of
illumination is validated only for those who can open themselves
completely to receive God's gift of understanding is then made
clear by the appeal of verse 23 and verse 24a. Verse 24b underscores the amazing extent to which God desires to unveil the
mystery of his kingdom through the parabolic teaching of Jesus
(**and still more will be given you** is possibly a Marcan addition). The only limiting factor is the degree of men's openness to
receive God's gift. Lastly, verse 25 indicates that where there is no
openness whatever, God's gift is already spurned and those who
have spurned it are in a worse state than before (**even what he
has will be taken away**): where there has been a beginning of
the openness that brings discernment, there is possible the fulfilment of the glorious promise implied in verses 21-22. On this
view of 4:21-25 the so-called Marcan parable theory of the
blinding of the crowd in 4:11-12 is obviously *not Marcan* at all,
and these sayings are to be associated with the parables that
follow (4:26-32), whose theme is the wonderful promise of God's
kingdom concealed in the ordinary everyday world of the hearer.

THE HARVEST GOD'S HANDIWORK **4:26-29**

This is the only parable in Mark that has no parallel at all in the
other Gospels, although Matthew's parable of the tares (13:24-30)
re-echoes its vocabulary (**sleep, sprout, blade, grain, harvest**)
and is distinctly reminiscent of it. Since it is peculiar to Mark,
and is prefaced with the formula **and he said,** which introduces
an independent saying, once more we do not know what its
original context was in the ministry of Jesus and so have no clear
pointer to its interpretation. Perhaps the most familiar approach
has been to fasten on to verse 28b **first the blade, then the ear,
then the full grain in the ear,** and to think of the parable as a

parable of growth. Jesus proclaims that the kingdom of God will
gradually evolve until its consummation. But the idea of a steady
development of the kingdom is a modern one, unsupported by
biblical evidence. In the forefront of Jesus' eschatological message
is rather the kingdom's imminence, the sheer unexpectedness of
its arrival, since it is God's to give in *his* time and not man's to
work out step by step. A similar parable in *1 Clement* 23:3 and 4
(from around AD 96) also describes various stages of growth, but
in fact the lesson drawn from it is that the kingdom is impending
in the very near future.

We may assume as a definite possibility that Jesus aimed this
parable at those of his contemporaries who felt that by their own
zeal for the Law, or for revolutionary political activity, or for the
preparation of the elect for the events of the end, they could by
themselves hasten the kingdom's coming. Against all such
strenuous human longings and aspirations Jesus teaches that the
kingdom of God, alike in its coming great future and in its silent
and concealed present in the world, is only at God's behest
(Bornkamm, pp. 72f.). But again it is important to ask what the
parable means for Mark in its present context.

26-29. the kingdom of God is as if: the parable, like most
others, is introduced without speculative preliminaries or prior
theological theory. The type of introduction that is employed
suggests that the kingdom is so radically different that its reality
cannot be described *in itself*, and yet at the same time it is inscribed on the commonplace things and events of daily life. The
variation of tenses between verses 26 and 27 denotes that when
once the farmer has completed the sowing, he can go about his
daily round for days and nights on end and simply leave it at that
(leave it, in the Semitic *milieu*, to God of course, and not to a 'law
of Nature'). **sleep and rise night and day: sleep** and **night**
are mentioned first no doubt because the process begins at the
close of that first busy day of sowing (verse 26), **he knows not
how:** a miracle happens in the earth silently and independently
of human resources. From Mark's standpoint this protects the
'secret' of the kingdom of God that can only be responded to and
believed in. **the earth produces of itself:** an answer to the
question implied in the immediately preceding **he knows not
how.** The clue to the parable lies in this statement. The focus in
verse 28 is not on the process of growth **first the blade, then the
ear, then the full grain,** but rather on the fact that all these

things take place spontaneously (Greek *automatē* = 'of itself'),
without human aid or force. This means that the kingdom's
coming depends on God's power alone to bring it, on which men
must simply wait. **but when . . . has come;** the closing words
he puts in the sickle, because the harvest has come are
from Jl 3:13, where the **harvest** is closely associated with the
final judgment. Here the note of judgment is muted and the
stress is on the end that comes at the decisive point. In terms of
the parable the expected conclusion follows very smoothly from
the initial action of sowing. The end is already concealed as
promise in the beginning.

The parable sustains Mark's view that the dawn of the kingdom
in its obscure beginnings is hidden from human eyes in the
ministry of Jesus. But since none-the-less it is there, the future
harvest of the kingdom God will produce can be awaited with
confidence. Mark's reader is thus challenged to see that all who
open themselves in faith to the future God will surely give may be
freed from frustration and anxiety even in the most straitened
present.

THE HIDDEN PRESENCE OF GOD'S COMING KINGDOM **4:30-32**

The parable of the mustard seed occurs also in Q (Mt. 13:31f.;
Lk. 13:18f.), where it probably stood alongside the parable of the
leaven, which conveys a similar message (Mt. 13:33, Lk. 13:20f.).
Its context, form, and meaning *as a parable of Jesus* are not at all
clear. It is highly questionable whether the comments about the
mustard seed being the smallest of all seeds and about the birds
nesting in the shade of the plant belonged to the original parable,
though they are included in Q and in the *Gospel of Thomas*.

30. The prefatory questions are expressed in the poetic form of
Semitic parallelism and are similar to parable-introductions
employed in rabbinic circles. Probably the whole passage goes
back to an Aramaic source (Black, *ARA*, p. 123). For Mark at
least, the questions will have demonstrated that the kingdom of
God cannot be mathematically studied or precisely defined.

31. It is like . . . seeds on earth: the mustard seed is not in
fact the smallest, but small enough apparently to have given rise
to a Jewish proverbial saying in Palestine, 'small as a grain of
mustard seed' (cf. Mt. 17: 20; Lk. 17:6). The descriptive commentary about its being **the smallest of all the seeds** is very

awkward grammatically and was probably added by way of explanation in an extra-Palestinian context where the proverb was unfamiliar.

32. Possibly the Q description of the grown mustard plant as a 'tree' (Lk. 13:19; Mt. 13:32) also suggests an extra-Palestinian touch. In Mark the grown plant is more accurately described as a herb or shrub (the shrub grows to a height of about 8 feet in Palestine). On the other hand, the idea in Q of the birds perching in its branches (to pick the seeds) appears to be closer to the facts than the Marcan idea of **the birds** nesting **in its shade.** All of this indicates that in the process of being repeated outside of Palestine the parable was subject to different adaptations of detail. In fact the closing words of Mk 4:32, **the birds of the air can make nests in its shade** echo Ezek. 31:6, and those of Mt. 13:32 and Lk. 13:19 echo Dan. 4:12, and since it is not characteristic of Jesus to refer to Scripture in his parables, these are most probably additions to the original.

In passages like Dan. 4:12 and Ezek. 31:6 the tree symbolises the protective care afforded by a great empire to its subject peoples. Accordingly, in view of Mark's interest in the movement of the gospel toward the Gentiles, it is possible that these last words of the parable symbolise for him a marvellous promise that is in part being fulfilled already through the Church's mission, the ingathering of the Gentile nations into the community of Jesus Christ (Nineham, p. 145). Most recent interpreters are agreed that such parables as those of the mustard seed and the leaven should be classed as 'contrast-parables'. The central point is the contrast between the insignificant and obscure beginnings of the kingdom in, with, and around Jesus, and the magnificent ending that God has in store for those who are prepared to trust him in the quite unspectacular present (see Jeremias, pp. 90f.; Bornkamm, pp. 71f.). But the Marcan perspective on the parable involves a transference of situation. The time of the beginning in which Jesus sowed the seed or brought the good news has now given way to the time of the Church's missionary promulgation of its message, and in this latter time, despite hindrances and failures in mission, the Gentiles are being brought within the scope of the kingdom (verse 32*b*). Consequently, as Schweizer correctly notes (*GNM*, p. 105), the challenge presented to the reader of this Marcan text is to see his own day in all its apparent insignificance, like the day of insignificant beginnings

in and around Jesus, as bright with the promise of the final consummation of God's purpose.

On this view we can dispense with the familiar understanding
of these parables as parables of growth. In the analogy of the
mustard seed with its dramatic portrayal of the *sudden* transformation of the seed into a great bush, there is no hint of the steady
evolutionary growth of the kingdom. Nor, since the transformation is entirely God's doing, is there any hint that the kingdom
is a moral or cultural goal toward which men can reach out by
dint of hard or even heroic endeavour. The kingdom is not something man earns, but something God gives. This does not mean of
course that men need only wait upon God's gift in complete
passivity. Rather openness in faith toward the future God alone
will bring releases men from illusory hopes of human progress in
the present and frees them for such active obedience to God's
will as can transform the present.

A THEOLOGY OF THE PARABLES 4:33-34

Mark here rounds off the section on parable-teaching with his
own editorial conclusion. It is often held, however, that verse 33
is a traditional statement reflecting accurately the original
purpose of Jesus in using parables: to communicate to people in
figurative language according to their capacity to understand. In
that case only verse 34 is redactional and corresponds to the
esoteric parable theory of 4:11f. (Rawlinson, pp. 58f.). On the
other hand, Taylor (p. 27; cf. Nineham, p. 132) suggests that
both these verses came to Mark from his tradition, and were
initially more closely connected with 4:1–9, verse 34 having
prompted Mark to insert 4:11f. and the explanation of the
parable of the sower in 4:13–20. But if in fact 4:11f. is not Mark's
own parable theory but a Church statement he proceeds to
radicalise (see above, p. 130), neither of these views is satisfactory.
Instead, verse 34 is then more in accordance with the traditional
Church position of 4:11f., and verse 33 represents Mark's conception of Jesus' parabolic teaching as a language aimed at all
people (in verse 33 **to them** = 'to the crowds'; cf. Mt. 13:34),
and adapted to their inability to comprehend the mysteries of
God directly (**as they were able to hear**).

33. With many such parables: implies that the Evangelist
is aware that he has reported only a few examples. His selection
of a few parables whose central point is the sowing of the Word is

in agreement with his steady interest in the teaching activity of
Jesus as the bearer of the good news. **he spoke the word:** here
again **the word** has its technical sense of the 'message of the
kingdom'. In the case of the parables, the medium is the message,
so to speak, for the Word cannot be grasped in itself but must be
clothed in a speech that men can understand (the Greek word
for **as,** *kathōs*, = 'in proportion as', indicates that his parabolic
mode of language is accommodated to the limits of human
understanding).

34. The first part of the verse only repeats in negative form
what has been said positively in verse 33. The second part of
verse 34 does not point up a contrast between two distinctive
modes of teaching, one for the crowd of outsiders and another
for the inner circle. There is, therefore, no inconsistency between
verses 33 and 34. Rather, the parabolic form of language is the
only appropriate form for all, including the disciples. Even they,
as 4:10 and 4:13 also make clear, stand in need of further
instruction. Only, by their very closeness to Jesus they are in a
position to receive his explanation of everything that pertains to
the message of the kingdom of God. This text then is about
continual dependence on Jesus for the Word. From Mark's
standpoint it comes as an invitation to the reader to recognise
that deeper understanding of that Word is open to men, but it is
conditional upon their being drawn into the company of Jesus
and their listening attentively to his living voice to the Church
(Schweizer, p. 107).

JESUS' GODLY CONTROL OVER WIND AND SEA 4:35-41

In Mark's Gospel there are some twenty miracle-stories as well as
three separate references to numerous healings by Jesus in
generalising summaries (1:32-34; 3:7-12; 6:53-55). To this
stock of materials Matthew and Luke do not add much; but they
do not subtract much from it either. John relates fewer miracle-
stories, but at least in the first twelve chapters of his Gospel they
are very significant for his theological purpose. Of course, miracle-
stories are by no means peculiar to the Gospels. They appear in
the *OT*, particularly in connexion with prophetic figures like
Elijah and Elisha (see e.g. 2 Kg. 4:35, 13:21). Tales of the
amazing deeds of wonder-working 'divine men' also feature
prominently in the Jewish and Greek literature roughly con-
temporaneous with the Evangelists. Whatever else may be said

then about the miracle-stories of the Gospels, it cannot be maintained that in themselves they prove the *uniqueness* of Jesus.

The 'stilling of the storm' (4:35-41) is the first 'nature miracle' related by Mark. Up to this point miracle-reports have been of Jesus' healings and exorcisms. The Evangelist himself would certainly not have distinguished between two orders of miracle but would have seen both alike as posing the question about God's action in Jesus. But the modern man does differentiate. He is somewhat less shy of healings and exorcisms, inasmuch as he feels that scientific analogies can be produced, or that they are subject in large measure to psychological explanation. Nature miracles, on the other hand, he is prone to dismiss altogether as impossible, or to rationalise away as legendary or hyperbolic accounts of originally perfectly natural happenings. Over against the supposedly scientific scepticism of the modern man in the street, however, today at the academic level (despite occasional bombshells from scientists, like the molecular biologist Jacques Monod in his *Chance and Necessity*), there is very much less inclination than formerly to subscribe to a doctrine of mechanical necessity, or a closed-shop view of the universe in which iron laws of nature are impenetrably fixed. To that extent it is no longer regarded as the better part of philosophical or historiographical (or even scientific) wisdom to decide in advance what is or is not possible. Accordingly, the present climate is in some respects more congenial than before to open enquiry into the miracle-stories of the Gospels.

These stories to be sure do not give us access to the thing in itself, to the miracle as an isolatable phenomenon. It may indeed be claimed that there is no such thing as a *past* miracle: if it happened at all, its traces are obliterated by the sands of time. In any case, were we able to lay hold of the miracle in itself we should then possess unequivocal proof of the supernatural, and proof and authentic faith in God are impossible companions.

What we do have in the Gospel miracle-stories is *testimony*. Since the Evangelists desire pre-eminently to testify to God's action in Jesus, the stories are for them worth reporting at all not for an extraordinary event lying behind them, but only in so far as they point away from themselves to God and become channels for his Word. David Hume's famous argument on miracles, whatever defects it suffers from by reason of his narrow definition of miracle as 'a transgression of a law of nature by a particular

volition of the Deity', does still pose for us the truly central
problem: the problem of human testimony. And in regard to the
miracle-stories the burning issue is: how do they stand as testimony?

On the matter of human testimony, we have grown accustomed to thinking that exact reproduction of the past is a definite
possibility and even a mark of quality. But the modern spirit of
such historical positivism is quite alien to the outlook of the world
of antiquity, to which the Evangelists belonged. When they
incorporated miracle-reports into their total witness to Jesus Christ,
they would not have thought to sift them in order to determine
precisely what was naked fact and what was mythical or symbolic
accretion. They would not have been bothered by the reality,
even if they had recognised it as we do, that these stories in the
course of being repeated and transmitted were increasingly
embellished and exaggerated (a process greatly accelerated in the
later apocryphal gospels). The testimony they bring is *believing
testimony*. They recount the miracle-stories, which may often have
originated from eye-witnesses among the fisher-folk and peasants
of north Galilee, not for the sake of the miracle in itself, but in
order to challenge the reader to say faith's Yes to the divine
reality to which the story is only a pointer.

These larger considerations we have to keep in mind in assessing
Mark's strategy as Evangelist. In 1:21–27 he connects a report of
a healing miracle of Jesus with his teaching activity in the synagogue. In chapter 4 the account of the stilling of the storm was
most likely linked with the parable teaching of 4:1–9 before
Mark, but its placement here in the Gospel would signify for
Mark that both miracle-report and teaching serve broadly the
same purpose. The miracle-story is but another mode of language
(more dramatic certainly but also in its own way more ambivalent), communicating like the parabolic teaching the mystery
of God's action in the world, a mystery that discloses itself only to
faith. Again, by his use of the secrecy motif, Mark subordinates
the miracle-stories to the way of the cross and restrains their use
as a type of propaganda for a 'divine man' Jesus that would make
faith unnecessary. Finally, in the passion story itself, the supernatural darkness and the rending of the Temple veil that accompany Jesus' death, according to Mark's report, are graphic
symbols for faith that the old order has passed and a new creation
has come. But the one miracle men demand as visible or tangible

proof of God's action in Jesus, that he should come down from the cross (15:32), is the very miracle that does not happen. Jesus dies, and his death it is that calls forth from a Roman centurion the faith that God's new order has arrived.

35–37. On that day, when evening had come: this rather precise notice of time Mark probably received from the tradition (together with other items of detail like the presence of other boats with Jesus), **on that day** referring back to 4:1–2, and 'when evening had come' being a part of the transmitted story, verse 38). **he said to them, 'Let us go across . . .':** the text shows no interest in Jesus' motives for crossing, and it is futile to speculate about them. What is important for Mark is that once more Jesus takes the initiative; the suggestion to *move on* is his. **just as he was in the boat:** without the words **just as he was** the Greek reads much more naturally. Whether added by Mark or not, they would have implied for him that the Jesus of the miracle-story is none other than the teacher of 4:1–34. This is borne out further by the rather unusual manner in which the disciples address Jesus in the midst of the storm as **Teacher** (verse 38). Just as in 1:21–27 the synagogue provides the setting for Jesus' teaching and the healing of the man with the unclean spirit, so here the **boat** provides the setting for his parabolic teaching (4:1f.) and the stilling of the storm. Thus 'synagogue' and 'boat' furnish the links for Mark between teaching activity and miracle-report. **a great storm of wind arose:** for a vivid description of how squalls suddenly blow up on the Sea of Galilee, see Rawlinson, p. 61.

38. The details in this verse do not necessarily uphold the historical authenticity of the account (cf. Taylor, p. 272). The story-teller too would know that the only place one could sleep in such circumstances was the high after-deck and that the leather or wooden seat (**cushion**), normally used by the helmsman, would be taken as a prop for the sleeper's head. Jesus' sleeping and the disciples' consternation are in turn reminiscent of *OT* ideas of the quietness of sleep as a mark of perfect trust in God (Ps. 3:5; 4:8; Job 11:18–19), and of the feelings of people in distress that God has turned his back on them or forsaken them (Ps. 35:23; 44:23f.; 59:4; Isa. 51:9a). **do you not care if we perish?:** the question is really a stern reproach (toned down to a prayer in Mt. 8:25, and to a fervent plea for help in Lk. 8:24), so little do the disciples in Mark know who he is or what is his authority (Cranfield, p. 174).

39. In stilling the storm Jesus assumes the authority that in the
OT is exercised solely by God. Behind this verse lie two related
sets of *OT* symbols: (a) **the sea** symbolises the primal chaos
which God struggles to control and out of which he creates an
ordered calm (Ps. 74:13f.; 89:9–13; 104:5–9; Job 38:8–11;
Jer. 5:22; 31:35); (b) the stormy deep also symbolises the trials
and tribulations of the righteous (Ps. 69:1f.; 14f.; 18:16), whose
only recourse is to trust in the God who alone can save him from
the great waters (Isa. 43:2; Ps. 46:1–3; 65:5; and particularly
Ps. 107:23–32). The words with which Jesus rebukes (cf. Ps.
104:6f.) the wind and addresses the sea, **Peace! be still!** are in
the Greek 'Silence! Be muzzled!' and the latter (cf. Mk 1:25)
features in wonder-worker stories almost as a technical term for
dispossessing a demon of his power. Possibly, therefore, the earliest
narrators of this story thought of Jesus overpowering a storm-
demon.

40–41. Have you no faith? the variant reading 'Have you
not yet faith?' has weighty MS support, is favoured by many
commentators, and is generally taken to mean: Has the 'secret'
of my (Jesus') authority still not dawned on you? In pattern and
stylistic traits this story, like other miracle-stories in the Gospels,
follows the same lines as Jewish and Greek parallels. But it
departs and goes its own way in the manner it handles the theme
of *faith* at the close, and it is here the narrator's special purpose
appears. However, the arrangement of the concluding verses is
rather strange. The questions of verse 40 fit better after the
disciples' reproachful question in verse 38 (the question, 'Why are
you afraid, O men of little faith?' is located there in Mt. 8:25f.).
Also the reverential awe and the question, **'Who then is this?'**
(verse 41) follow more naturally after the closing words of verse
39, **there was a great calm** (again they do so in Mt. 8:26f.).
Accordingly, the ordering of verses 40–41 in Mark appears to
constitute this a separate little concluding act through which the
Church of Mark's time can feel itself directly addressed. It is the
living Christ who comes to them with his searching questions that
contrast their fearfulness in crisis with the lifegiving power of
Christian faith. The awe that is felt is then a response to the one
who visits them challengingly afresh as the Great Questioner, in
whose presence they can only ask among themselves whether he is
not the one possessed of the divine authority to create calm over
the stormy waters on which the tiny vessel of the Church (very

early in its history pictured as a ship) is sailing. On this view the whole story is transformed into a summons to the readers to submit in faith to the protective and saving grace still offered by the living Christ to his obedient followers in the Church.

A RESTORED DEMONIAC BECOMES ENLISTED MISSIONARY 5:1-20

In regard to its literary structure this extraordinary story has some most unusual features. Verse 2 tells us that on leaving the boat Jesus was met by a man from the tombs. Yet in verse 6 the same man sees Jesus from afar and runs to him. Presumably verses 3-5 (not essential to the story), describing the typically fearsome life of demoniacs among the tombs, were interpolated as intensifying this man's plight and showing how great the miracle must be that could cure one so far beyond all human help. Then verse 6 would have been added as taking up and expounding verse 2 (**there met him**). Verse 8 is an explanatory comment from a narrator who forgets that in the typical exorcism story the demons tremble in the presence of Jesus *before he speaks*.

If verses 11 and 14 belonged to the scenery of the initial story of the healing of the demoniac, they might point to the originality also of the account of the swine rushing headlong into the water. On the other hand they would equally make its later insertion easy. But the awkward fashion in which the phrase **and to the swine** is tagged on in the Greek of verse 16b (which reads 'and concerning the swine') strongly suggests that the report about the swine was a later addition, in which case verses 11 and 14a may be accommodations to the addition. The inclusion of this brief story, and especially the detail of the excessively large number of the herd, may then have been prompted by the name of the demon, **Legion; for we are many** (verse 9). The desired effect of the inserted story would be to provide visible proof of the exorcist's victory over the whole mob of demons.

Verse 15 is strange as it stands in context immediately preceding verse 16, for it really makes verse 16 redundant. There is no need for them to be told since they have seen the healed demoniac already for themselves. Perhaps the original story ended with verse 15. But verse 15 does not go very well either with verse 14. One must assume a considerable lapse of time for the herdsmen to spread the news in the city and country districts and for the people they inform to get back to the scene. Yet when they do they find the healed demoniac still sitting near to Jesus. Probably verse 15 is an insertion, therefore, and it reveals traces of Mark's editorial activity—'they came to see Jesus' (Greek = **they came to Jesus**) may be a Marcan correction of 'came to see what it was that had happened' (verse 14), in order to turn the searchlight on Jesus rather than on the miracle itself. The verb **saw** in the phrase **saw the demoniac** occurs elsewhere in Mark at 3:11; 5:38; 16:4, and is a different verb from that used in verses 14 and 16. The Greek verb in **they were afraid** signifies religious awe for Mark (see especially 4:41 and 16:8) and would here denote awe before the mystery of Jesus' authority. Finally, verses 18–20 do not belong to the miracle-story proper, but from their style and vocabulary appear to be a Marcan conclusion.

This relatively long and detailed narrative has been built up to its present form in various stages, although it is no longer possible to determine each stage precisely. Commentators who hold that the whole account as we have it is a unity based on eye-witness (even Petrine eye-witness: see Cranfield, pp. 175ff.; Taylor, pp. 277ff.) are hard pressed to account for what happened to the ill-fated herd of swine (which on the face of it does little credit to Jesus in his treatment of animals). Neither the common explanation that the paroxysm of the demoniac, as he hurled himself toward the pigs, caused them to stampede into the water (see e.g. Taylor, pp. 282f.), nor the less common one that the only way Jesus could reassure the man and cure him was by allowing the demons to enter the pigs (one man in Jesus' eyes being infinitely more valuable than many pigs), is very plausible. On the view brought forward above, the problem does not arise at all, or is erased by a literary critical review of the passage. An old Palestinian folk-tale about a herd of swine has been joined to a story of Jesus' healing of a demoniac.

1. the country of the Gerasenes: probably the correct reading in Mark and Lk. 8:26, although some texts have Gergesenes (a conjecture of Origen's, stemming probably from Gen. 10:16), and Matthew has Gadarenes (Mt. 8:28). Gadara is some eight miles from the lake, but its 'territory' may have stretched to the shore. Gerasa, however, is over thirty miles to the south-east of the lake, too far away for the setting of the story which demands a city in the vicinity of the lake with a precipitous slope down to the water nearby. That Mark has taken over the name Gerasa from the tradition, and yet thought of it as close to the lake (verse 14), does not say much for his acquaintance with Palestinian topography. Probably all that concerned him was that the story was set in the partially Gentile territory of the Decapolis.

2–5. Cemeteries were believed to be the abode of demons (verse 2). Verses 3–5 are an addition to the original story (see above). They vividly describe the utter lostness of the man, 'as good as dead', as he wanders among **the tombs** (rock tombs or caverns). The reason for the inclusion of those verses is quite simply that the more forlorn the man's condition is shown to be, the greater the miracle needed to heal him.

6. Coming after the added verses 3–5, this verse resumes and develops verse 2 (see above). **worshipped him:** the Greek word means 'knelt before him' in an act of homage, and shows that immediately, before any dialogue, the demon profoundly respects the power of Jesus.

7. Bears a striking resemblance to 1:24, except that here the demon addresses Jesus as **Son of the Most High God:** the title 'Son of God' appears as an utterance of unclean spirits in the Marcan summary of 3:11, and its occurrence here in 5:7 may be due to Mark. **Most High God** is a designation particularly suited to the Gentile territory in which the story is set (for the application of the title by pagans to the God of Israel, see Dan. 3:26; 4:2). One should scarcely assume, however, that Mark wished to classify the demon as a 'Gentile demon', or the demoniac as a pagan. The first ploy of the demon was to get the name of his opponent right in order thereby to disarm him of his power. Failing in his attempt to overcome the exorcist, and apparently more than ever conscious of his mighty power, the demon then implores Jesus in strong language, **I adjure you by God, do not torment me** (Matthew regards the punishment as a foretaste of the pain to be suffered in the final judgment of God, Mt. 8:29; cf. Rev. 18:7f.; 20:1–3, 7–10).

8. An interruption of the original story, which centred upon the ongoing conversation between the demoniac and Jesus. The insertion comes as a reminder that all that is really needed to expel the demon is a word of command from Jesus.

9. Part of the strategy of the exorcist was to find out the demon's name in order to gain control over him. For the first narrators of this story **Legion** may have been thought of as a *boast* of the demoniac whereby he unwittingly divulged his name, or as an evasion (see the suggestion of Jeremias, *JPN*, p. 30, note 5) that

the Aramaic behind the Greek word *Legiōn* could also mean
'soldier' and that the demoniac was really refusing to give his
name by describing himself simply as one of a great company
(cf. Nineham, p. 154). For Mark, however, the question by Jesus
and the immediate admission of the demon's name no doubt
illustrate Jesus' amazing authority. A Roman legion normally
consisted of some six thousand men, but 'legion' was probably a
by-word for a 'very large number' (cf. our use of 'regiment').
Whether the name Legion gave rise to the detail of the **two
thousand** pigs in the associated folk-story, or whether the number
of pigs suggested the name Legion for the demoniac, is hard to say.

10–13. The request of the demons not to be sent out of the
country is a familiar feature of exorcism-stories. Demons about to
be expelled plead to remain in their familiar habitat. Here from
the viewpoint of the Jewish folk-tale it would be particularly
appropriate that they should wish to remain in what was largely
Gentile territory. The old story concluding with the report of the
fate of the herd of pigs would have been particularly satisfying
and amusing to Jewish hearers, since pigs were abominated as
unclean animals, and according to Jewish belief there would be
no place for pigs in the messianic age. It is unlikely that in re-
counting the story Mark would have any such piece of messianic
symbolism in mind. Probably he saw it as an impressive confirmation of Jesus' unprecedented authority (stories of exorcised
demons knocking over statues or jugs of water illustrate both the
extreme viciousness of the demons and the enormous power of
the exorcist).

14–17. For the questions raised by the arrangement of verses
14–16, see above (pp. 146f.). **and they were afraid:** from Mark's
standpoint, not about the further loss of property, but in confrontation with Jesus' supreme authority. But neither their fear
nor the corroborative account of what had happened (verse 16)
opens their eyes to who Jesus really is; instead they want to be
rid of him.

18–20. The desire of the people of the neighbourhood to be rid
of Jesus (verse 17) acts as a foil to the reaction of the healed
demoniac. His entreaty to Jesus **that he might be with him**
exemplified for Mark the only true response to the miracle: the
faithful following of Jesus in discipleship to him. Jesus' refusal
(verse 19) is yet another example of his sovereign authority to
call or reject whomsoever he chooses; but since in the Gospel no

healed person ever goes 'with Jesus', the thought may have been present to Mark that the healed demoniac would have been a standing advertisement among the disciple band for a 'divine man' Jesus of miraculous power. The all-important thing for the Evangelist is not propaganda for the miracle but the spreading of the good news of all that is happening through God's grace and mercy (**the Lord** here = God, see also 1:25, 44; 3:12, etc., and cf. Lk. 8:39), and the man is commissioned to preach (the Greek word for **tell** in verse 19 is used elsewhere of announcing the Church's missionary message, e.g. Ac. 17:30; 26:20; 1 C. 14:25; Mt. 11:4; cf. Mk 1:45. The word for **proclaim** in verse 20 is the usual one in the *NT* for 'preaching the gospel'). The change from **Lord** (verse 19) to **Jesus** (verse 20, **began to proclaim how much Jesus had done for him**) serves to illumine the Marcan idea that in Jesus quite particularly and concretely the very grace and mercy of God are experienced. Accordingly, Mark viewed the man's action positively (verse 20 begins with **and** not *but*) as an obedient response to Jesus' command. This is preferable to the suggestion that Jesus asked the healed demoniac to keep the word within his own family, *but* he disobeyed and spread it widely (thus breaching the 'secret').

Verses 18–20 may reveal that the churches of the predominantly Gentile area of the Decapolis (a group of ten towns lying mainly east of the Jordan) adopted the story of Jesus' healing of the Gerasene demoniac to explain how the Christian mission began in that region (Lightfoot, *HIG* pp. 89f.; cf. Nineham, p. 151). Mark himself may have regarded it as the inauguration of the mission to the Gentiles (whereas foreigners from beyond Jordan came to him (Mk 3:8), it is only now Jesus has moved out into their territory, cf. 5:1). It is uncertain how much the story owes to the influence of Ps. 67:7 LXX (= Ps. 68:6 in *RSV*): 'God makes the solitary dwell in a house, leading forth mightily them that are bound, and also them that behave rebelliously and that dwell in tombs', or how much, therefore, the demoniac's wonderful restoration (verses 15, 19–20) may have presented a paradigm of conversion (Cranfield, p. 180).

Much less hesitantly we should say that Mark has turned the story to his own use in that it preserves for him the truth that the miracle in itself is ambivalent as a sign. Some are afraid of the authority manifest in the miracle, but remain eager to keep Jesus at arm's length (verses 15–17): the only fruitful outcome is when someone opts to be 'with Jesus' and is called to proclaim *the good news of all that the Lord is doing in Jesus.*

JESUS' POWER TO SAVE FROM SICKNESS AND DEATH 5:21-43

The materials from 4:1–5:20 have been connected with the lake. Possibly the account of the raising of Jairus' daughter (set also by the lake after the journey from the eastern shore, verse 21) was already combined with 4:1–5:20 in the tradition. On the other hand the secrecy motif is given such prominence in 5:43 that Mark may have included 5:21–43 as a suitable conclusion to the miracle-stories of the stilling of the storm and the healing of the Gerasene demoniac. In 5:21–43 the healing of the woman with the haemorrhage (5:25–34) takes place after Jairus' visit to and fervent request of Jesus (5:21–24), and while Jesus is on his way to Jairus' home. A number of commentators hold that the whole episode goes back to eye-witness testimony and that events actually developed in this way (see e.g. Taylor, pp. 289ff.; Cranfield, pp. 182ff.). But is it historically probable that the same Jesus who forbids any of the crowd to follow him (verses 37–38) should have allowed the crowd and what transpired in its midst (5:24–34) to impede his progress to Jairus' home, especially in the light of the extreme urgency of Jairus' plea about his daughter? There are on the contrary very strong grounds for thinking that Mark himself has intercalated the story of the healing of the woman into the story of the raising of Jairus' daughter. At the close of the former (verses 32–34) the question of faith or belief is uppermost, as it is also in verses 35–36; the language of verses 25–34 is straightforward but standard Hellenistic Greek, while the rest of the passage has a cruder (Semitic) syntax; Mark elsewhere employs the method of insertion (cf. 3:22–30; 6:14–29; 11:15–19; 14:1–11, 53, 72), not only to fill up an interval in time, but where two items complement each other in meaning.

21–24. After his brief incursion into Gentile territory, Jesus is now back on Jewish ground at a place not stipulated, by the sea (often assumed to be Capernaum). **Then came one of the rulers of the synagogue, Jairus by name:** the **synagogue** normally had two officers, the ruler or president, and the attendant (*hazzan*). The ruler was responsible for making arrangements for public worship, but not for its conduct. Some synagogues may have had more than one ruler (cf. Ac. 13:15), who acted jointly as a board or in rotation. Alternatively the Greek phrase in verse

22 may = 'one who belonged to the class of synagogue rulers' (Rawlinson, p. 66). What is important for the story is that he was a man of high standing in the Jewish community. The name of the man is wanting from Mt. 9:18 and from a number of mss of Mark: it may have been brought into Mark by assimilation from 8:41. It is quite unlikely that it was introduced as a symbolic name (Hebrew *ya'îr* = 'he awakes'). According to the story it is not the synagogue ruler who is the 'awakener'. **seeing him, he fell at his feet:** the act of obeisance to the healer was a regular feature of healing and exorcism stories. Here the fact that homage is paid by a man of such status heightens the impression of Jesus' exceptional authority. **is at the point of death:** 'at her last gasp' (Johnson, p. 106). Matthew, who presents a much condensed version of Mk 5:21-43 (Mt. 9:18-26), reads here 'has just died' (Mt. 9:18). **lay your hands on her . . . made well, and live:** the laying on of hands was familiar in the Jewish context in connexion with sacrifice, blessing, and ordination, much less familiar in connexion with healing (see Johnson, p. 106, and also for an interesting parallel to the synagogue ruler's request here, see the *Genesis Apocryphon* from Qumran). But it is common enough in Mark's healing stories (cf. 6:25; 8:25). According to the present passage (see also verses 30–34) the realm of the physical is not excluded from God's action in Jesus. In this regard the terms **made well** and **live** may include both physical well-being and salvation and (eternal) life in the religious sense.

25–26. Mention of the long duration of the ailment, here **twelve years,** is commonplace in healing stories. Doctors in the Near East have often been adversely criticised both for the cost of their services and their conflicting diagnoses and unhelpful prescriptions (cf. *Qid.* 4:14, 'the best among doctors is worthy of Gehenna'; see also Rawlinson, p. 68). The interest of the present story lies not of course in denigration of the medical profession, but in stressing that *human* resources and skill had not availed the woman in her chronic ailment.

27–31. the reports about Jesus: in Greek literally = 'the things concerning Jesus'; here = 'information about Jesus with particular reference to his healing ministry'. **came up behind him:** possibly out of shyness because the nature of her illness made her ceremonially unclean (Lev. 15:25–27). **touched his garment:** a crude feature, very common in ancient healing stories, that for us today savours of magic or superstition (cf. Ac.

5:15; 19:12). **for she said ... made well** (verse 28): an insertion into the story explaining the woman's motivation, and probably understood by the Evangelist as an incipient expression of her faith (cf. Mk 6:56), preparing the way for Jesus' final commendation of her in 5:34. In Mt. 9:20 and Lk. 8:44 it is the tassel of Jesus' robe she touches. **and immediately ... her disease:** modern attempts to attribute her immediate cure to the force of auto-suggestion are quite beside the point. The following verse (30) shows at once that in the story her cure is effected by the healing power that goes out from Jesus. **perceiving in himself that power had gone forth from him:** more literally the Greek = 'the power that proceeds from him (i.e. by reason of his being who he is) had gone forth'. In the Hellenistic context this could readily have been understood as the transmission of impersonal substance or energy; but here the 'power' is directly associated with the person of Jesus. It is idle to speculate about the extent to which Jesus' *feeling* or *knowing* here is the feeling or knowing of God in him. Jesus is not here portrayed as a superman with supernatural knowledge (Schweizer, *GNM*, p. 117). His question **'Who touched my garments?'** does not imply superhuman knowledge but shows that he *seeks* an answer (Taylor, p. 292). The disciples' remonstrance (verse 31, omitted in Mt. 9:20–22 and toned down in Lk. 8:45) arises from their all too human scepticism, which fails to appreciate that what is impossible for men, is possible through the divine will to reach people.

32–34. Only with these concluding verses is the old healing story, with its crude and primitive traits, 'domesticated' by being brought under the question of *faith*. It is Jesus' *look* that sets things in motion. His eagerness for encounter makes encounter possible, and paves the way for a dialogue in which *faith* is shown to be something more, or other, than merely trust in the miracle-worker. Moved by awe (**in fear and trembling**) in regard to Jesus' authoritative power, the woman openly and honestly ascribes everything to him and claims nothing for herself (**told him the whole truth**). **Daughter, your faith has made you well:** the affectionate mode of address denotes that the crucial thing has happened: she has been brought into close personal relationship with Jesus. From within that relationship faith can be understood as the openness to receive God's gift of *salvation* made freely available in Jesus. The Greek word for **Made you well** (*sōzein*, cf. *sōtēr* = Saviour) connotes not only physical health but also salvation in the religious sense. Accordingly, the **faith** that is spoken of here relates not only to the inward spiritual side of man's life but to all aspects of it, including the *bodily*. **go in peace and be healed of your disease:** by this command Jesus emerges clearly as the bestower of peace. **Go in peace** is a common formula of farewell (Jg. 18:6; 1 Sam. 1:17), but in the *NT* (cf. Lk. 7:50; 8:48; Jn 14:27; 16:33; 20:19, 21, 26) the word **peace** (like the Hebrew *shālôm*) means not just freedom from inward anxiety, but that *wholeness* or *completeness* of life that comes from being brought into a right relationship with God. The closing statement **be healed of your disease** places the healing within the wider orbit of God's offer of salvation, and thereby diverts attention from the miracle itself to Jesus' own gracious word. Accordingly, the story becomes for Mark's readers an invitation to the continual dependence on the word of Jesus that enables men to receive God's gift of salvation.

35-36. This main story is now resumed at the very point where it has just been disclosed that the all-important thing is faith's dependence on Jesus' life-giving word for salvation. Now come the visitors from Jairus' house with the bleak message that his **daughter is dead,** and the *faithless* remark that it is a waste of time to bother Jesus any further. They are the representatives of all who measure God by human standards and set their own limits in advance to what is possible for him. By contrast Jesus will not allow that even the spectre of death is an insurmountable obstacle for faith. He therefore refuses to be tempted by the voice of faithlessness (the Greek word for **ignoring** may also mean 'overhearing', but the translation 'ignoring' is not ruled out by the fact that Jesus does answer the message, for 'ignoring' implies that he pays no heed to its sinister destructive threat). Against the shattering word of the child's death, Jesus' own word **'Do not fear, only believe'** keeps faith and hope alive. These two verses then furnish a clue to the way the story, as intended by Mark, should be interpreted. The Evangelist regards the episode not as a resuscitation from seeming death but as a *raising from the dead*, and the theme is the confidence in God that is not overcome even by death.

37. Peter and James and John are the only ones present also with Jesus at the transfiguration (9:2), in Gethsemane (14:33), and (together with Andrew) on the Mount of Olives (13:3). The fact that the intimate disciples alone accompany Jesus was

probably taken by Mark to indicate that only to the follower is it
given to understand the 'secret', here the ultimate 'secret' of God's
victory over death in Jesus. Also the Church that heard this would
have been reminded that it was the community of the resurrection.

38. The public display of mourning and lamentation is in
conformity with Palestinian custom (cf. *Ket.* 4:4, 'even the poorest
in Israel should hire not less than two flutes and one wailing
woman'). In the present context it points up graphically the
contrast between those who are overwhelmed by the anguish of
death and the quiet assurance of Jesus and his word.

39. The child is not dead but sleeping: on the assumption
that the verb **sleeping** refers to natural sleep, it is frequently
suggested that the child was in a coma, that the members of the
household had come to a premature conclusion about her state
(verse 35), and that Jesus ignored their message because he was
aware of it (verse 36). But how would Jesus have known that the
child was merely comatose before ever he had gone in to see her
(verse 40)? The very fact, however, that such an interpretation is
possible shows that we can no longer determine what the original
facts were. Fortunately the meaning of the story for Mark or his
readers is not dependent on our ability to reconstruct what
happened. Clearly the Evangelist understood the story as describing a resurrection (see on 5:35-36).

When Jesus speaks of the child as **sleeping,** he is expressing
the conviction (over against the mourners) that death is not just
the grim finality it appears to be, but the prelude to resurrection
life. His words therefore correspond to the widespread Christian
thought that death is only a temporary 'sleep' (the Greek verb
in Mk 5:39; cf. Eph. 5:14; 1 Th. 5:10, is not the one generally
employed, e.g. in 1 C. 11:30; 15:6; 1 Th. 4:13-15), in hope of
the coming resurrection, a hope validated for the Church of
course by Easter. Accordingly, Jesus appears here as faith's
spokesman.

40. And they laughed at him: with the mocking laughter of
those who are governed only by what their eyes see, and who
cannot imagine that God might smite death with resurrection.
but he put them all outside . . . where the child was: only
the select few are allowed to be witnesses to the miracle. It is not a
public spectacle for the crowd but a revelation for those who are
in the company of Jesus.

41-42. The brief report of the miracle has much in common with other ancient wonder-stories, the physical contact (**taking her by the hand**), the vivid description of the practical effect (**the girl got up and walked**), and the response, here portrayed in very forceful language (**they were overcome with amazement**), suggesting the exceptional nature of the miracle. The Aramaic words, **Talitha cumi** (omitted by Matthew and Luke), may have been retained in the story by Greek-speaking Christians in deference to the known custom of wonder-workers of using formulas in a foreign tongue, or simply to preserve a sense of mystery. But here the formula is translated for the benefit of Greek-speaking readers, and the addition of the words **I say to you** serves to emphasise that the very command of Jesus is in itself efficacious. **for she was twelve years old:** appears to be an explanation of her walking, since the various words used of her could denote an 'infant' as well as a 'grown child'. The correspondence of the child's age with the **twelve years** of the woman's ailment (verse 25) is probably a coincidence rather than a deliberate assimilation.

43. The request to **give** the child **something to eat** is not so much a testimony to Jesus' very human concern for the child's needs as impressive confirmation of her restoration to normal bodily existence, i.e. confirmation of the reality of the miracle. In view of the previous public display of mourning (verse 38), the exceptional character of the miracle and its exceptional fascination stand out in the narrative. All the more striking, therefore, is the closing injunction to secrecy or silence. For the Evangelist the story of even so great a miracle is not to become propaganda for the great miracle-worker. Rather it is to bear witness to the power of God that goes forth in this Jesus to all who believe.

The whole story presents enormous difficulty to people today, the more so because we come to it with the question uppermost in our mind about whether originally it happened precisely so. But even if the miracle itself were proven, we should then only have an isolated, local instance of the restoration of a child to normal day-to-day existence—and that might merely teach us in the presence of death to expect a similar kind of *physical* miracle. Such expectation (doomed to disappointment!) is to be sure radically different from the faith that is not broken by death but goes on believing in God's power to conquer it and to bestow that *new life* (of the resurrection) that unimaginably transcends our present

everyday existence. Just as by their familiar saying that God
alone has 'the three keys, the key to the rain, the key to mother-
hood, and the key to giving new life to the dead' (SB 1, p. 523),
the rabbis were really testifying to the universal range of God's
power, so the Evangelist would have understood this story (whose
historical credentials he would not, like us, have paused to
question) as paradigmatic for faith, faith in God's victory over
death. As the account of the healing of the woman becomes for
Mark a summons to that fellowship with God that makes authentic
life possible (see on 5:32–34), so now this associated story symbolises that the life God gives through Jesus is stronger than death
itself. So Mark's reader is asked to believe in the creative power
of God's word in Jesus, as well in the face of death as in everyday
living (see Schweizer, *GNM*, pp. 120ff.).

THE REJECTION OF JESUS ONCE AGAIN, BY HIS OWN HOME FOLK
6:1–6

The Evangelist appears to have attached a special significance to
this episode (Lightfoot, HIG, pp. 182ff.). Just as 3:6, reporting
the rejection of Jesus by the Jewish authorities, comes at the close
of an earlier section of the Gospel, so now 6:1–6, reporting his
rejection by his fellow citizens, concludes a section that has dealt
with his mighty works. In each case we may perceive the shadow
of the cross already falling upon Jesus' ministry. It has been
suggested that this brief report represents an ideal scene constructed around the originally 'floating' proverbial saying of
verse 4 (Bultmann, *HST*, p. 31). But one can scarcely imagine the
Church applying a proverb about a **prophet** to the Jesus whom
it regarded as so much more than a prophet, and then extracting
from the proverb a story of his failure (verse 5a). Most probably,
therefore, the fact that Jesus taught in his native place *without
success* was a fixed datum of the tradition to which the proverb of
verse 4 was added as a 'summarizing slogan' (Schweizer, *GNM*,
p. 123). Knowing only the one fact of Jesus' failure **in his own
country** (see Haenchen, p. 220), Mark has shaped up the story
in his own way (as have Matthew and even more notably Luke,
cf. Mt. 13:53–58 and Lk. 4:16–30, where it prefaces the whole
Galilean ministry and is transformed into a success story, reflecting the Gentile mission and anticipating Christ's triumph in
the resurrection). Marcan redactional touches are prominent in
the report, e.g. in the transitional verse 1, in the bringing to-

gether of Jesus' teaching activity and his mighty works in verse 2,
in the mention of **his own kin** (peculiar to Mark) in verse 4,
and in verse 5*b*.

1. He went away from there ... to his own country:
the Evangelist's concern is not with a chronological sequence of
events, but with *theological* connexions: Jesus' mighty works (even
the raising of Jairus' daughter) do not automatically produce
faith. Indeed it is possible for his fellow countrymen to note these
works and yet to label him as ordinary and so repudiate his claim.
The verb **went away** is redactional (cf. 1:28, 29, 35, 38; 2:13;
3:6; 6:12, 34, 54; etc.), as is also the phrase **from there** (cf. 7:24;
9:30; 10:1). From 1:9 and 1:24 the reader of Mark knows that
his own country is Nazareth (cf. Lk. 4:16). There is no indication of the purpose of Jesus' visit, although the verb **came**
signifies for Mark 'came as the bearer of the good news' (see
comments on 1:9, 14). **his disciples followed him:** a Marcan
redactional feature (omitted in Mt. 13:53 and Lk. 4:16), not
only preparing the way for the next section (6:7–8:26) in which
the discipleship theme is very prominent, but reminding the
reader that *Jesus has chosen his own to follow him*, 'his own' do not
necessarily choose him.

2. on the sabbath he began to teach in the synagogue:
almost an introductory formula for Mark (cf. 1:21, 39; 3:1),
with his typical stress on the teaching activity of Jesus. The
question whether Mark knew the content of Jesus' synagogue
sermon (cf. Lk. 4:18–21) is irrelevant, since his reader has in any
case been made aware that Jesus preached the mystery of the
kingdom of God (1:14f.; 2:16f.; 4), with an unprecedented
authority (1:22, 27). **many ... were astonished:** the **many**
denotes for Mark not the majority who were impressed over
against the minority who were irritated (Rawlinson, p. 73,
Taylor, p. 299), but rather the 'whole crowd' attracted by Jesus'
fame (cf. 1:34f.; 2:2, 13; 3:8, 20; 4:1; 5:21, 24). The verb **were
astonished** figures prominently in Mark (cf. 1:22; 7:37; 11:18).
Astonished questioning about the identity of the miracle-worker
is the typical climax of the miracle-story (cf. 1:27). **Where did
this man ... by his hands:** elsewhere in Mark the first
question is 'what'? (1:27) or 'who?' (2:7; 4:41). Here the first
question is the question of origin or source (the Greek word for
Where? literally ▬ 'whence?') which is particularly well adapted
to the succeeding question about Jesus' lineage in verse 3. It is

quite appropriate for the people to ask about his **wisdom,** since
they have just listened to a sample of his teaching. But the
expression of amazement at his **mighty works** is nothing other
than the Evangelist's reminder to his readers that Jesus' mighty
works come under the cover of his teaching activity, and both
alike are related to the mystery of the kingdom of God. So the
reader is constrained to ask why the one so authoritative in word
and deed (described in chapter 5) should be so harshly rejected
in Nazareth.

3. The word translated **carpenter** is a general word referring
to any kind of artisan in stone or wood or metal, and the Church
fathers understood it in various ways, e.g. 'smith', 'maker of
ploughs and yokes', 'builder' (see Rawlinson, p. 74). **the son of
Mary:** the textual tradition, not unexpectedly, reveals a number
of variants: 'the son of the carpenter' (cf. Mt. 13:55), 'the son of
the carpenter and of Mary'; and 'the son of Joseph' (Lk. 4:22;
Jn 6:42). The reading 'son of the carpenter' is well attested, and a
fairly cogent argument can be adduced in its favour (see Taylor,
p. 300). Accordingly, it is by no means certain that the original
reading in Mark is that of *RSV*, **the carpenter, son of Mary.**
If it is, it is most unusual. Among the Jews a man is called after
his father. Must we suppose then that Joseph was dead by this
time (but see Lk. 4:22)? Or is a slur intended by naming Jesus
after his mother, in order to render his paternity suspect? Or
again is Mark's omission of the father meant to suggest that only
God is the father of Jesus (Robinson, *PHM*, p. 81, note 1)? Or is
the reading, **the carpenter, son of Mary** a dogmatic correction
to preserve the doctrine of the Virgin Birth (Johnson, p. 112;
Klostermann, p. 55)? One thing at least seems certain, that the
Evangelist himself was not responsible for such a dogmatic
correction, since for him the whole thrust of the question in
verse 3 is to show that those who ask it *cannot believe because of the
all too human connexion of Jesus with an ordinary family.* Their question
shows in fact how in their case amazement at Jesus' authoritative
words and deeds leads not to faith but unfaith. **brother of James
… Simon:** only here (= Mt. 13:55) are the four brothers
named together in this way, although the 'brothers of Jesus' are
mentioned also in Mk 3:31, Jn 2:12; 7:3, 5, 10; Ac. 1:14, 1 C.
9:5; Gal. 1:19. There is no trace here or elsewhere in the *NT* of
the later ecclesiastical tradition of the perpetual virginity of Mary.
'The Jesus without brothers and sisters, the singularity of whose

birth was not profaned or reduced to ordinary human level by later normal births of Mary, is really the incomparable exception, even and precisely as a real human being, while the people of Nazareth argue with the exact opposite: as a human being Jesus is not the exception, but the normal case' (E. Grässer, *NTS* 16 (1969–70), p. 15). **they took offence at him:** the Greek word so rendered (*eskandalizonto*, from which is derived our term 'scandal') is really much stronger in meaning, and in the vocabulary of the early Church referred to those who rejected outright the claims of the gospel (cf. 1 C. 1:23; Gal. 5:11). So this story, which certainly did not conceal the harshness of *Jesus*' own people's refusal to accept him, might well have brought consolation to early Christian missionaries in days when their message was spurned or denied.

4. The proverbial saying (cf. the similar but shorter version in Lk. 4:24) appears in different forms on the lips of Jesus in Mt. 13:57 and Jn 4:44, as well as in a papyrus from Oxyrhynchus and in the apocryphal *Gospel of Thomas* ('There is no prophet acceptable in his own neighbourhood, nor does a physician do healings among those who know him'). As it stands in Mark, it is a mild statement when compared with their being scandalised by Jesus, and as we noted, it is best to regard it as a summarising slogan about a common human experience, that was attached early in the process of transmission to the rejection report. **among his own kin:** occurs only in Mark and seems to be a redactional touch, either echoing the negative stance of the relatives already described in 3:21, 31ff., or simply as an accommodation to the situation Mark took to be implied by the question about Jesus' family in verse 3.

5–6. And he could do no mighty work there: a very old and almost surely authentic piece of tradition, considerably toned down in Mt. 13:58, 'and he did not do many mighty works there because of their unbelief'. We should not subject this statement to psychologising interpretation, as if it were saying that Jesus could not cure those who had no confidence in him. Rather, in terms of the Marcan account, Jesus' authoritative words and works led the people of Nazareth not to faith but un-faith. Scandalised by his humanity, they could not understand how God should speak or act in this one (verse 3). Among those who had looked upon Jesus and had already dismissed him with a commonplace tag ('the carpenter'), 'mighty works' are useless and impossible, since their very purpose is to seek out the response of faith. That the essential point of the story is in fact the problem of faith or unfaith, belief or unbelief, is borne out by the closing affirmation **and he marvelled because of their unbelief** (verse 6a). **except that he laid his hands . . . healed them**: this mitigation of Jesus' failure is not quite congruous with the apparently total impenitence of the people of Nazareth reflected in verses 3 and 6a. However, these words are reminiscent (in a negative way) of the Marcan summaries of Jesus' healing activity (1:32ff.; 3:7–12; 6:53ff.), and he may have wished to show that Jesus' possibilities of healing action were only limited, not completely closed. On the other hand, in view of the Marcan emphasis on the **unbelief** of the people of Nazareth, verse 5b was possibly inserted in the tradition before Mark, or by some later redactor after Mark. **And he went about among the villages teaching** (verse 6b): not even rejection and failure in the home territory impedes the progress of the good news brought by Jesus.

It is stretching things too far to suggest, mainly on the basis of 3:21, 31–35 and the redactional **among his own kin** in 6:4, that Mark's animosity to the relatives of Jesus amounts to a polemic against the Jerusalem church, where James the Lord's brother became so important, and that he issues a manifesto against the jurisdictional hegemony of the mother-church (see J. D. Crossan, *NovT* 15 (1973), pp. 110ff.). In fact the relatives of Jesus are not *actors* in this story, but feature only in the question (verse 3) posed by the **many** (verse 2). Rather, for Mark the people of Nazareth represent in their own way the blindness of the world. They want an altogether glorious, supernatural Jesus whose credentials will be obvious to all, and refuse to believe that God discloses himself in the humanity of this one who is the member of a humble family and whose way, according to Mark's testimony, is the way of the cross.

MISSIONARY OUTREACH AND THE DISCIPLES' LACK OF UNDERSTANDING 6:7–8:26

MISSIONARY MARCHING ORDERS OF THE TWELVE 6:7–13

The section of the Gospel that closes at 3:12 ends with a Marcan summary of Jesus' healing activity, and is followed by a new section that opens with the appointment of the Twelve ('and he appointed Twelve, to be with him and to be sent out to preach, and have authority to cast out demons', 3:14). So now, after a brief Marcan summary in verse 6b, a new section opens with the sending out of the Twelve.

The narrative of 6:7–13 is brief, cryptic, and rather puzzling. Mark's own hand is very much in evidence in verse 7 (in the calling to Jesus of the Twelve, cf. 3:13, 14, 16; in the prominence given to the **authority** possessed and bestowed by Jesus, cf. 1:22; and to exorcism of **unclean spirits,** cf. 1:23), and again in verses 12–13 (in the stress on preaching and repentance, with no account of the actual content of the preaching; in the brief summary report of successful exorcisms and healings). Verses 8–9 read like an elementary manual for Christian missionaries. If the instructions of these verses belonged to Jesus' own situation, we should need to suppose that his disciples owned more possessions than allowed here, and that is doubtful (see Schweizer, p. 128). In the light of these and other considerations, like the fact that nothing at all is said of why, when, or where Jesus sent out the Twelve or of what he did in their absence, it may seem tempting to follow the view that the whole incident is unhistorical (see e.g. Wellhausen, p. 44). But on the other hand, the saying of verse 11 has an authentic ring (and as a saying of Jesus certainly pre-supposes some such mission of his disciples in the course of his ministry). Its sense of eschatological urgency is very strong and it expects judgment to follow immediately upon *one* presentation of the message of repentance, and that scarcely accords with the Church's situation. Moreover, the sending out of the Twelve is exceptionally well attested in multiple layers of the Gospel tradition, in Mark, Q, and the material peculiar to Matthew and Luke. In fact, whereas Lk. 9:1–6 is based on Mk 6:8–13 (except that Luke omits reference to the sandals, the preaching of re-pentance, and anointing), the mission discourse that Luke places in the context of an address to the seventy (Lk. 10:1–16) appears to possess more primitive Palestinian features than Mark's account and so is probably the earliest form. It forbids sandals and greetings on the road, Lk. 10:4; the Semitic formulation 'son of peace' and the notion that the 'peace greeting' remains on the hearers or returns to the disciples (Lk. 10:6), the kingdom of God as the content of the message (Lk. 10:9, 11), and the fact that only later do the disciples discover their power over unclean spirits, all these seem to be older traits.

We may suppose that, together with the sayings of verses 10–11, Mark has taken over from his tradition a set of Church instructions for missionaries that is slightly more advanced than the form in Lk. 10:1–16, and has woven them into a framework of his own composition. Since, looked at historically, the narrative does not appear to belong to any specified point in the ministry (Taylor, p. 303), we have to watch the more closely for typically Marcan theological connexions.

7. This verse, as we noted, consists of Marcan redactional elements. The exception is the sending out of the disciples in pairs, a practice which the Church followed in its mission, according to Ac. 3:1–10; 8:14–25; 11:30; 12:25; 14:28; 15:40–17:14; cf. 1 C. 9:6). As Mark has it, the focus of interest is the **authority** bestowed by Jesus. The one possessed of unique authority himself, alone empowers his followers in the warfare against all evil forces. Just as in Mark Jesus' mighty works against the demons are associated with his preaching-teaching activity, so must healing and exorcism form part of his disciples' preaching mission (see verses 12–13). Preaching and the bringing of God's healing power to bear on needy lives go hand in hand.

8–9. Only by complying with the command to renounce all accoutrements and material resources, except the barest minimum, could the missionaries of Jesus intimate their abandonment of human or worldly power and their dependence upon their Lord. **except a staff:** even this is forbidden in Mt. 10:10 and Lk. 9:3; so also are shoes forbidden in Q (Mt. 10:10 = Lk. 10:4), whereas Mark permits **sandals** (verse 9). It is questionable whether the permission to carry a staff and wear sandals (presumably to ward off wild animals or snakes) is in Mark's version an intentional blow at the fanaticism that thinks of faith itself as a magical protection against all ills (see Schweizer, p. 130). The wearing of sandals (necessary for a *longer* journey) hardly belongs to the primitive Palestinian situation reflected in Lk. 10:1–16. But neither is this or any other injunctions in the missionary charge in Mark appropriate to the geographically extensive Pauline mission. The permission to take a staff and wear sandals could only have been added to the more primitive tradition then within a Church that could not picture a missionary going barefoot or without a staff. **no bag:** most probably the beggar's bag, like that carried by Cynic preachers, rather than the provision-bag such as shepherds carried ('provision-bag' would not suit the com-

mand to take no bread). **no money in their belts:** the Greek =
'not a copper coin in their girdle' (the girdle being made of
cloth). **and not put on two tunics:** with this phrase in the Greek
(literally = 'do not put on') there is a sudden change from
indirect to direct speech, which accords with the opening charge
of the earlier Q version, 'do not take' (Mt. 10:10 = Lk. 9:3),
except that in Q it is the *possession* of the tunic(s) (inner garment
worn next to the skin) that is forbidden. Here they are asked
simply not to burden themselves needlessly with extra clothes.

10–11. And he said to them: a formula introducing an
originally independent saying (cf. 2:27, 4:21, 24, etc.). **where
you enter . . . place:** they are not to seek out more luxurious
quarters in any given locality but are to be content with the most
humble hospitality. This, rather than the length of time they
should stay in any particular lodging (a subject much discussed
by the rabbis), appears to be at issue here (cf. the rules laid down
for travelling apostles and prophets in the *Didache* 11:3–12:5, a
Christian work from around the middle of the second century, in
which it is said that an evangelist, if he stays more than two or
three days, is a false prophet). **And if any place . . . testimony
against them:** the immediacy suggested by this verse is in marked
contrast to verse 10. Here everything depends once-for-all on
men's direct response (or rather lack of it) to the disciples'
message. For preacher and listener there is but a solitary encounter. The command to **shake off the dust** has behind it the
practice of strict Jews who did just that when they returned from
Gentile regions to Palestine to indicate that the Holy Land was
not to be contaminated with the dust of pagan places. In the
present context the gesture is possibly meant as a symbolic act
against the impenitents, signifying that God's judgment was
impending for them (**a testimony against them**). But the
Greek words translated in *RSV* **a testimony against them** may
also mean a 'testimony to or for them', and probably the gesture
is meant to show that the disciples have done all they could in
proclaiming the message and the final outcome now lies between
their hearers and God.

12–13. In these verses, Marcan in style and vocabulary and
ideas (except perhaps for the anointing with oil), the disciples are
depicted as entering into the full range of Jesus' own ministry;
their mission, like his, is mission in word and deed. **preached that
men should repent:** here too, as in the case of Jesus, Mark is

more interested to report their preaching activity than to describe
the content of their message (described as 'the kingdom of God'
in Lk. 9:2 and as 'the near approach of the kingdom of God' in
Mt. 10:7). There may be something in the suggestion that for
Mark the Twelve are able, like John the Baptist, to preach only a
mission of repentance, until after the passion and death of Jesus
when the *full gospel* had been revealed to them (Lightfoot, p. 106,
note 2; also Nineham, pp. 170f.). But since for Mark the good
news of Jesus Christ and the good news brought by Jesus are in
closest continuity, and since the message of Jesus centres upon
the mystery of the kingdom of God (chapter 4) and includes the
call to repentance (1:15), the Evangelist probably has the distinctively Christian message in mind here. **anointed with oil:**
the use of **oil** as an emollient is found in Lk. 10:34. Only here
and in Jas 5:14 in the *NT* is anointing with oil associated with
healing of a miraculous sort. The oil is apparently an outward
symbol of the gracious and efficacious word that makes the
healing possible.

It has been observed that this whole episode should be a decisive
stage in the development of the Gospel, whereas in fact nothing
seems to result and the disciples' blindness is soon uppermost
again (6:47–53). The inference to be drawn from this, however,
is not that the event is unhistorical, or even that Mark was very
short on information or his church relatively uninterested in this
piece of tradition (cf. Nineham, p. 168). To be sure the missionary
charge reported here would scarcely have been relevant to the
situation of missionaries from Mark's church. But what the
Evangelist wants to communicate to his readers is that all mission
can only be initiated and empowered by God's word in Jesus.
For that enabling word no human power, resource or ingenuity
can ever be substitute. The missionary is altogether dependent
on the archetypal missionary; the living word of the living Master
is their instruction, their comfort and their inspiration. His
failure (verse 5) is their failure (verse 11; here is the connexion
with the preceding story of Jesus' rejection in Nazareth); his
success, their success (verse 13). 'The mission of the disciples is an
introduction to the fate of the Master, and therefore training
for following him. As such it has a fundamental significance'
(E. Grässer, *NTS* 16 (1969–70), p. 22).

THE DIRE FATE OF THE BAPTIST, JESUS' FORERUNNER 6:14-29

The account of Herod's opinion about Jesus and of the execution of John the Baptist is sandwiched between the sending out of the Twelve (6:7-13) and their return (6:30) It is true enough that Mark thus fills in the interval. But it is hardly enough to describe the report as an 'interlude' (Taylor, p. 307). We have to ask further why Mark included just this report just here (see notes). No doubt he received from his tradition the brief notice on Herod's view of Jesus (verse 16), which provides him with his *entrée* to the story of John's death. But verse 15 corresponds closely to 8:28*b* (the estimates of Jesus put forward here having belonged originally to the context of 8:27ff.), whereas verse 14 corresponds to 8:28*a*, though its several Marcan traits clearly show that it has been expanded by the Evangelist into a preface to what follows.

The story of John's fate is told elsewhere also by the historian Josephus (*Ant.* XVIII.5, 2), in a version that reveals numerous discrepancies with the Marcan record. According to Josephus, it was the daughter of Aretas, the king of Arabia, whom Herod had married, but he was subsequently captivated by Herodias, the wife of his half-brother, also called Herod, and she consented to elope with him on condition that he divorced Aretas' daughter. When the latter informed her father, he made war on Herod and defeated him. Josephus locates John's imprisonment and execution in the fortress of Machaerus (the Marcan record, verse 21 particularly, is consonant only with Herod's palace in the Galilean capital of Tiberias), and attributes them to Herod's fear that his influence with the people might lead to an insurrection. Lastly, Josephus is silent about the banquet (Mk 6:21) and the dancing (Mk 6:22). The dancing of a Herodian princess in the midst of a carousal is an improbably bizarre touch, which could forthwith be dismissed as fictional, were it not a known fact that the excesses of the Herodian court were in most respects quite notorious (see S. Perowne). It is barely worth while trying to reconcile the accounts of Josephus and Mark. They are written from entirely different perspectives (see Rawlinson, p. 82). As an historian working some sixty years after the event, Josephus is concerned to trace the political causes of Aretas' campaign against Herod. Mark's narrative is a carefully constructed literary product which almost surely came to him already in written form. But it bears the stamp of a popular folk-tale arising probably in the

circle of the Baptist's disciples and gathering legendary accretions
at the earlier stage of oral transmission. It purports to paint in
vivid colours the awful enmity of secular worldly powers to the
unworldly religious man (in his innocence and defencelessness).

14. King Herod heard of it: in Mt. 14:1 and Lk 9:7 Herod
is correctly designated 'tetrarch'. Mark's **king** may, however,
reflect popular usage. The Herod in question is Herod Antipas,
who ruled Galilee and Perea from 4 BC to AD 39. The Greek has
no equivalent to the words **of it.** What Herod heard is therefore
not stated, and there is no support whatever from verses 14–16
for the view that it had anything to do with the mission-tour of
the disciples. Mark's reader does not of course require to be told
what Herod heard—he knows it already from the preceding
chapters of the Gospel. **for his name had become known:**
Mark is fond of inserting explanatory comments introduced by
the Greek particle *gar* = 'for' (cf. 1:22; 2:15; 3:10, 22; 5:8, 28;
6:17, 20, etc.). The **name** (cf. also 9:37-39, 41; 13:6, 13) is
synonymous with the total person as expressed in his word and
deed. **Some said...are at work in him:** most MSS read 'he
said' (i.e. Herod), but this is an assimilation to the singular of
the verb 'heard' (**Herod heard**), and the plural 'they said' with
the subject unspecified (= 'people were saying') is most probably
correct; it matches the twice-repeated **others said** of verse 15.
Having begun with the reference to Herod as no more than an
anticipation of the verse (verse 16) he needs to lead into the story
of John's execution, Mark at once turns the searchlight away
from the king to the all-important question of *who Jesus is* in the
eyes of the people generally. The Evangelist issues no invitation
to his readers to probe the subject of Herod's guilty conscience,
although the old story he derived from the tradition has its own
observations to make on the subject (verse 20). The first suggestion of the people that Jesus is John the Baptist 'raised from the
dead' is consistent with Mark's prefatory affirmation that only
after John had been 'delivered up' did Jesus begin his ministry
in Galilee (1:14). There is no record of the Baptist's having
worked miracles during his lifetime, but the thought that the
Baptist *redivivus* would have had mighty **powers at work in him**
is quite natural.

15. But others said, "It is Elijah ... prophets of old": the
belief in the return of **Elijah** ... is attested in Mal. 3:1; 4:5.
Whereas here, according to a popular conjecture, Jesus is the

returned Elijah, in Mk 9:13 Jesus alludes to the death of the
Baptist as Elijah. According to another estimate, Jesus is a
'prophet' (cf. Lk. 13:33; 24:19). The appearance of the coming
prophet is predicted in Dt. 18:15, and among the Qumran
sectarians a prominent role was assigned to the 'eschatological
prophet' in the drama of the last days.

16. when Herod heard of it: the return to Herod is somewhat awkward, and lends credence to the view that Mark was
responsible for introducing verses 14*b* and 15 from 8:27f. (Once
again there is no mention of what Herod **heard;** there is nothing
in the Greek corresponding to **of it.**) These words merely pick
up the opening words of verse 14, and it does not follow that
Herod's own response to Jesus was formulated in the light of the
popular reaction of verses 14*b*–15. **John, whom I beheaded,
has been raised:** a guilt-ridden Herod could possibly have
imagined that John had come back to life to haunt him. Or, since
in his introduction Mark associated the beginning of Jesus'
mission of preaching very closely with the Baptist's being delivered
up (1:14), it may be he thinks of Herod as saying: 'It is John the
Baptist all over again!' (see Rawlinson, p. 79). No sooner is one
call to repentance extinguished than another comes to take its
place, and to disturb the populace afresh.

The popular estimates of who Jesus is (they acknowledge the
presence of some supernatural power in him) challenge Mark's
readers to go further and ask whether any label out of the past
is at all adequate to describe this Jesus, in whom God is acting
in a **new and unexpected way,** the way of suffering and the
death of the cross (cf. 8:27–31), of which the divinely willed
(cf. 1:14) fate of the Baptist, now narrated in verses 17–29, is the
precursor.

**17–18. for the sake of Herodias, his brother Philip's
wife:** according to Josephus (see above), **Herodias** was not the
wife of his brother Philip (tetrarch of Iturea and Trachonitis),
but of another (half-) brother, Herod. Philip in fact was the son-
in-law of Herodias, having married her daughter Salome, named
by Josephus as the girl in the story. Mark appears then to have
confused Herodias' husband with her son-in-law. In any case
Herodias was a grand-daughter of Herod the Great and Mari-
amne, and therefore a niece of the Herod (Antipas) mentioned
here. In order to marry her Herod Antipas had divorced his own
wife and taken Herodias from his half-brother. **John said ...**

brother's wife: it was forbidden by law to marry a **brother's wife** (Lev. 18:16; 20:21), and with prophetic forthrightness John had said so much. Herodias appears simply to have deserted her husband, or perhaps divorced him according to the provisions of Roman law.

19–20. There is a certain resemblance between **Herodias** and Jezebel (1 Kg. 19:2), and Herod's vacillation matches that of Ahab (1 Kg. 21:4ff.). The development of the story probably owed something to *OT* prototypes. Herod's protection of John from the vengeful desire of Herodias, out of respect for the man and his message, only serves to make his ultimate surrender to her whim all the more sinister. Knowing the good when he encountered it, he had none the less by his previous actions put himself too securely in the grip of evil to remain faithful to his own better judgment. The latter part of verse 20 is awkward in Greek, although the mingled feelings in Herod of 'perplexity' and 'glad response' to John are not impossible. But there is large textual support for another reading: 'Once having heard John, he heard him frequently and heard him gladly.'

21–22. Would Mark have thought of the incalculable difference between this pretentious wordly banquet, in which the forces of evil are so obviously at work, and the simple but altogether satisfying feast of loaves and fish, in which the power of God himself is at work (6:33–44)? **when Herodias' daughter came in and danced:** besides this, the MSS attest other variant readings: 'when the daughter of Herodias herself came in', which may also be translated 'when her daughter Herodias came in' (but that involves Mark in attributing to Salome the name Herodias); 'when his daughter came in', i.e. the natural daughter of Herod Antipas, in which case 'mother' must be loosely used in verse 24. The variants reflect the confusion in the Marcan version of the story itself about the complex relationships within the Herodian family. The picture of a Herodian princess dancing before such an audience is outrageous. In context it shows to what low devices (the daughter's dance presumably of Herodias' devising) wickedness will stoop to gain its objective.

23. Herod's vow to the girl is strikingly reminiscent of the language of Est. 5:3; 7:2, betokening once more the story's indebtedness to *OT* models. Those who told this story would not have paused to reflect that as a puppet of Rome, Herod had not the ghost of a chance of giving **half of** his **kingdom** away.

24-28. It is the **mother,** plotting behind the scenes (verse 24) who is the real sinner (cf. verse 19). In the climax of the story, Herodias' nefarious design is accomplished with astonishing speed (note the repeated use of **immediately** in verses 25 and 27). Herod plays his part by surrendering at the decisive moment to his lower nature and allowing his grandiose promise to the girl and his big reputation with his fellow-revellers to overcome his regard for John (verse 26). The gruesome details of verses 27–28 are presented shockingly, and nothing at all is said in praise of John. This is because the story's searchlight is turned fully upon the world's bitter hostility against God's true spokesmen.

29. The Greek word for **body** is the same as that used of Jesus in 15:45. The loving attention paid by John's **disciples** to his remains anticipates the story of Jesus' burial (15:42ff.). The fate of the Forerunner presages Jesus' own fate. But if burial is the end of John, it is not so of Jesus (cf. 16:1–8.)

This is the only story in the Gospel that is not centred upon Jesus, although of course for Mark the death of the Baptist and the message and mission of Jesus culminating in the cross are theologically closely integrated, directly related as they are to the will of God (see 1:14, and cf. 9:9–13). But why has the Evangelist connected the account of John's execution with the sending out of the Twelve on mission? In facing the menace of the world's might, the prophet and his disciples in their weakness appear to be quite ineffective. As the archetypal missionary himself had to endure the repudiation of his claim in Nazareth (6:1–6), so his missionary followers must encounter the severest setbacks, the opposition of a hostile world being what it is (6:17–29). But there is hope: in verses 14–16 Mark shows that the world is not easily rid of its prophets like John, and so challenges his readers to recognise that the mission of the Church is guided and inspired by the *risen Jesus* (Best, pp. 119f.). The mission marches forward, despite all resistance, as is symbolised by the fact that Jesus now moves out with the good news into predominantly Gentile territory (cf. 6:45; 7:24, 31; 8:27).

THE DISCIPLES' RETURN: MIRACLES MISUNDERSTOOD **6:30-52**

In style, vocabulary, and content verses 30–31 are Marcan. They form a transition, verse 30 picking up the theme of the mission

of the Twelve (6:7–13), and verse 31 providing a good reason
(the request of Jesus himself) for the disciples' removal to a
lonely place, which is the setting (verse 35) for the miracle of
the feeding of the five thousand.

30–31. Except for **apostles,** all the words in the Greek of
verse 30 are typically Marcan (**returned,** cf. 2:2; **told,** cf. 5:14;
all that they had done, cf. 3:8; **taught,** cf. 1:21). Mark certainly tells the barest minimum about the mission of the Twelve,
only that at least they have been faithful to their commission to
perform healings and preach or teach. So little does he make
of its significance that in what follows it is as if it had never
happened. In fact he will shortly dwell on the blindness of the
disciples (6:52), so important to him in this section of the Gospel.
From Mark's standpoint, the emphasis in verse 30 is on the
missionaries' accountability to Jesus alone, the one who sends
them out and to whom they must report back. The term **apostles**
is used only here in the Gospel. In the NT it is often applied to a
wider circle than the original Twelve (1 C. 9:5f.; Ac. 8: 4f., 26,
40; 15:39). But Paul's desire to broaden the concept of apostleship (1 C. 15:7; Rom. 11:7; 2 C. 8:23; Phil. 2:25) and his stout
defence of his own special apostolic credentials (1 C. 15, and
Gal., especially chapter 1) points to a situation in which the word
was being reserved as a technical and official title only for the
Twelve. Behind the NT word 'apostle' (Greek *apostolos* = 'one
sent') possibly lies the Hebrew *šaliah* (Aramaic *sᵉlîha*), the
authorised representative of a private person or of a community
(e.g. the synagogue community) sent out to fulfil a particular
commission, but with the authorisation lapsing at the closure of
his task. (See Schmithals for the entirely different view that the
NT idea of apostleship stems from gnostic or proto-gnostic
notions of the 'heavenly emissary'.) Whereas Jesus himself is
unlikely to have regarded the Twelve as his *šelûhim* ('official
agents'), it is possible that the Jewish-Christian Aramaic-speaking
church in Jerusalem did so regard them. Here in Mark, however,
apostles is not employed as a technical or formal title, but
rather refers to their function as missionaries 'sent out' to exorcise
demons and to preach. Mark may in fact use the word **apostles**
in verse 30 in preference to 'disciples' (Greek *mathētai*) since the
latter has just been applied to the followers of John in verse 29.

Except for the Greek verbs for **rest** and **have leisure,** verse 31
contains Marcan elements, **come away** (Greek *deute*, cf. 1:17),

by yourselves (Greek *kat idian*, cf. 4:34), **to a lonely place** (*eis erēmon topon*, cf. 1:35), **for they were** (Greek *ēsan gar*, cf. 1:22), **going** (Greek *hypagō*, cf. 1:44). If Jesus' request to the disciples to seek rest in a lonely wilderness place stood in some form (here adapted by Mark) in the tradition, those who transmitted the tradition would have seen in it simply Jesus' lively concern for the physical welfare of the disciples. It is doubtful whether Mark himself would have understood verse 31 typologically as alluding to the sabbath rest of the people of God (cf. Heb. 4:9), or to the little Church on which the peace of God descends in its apartness over against the busy world, symbolised by the crowd **coming and going.** What is clear enough is that their departure to a wilderness spot (verse 32) is attributed by Mark in verse 31 to a command of Jesus. He is responsible for the movement of his disciples.

Verses 32–33 may contain fragmentary items of tradition, but the picture of the crowds converging on Jesus in verse 33 is peculiar to Mark (cf. Mt. 14:13f.; Lk. 9:10f.), and suits well his customary stress on the magnetism of Jesus for the people at large. The wilderness place they made for (unspecified in verse 32) is named by Luke as Bethsaida (Lk. 9:10), situated on the north of the lake probably by the mouth of the Jordan. As verse 45 shows, Mark does not locate the feeding at Bethsaida. He may have thought of the western shore, the journey of verse 32 implying that they moved only a short distance along that shore with the crowds able to keep them in view and get ahead of them (verse 33). From such a spot, Bethsaida may be appropriately described as 'across the lake' (verse 45). If Mark had thought like John (6:1, 17) of the feeding as occurring on the eastern shore, then the statement of verse 45 about a journey to the opposite side, to Bethsaida, would be extremely misleading. The complexities of the textual tradition in verse 45 in fact betoken the problematic nature of the geographical notices here in Mark (in 6:53 the disciples land south of Capernaum and do not arrive at *Bethsaida* until 8:22). Presumably the Evangelist lacked precise information on or set little store by the topography of the lakeside towns. Verse 34 possibly serves as the opening of the miracle-story proper.

In verses 34–52 the two miracle-stories of the feeding of the multitude and the walking on the sea are narrated. John 6 reports the former in a rather different form, the author being dependent

most likely on a tradition independent of the Synoptic Gospels.
Significantly Jn 6:1–21 also follows the same sequence of events
as Mk 6:32–52, the journey to the eastern shore, the miraculous
feeding, the re-crossing of the lake, and the walking on the sea.
We may therefore suppose that the tradition aside from and
before Mark had associated these stories (Schweizer, p. 137).
But Mark himself has forged his own close *theological* link between
them with the reference back to the miracle of the loaves in
verse 52, after the walking on the water.

Miraculous feedings similar to the one reported here of Jesus
were common in antiquity, not least in Jewish and Greek literature. The provision of abundant food to Israel in the wilderness
was understood as a mark of God's saving grace to his people in
rescuing them from bondage in Egypt, a central theme of the *OT*
(see e.g. Exod. 16 and Num. 11; and cf. e.g. Neh. 9:15; Ps.
78:17ff.). Moreover the stories of Elijah (1 Kg. 17:8ff.) and
Elisha (2 Kg. 4:1ff., 42ff.) affords parallels to Mk 6:34–44. The
whole character of the story is such then that from the very first
it would appear to have been related as a miracle-story. Certainly
Mark interpreted it as the report of a miracle, albeit a miracle
misunderstood, as verse 52 indicates. Attempts to reconstruct the
original incident which gave rise to the story are accordingly
hazardous indeed, not to say pointless. One suggestion is that
Jesus was confronted with a mob of zealot-like revolutionaries in
the wilderness, and countered them with the use of symbols that
came to be connected with his suffering and death (T. W. Manson, *TSM*, pp. 69–71). The suggestion of course leans very
heavily on Jn 6:15; there is no hint of a *revolutionary* crowd in
Mark. It has also been held that Jesus was actually host at a kind
of love-feast, at which spiritual if not physical hunger was satisfied
by the crowd's partaking of fragments of the broken and blessed
bread; or that Jesus celebrated an 'eschatological sacrament'
with a relatively small number in the wilderness, in anticipation
of the coming messianic banquet in the new age (see 1 *En.*
62:14; 2 *Bar.* 29:8; *Sib. Or.* 3:46–49; cf. Jn 6:30–34, 48–51;
Mt. 8:11 and the parable of the great supper in Mt. 22:1–14).
Finally, the rationalisation that the episode was an 'idyllic
expression of good comradeship' (Taylor, p. 321), each person
sharing out the little food he had with others, removes us further
than ever from Mark's conception of a miracle which the disciples, in their unshakeable obduracy and obtuseness, fail to

comprehend. It is also incongruous with the fact already noted that the story would appear to have been related from the outset as a miracle-story. In the early Church the story was no doubt an often repeated tale, with its echoes of the *O T* and its assurance of spiritual nurture of the faithful with heavenly food in the 'desert' of this present world. An account exists in all four Gospels and was moreover told in two different versions (cf. Mk 8:1–9). Hand in hand with its popularity went apparently its progressive assimilation to the Church's Eucharist (see verses 39 and 40, and also Jesus' actions at the Last Supper, verse 41, cf. Mk 14:22 and 1 C. 11:23f.).

34. he had compassion on them . . . taught them many things: in an earlier stage the story possibly pictured Jesus as moved to pity only by their physical need (cf. 8:2). Here he sorrows over their 'lostness' (for the notion of **sheep without a shepherd** see the LXX of Num. 22:17; Ezek. 34:5; 1 Kg. 22:17; Zech. 13:7). Characteristically Mark stresses Jesus' teaching activity and brings it into close contact with his mighty works. What follows is an account not of the content of Jesus' teaching but of a miracle. Did Mark want his readers to recognise that the first priority for the Church is not communication or discussion of what Jesus had once said, but the proclamation of a *living Lord* who makes the 'miracle' happen for men in the present by bringing them God's love?

35–37. when it grew late: the note of time (probably late afternoon) is germane to the story. The pangs of hunger increase in the crowd as the day wears on. Jesus' response (**"You give them something to eat"**) to the disciples' request that the crowd be sent away to the farms (the Greek word translated **country** in *RSV* = 'farms') **and villages,** implies that as God's representative Jesus deems to be immediately possible what the disciples imagine is beyond them. Their counter-question, possibly tinged with sarcasm (**'Shall we go and buy two hundred denarii worth of bread?'**), indicates that they still operate only at the level of what is *humanly* possible or rather impossible. For them it was quite impossible because they would not have had among them the sum of about £20 (the denarius, worth close on two shillings or ten new pence, was a labourer's daily wage, Mt. 20:2ff.).

38. How many loaves . . . five and two fish: the command to **"Go and see"** means evidently that they are to look in the

boat for provisions. The **loaves** were made of wheat or barley
in the form of round cakes, and were broken for eating. The **fish,**
pickled or smoked, was no more than a relish for the bread. Since
the story is set in a locale where fishing was an important industry,
it is quite aposite that fish together with bread should provide
the simple fare for this common meal. Early Christian art, of
course, furnishes many examples of bread and fish as symbols of
the Eucharist. The incredibly small amount of food, one loaf per
thousand people and two fish among five thousand, heightens the
miraculous nature of the feeding.

39-40. upon the green grass: hardly an eye-witness recollection of the event's having occurred in the spring, nor indeed a
symbol of the spring-time Passover season (cf., however, Jn
6:4), or of the transformation of the desert into a fertile land
sometimes expected in apocalyptic circles (see Schweizer, p. 139);
but probably only a 'pictorial touch' (Rawlinson, p. 87), indicating that they sat down on a suitable piece of ground without
spreading any cloth. Jesus' word of command (verse 39) is
enough in itself to make things happen and the vast company is
soon disposed in groups, **by hundreds and by fifties:** this
arrangement may recall the groupings of Exod. 18:21 (cf. the
War Scroll from Qumran, 1QM).

41. The way this verse is framed suggests it has been aligned
with the actions of Jesus at the Last Supper as described in Mk
14:42. The dividing out of the fish takes places only as a sort of
addendum, after the blessing, breaking, and distribution of the
loaves is completed. **he looked up to heaven:** whether this is
intended to denote how the miracle of the multiplication of the
food was effected, or is simply a normal gesture in prayer (cf.
Job 22:26; Lk. 18:13; Jn 11:41) is not entirely clear. The latter
is more likely, since otherwise Jesus acts according to the usual
manner of the host at a Jewish house-meal, where before the
breaking and handing out of bread to the guests the familiar
thanksgiving was: 'Blessed art thou, O Lord our God, King of
the universe, who bringest forth bread from the earth.' The
gesture of looking heavenward later passed into the Church's
liturgy, the celebrant of the Mass being directed in the Roman
canon to raise his eyes before the consecration of the host. So
natural in the situation depicted in the story is the passing of the
bread by Jesus to the disciples and their taking it in turn to the
crowd that it is not necessary to suppose the description has been

determined by the subsequent practice of the Church whereby
the deacons distributed the bread at the Eucharist. That the
early Christian reader of the story would have taken mental note
of the association between the two is of course another matter.

42-44. and were satisfied: this detail in the story suggests
that it was told and understood as a miracle-story, and weighs
against the view that it had its ultimate origin in an 'anticipatory
sacrament' in which through the distribution of a *morsel of bread*
Jesus consecrated his disciples as partakers in the coming messianic feast (Schweitzer, *MKG*, pp. 103ff.), unless of course one
wishes to think of the multiplication of the bread to satisfy physical
need as a later materialisation of the tradition (Taylor, p. 321).
The preceding notes have suggested that the story told from the
outset of an ordinary meal at which hunger is assuaged by a
miracle. **And they took up . . . of the fish:** verse 43 may have
been influenced by 2 Kg. 4:43f. The fact that they finish with far
more food than they had at the outset not only confirms the
miracle but pays tribute to the generosity revealed in this mighty
work. The Greek word for **baskets** here is different from that
used in 8:8; 20. On the question of a possible symbolic significance
in this and in other items in the story see notes on 8:1-9. **And
those . . . five thousand men:** information on the size of the
multitude has been held back to the last moment, and surprises
the reader all the more with the greatness of the miracle. We
cannot be sure whether the Greek word for **men** excludes women
and children. Here, as elsewhere, Matthew heightens the miraculous element by speaking of 'five thousand men, not counting
women and children' (Mt. 14:21).

The motif of astonishment, usual at the close of the miracle-
story, is omitted from this one. Attention is thus riveted entirely
on the miracle (and on the associated notice about the blindness
of the disciples in verse 52), so that the reader is clearly asked to
see in it by faith what the disciples cannot see. Jesus appears in
this story not as the one who presides at an 'eschatological sacrament'; nor yet as just the uniquely authoritative Teacher of the
lost and leaderless crowd. Rather he appears as the one in and
through whose *word and deed* God's own Word is offered to the
multitude in all its creative power. But only those who have the
eyes of faith to see and understand can accept the gift. The blind
disciples for their part still refuse to trust Jesus to do what needs
to be done, and in the extremity of their situation reckon about

merely *human* supplies and resources (see the question of verse 37, and cf. verse 52).

While the story of the walking on the water was probably connected with that of the feeding in the tradition before Mark (see above, p. 173), the Evangelist himself clearly wanted them to be interpreted together (see especially verse 52). The story of the walking on the water is, however, itself composite. It seems that a detail or two from a story of rescue and storm-stilling (verse 51), possibly derived from some such report as Mk 4: 37-41 contains, have been fused with a longer account of an epiphany of Jesus to his own on the water. The somewhat mysterious words at the close of verse 48, **He meant to pass by them,** certainly do not suggest a situation of alarm and urgency in which the disciples needed to be rescued. Conceivably then with the addition of verse 51 to the original epiphany story, the description of the disciples' rowing into a contrary wind was inserted to prepare for the new conclusion in verse 51: **and the wind ceased.** Thus the story of an appearance on the water becomes also a storm-stilling and rescue.

Noting the enormous difficulties of the whole account, V. Taylor nevertheless wishes to hold that this story too originated from 'actual events remembered and interpreted'. But to say what these events were he has on this occasion to resort to rationalisation (against his usual judgment): 'The action of Jesus in wading through the surf near the hidden shore was interpreted as a triumphant progress across the waters' (p. 327). It has also been suggested that Jesus was walking on a reef or on a hidden raft, or that he was walking *by* the sea (the Greek preposition *epi* meaning 'close by' or 'near to' as well as 'on'). But it is more pertinent to this story (as to the report of the storm-stilling in 4:37-41) to take account of the *OT* symbolism behind it. God's control over the sea is illustrated by his ability to walk on or through the waves (Job. 9:8; Ps. 77:19; Isa. 43:16). Lohmeyer (p. 135) has proposed that the sea is a symbol for death (Ps. 18:15-17; 69:2-3) and that Jesus is here presented as the conqueror of death (cf. Sir. 24:5, where Wisdom walks in the depths of the abyss), which might support the view that the story was originally a *resurrection-appearance* story (cf. Jn 21:1-14). But more probably what the account depicts is an epiphany of the earthly Jesus as divine wonder-worker (Schweizer, p. 141).

45-47. On verse 45 see notes to verses 32-33. No indication is given in verse 45 of why Jesus should dismiss the crowd or why he should want his disciples out of the way first. To suppose that the notice of Jn 6:15 is historical and that Jesus (here in Mark's report) hurried the disciples away to prevent them from catching the contagion of the crowd's revolutionary designs, is purely speculative. In fact the explanation given in verse 46 (possibly by Mark) for the crowd's dismissal is that Jesus **went into the hills to pray** (for Mark an indication of the real source of his power; cf. 1:35). The link verses 45–46 seem to be somewhat contrived and we should probably think of them as designed chiefly to provide the necessary setting for a story that demands the separation of Jesus from his disciples for a while. **when evening came:** shows how ill-fitting the successive stories are from the point of view of chronological sequence. If they were already well out on the lake by evening, they must have set out in broad daylight; yet before the feeding started it was already late (verse 35). **out on the sea:** the Greek means literally, 'in the middle of the sea', but the phrase can denote simply 'on the water' and so they are separated from Jesus on the land. Their loneliness and isolation is thus emphasised, and the early Christian reader could well have thought of the littleness of the vessel of the Church on the perilous sea of the world.

48. about the fourth watch of the night: around 3 a.m. The Roman reckoning of time is used here; the Jews divided the night into only three watches. **he meant to pass by them:** sometimes translated 'he was on the point of passing by them'. But the Greek verb for **meant to** normally denotes a set intention or desire, and = 'he wanted to'. So the puzzling question of Jesus' motive for passing by arises, and many conjectures have been made, e.g. he wished to demonstrate that he was Lord of the water; as Yahweh passed by Moses on Sinai (Exod. 33:18ff.) and Elijah on Horeb (1 Kg. 19:11ff.), so Jesus wishes to manifest the divine glory of the Son of man. Whatever the intention of these words in the original story, Mark himself probably thought of Jesus as putting their faith to the test, since for him the account becomes an example of man's incredible blindness.

49–50. they thought it was a ghost ... 'Take heart, it is I; have no fear': it is possible for them to feel they are in the presence of the supernatural or the miraculous, and yet, so far from believing in Jesus, only be gripped with terror. The miracle itself gives no guarantee that faith will arise from it. In the

Emmaus story the stranger who walked with the disciples is recognised as Jesus only when he breaks bread with them (Lk. 24:30-31). Here Jesus' *word* is enough. The Greek for **it is I** is literally **I am,** almost a revelation formula (see Exod. 3:14 and cf. Mk 13:6; 14:62; Lk. 24:39; Jn 6:35; 8:12, etc.).

51-52. Only when Jesus is *present* with them in the boat can everything become calm and peace descend. But even yet, as the Marcan conclusion demonstrates, they cannot grasp what the presence of Jesus should mean to them, for they are merely amazed and confused. So great is their blindness that it can only be attributed to a preternatural *hardening* (cf. 3:5).

The combined stories of the walking on the water and the miraculous feeding are more closely related to the theme of mission, central to Mark's interest in 6:7-8:26, than is usually recognised. Mark's reader is challenged to see what the disciples here cannot comprehend, that there is entrusted to the community the immense privilege and responsibility of offering to the multitude outside the living Word that alone can satisfy their hunger. If enthusiasm wanes in face of the world's opposition, those in the community should take heart and endure with patience, knowing they are not called to 'go it alone', for the Lord whose Word they have to proclaim will be present with them, even when the hour is late and they are wearied, to renew them for their task.

CROWDS CARRY INVALIDS EXPECTANTLY TO JESUS **6:53-56**

This section resembles the generalising summaries of 1:32-34; 3:7-12; and 6:33, and is no doubt due to the Evangelist's redactional activity. The details of verse 56 may have come to Mark from the tradition (based here on accurate knowledge of what took place at this point in the ministry, according to Taylor, pp. 331f.), or some brief notice of Jesus' work in **Gennesaret** may have been available to him, but it is just as likely that he was dependent for this summary report on items from stories previously narrated in the Gospel (e.g. 2:1-12; 5:25-34). The summary portrays the extent of Jesus' fame as a wonder-worker and his drawing-power as such for the crowd. If we are right in thinking that Mark considered the miracle in itself an ambivalent sign then he will have regarded this report negatively as a further illustration of the blindness of the world, like that of the disciples in 6:30-52 (to come to Jesus only for physical healing is not yet to believe in him for who he really is, see Schweizer, p. 143), and not in fact as 'a fully personal faith-response to Jesus' person and ministry' (Nineham, p. 186).

53–56. they came to land at Gennesaret: in verse 45 it was reported that they were making for Bethsaida, but Jesus appears there only at 8:22 and here now they land at a quite different locale. We do well not to judge Mark by the coherence of his geographical (or chronological) notices. **Gennesaret** is a fertile plain, lying to the south of Capernaum: Josephus called it 'the ambition of nature'. **the fringe of his garment:** probably the tassel which every male Jew was required to wear (Num. 15:38–41; Dt. 22:12; cf. Mk 5:27). **As many as touched it were made well:** comes almost incidentally as conclusion to the picture of the crowd's flocking to Jesus. Mark acknowledges Jesus' healing power, but gives no indication here that those who experienced it attained to a deeper insight into the meaning of his person. In the light of 5:18–20 it may be that Mark thought of the healed ones from the crowd as *potential* believers.

JESUS' ABROGATION OF STRICT JEWISH LEGALISM AND MEN'S INABILITY TO UNDERSTAND **7:1–23**

The whole passage as it stands in Mark should be interpreted as a single unit. Its composite nature is clear enough. Verses 9–13 are a sort of doublet of or parallel to verses 1–8; verse 9 picks up and repeats verse 8 in a slightly different form; verse 20 is doublet of verse 15*b*. The hand of Mark is in evidence in various places in the composition. Verses 3–4 are a parenthetical explanation of Jewish custom for the benefit of his Gentile readers, inserted by the Evangelist between the scene set in verse 2 and the question of defilement in relation to the tradition of the elders in verse 5. There are seams in the narrative at verse 6 and verse 9, where the phrase **and he said to them** introduces in each case probably a different item of tradition. Verses 14, 17–18*a* are characteristically Marcan in language and ideas and bear a close similarity to his treatment of the parabolic teaching of Jesus in chapter 4. Here too the Marcan motif of the disciples' blindness is brought to the forefront. After what appears to be an explanation on the part of the Church in verses 18*b*, 19 (cf. Mk 4:14–20) of the saying of verse 15, Mark inserts in verses 20–23 a further exposition consisting of a catalogue of vices that possibly betrays Hellenistic influence.

The various stages in the composition of the whole discourse are virtually impossible of recovery. Many commentators hold that the basic section was verses 1–8 (verses 3–4 of course being a Marcan explanatory insertion), originating in the Palestinian church in Bultmann's view (*HST*, pp. 17f.), and designated a 'pronouncement-story' by Vincent Taylor (pp. 334 and 342). To this Mark attached verses 9–13 and then appended verses 14–23 because of their topical similarity (see also Montefiore, Vol. 1, pp. 132–66; Haenchen, pp. 260–71). Another possible and perhaps preferable view is that the initial nucleus consisted only of the question of verse 5 and Jesus' reply in verse 15, for which the Church in the tradition prior to Mark had provided the setting described in verses 1–2 (see Rawlinson, p. 93). As a later development, the portrayal of Jesus' broad attack on the scribal tradition in verses 6–8 was interpolated as providing an answer to the large general question of verse 5, whether by some branch of the Church before Mark or by the Evangelist himself is hard to say. Lastly, since Mark for his part wanted to close the controversy story with his customary motif of the disciples' blindness, all the more reprehensible here in the light of the shining clarity of Jesus' statement in verse 15, he did not keep the concrete illustration of the futility of scribal legalism in the **Corban** case to the end, but inserted it in verses 9–13 (see Schweizer, pp. 145f.).

How far has this composite passage, with its Marcan editorial features, preserved elements of early Palestinian tradition or behind that of the original words or attitude of Jesus himself regarding the Law? The notice that Jesus' **disciples ate** (on a specific occasion) without ritual cleansing of **hands,** is widened in verse 5 to the larger question of why they did not in general conform to **the tradition of the elders,** i.e. the oral law that had grown up through the discussion of rabbis or scribes over many years alongside the written Law. No doubt the question of the validity of the oral tradition was frequently asked by early Jewish Christians. But the keeping of the Law, in its written and oral sanctions, was a problem far beyond Palestine, as Paul's experience shows. Moreover, there is no clear evidence that lay Jews at the time in question followed the requirement of ritual cleansing before food. Accordingly, unless we postulate the existence of a school of scribal rigorists who insisted on this in the age of Jesus, we cannot say with any assurance that the ritual hand-washing dispute, in relation to the question of the oral tradition, emanated from the Palestinian church.

Jesus' response to the question of why the disciples do not keep **the tradition of the elders** in verses 6–8 comprises first a citation from Isa. 29:13, and then a charge against the Pharisees that they follow the oral precepts transmitted by men. The form of the citation deviates extensively from the Hebrew and follows the LXX with one or two minor modifications. It is hardly a 'proof from prophecy' marking out the Pharisees as the very hypocrites (saying one thing and meaning or doing another) described in advance by Isaiah, but rather functions as a description of their unworthy devotion to merely human ordinances. Exactly where it departs most notably from the Hebrew is the quotation from Isa. 29:13 most apposite to the context: 'The doctrines they teach are nothing more than human precepts.' In this Greek form it could hardly have come from the lips of Jesus, but may have been adopted from liberal Hellenistic Jewish quarters (Schweizer, p. 145) as part of the polemic of Gentile Christians against the restrictions of the Law and its scribal applications.

The section of the **Corban** case (verses 9–13) purports to provide a concrete illustration of how the Pharisees let their oral tradition take precedence over Moses or the Torah. What it really does is to show Jesus opposing the practice of obeying one provision of the written Law on oaths (Dt. 23:21–23; Num. 30:2) by cancelling out another provision on a son's responsibility to his parents (Exod. 20:12; Dt. 5:16, etc.). But according to the Mishnah, the later rabbis at any rate wholeheartedly agreed that filial piety was of supreme importance. It is just possible, however, that in Jesus' day there were some stricter rabbis so addicted to the Law of oaths that they allowed it to overrule the humanitarian considerations inherent in the chief commandments like 'honour your father and your mother'. Possibly also there is something in the ingenious suggestion that someone who in a fit of temper had vowed not to support his parents had provided a *cause célèbre* for discussion in the bazaars of Galilee (Rawlinson, p. 95; also Nineham, pp. 190f.), and Jesus addressed his statement on Corban directly to this. But against these conjectures, the Corban case presented here seems both extreme and hypothetical. As Schweizer observes (pp. 145f.), the issue for a Pharisee would have been that obedience to God took precedence even over love to father or mother, and this corresponds to the attitude and call of Jesus (Mt. 10:37; Lk. 14:26). The provenance of this piece of tradition therefore remains uncertain.

In the saying of verse 15 we come closest to Jesus' own stance. The saying could hardly have been understood from the first as unambiguously sweeping aside large areas of the written Law. Otherwise it is hard to see why the early Church, with such an absolute word of the Lord to guide it, should have continued to engage in disputes about the Law's validity. Its more radical implications (see verse 19, **thus he declared all foods clean**) 'would be drawn out only slowly and painfully over many years of controversy' (C. E. Carlston, *NTS* 15 (1968–9), p. 95). Probably Jesus initially intended to state in regard to the food laws that inward pollution is more serious than any pollution from outside. Nevertheless, the final solution represented here in Mark is not necessarily inconsistent with the basic posture of Jesus during his ministry, for he did consort with sinners who did not keep the food laws, and he did oppose the view that punctilious observance of the regulations of the Torah is a prior condition of God's gracious action. Finally, verses 18*b*–19 and verses 20–23 should be regarded as radical interpretations of the statement of verse 15, probably current in the Gentile Church (Rawlinson, pp. 96f.).

The passage contains echoes of former controversies between the Church and the representatives of a legalistic Judaism. But by the time Mark's Gospel was written, the Church had already settled the dispute by claiming its liberation from the Law. So the Evangelist sees here an emphatic declaration that the old way of the Law is *passé*. Above all, by stressing the blindness of the disciples he shows that the new dispensation of freedom brought in by Jesus makes it easier for the world to reject him than to understand and accept him. The story of the Syrophoenician woman that follows suggests that only on the basis of new insights from outside the pale of Judaism does faith arise.

1. These materials have come to Mark without note of time or location. His reasons for placing them here are not connected with accurate chronology but with his theological intention. **The scribes, who had come from Jerusalem:** their presence here denotes for Mark that the heart of the official opposition to Jesus comes from the city where his death will be encompassed.

2–4. What is at issue is not the question of hygiene generally, but of *ceremonial* cleanness or defilement. **some of the disciples** (verse 2; cf. **your disciples** in verse 5). The practice not of Jesus himself but of his followers (in the Church) is the matter for debate. **ate with hands defiled,** that is, unwashed: 'unwashed' is Mark's explanation for the benefit of Gentile readers of what it means to eat **with hands defiled.** The word translated **defiled** means literally 'common' or 'secular' as opposed to 'holy'. The common or secular was not in and by itself unclean, but became 'impure' in circumstances where a legal rule required ritual cleansing or consecration. It is the notion that God comes only to the man who is already sacred in the ritual sense that Jesus is pictured as resisting in the passage. **unless they wash their hands:** the word left untranslated by *RSV* because of its uncertain meaning is *pygmē*, literally = 'with the fist'. It probably represents an attempt on Mark's part to explain some technicality that even in Mark's time the Church no longer understood. The numerous textual variants certainly show that it was obscure from an early date (see Taylor, p. 335). Whether it refers to rubbing the fist on the palm of the hand, or to pouring water over the clenched fist, or to washing up to the wrist is impossible to determine. **when they come from the market place:** where by rubbing shoulders with people in the crowd they might have touched a Gentile or a Jewish sinner who was unclean, and so incurred ritual defilement themselves. They purify themselves: some MSS read 'baptise', i.e, 'bathe' themselves, but the much less familiar Greek word = 'sprinkle' or 'wash' themselves (here rendered **purify**) is more likely the correct reading. The account of Jewish custom given in verses 2–4 is difficult to square with the known facts. According to the Talmud (the Palestinian Talmud dates from around AD 450 and the longer Babylonian Talmud from around AD 500), in the time of Jesus only the priests were required to make an ablution before partaking of the sacrifices (cf. Lev. 22:1–16). From all we can gather the obligation of ritual washing was not extended to laymen, including scribes and Pharisees, until shortly after AD 100 (see *Ab.* 1:1). If the story about the ritual handwashing dispute (verse 2) is historical, then we must suppose that even in Jesus' day a minority of lay pietists voluntarily took upon themselves the prescription of ritual ablution for priests, perhaps before entering the Temple or participating in a sacred rite. But Mark's explanatory comment that **the Pharisees and all the Jews** followed the practice

could not apply to the age of Jesus. The ironical and polemical
tone of verses 3-4 in fact suggests that this detailed description of
Jewish ritual customs, so fastidiously observed, in fact suggests
not so much past historical reality as a Church context in which
all legal scrupulosity was already deemed absurd and quite
irreconcilable with the Church's own very different concerns.

5. The specific occasion and question presupposed by verse 2
is now broadened out into the larger issue of the validity of the
scribal tradition (transmitted orally until codified in the Mishnah
around AD 200 and held to be binding, like the written Torah,
by scribes and Pharisees).

6-8. An answer to the question of verse 5 is now furnished by a
particular use and application of Isa. 29:13, which here appears
in its Greek form and has been appropriated by Gentile Christianity from liberal Hellenistic Judaism (see above, p. 182). The citation is a typical prophetic denunciation of outward observance of
religious ordinances that is not accompanied by total life-commit-
ment to the one who is the true object of religious devotion. Concentration upon external acts of piety to the neglect of true
holiness is now equated here with submission to a scribal tradition
that is of merely human manufacture (**the precepts of men,**
verse 7; **the tradition of men,** verse 8)—such submission means
forsaking the true **commandment of God,** which requires
something immeasurably greater and deeper than surface efforts
to satisfy him.

9-13. As introduced here, Jesus' words on the **Corban** case
afford a particular example of the way the scribes and Pharisees
elevate the **tradition of** men above **the commandment of God.**
You have a fine way . . . your traditions: the Greek adverb
used ironically here (*kalōs* = 'well', here translated **you have a
fine way**) has been added to verse 6 (**Well did Isaiah prophesy**)
to commend the truth of the prophecy, and this coupled with the
fact that 'the tradition of the elders' (verse 5) is here called **your
tradition** supports the view that verses 9-13 are a later insertion
(Schweizer, p. 146). **Moses said . . . surely die:** the quotations
in verse 10 from the Law of Moses, enjoining love to father and
mother, correspond almost word for word with the LXX of Exod.
20:12 and 21:16 (17). **Corban (that is, given to God):** the
RSV **given to God** reproduces Mark's single Greek word =
'gift' or 'offering'. It is sometimes held that **Corban** here means
a 'votive offering' (cf. Ezek. 20:28; 40:43), so that the man is

threatening to give his earnings to the Temple treasury and thus deprive his parents of their due support. However, on the rather late second-century evidence of the Mishnah tractate *Nedarim* ('On Vows'), the practice of Corban allowed a man to vow over his property to God and so prevent its use by those who had a legitimate claim on it. A recent discovery suggests that the same practice obtained also in the time of Jesus. An inscribed ossuary-lid found in a Jewish tomb near Jerusalem dating from the beginning of the Christian era carries words that may be translated: 'All that a man may find to his profit in this ossuary is an offering (**Corban**) to God from him who is within it' (Fitzmyer, pp. 93ff.). 'Corban' is a dedicatory formula that puts a ban on something, reserving it for sacred use and withdrawing it from the profane. At any rate in verses 10–12 Jesus is portrayed as condemning outright the subordination of filial responsibility to any such abstraction as the law of the irrevocability of oaths (here assigned to 'the tradition of men'). But according to the evidence of the Mishnah (*Nedarim* 8:1ff.), the later rabbis shared Jesus' attitude and ruled that no vow made to the detriment of father or mother could be abrogated (see also above, p. 182). The Church which cherished the report of verses 9–13 no doubt did so not because it pictured Jesus as one who beat the rabbis (in advance) by his superior skill in deciding the 'weightier matters of the Law', but rather as one possessed of that intuitive awareness of God's will that enabled him to put *human needs and interests* above everything else.

14–16. Verse 14 is a Marcan editorial transition that picks up again the question of verse 5 and leads to the statement of verse 15. **he called the people to him again:** the **again** does not necessarily refer back to a similar previous episode, but is simply a connective particle or denotes for Mark that *as usual* Jesus takes the initiative in seeking to reach the people, in this case *all* the people. The summons to all to **hear** and **understand** suggests that the saying of verse 15 is not only of universal import but in its parabolic nature demands an intent and faithful hearing. The statement of verse 15 is found in a simpler form in the *Gospel of Thomas* (83:24–27). It is important to notice that it does not evaluate the inward spiritual life of man more highly than his bodily life in the world. Rather it affirms the goodness of God's creation. The material gifts that sustain man's life are good, and so the threat to his existence does not come from externals but from the inward

disposition of his heart. Apparently the Church did not accept
this all at once. Paul had to struggle to maintain table-fellowship
between Gentile and Jewish Christians (Gal. 2:11–13; Rom.
14:14), and according to Ac. 10:1 Peter needs to have a revelation from heaven before he can associate with a Gentile. But
when the Church did understand the saying of verse 15 in its
radicality, it understood also that it dispensed with food regulations and taboos as a means of justification, that it swept away
great tracts of the written Law of Moses, and in fact rendered the
Law itself obsolete. Verse 16, 'if any man has ears to hear, let
him hear', wanting in some manuscripts, is omitted in *RSV*. But
it can be retained as a Marcan reinforcement of the summons of
verse 14 (**hear and understand**), and so as confirming that
Jesus' teaching is parabolic and not easily grasped.

17–18a. Mark relates Jesus' discourse to a central motif of
the Gospel, private instruction and explanation to the disciples
and their persistent blindness. By calling a **parable** what is more
a straightforward statement (verse 15) than figurative language,
Mark is able to stress how blind the disciples really are and to set
the stage for the expositions that follow. **are you also without
understanding? also** here indicates that the disciples are just
as dull and uncomprehending as the crowd of people (cf. Mt.
15:16, where the more temperate 'even yet' modifies the criticism
of the disciples' blindness). They too can grasp the meaning of
God's Word in Jesus only with the help of God himself. The
fact that they receive special instruction indicates with Mark not
that they enjoy a special position which merits it, but that, as
the bearer of God's Word, Jesus tries everything to reach the
world.

18b–20. Verses 18*b*–19 are a rather crude explanatory comment (Taylor calls it a 'Christian targum', p. 343) on Jesus'
statement by a church, probably Gentile, that has already
abandoned the food laws. The intention is to affirm that the
eating, digesting, and excreting of food is a wholly physical
process, that has nothing to do with the quality of a man's life.
Thus he declared all foods clean: the *RSV* offers here a free
rendering of the Greek which reads only 'cleansing all foods'.
It has been proposed (Black, *ARA*, p. 159) that the Greek is a mis-
translation of an Aramaic phrase ('all the food being cast out and
purged away'), in which case the initial force of the words would
have been to suggest that since all foods become excrement any-

how, there is no distinction among them. But the present participle 'cleansing' is related to the subject of the verb 'said', i.e. Jesus. *RSV* therefore is most probably correct, and the words are either a Marcan 'footnote' or a later marginal gloss, asserting that Jesus absolutely abolished all food laws. **And he said ... defile a man:** the formula **and he said** introduces yet another exposition, most likely from Gentile Christianity, which now sets over against the biblical concept of ritual uncleanness the idea that *morality* (or immorality) proceeds from within, from the very heart of a man's being. In the list of crimes the first six nouns are in the plural, denoting *repeated* acts, and the second six in the singular, denoting different kinds of vice. The list is without parallel in the teaching of Jesus. Similar catalogues occur in the *Manual of Discipline* from Qumran (1QS 4:9-11) and in Rom. 1:29-31; Gal. 5:19-23 (cf. 1 Tim 1:9-10; 2 Tim. 3:2-5); they betray the influence of Hellenism and are characteristic of the Hellenistic world generally.

Located where it is in the Gospel, the section 7:1-23 serves to show for Mark that the old day of the Law's sovereignty has passed, and that with Jesus the new day of freedom from the Law's restrictions has come. Consequently, without imposing prior conditions, without demanding the fulfilment of external acts of piety, to the patent absurdity of which this passage seeks to point, without asking for 'works' in advance, God now offers his Word freely and graciously to all who are prepared to believe that the barriers of legal righteousness are broken down. The Evangelist follows this section immediately with the story of the healing of the Syrophoenician woman's daughter in 7:24-30, since the latter demonstrates how the boundaries of Judaism are transcended, and God gives his healing grace to those Gentiles who could only appear to be defiled in Jewish eyes. To be sure the new way and the new dispensation of Jesus, in which faith discovers its genuine freedom (and ethical responsibility) before God, are no soft option. It is difficult to comprehend and accept that God's action in the world is not at all dependent on man's striving to keep the requirements of the Law, written and oral. This Mark wants to show by the searching question of 7:18: **'Then are you also without understanding?'**

THE LORD'S SAVING RESPONSE TO A BELIEVING GENTILE 7:24-30

The disciples' inability to understand that God's Word in Jesus has overcome the Jewish legalism, somewhat polemically described in the preceding section, acts as a foil to the readiness of a Gentile woman, who stands quite outside the Law, to believe that Jesus can forthwith meet her need. The conclusion (verses 29–30) leaves no doubt that the story is a miracle-story, but neither the miracle itself nor its effect is dwelt upon, and the emphasis is entirely on the statement of Jesus in verse 27 and his brief ensuing dialogue with the woman in verses 28–29. These verses 27–29 relate to the subject of the relative position of Jews and Gentiles in God's economy of salvation and the story must have been told from the outset in connexion with this controversial issue of the Jew–Gentile relationship. The opening verse 24 indicates a shift of scene for Jesus' ministry from the Galilean to the part-Gentile territory of Tyre and Sidon, and this is crucial for Mark's view of the story as reflecting a shift from the domain of the Law to the domain of the *gospel*. No hint is given in Mark of the motives for Jesus' move (e.g. to escape from Herod's hostility, or to avoid arrest), and any attempt to estimate what they were depends on conjecturally filling in the gaps in Mark's witness. Nor is there any indication in Mark that Jesus conducted a lengthy and extensive mission outside of strictly Jewish territory (although he appears to have had one or two stories like the present one set in (semi-)Gentile regions). From Mark's standpoint it is enough that a single story of Jesus' incursion into an area beyond the strict borders of Israel and of a miracle granted to the faith-response of a Greek woman should stand as a representational symbol of the truth that God acts healingly in Jesus toward those who have the courage to expect and believe that his action is not conditioned by the observance on their part of a specific set of legal rules.

24. And from there ... Tyre and Sidon: the description **Tyre and Sidon** embraces the whole of Phoenicia. A number of MSS omit the words **and Sidon,** which may have been an assimilation to the mention of Sidon in Mk 7:31 (see notes below). On the other hand, if the words stood in the original text, their later elimination could be explained as a correction in the light of the statement of 7:31: 'he returned from the region of Tyre, and went through Sidon.' Presumably Mark was not so much concerned to furnish a coherent geographical scheme (he may not have had the requisite information or knowledge to do so), but was content to serve notice that Jesus crossed the boundary into territory to the west and north of Galilee, which if it was by no means completely Gentile was not strictly Jewish either. **and he entered ... not be hid:** conjures up a picture of Jesus' magnetic attraction for the crowd even *outside of Israel*. Wherever he moves something of his glory shines through and constrains the people to flock around him.

25–26. His presence is enough to make things happen at once. The woman who pays her respect and assumes the posture of a supplicant before him (verse 25) is carefully described in verse 26 as a non-Israelite. **a Greek, a Syrophoenician by birth:** the word for **a Greek** (*Hellēnis*) refers to her religion; she is a pagan, a Gentile. By nationality she is a Phoenician from Syria as distinct from a Liby-Phoenician or Carthaginian.

27. Since now for the first time in the Gospel it is a *Gentile* who has requested of Jesus healing for her daughter, a measure of suspense is created in the story as to what his response to such a person might be. **Let the children first ... to the dogs:** the **children** are clearly Jews and the **dogs** Gentiles. The statement **let the children first be fed** (with the bread of the gospel that satisfies their deepest need) is of doubtful authenticity as a word of Jesus. It implies that it will be all right for others to be fed once the Jews have already been fed, and seems to reflect the demeanour of a Church that is acquainted with the Gentile mission and with the standpoint, 'to the Jew first and also to the Greek' (Rom. 1:16). Accordingly, these words, with their implicit promise to the Gentiles, somewhat blunt the edge of the woman's retort as an expression of Gentile hope and expectation. The clause does not occur in Matthew (15:26), and while his version of the incident differs from Mark's, the wording of the second part of this saying corresponds exactly to Mark's. Moreover the Greek word for **be fed** (= 'be fully satisfied') is the same as that used in the story of the feeding of the multitude (Mk 6:42). Possibly, therefore, Mark may himself have introduced the words **let the children first be fed** (see Schweizer, *GNM*, p. 152). By reason of its apparent harshness, Jesus' reply has perplexed the commentators. Jewish writers sometimes applied the description **dogs** as a term of approbrium to Gentiles. Numerous attempts have been made to tone down the seeming rudeness of the saying by suggesting, e.g., that Jesus spoke in half-jest; that he wanted to test the woman's faith; that he was here wrestling with himself about the scope of his mission. Probably too much has been made of the term 'dogs' here as an insult. The diminutive of the noun for 'dog' is used, and the story clearly envisages household pets, and not the pariah dogs that roamed the streets. The saying does raise the question of Jesus' attitude to the Gentiles. In his parallel account, Matthew reports that Jesus said: 'I was sent only to the lost sheep of the house of Israel' (15:24). Since Matthew strikes a thoroughly universalist note elsewhere in his Gospel (e.g. 28: 18–20), it is reasonable to suppose that he is here faithfully reporting very ancient tradition and probably Jesus' own words. If that is so, then Jesus thought of his own, and his disciples' mission as confined to the house of Israel, and this same perspective is implied in Mk 7:27. Beyond that, however, Jesus may have shared the old prophetic view that on God's day when his purpose was finally consummated, the Gentiles too would be brought into the fold (Isa. 19:19–25; 66:19f., Mic. 4:1f.; Zech. 8:20ff.; see Jeremias, *JPN*, pp. 56ff.; cf. Nineham, p. 199). No doubt the Evangelist himself saw in the saying and its sequel an exceptional illustration of the truth that the gospel was intended for *all*.

28. Yes, Lord ... crumbs: the term **Lord** is here simply the customary Gentile mode of address = 'sir'; it is used nowhere else in Mark in this sense. It is not the *wit* of the woman's reply that is important in the Marcan story. Rather it shows that she claims nothing as by right or by performance and is an exemplar of humility and openness to receive whatever is granted. The woman's words may have had a certain apologetic value for Gentile Christianity as a defence of the 'Jewishness' of Jesus, for here a Gentile acknowledges the distinction between Jew and Gentile and yet expresses dependence on the Jesus who speaks out of Israel (see verse 27).

29–30. In the conclusion the healing of the **daughter** is not played up. There is no mention of astonished bystanders. Nevertheless, it is quite unlikely that Mark regards the story as an example of Jesus' supernatural knowledge or his 'telepathic awareness of what is happening' (Taylor, p. 351). It is rather the account of a miracle of healing at a distance (cf. Mt. 8:5–13), by which *the wall of partition between Jew and Gentile is broken down*.

In this story the new dispensation pointed to in 7:1–23 is seen in operation. Matthew's report of the incident describes explicitly the woman's importunity (15:23) and her faith (15:28). But for Mark her faith is no less real. She comes making no legal claims and pleading no special merits, but just as she is, empty-handed and in need, and dares only to expect God's gift in Jesus. Thereby is exemplified the contrast between Jewish legalism and the faith that waits on God.

THE EARS OF THE DEAF OPENED 7:31-37

The preceding report illustrated how God's Word in Jesus could break down ancient boundaries. But the boundary wall of the world's apparently impenetrable incomprehension remains, its inability to hear aright and understand (cf. 7:14, 18). Mark now adds a story that offers the reader an anticipatory glimpse of God's will and God's power through Jesus to overcome even this obstacle and open deaf ears. The importance of the peculiar geographical notice (see notes on 7:31) with which he introduces the miracle of the healing of the deaf man is just that it locates the episode in predominantly *Gentile* territory, for the next chapter will again dwell upon the lack of understanding of the *Pharisees and the disciples*. The elements of the miraculous are decidedly more prominent in this account than in the previous one (7: 24-30). Hence Mark closes with his distinctive stress on the 'secret' (which none-the-less can hardly be suppressed, verse 36). This story is in fact remarkably different in character from the preceding. It is more primitive in that it contains the familiar features of comparable Jewish and Hellenistic tales of wonder-workers, the prodding of the ears, the use of saliva, the physical touching, the healer's groaning, and the use of a curative formula (*Ephphatha*, verse 34). Such a story may well have first circulated among the peasant folk of north Galilee, and its crasser details may have offended Matthew and Luke, who omit it. But it also has a strong 'biblical' ring in that it ends in Mark's record (verse 37) with a clear echo of Isa. 35:5 (cf. Isa. 29:18), and its language generally is reminiscent of LXX.

31. To go from the territory of **Tyre** by way of **Sidon** to the **Sea of Galilee** is like travelling from Cornwall to London *via* Manchester (Rawlinson, p. 101). **Through the region of Decapolis:** the Greek means literally 'in the middle of the Decapolis district', i.e. on the eastern shore of the lake in largely Gentile land. This improbable itinerary (whatever else its connotation or intention) does at least allow Mark the Gentile setting he wants at this juncture in his Gospel, and provides a spot by the lake for the second account of the feeding of the multitude in 8:1-10.

32–35. an impediment in his speech: the rare Greek word used here means literally 'speaking with difficulty'. It occurs in the LXX only in Isa. 35:6 where it translates a Hebrew word meaning 'dumb', and Mark probably derived it from there. The meaning 'speaking with difficulty', with **an impediment in his speech**, accords with the later description of the healed man, **he spoke plainly**. But in the view of the different and more regular word for 'dumb' in verse 37, it is likely that the story was understood in the tradition, if not by Mark, to refer to the healing of a deaf-mute. **taking him aside ... privately:** at the pre-Marcan stage this may have suggested only that the healer's technique was his own business and not for all to see, but it also conforms well with Mark's interest in the secrecy motif! Jesus does not make an exhibition of his power to the multitude. **spat and touched his tongue:** physical gestures and contact are essential to this story, since Jesus cannot communicate in speech with the deaf man. Spittle was believed to possess healing properties in antiquity (see Tacitus' account of how Vespasian cured a blind man with spittle in Alexandria, *Histories*, 4:81; cf. Mk 8:22–26; Jn 9:6), and also to have a magical effect in expelling demons. **looking up ... he sighed:** the upward look (cf. 6:41) indicates the transcendent source of the healer's power. Jesus' 'sighing' could be a 'groaning of the Spirit' (cf. Rom. 8:23, 26) in inarticulate prayer (Rawlinson, p. 102), but is more likely a groan of lament that such suffering as this is contrary to God's will for his creation. **Ephphatha ... be opened:** on the retention of the Aramaic word in the healer's pronouncement, see on 5:41. The form of the command implies that Jesus is acting here as an exorcist and that the man's disablement is attributed to demon-possession. This is borne out by the statement, **his tongue was released:** the Greek = 'the bond of his tongue was loosened'. What had caused his speech difficulty was 'binding' by a demon.

36–37. We charged them to tell no one: the insertion of the injunction to 'secrecy' represents Mark's warning to his readers that the miracle itself is not the decisive thing, and that admiration for Jesus merely as wonder-worker does not come near the truth that waits to be revealed (when his way to the cross is complete). Nevertheless, in the remainder of the verse Mark also shows that the full and final revelation which is pending cannot even now be completely suppressed—so great is the divine authority in Jesus. **he has done all things ... dumb speak:**

the astonishment of the people who make this statement is described in such strong terms that verse 37 may very well have stood initially as the conclusion to a *series* of miracle-stories (rather than to just this one). Initially also, with its reminiscences of Isa. 35:5 and Wis. 10:21, it probably testified to the messianic fulfilment of prophecy in Jesus. But for the Evangelist himself (not nearly so interested as Matthew in the precise fulfilment of *OT* predictions; see Anderson, *UOTN*, p. 28off.) it was hardly as miracle-worker that Jesus fulfilled God's saving purpose, but as the one who took the way of the cross (cf. Mk 8:31). Consequently, Mark would have thought of verse 37 as testimony only to the fact that Jesus' words and deeds were in accordance with the will of God expressed in Scripture.

THE FEEDING OF THE FOUR THOUSAND 8:1–10

The possibility that two separate feeding incidents (cf. 6:34–44) took place in the course of Jesus' ministry cannot be arbitrarily ruled out. But two facts make it highly improbable that the two stories reflect two different episodes. First, the disciples' bewilderment about what is to be done, evident from their question in 8:4, would be inconceivable on top of a previous miraculous feeding. Secondly, the correspondences in detail between the two accounts strongly suggest that they are duplicate versions of the same story—the compassion of Jesus, the dialogue with the disciples and the latter's perplexity, the thanksgiving and breaking of the bread and its distribution by the disciples, the separate action of the blessing and handing out of the fish, the satisfaction of the crowd's hunger, the gathering of the left-over fragments, and the journey across the lake—all these are repeated here from the first story.

Not only do these two stories correspond closely with each other, but the materials that follow in 8:11–26 also match the development of chapter 7. The dispute with the Pharisees about a sign from heaven in 8:11–13 parallels the controversy with them in 7:1–23; the section on the leaven of the Pharisees (8:14–21) parallels the story of the Syrophoenician woman (7:24–30); the healing of the blind man at Bethsaida (8:22–26) parallels the healing of the deaf man (7:31–37). Whether Mark had at his disposal two separate written cycles of material (6:35–7:37 and 8:1–26) is quite uncertain. It does appear that he possessed two accounts of the miraculous feeding which he

believed related to two separate episodes. To the first account
he appended the stories of chapter 7. To the second account
(8:1-10) are appended stories (the demand for a sign 8:11-13,
and the discourse about bread, 8:11-21) that seem to have been
associated with each other and with Peter's confession (cf. Jn
6:30ff.) in the tradition before Mark. Accordingly, it is as likely
that 8:1-26 has influenced the shape of 6:35-7:37 as the other
way round.

We might best think of Mark as having been the first to bring
8:1-26 into close proximity with 6:35-7:37 and as having so
extensively edited or rewritten particularly the stories of 8:
14-21 and 8:22-26 as to impose on them his own leading ideas,
especially the awesome blindness of the disciples and God's
power in Jesus to eradicate even that eventually. It is as if by this
juxtaposition the Evangelist wanted to keep his reader in suspense
by imposing a double restraint on the disclosure of the 'secret'
until it can begin to be revealed who Jesus really is from 8:31 on,
and as if he desired to make doubly sure of driving home the
lesson that to 'see' (cf. 8:22-26) and understand that revelation
is the real miracle of grace granted by God.

1-3. in those days: no more than a vague linking phrase.
In fact no notice is given of the setting or time of the event. It is
doubtful, therefore, whether Mark particularly wants to stress
here a Gentile setting for this account (as against the Jewish
setting of the previous account). **have been with me now ...
nothing to eat:** in 6:34 Jesus' pity is evoked by the spectacle
of a leaderless host without a teacher to guide them, here simply
by their physical hunger. In 6:35f. the disciples draw to Jesus'
attention the hunger of the crowd, here Jesus himself takes the
initiative, as indeed he does at first in calling the disciples to him
(verse 1). In this form of the story all the action is with Jesus; the
disciples play a more passive role. **if I send them away ...
have come a long way:** these words are simply a further illustration of Jesus' compassion in the face of extreme human need and
not an indication of his hesitation about what to do. In the light
of what follows he is not the one who needs to hesitate.

4-5. The disciples' question once again reveals that they
reckon only at the material and human level (cf. 6:37). The
very thing, namely the incredible stupidity involved in the
disciples' repetition of the question, that some commentators try
to *explain away* (see Taylor, p. 359) as due either to confusion

between the two accounts or to the lapse of a long interval between the two miracles, is precisely what Mark is eager to corroborate by a twofold emphasis (i.e. the disciples' lack of understanding). **in the desert:** only now do we learn that, as in 6:35, the setting for the miracle is a desert place. **how many loaves have you?** agrees verbatim with 6:38.

6–9. There is no mention of the 'green grass', the 'companies', or the arrangement 'by hundreds and by fifties' of the previous story. Whereas in 6:41 Jesus 'looked up to heaven and blessed' before breaking the bread, here he first 'gives thanks'. Otherwise the two narratives agree closely in respect of the distribution, the appeasing of the multitude's hunger and the taking up of the fragments with of course a change of the number of loaves from five to seven and of baskets from twelve to seven. Schweizer (*GNM*, p. 157) notes that the statement of verse 6, **having given thanks, he broke them and . . .** corresponds exactly with 1 C. 11:24 and asks whether the church that transmitted the story in this form may have used it as a liturgy for the Lord's Supper, whereas the church that told and handed on the story of 6:32–44 used a rather different liturgy. The fact that the distribution of the bread (verse 6) is kept quite separate from and concluded before the distribution of the fish (verse 7, cf. 6:41), probably betrays the accommodation of the story to the Church's eucharistic practice. **there were about four thousand people:** cf. 6:44. Divulged only at the end, the large number again dramatises the outstanding nature of the miracle.

10. sent them away: Jesus controls the movements both of his disciples (verse 1) and the crowd—they come and go at his behest. **the district of Dalmanutha:** no such place is known to us. Not surprisingly there is some textual warrant for alternative readings like 'Mageda', 'Magedan' (Mt. 15:39 has 'Magadan', also unknown), and Magdala, and a great variety of modern conjectures have been made. Once more, it appears Mark's knowledge of the geography of the lake and the lake towns was to say the least, quite vague. Possibly all that concerned Mark as redactor was that the lake and its surrounding territories, some Jewish, some mainly Gentile, was an ideal setting for those frequent journeyings of Jesus and his disciples to and fro which demonstrate that from first to last the gospel has its own irresistible missionary momentum.

From as early as the fourth century it was thought that Mark

intended the feeding of the five thousand to symbolise the giving
of the Bread of Life to the Jews and the feeding of the four thousand
the giving of the Bread of Life to the Gentiles, and thus to demonstrate to the disciples the universality of Jesus' power. Puzzled
by Mark's recording of the two stories in such close proximity
in what is after all a quite short work, modern critics too have
found in them an extensive symbolism. In the first the five
loaves distributed among the five thousand have been taken to
represent the five books of the Law given to the Jews, and the
twelve baskets to represent the twelve tribes of Israel. In the
second the four thousand receive seven loaves, reminiscent of the
seven deacons in Ac. 6:1–6, the mission of the seventy in Lk. 10:
1ff., the seventy traditional divisions of the Gentile world, the
LXX, and possibly also the seven spirits of God mentioned in
Revelation. Confirmation of this symbolism has also been sought
in the different words for basket in the two stories, in 6:43 the
kophinos being thought to be a special Jewish type, and in 8:8 the
spyris an ordinary type, possibly a fish-basket. (For a balanced
discussion of the symbolical interpretation, see Nineham, pp. 103f.)
But as 7:24–30 shows, Mark knew how to give a story an explicit
Gentile setting and to relate it rather openly to the Church's
Gentile mission when he wished. He has not done so here, and
the close correspondence between the two stories, both set simply
'in the desert', militates against the view that Mark has designed
a study in symbolical contrasts. In fact it becomes clear with
8:14–21, especially verses 20–21, that the Evangelist's basic
intention is to bear a dual witness to the disciples' non-understanding. It can of course also be said that neither of these stories
is unrelated to the theme of mission and the gospel's power to
satisfy all needy people, Jews or Gentiles.

JESUS' REPUDIATION OF THE DEMAND FOR A SIGN **8:11–13**

The demand for a sign was most likely associated with the feeding
of the multitude in the tradition (cf. Jn 6:5–14, 22–30). But this
little section, in which Mark provides his own framework for the
saying of verse 12, fits well with his purpose. On the negative
side, the Pharisees appear, like the disciples in 8:1–10, as representatives of the blindness of the world. On the positive side, the
statement of verse 12 furnishes the Evangelist with the corroboration he needs of the truth that for those who have eyes of faith to
see, God's activity in Jesus is concealed in the earthly and com-

monplace, in the breaking and distribution of bread. Everything hinges here of course on the saying of Jesus, which appears in Q (Lk. 11:29 = Mt. 12:39) with the addition of the important exception, 'except the sign of Jonah'. Mark may have omitted the exceptive clause because for him the mighty works so far narrated in the Gospel were sufficient indication for faith that God's power was active in Jesus (Perrin, pp. 192ff.), and no other sign was necessary. On the other hand, it may have been omitted in the tradition before Mark since even then it was no longer understood (Lk. 11:32 explains it as a reference to Jonah's *preaching*; Lk. 11:30 relates it to the parousia of the Son of man; Mt. 12:40 refers it apparently to the death, entombment, and resurrection of the Son of man. See Schweizer, *GNM*, p. 158). In other respects the form of the saying in Mk 8:12 appears to come closest to Jesus' original pronouncement—the 'Amen' at the beginning of the sentence (Greek *amēn* = *RSV* **truly**); the Greek words 'if a sign shall be given to this generation' (*RSV* **no sign shall be given to this generation**) reflecting the idiomatic Hebrew manner of making a solemn asseveration, 'may I be accursed if God shall give a sign'; the passive **shall be given** representing the Hebrew, 'God shall give'. These point to the authenticity of the form of words in Mark.

11. the Pharisees came: in characteristic Marcan fashion, **the Pharisees** appear as if from nowhere, since at this point in Mark Jesus is in non-Jewish territory. Although the saying of verse 12 was earlier connected with the miraculous feeding in the tradition, Mark here provides a setting by introducing the Pharisees as typical opponents of Jesus and as representatives of 'this generation'. **seeking from him a sign from heaven, to test him:** the fundamental Marcan conception is that the miracles are *dynameis* ('mighty works'), through which faith is challenged to discern God's action in Jesus. With this conception, particularly prominent in chapters 6–8, the Pharisees' illegitimate demand for a **sign** (*sēmeion*) is now demonstrated to be at variance (Kertelege, pp. 89, 165, 170f. Behind the Greek word *sēmeion* is the Hebrew *ōth*, which in both the *OT* (cf. Isa. 7: 10ff.; Dt. 13:1–2) and rabbinic literature is understood as a sign validating or negating the trustworthiness of a prophetic messenger or teacher. What is being sought by the Pharisees here is a sign **from heaven**, an open and visible guarantee from God (cf. Mk 12:30) that Jesus is to be trusted. Probably, in view of the implied contrast in Mark between 'mighty work' (*dynamis*) and 'sign' (*sēmeion*) and of the use of the latter word in the apocalyptic materials of chapter 13 (Mk 13:4, 22), the sign expected would have consisted of a spectacular and portentous heavenly miracle of an apocalyptic kind (Schweizer, p. 159). Mark has construed the Pharisees' demand for such a sign as a desire to **test** Jesus (to 'tempt' him, 'try to prove him'). While the use of the same verb (*peirazein*) as in the temptation story (1:13) implies that the Pharisees are aligned with Satan and his work, 8:11–13 can scarcely be enlisted to uphold the opinion that 'the whole Gospel is an explanation of how Jesus was tempted' (Mauser, p. 100; cf. the counter-arguments in Best, pp. 25ff.). Rather, the issue here for the Evangelist is the legitimation of Jesus' *authority* and the question of faith or unfaith in regard to it. Faith ceases to be faith when it clamours for visible or tangible proof. The essence of unfaith is to put God to the proof, to lay down prior human and worldly conditions for believing in the God who himself offers his Word freely and imposes no prior conditions on men (cf. 7:1–23). According to the Evangelist, it is the *hidden* presence of God in Jesus' earthly activity, even in his mighty works, that calls to faith and creates its possibility.

12. Mark has connected Jesus' broader application of the demand for **a sign** to **this generation** with the Pharisees, thereby presenting them as an example of the world's blindness. By this saying, Jesus no doubt meant originally to declare that it is not God's way to compel belief by the ocular demonstration of marvels designed for the purpose. In its Marcan context it clarifies the contrast between the summons to faith presented in God's miraculous gift of bread (8:1–10) and man's reluctance, in his faithlessness, to say Yes to God until he has shown his hand in extraordinary and 'unworldly' displays of power.

13. Verse 13 may be a doublet of verse 10. But Jesus' abrupt departure from the Pharisees may also signify for Mark that those who do not have the courage to trust him are left behind and cannot follow him.

The short section 8:11–13 is very significant for the Evangelist. It provides a bridge between the feeding of the four thousand (8:1–10) and the discourse on the loaves (8:14–21). The lack of perception of the Pharisees and of the disciples must both alike be rebuked. It also protects the Marcan notion that the miracles or mighty works are not overt *proofs* of God's action in Jesus.

They are inherently ambiguous and may or may not elicit a
believing response. So the Evangelist safeguards the 'scandal' of
the humanity of Jesus against all pictures of a purely prodigious
wonder-worker. Does he in 8:11-13 also cast a side-glance at
some in his community who were allowing their zeal for mission
to be eroded by passively waiting on apocalyptic portents (cf.
chapter 13)?

THE MIRACLE OF THE LOAVES AND THE DISCIPLES' REMARKABLE
INSENSITIVITY 8:14-21

Indications of any coherent chronological sequence in Mark are
once again lacking at this point. It seems incredible in the light of
their so recent experience of the crowd's needs that they should
now have **forgotten to bring bread** (verse 14). Mark has
apparently picked up verse 14 from the tradition and inserted it
here as introduction to what is his own relatively free composition
in verses 16-21, highlighting the disciples' continuing incomprehension. Certainly, since Mark was the first to bring the accounts
of the two feeding miracles into close proximity, he has been
responsible for the double questions and answers of verses 19-20.
If one wishes to defend the substantial historicity of the whole
episode, including the difficult saying of verse 15 (**beware of the
leaven . . .**), then one must account for the fact that verses 16-21
seem to be quite unconnected with the warning about the leaven,
and relate obviously to the disciples' lack of bread. The psychologising explanation that the disciples were 'so preoccupied with
their own problem and the resulting recrimination among themselves that they failed to heed at the time what Jesus was saying
to them' (Cranfield, pp. 259f.) is something of a *tour de force*.
Probably Mark found the saying about the 'leaven' (verse 15)
in the tradition. It was possibly already connected with the
situation described in verse 14 through association of ideas, the
'leaven' with the 'bread' or 'loaf'. In that case the traditional
item of verse 15 has become entirely subsidiary to verse 14 and
Mark's use of it as preface to verses 16-20, in which he expresses
his main intention, is to stress the disciples' lack of understanding.
It is noteworthy that if the saying of verse 15 is bracketed out the
story is then complete and coheres in itself.

**15. Take heed, beware of the leaven of the Pharisees
and the leaven of Herod:** some manuscripts and versions read
'of the Herodians', but this is probably through assimilation to

3:16 and 12:13, and does not in any case materially alter the sense. That this originally independent saying occasioned difficulty from the earliest stage is clear from the fact that Matthew has 'beware of the leaven of the Pharisees and Sadducees' (16:6) and later interprets the 'leaven' as the *teaching* of both these groups (16:11f.), whereas Luke speaks only of the 'leaven of the Pharisees' and refers it to their *hypocrisy* (12:1). Among the rabbis leaven frequently symbolised the evil or vicious side of man's nature, and a similar metaphorical usage occurs also in the *NT* (cf. 1 C. 5:6-8; Gal. 5:9). **The leaven of the Pharisees and ... of Herod** would then signify man's inclination to impress both God and fellow-men with outward worldly show (the **Pharisees** by external acts of legal observance and **Herod** by the arrogant exercise of secular authority). In its present context, however, the saying does seem to be peripheral to Mark's leading purpose, although it may have occurred to him that the idea of steady growth or progression in the figure of the leaven was apposite to the progressive blindness of the disciples, which now in verses 16-20 reaches its worst level and evokes from Jesus the severest reproach so far administered in the Gospel.

16. And they discussed ... no bread: many MSS read 'we have no bread', and most of them also insert the present participle of the verb 'to say' (*legontes* = **saying**). This is the reading followed by *RSV*, in which case an ellipse has to be understood— 'they discussed among themselves, saying: (the Teacher speaks about the leaven) because we have no bread'. Adopting this same reading, Moffatt renders it, 'Leaven?' they argued among themselves, 'We have no bread at all!' This reading and the resultant translations do forge some kind of rough connexion between the saying of verse 15 and what follows in 17-21. But the words **saying** and **we have** are probably due to assimilation to Mt. 16:7, and the more probably correct reading is 'they disputed with one another because (or 'as to the reason why')they had no bread', in which case there is no very obvious connexion with the saying of verse 15, but a quite natural connexion with verse 14. Presumably the link with verse 14 is uppermost in Mark's mind, especially since he derived both 14 and 15 from the tradition, and may have understood 15 only in the sense indicated above (see note on 8:15).

17-18. For the Evangelist the point of the questions posed by Jesus is that his mighty works, like his parabolic teaching (cf.

chapter 4), are a metaphorical language which should reveal the truth but in fact obscures it, which should call forth understanding but in fact is met with a blatant lack of it. The fact that Jesus should pursue so many questions with his disciples (verse 17–21) serves not only to underscore the earnestness of God's longing to reach them with his Word in Jesus, but their own obduracy and dullness as well. Even God's free gift of bread for the hungry crowds has been wasted on them. The question **why do you discuss the fact that you have no bread?** makes it plain that they still operate at the level of very mundane and material calculations. The words **do you not perceive or understand?** recall the language of the LXX (cf. Isa. 6:9f; Jer. 5:21, Ezek. 12:2), but it is not certain that Mark thinks of the disciples' failure as a failure to perceive in Jesus the one greater than Moses who brings to fulfilment the great saving event of the Exodus (cf. Nineham, p. 213). To judge by what has gone before in the Gospel, it is rather the mystery of the kingdom's hidden power and presence in Jesus they cannot comprehend. **Are your hearts hardened?** the question carries the sternest rebuke. Despite God's specially strenuous efforts to communicate his truth to them in Jesus, their astonishing lack of perception and insensitivity (hardness of heart) has left them in no better place than those outside (4:11b, 12). **And do you not remember?** a lapse of memory so shortly after two amazing miracles of feeding is inconceivable. The question is therefore indicative of editorial activity, and leads into the further questions about the miraculous feedings.

19–21. The correspondences between the questions of verses 19–20 and the two different accounts of the healing of the multitude (in the exact replication of numbers and the words for 'basket') are further evidence of editorial compilation. In verse 21 the **not yet** (**'Do you not yet understand?'**) paves the way for a new stage in which Jesus openly discloses himself (8:31f.).

In this section Mark is at pains to show that the disciples' misunderstanding is apparently ineradicable. The succeeding story of the healing of the blind man at Bethsaida suggests that thing short of a miracle of God's grace can bestow believing-understanding on those who have eyes yet do not see.

THE EYES OF THE BLIND OPENED 8:22–26

This account and the account of the cure of the deaf-mute in 7:32–37 are both peculiar to Mark and form a pair of stories which parallel each other rather strikingly in both language (see Taylor, pp. 368f.) and content. Both have affinities with Jewish and Hellenistic healing stories, perhaps especially the latter, and feature such secular peculiarities as the use of saliva and the laying on of hands. So close are the two reports they are often assumed to form a doublet, referring to one and the same incident. If, however, they circulated originally as two separate accounts of two different episodes, they have patently been assimilated to each other, most likely in the process of transmission. How far Mark himself may have contributed to the assimilation it is not easy to say. We can regard the Evangelist as responsible for the placement of the story of the healing of the blind man here. It matches his placement of the story of the deaf-mute at the close of the first 'feeding cycle' (cf. 6:35-7:37). Probably the opening words and the closing command are also due to Marcan redaction.

22. And they came to Bethsaida: Bethsaida was a large bustling town, yet the story speaks twice of **the village** (verses 23 and 26). The story has evidently come to Mark from the tradition with no note of place or time. He prefaces it with the short notice of the arrival at Bethsaida for which the disciples had actually set out in 6:45, and mistakenly regards the city of Bethsaida as the village of the story. The difficulty is hardly overcome by conjectural attempts to identify a *village* of the name Bethsaida on the west side of the lake, nor by taking the words **and they came to Bethsaida** as the conclusion of section 8:14-21, for even then there is nothing to indicate that Mark would not have thought of Bethsaida as the setting of 8:22-26. The verbs **brought** and **begged** are impersonal plurals, with no subject specified, hence the *RSV* **some people**.

23-25. The removal of the man to a private place, the gestures, and the address to him follow the same pattern as Jesus' actions toward the deaf-mute (7:33). There, however, Jesus' address consisted of a command 'Be opened'. Here it is a question, **'Do you see anything?'**, and the question leads up to a rather unusual element in the story—the eventual healing is effected only in two distinct stages and after Jesus has *twice* laid his hands on the man. The Greek word **he looked up** is used again in 10:51f. of the recovery of sight, but here it appears to denote simply the reflex action of raising the head. Behind the *RSV* translation **I see men; but they look like trees, walking** stands an awkward Greek sentence literally = 'I see men for (or 'that') like trees I

see them walking'. Awkward though it is, as the more difficult
reading this is to be preferred to the simpler variant attested by a
number of MSS, 'I see men walking like trees'. The meaning is
accurately enough presented by *RSV* or by Moffatt's even freer
rendering, 'I can make out people, for I see them as large as trees
moving.' **Like trees** is a not unnatural description of the blurred
and dimly seen shapes of men moving around. That 'the man
was not born blind', as Taylor suggests (p. 371), is a scarcely
warranted inference from verse 24. A Greek inscription records
an interesting parallel. In the Temple of Asclepios at Epidaurus
the god runs his fingers over the eyes of the blind Alcetas of
Halice and 'the first things he saw were the trees in the Temple
precincts' (see Rawlinson, p. 108). Only after the repeated action
of Jesus, when **again he laid his hands upon his eyes** is the
man's sight restored. The cure, it is implied, is gradual. Did Mark
himself detect in the *gradual* nature of the cure in this story a
symbolic parallelism with Jesus' gradual opening of the disciples'
eyes to the truth about himself in the next section of the Gospel
(8:27–10:52), to which 8:27–9:1 stands as preface? (The detailed
case for such parallelism is made by Lightfoot, *HIG*, pp. 90f.,
cf. Nineham, p. 218.) Probably, as frequently in such popular
stories, the gradual cure suggests no more than the intractable
nature of the malady and so in the end magnifies the healer's
miraculous power. For Mark it would have meant that just as
physical blindness is extremely hard to remove, so the world's
spiritual blindness can be overcome only through the divine
miracle whereby God now chooses to reveal himself in Jesus
(8:27–9:1). Mark allows nothing to distract attention from this
one nodal point, that it takes a miracle of God to open blind eyes,
for there is no mention at all in this report of the reaction of the
healed man or the people.

26. When Jesus **sent him away to his home** he must have
known that any command to silence was futile since silence
could by no means be ensured. Accordingly, we may suppose that
the injunction to secrecy implied presumably in the words **do not
even enter the village** is an editorial reflection of the Evangelist's secrecy motif. The physical miracle in itself has news value,
but it is not the good news, and so must be suppressed. The good
news arises with the Word given to and through Jesus (8:31)
and his call to obedience to it (8:34ff.) and this is *the miracle* that
has to be proclaimed. Many MSS attest the reading followed by

RSV but there is some textual support also for 'tell no one in the village', which may well be correct in view of the unusual Marcan use of the Greek preposition *eis* ('into') to mean *en* ('in'). With this reading the injunction to secrecy is sharpened.

THE WILL OF GOD FOR JESUS AND HIS DISCIPLES: THE WAY OF SUFFERING 8:27–10:52

Characteristics of this division of the Gospel

Up to this point the Gospel has been concerned chiefly with the divine authority of Jesus. His authority expresses itself in his disputes with the Jewish leaders. So radical is his conflict with them that in fact the representatives of religion conspire with secular powers to destroy him (cf. 3:6). Already therefore the shadow of the cross has fallen across his pathway. Now in this new section the mere shadow becomes an inescapable reality. The divine necessity of the cross is openly declared (8:31f.; 9:31; 10:33f.). Whereas previously the Jewish leaders have moved against him, he now moves against them, not with the weapons of the warrior, the teacher or the wonder-worker, but paradoxically of the one for whom it is divinely ordained to suffer and to die. The earlier part of the Gospel consists of a varied collection of stories relating to different facets of Jesus' ministry, his controversies with the Jewish authorities, his teaching activity and his mighty works. Now this relative diffuseness gives way to a massive concentration on the theme of his passion as willed by God. It is, however, a mistake to think of 8:27–10:45 as mainly an exposition of the Person of Christ in isolation. The Evangelist is no speculative theologian interested in high doctrine of christology for its own sake. Rather he is an adventurous Christian who here makes his distinctive contribution to the life of the Church of his day by portraying Christ in the company of his group of disciples, seeking to draw them out and lead them on, in the face of their persistent protestations, to recognition of the truth that the cross God willed for the Master and which he alone in the first place knew how to endure, presents an inescapable call to his followers to travel the *via crucis* also. His disciples, in particular the Twelve (9:35; 10:32) and their leading spokesmen like Peter (8:32f.; 9:2–5; 10:28) or the sons of Zebedee (9:2, 38;

10:35–41), have a long hard apprenticeship to go through in renunciation, disciplined service, and humility before God's mission in Jesus is fulfilled.

Previous to this division of the Gospel, Jesus' divine authority has been enclosed also in his teaching and mighty works. Both teaching and mighty works the Evangelist has construed as different modes of the same metaphorical language, which conceals the mystery of the kingdom's presence and power in, with and around Jesus, requires the eyes of faith to pierce the veil, and so shows up the blindness of the world for what it is. Hence the 'secret', which has been given such prominence in Jesus' repeated commands to silence, has checked all interpretations of the miracle-stories as propaganda for a mighty wonder-worker and all notions that God's action in Jesus could simply be viewed by everyone as a worldly spectacle. Moreover the 'secret' has imposed a 'not yet' upon the reader of the Gospel and has kept him waiting toward the full disclosure. Now in 8:27–10:45 the disclosure does come. The invitation to faith becomes an invitation to learn what faith in Jesus must look like *in action* in order to remain faith: it inevitably involves cross-bearing. To the open declaration that the way of the cross is the only way for Master and follower (8:32), the disciples react as the natural man inevitably reacts. Their failure now is not a failure of theoretical understanding, but a failure of nerve and courage to accept so costly a discipleship. Knowing him formerly, they really did not know him. Knowing him now with greater clarity, they really *do not want* to know. They vehemently refuse to tolerate the thought that obedience to God's will must mean forsaking their worldly securities and their worldly ambitions for both Jesus and themselves, and taking a road of peril, obscurity, and sacrifice, which by their own earthly standards seems altogether unlikely to achieve anything, least of all to win victory for God's purpose. 'The Marcan narrative becomes at this point virtually an impressive sermon addressed to the reader' (Rawlinson, p. 108). It is a 'sermon' different in shape and structure from the preaching of the apostles, but it sounds the same note and might almost be regarded as a *midrash* on 1 C. 1:21–24: 'For since, in the wisdom of God, the world did not know God through wisdom, it pleased God through the folly of what we preach to save those who believe. For Jews demand signs and Greeks seek wisdom, but we preach Christ crucified, a stumbling-block to Jews and folly to Gentiles, but to those who are called, both Jews and Greeks, Christ the power of God and the wisdom of God.'

It has long been recognised that the episode of Caesarea Philippi and Peter's confession (8:27–9:1) stands as a watershed in the Gospel. But is it a *biographical* turning-point? Many have so viewed it, holding that not only this great crisis in Jesus' ministry but also the ensuing sayings and incidents which occur during Jesus' fateful journey to Jerusalem are firmly based historically and stem indeed from Petrine reminiscence. Now Peter did confess Jesus as the Christ, and Jesus did rebuke him (see notes below). But it is another thing to maintain that in structuring his Gospel Mark himself looked upon and wanted to recollect Caesarea Philippi and what happened there as the great *past* historical hinge between the two sides of Jesus' ministry: pre-Caesarea Philippi when he went unrecognised, and post-Caesarea Philippi when he was recognised for the *first* time. As a man of practical concern for the life of the Church in his time, Mark appears in fact primarily to offer in 8:27–9:1 a paradigm of how faith, whenever and wherever it does recognise who Jesus is, must express itself in a sacrificial following of the Master. Those who support the biographical approach have generally tended to pay insufficient heed to the difference between tradition and redaction. Consequently they have here stressed very heavily the decisiveness of the confession of Peter to the comparative neglect of how in Mark it is not the confession that functions positively for Mark, but instead its radical overthrow by the word about the coming suffering and rejection of the Son of man. They have then gone on to explain Peter's confession as the end-result of a gradual process by which those disciples, who must have followed him in the first instance because they were impressed by his greatness, became more and more convinced that he was indeed the Messiah and the one to fulfil the ancient prophecies (see e.g. Taylor, p. 375). But where is the evidence of this steady progress in understanding culminating in Peter's words? Does not the picture arise from a modern estimate of the psychological probabilities in the situation of Jesus and his disciples? Certainly in Mark's Gospel there is not a word about any preparation of the disciples for their call. It is in fact the blindness of the disciples that reaches its height in 8:1–9, 14–21, to be followed by a story that shows how only a miracle of God can open blind eyes, a miracle that has not yet happened for Peter obviously, according to 8:33.

The materials of 8:27–10:52 have for the most part come from the tradition, and while a solid historical substratum no doubt underlies many of the sayings and incidents, the preaching and catechetical interests of the Church as well as the editorial purpose of the Evangelist appear to have played their part in the formulation of the section. From what has been said above, we may judge that the Evangelist thought of the section first and foremost less as a faithful account of the past than as a word in season, or indeed a sermon, to the Church of his own day: in short that his interests were rather less historical than expository (see Rawlinson, p. 110).

Son of Man

The designation 'Son of man' has appeared twice before in Mark (2:10, 28), but now it comes much more to the forefront (8:31; 9:31; 10:33; cf. also 8:38; 9:9; 10:45). In Mark as in Matthew and Luke it occurs only on the lips of Jesus as a self-designation. The designation, which in Hebrew and Aramaic means simply 'man' or 'individual man' (cf. Ps. 8:4; Ezek. 2:1 etc.), is used very frequently in the Gospels, sometimes in sayings referring to the Son of man's returning in glory and for judgment at the end of the age, sometimes in sayings connected with the passion of Jesus, sometimes in statements about the earthly Jesus and his lot. Beginning from the premise that Son of man is an apocalyptic title describing the heavenly figure who will come to judge the world, some scholars have argued that Jesus cannot have spoken of the Son of man at all, mainly on the ground *either* that only after Easter and on the basis of the resurrection appearances did the Church identify him with the heavenly Son of man, and as a result the title infiltrated many different strands of the Gospel tradition (e.g. H. M. Teeple, *JBL* 84 (1965), p. 236; N. Perrin, pp. 164–99); *or* that Jesus' use of an apocalyptic title like Son of man would be quite incompatible with his authentic and *unapocalyptic* message of the kingdom of God (Vielhauer, *ZThK* 60 (1963), pp. 133ff.). But against any such radical conclusion stands the incontrovertible fact that outside the sayings of Jesus, the name Son of man has vanished from the usage of the Church almost without trace (see only the dubious exceptions of Ac. 7:56, where there is an alternative reading 'Son of God', and Rev. 1:13 where 'one like a son of man' is hardly a title but a piece of descriptive *OT* symbolism; cf. Ezek. 1:26; Dan. 7:13). That

the term is not predicated of Jesus and finds no place in the confessions of the Church (unlike 'Christ' and 'Son of God') is very
strong evidence indeed for its authenticity as a self-description
employed by Jesus.

Other scholars again hold that only those sayings which
announce the return for judgment of the heavenly Son of man
are authentic, but in all such apocalyptic statements Jesus *is in
fact referring to a heavenly being other than himself* (see e.g. Bultmann,
HST, pp. 121ff.; Todt; Hahn). This hypothesis also means subscribing to the view that it was belief in the resurrection of Jesus
that led to the identification of Jesus and the Son of man and so to
the extensive placing of the term on his own lips even in non-
apocalyptic sayings. But the Achilles' heel of such a position is
that one might have expected the rather sensational post-Easter
discovery that Jesus *is* the Son of man to receive explicit formulation in the Church's confessions. It does not do so. We nowhere
read 'Jesus is the Son of man' or 'I am the Son of man' or even
'Jesus, the Son of man', or 'I, the Son of man'. Instead, according
to the Gospel tradition, the term is used with absolute consistency
in the third person as a piece of self-description. Besides, the
statements of Mk 14:62; Mt. 5:21ff.; 11:11; Lk. 11:20; 17:20f.
seem to militate against the view that in apocalyptic sayings
regarding the Son of man Jesus was referring to a coming heavenly
figure greater than himself.

On the likely assumption, therefore, that Jesus himself was
originally responsible for taking up the term as a self-description,
the majority of interpreters have favoured accepting the class of
apocalyptic statements as the most probably genuine and have
sought the background for and the explanation of Jesus' use of
Son of man in Jewish apocalyptic literature, particularly in Dan.
7. Son of man terminology occurs outside of Daniel in *1 En.* 37–71,
the so-called *Similitudes of Enoch*, and in *4 Ezra*. The latter work
is most likely post-Christian, so its picture of the Son of man
rising from the sea to destroy his enemies is not relevant to Jesus'
use of the title. Similarly the *Similitudes of Enoch* have come to us
only from very late Ethiopic manuscripts as part of the canonical
literature of the Abyssinian Church. Also we are now aware
that they were unknown at Qumran (where the rest of the Enochic
writings were treasured), and it is a fair presumption that they
were not yet written. Accordingly, only Dan. 7 is left as a possible
source of Jesus' usage, and it is generally held that he picked up

the Son of man terminology from Dan. 7:13 and applied it to himself as the one who would come on the clouds of heaven for the final judgment, while at the same time he allowed it to refer to himself in the course of his earthly ministry as Messiah. But on this view of Son of man as a high apocalyptic-messianic title on Jesus' lips, what is then to be made of the strange combination of heavenly glory with rejection and death, for example, in the threefold prediction of the passion in Mark: 'The Son of man must suffer'? The case put forward for the notion of a *suffering Messiah* in pre-Christian Judaism (see e.g. Jeremias *SG*, chapters 3–4) has by no means been established (see Hooker, *JS*). Again, aside from a few residual traces surviving no doubt from the early Palestinian stage of the Church's existence (Ac. 3:26; 4:27, 30), the Isaianic theme of the Suffering Servant appears to have had scarcely any impact on the Church's christology, nor can it easily be shown that it had an impact upon Jesus himself. From a quite different angle, the difficulty of those statements which connect the Son of man with suffering and death, or with earthly lowliness and obscurity, would be overcome if 'Son of man' could be taken in such cases as a circumlocution for 'I'. There is some evidence to suggest that under certain conditions this was possible, just as the Aramaic expression 'that man' could mean 'I, the speaker' (see G. Vermes in Appendix to Black, *ARA*, pp. 320ff. Note also the shift from the 'Son of man' in Lk. 12:8 and Mk 8:38 to 'I' in Mt. 10:32). Possibly, however, as many would hold, there is no need to look beyond the book of Daniel for background evidence of how Jesus could have associated the heavenly glory of the Son of man with suffering and death. In Dan. 7 a whole catena of ideas surrounds the imagery of the heavenly figure who comes with the clouds to the Ancient of Days, notably the thought that the figure is synonymous with 'the saints of the Most High', the righteous remnant of Israel who receive the kingdom and are thus vindicated only after enduring a great tribulation (Dan. 7: 21f.; cf. 7:25). Founding upon this, as the one who summed up in himself the 'faithful Israel', Jesus could have spoken not only of the coming glory of the Son of man but of his suffering and death as the divinely decreed prelude.

There is another leading view of the background of the term 'Son of man' and of its meaning on the lips of Jesus. It has been argued that only those sayings which refer to earthly lowliness (e.g. Mt. 8:20 = Lk. 7:58) are authentic utterances of Jesus (see

especially Schweizer, *GNM*, pp. 168ff.; also *Jesus*, pp. 18ff.), and
that Jesus' usage derives from the book of Ezekiel where the
prophet is called Son of man some eighty-seven times. It is as the
'son of man' identified with men, that he has to undergo suffering
for the sake of his people (4:9ff.; 5:1ff.; etc.). On the basis of
Ezekiel's experience and passages from the Jewish apocryphal
and pseudepigraphical literature, like Wis. 2–5, Jesus believed
his destiny was to consummate in himself the sufferings of the
prophets and martyred righteous of Israel. As *the* faithful witness
he would have understood that he had a supreme part to play in
God's final judgment, speaking for or against men before God,
according to their positive or negative response to his call. With
Jesus during his earthly ministry, therefore, the title Son of man
would have been primarily a title of lowliness and humiliation,
only redolent also now of everything that his ministry and message
implied of the nearness of God's coming judgment. Later the
Church elevated Jesus himself to the position of Judge, and spoke
of the approach of the heavenly Son of man. Accordingly, the
Son of man sayings which manifest a strong apocalyptic trend
may be attributed to Christian prophets and preachers.

In an article called 'Exit the Apocalyptic Son of Man' (*NTS* 18
(1971–2), pp. 243ff.), R. Leivestad has argued rather persuasively
for a position akin to Schweizer's. He holds that the titular application of the term 'Son of man' in pre-Christian Jewish apocalyptic
literature has not been established, that Jesus did use it as a self-
designation, but *without any titular force and simply as a periphrasis for
'I'*. It denotes his identification with the sons of men. 'The Son of
man is he who is a friend of sinners. The Son of man is he who
came to serve and give his life. The self-designation is an evidence
of his self-dedication to men' (Leivestad, op. cit., p. 267).

Even from a brief description of representative views it is
apparent that, in our present state of knowledge, the vexed
problem of the Son of man as self-description of Jesus has not
yielded to any definite resolution. Given the diversity of roles
or functions of the Son of man in the various classes of sayings
it is hard to avoid the conclusion that the Church has modified,
revised, or even framed at least a number of these sayings in one
or other of the groups. So far as historical research into the earthly
ministry of Jesus is concerned, therefore, it is a reasonable axiom
of procedure not to let the designation Son of man, hedged about
as it is with such great uncertainty, determine our picture of Jesus

of Nazareth, but to allow more readily verifiable data from other strands of the Gospel tradition to inform our understanding of what Son of man might mean in its various contexts.

How does Mark regard the term Son of man? As used in Mark, the title, it is frequently maintained, has the same representative or corporate character it had in Daniel. As *the* final representative of the righteous nucleus of Israel, Jesus enters his triumph as the leader who suffers for and with the people of 'the saints of the Most High', the elect community. Now it is true that in 8: 27–10:52 Mark is much concerned to proclaim the necessary continuity between Jesus' way of the cross and the cross-bearing of his disciples, and the essential unity of Jesus and his community in tribulation and affliction. But it cannot be proven that Mark had the Danielic imagery in mind, and in any case it is fair to claim once more that it is less the title Son of man that illumines the theme developed in 8:27–10:52 than the theme of the solidarity of Jesus with his followers in suffering that illumines the title. Again, the opinion has gained ground of late that it is the element of authority that links all usages of the term together in Mark (Hooker, *SMM*; Martin, pp. 191f.) As the all-powerful Son of man authorised by God, Jesus exercises the divine prerogative of forgiving sins in his earthly ministry and confidently expects in submitting to the enemies who deny his prerogative that his authority will become universal when he comes in power and exultation. But, on the contrary, Mark's problem is *not* to establish the *heavenly* authority of the Son of man in spite of denials of it. Rather it is to protect the truth first of all that the divine authority belongs to the 'man' who identifies himself with all the sons of men, and so is a 'secret' that cannot be understood; and, secondly, to show how great a stumbling-block it is to the world when the 'secret' is unfolded that the God whose authority resides in Jesus permits himself in lowliness and humiliation to be rejected. It is in the interest of preserving this message that in 8: 27–10:52 Mark is at pains to suppress all false and premature notions of heavenly glory and victory (8:30, 33; 9:9, 11–13; 10:17–22, 23–27, 28–31, 35–45). The same interest may be served for the Evangelist by such a saying as 8:38 (cf. 14:62) in which the shift from 'I' to 'Son of man' may suggest not an unbroken continuity between the heavenly Son of man coming in glory and the one who has been Son of man *in that sense* all along, but the supreme paradox that the promise of God's victory comes through the lowly one at whose call to be lowly and insignificant men take offence.

A HARD APPRENTICESHIP FOR THE DISCIPLES AND THEIR LEADING REPRESENTATIVE 8:27-33

It is very difficult to reconstruct the tradition behind these verses. Jesus' words of rebuke to Peter in verse 33 would appear to be an indisputably historical trait, as Karl Holl's very pertinent question suggests: 'Who from the primitive community would have dared to call the revered Kephas Satan?' No response of Jesus to Peter's confession in verse 29 is recorded (contrast his positive response in Mt. 16:13-23), and possibly verse 33 represented the original response. At any rate the charge to secrecy in verse 30 is almost certainly a Marcan editorial insertion. Marcan editorial touches may further be discernible at the beginning of verses 31 and 32 (**he began to teach them; he said this plainly**. See Schweizer, *GNM*, p. 166), and it is also doubtful whether in the saying of verse 32 Jesus would have referred so explicitly or precisely to the resurrection (see notes). While presumably Peter must have said something like what he says in verse 29 (**You are the Christ**) to occasion the rebuke of verse 33, Jesus' placing of the question in verse 29 (**who do you say that I am?**) would appear to be somewhat artificial, inasmuch as the Jesus of history was apparently very reticent about the use of titles. The question and answers of verses 27-28 are reminiscent of 6.14-15 and may be modelled on it. Since the Evangelist himself has only a vague interest in and knowledge of geographical details, the location of the episode in the neighbourhood of Caesarea Philippi is likely to have been a well-established datum of the tradition. All in all the narrative of 8:27-33 gives a strong impression of resting on a solid historical foundation, although once again we have to scrutinise closely what Mark himself is making of it.

27-28. the villages of Caesarea Philippi: the territory of the city-state of Caesarea Philippi, rebuilt by Herod Philip in honour of Tiberius. Its previous name of Paneas survives today as Banyas. A grotto of Pan stood nearby and the cult of the emperor was practised there. It is unlikely that either Mark or his readers would have thought of an implied contrast between the false gods of the pagan cults and the true agent of God, Jesus. **on the way he asked his disciples:** the fact that the incident takes place **on the way** may signify for Mark that only those who 'follow' Jesus on the road he has to travel (in 10:32f. the road to Jerusalem and death) can really learn of him. In Jewish practice it was the rabbi who was questioned by his pupils. Here Jesus questions his disciples. Here as elsewhere in Mark it is Jesus who initiates dialogue and does all he can to lead men on to the truth about himself. On verse 28 see notes on 6:14-15.

29-30. he asked them, 'But who do you say that I am?' with the question of verse 27 (**who do** *men* **say that I am?**) and the answers of the generality of men brought forward by the disciples in verse 28 the discussion has moved in the realm of opinions, theories, and labels. At this level the people are interested but uninvolved spectators who in effect dispose of Jesus' claim upon their lives by labelling him in advance without encountering him. But in verse 29 a distinction is now drawn between the people generally and the disciples. Faced with Jesus himself they are put on the spot and constrained to come to a decision that immediately and directly involves 'saving life or losing it' (cf. verse 35). The singling out of the disciples introduces the reader at once to the prominent theme of 8:27-10:52, Jesus' instructions to his followers on what discipleship means. **Peter answered him, 'You are the Christ':** in the *Gospel of Thomas* Peter replies to a similar question of Jesus that he is like a righteous angel; Matthew compares him to a philosopher, and Thomas acknowledges that he is unable to say what Jesus is like. A later apocryphal passage such as this no doubt presents a gnosticising interpretation of the Synoptic materials, and sheds no light on the original event, but it does show how freely the tradition could be adapted to suit particular theological perspectives. Here Peter calls Jesus **the Christ,** i.e. the Anointed One (Hebrew *māšiaḥ* = Messiah). In the time of Jesus, Jewish messianic expectation was fluid and varied. The Qumran sect awaited not only a lay or royal Messiah of the house of David but a priestly Messiah of the house of Aaron, as well as an eschatological prophet who would figure largely in the last days. On the lips of Peter the title 'Christ' would have referred to the messianic Son of David (cf. Mk 10:47; 11:10; 12:35). The coming of a Davidic Messiah, who would restore the political fortunes of Israel and establish her national supremacy over the world, was a widespread hope (Pss. 18; 78:65-72; Am. 9:11-12; Isa. 9, 11; Zech. 4:6-10; cf. *Ps. Sol.* 17:5-8, 23-28, 32). The political implications of the title probably explain why Jesus does not appear to have appropriated it during his ministry and why (if verse 33 formed the original response to verse 29) he severely reprimanded Peter for using it.

However, we must distinguish between tradition and redaction. Whatever Peter's confession may have meant in the setting of Jesus' ministry or within the Church that transmitted the tradition, it is important to ask also about Mark's standpoint. According to T. J. Weeden (*ZNW* 59 (1968), pp. 145–58; see Introduction, pp. 49ff.), Peter appears here for Mark as the mouthpiece of those heretical opponents in his congregation who as charismatic leaders claim to be following Jesus' example as thaumaturge, in which case Peter is acknowledging Jesus as a 'divine man' or wonder-worker. But with Mark the title 'Christ' is not a disreputable one. While he exercises a good deal of reserve toward it, he does not spurn its use (see 1:1; 14:62). Peter's fault, therefore, in this section of Mark is not that his understanding and confession are unorthodox or heretical. Rather they are altogether too orthodox, since after all 'Christ' was a long-hallowed designation. So Peter and the rest have to be taught that Jesus is not exhausted by the old and the orthodox, and that they have a long way to go in discipleship before they comprehend the sheer newness and unexpectedness of God's lowly way of suffering with the world in Jesus. **and he charged them to tell no one about him:** the word **charged** is a strong one in Greek, carrying the sense of 'strict warning' or even 'denunciation' (cf. 1:25; 3:12; 4:39; 8: 32–33; 9:25; 10:13, 48). The stern command to secrecy after Peter's confession stands for Mark as a bridge between Peter's outmoded standpoint and the new divine truth of the way of the Son of man, a truth that remains scandalous to the natural man with his worldly desires and can only be revealed to faith (verse 33).

31. he began to teach them that . . . : the Greek verb **began** here does not indicate for the Evangelist a chronological turning-point at which Jesus now taught in this way *for the first time* (contrast Mt. 16:21). The verb is characteristically Marcan, occurring approximately twenty-six times (e.g. 1:45; 2:23; 4:1; 5:17, 20; 6:2, 7, 34, 55; etc.), most frequently simply as a redundant auxiliary verb with no special force. If it has any force for Mark here, it would tend rather to denote the new and unprecedented content of Jesus' teaching. The teaching is expressed not as a direct saying of Jesus, but indirect speech (**began to teach them that . . .**) and reads like a Church statement of faith, possibly developed from a less detailed original saying about the suffering and rejec-

tion of the Son of man. It is not at all improbable that, in the light
of the prophets and the suffering righteous of Israel before him,
Jesus foresaw disaster for himself. While **the elders and the chief
priests and the scribes** may only be a way of referring to the
Jewish Sanhedrin, it seems likely that Jesus' basic saying would
have been confined to the familiar Jewish expression, **suffer
many things,** and that the specifics reflect the language of the
Christian community. This would apply even more to the prediction, **after three days rise again:** whereas it is not impossible
that Jesus could have expected an ultimately victorious outcome,
it is unlikely that he would have prophesied his resurrection so
precisely, since then the complete bewilderment of the disciples on
Good Friday and their continuing doubts despite the Easter appearances would be incomprehensible. The difficulty is hardly
eradicated by the suggestion that the phrase **after three days**
(elsewhere 'on the third day', cf. Mt. 16:21; 17:22; 20:19; Lk. 9:
22; 18:33) might have meant for Jesus simply 'after a short interval' (cf. Hos. 6:2). **the Son of man must suffer:** the injunction
to silence in verse 30 has paved the way for the new designation
'Son of man'. What is to be said by Jesus and about him cannot
be exhausted in old formulations and titles like 'Christ'. The designation 'Son of man' was mysterious enough and probably unfamiliar enough to protect Mark's interest in the 'secret', and to
provide at the same time a vehicle for communication of the truth
that God surrenders himself, through Jesus' identification with the
sons of men, to suffering and defeat. When it is said that **the Son
of man must suffer,** this **must** does not rule out all freedom of
choice and decision on Jesus' part (cf. Mk 14:35f.). Neither for
Jesus nor the Church nor Mark was it the necessity imposed on
Jesus by a blind fate or even an incomprehensible 'divine must'
applied to the horrible and puzzling event of the passion. The
'must' is related to Scripture, not to particular passages like the
Servant Songs of Isaiah or Dan. 7 or the 'stone' passage of Ps.
118:22, but to a whole set of ideas concerning the persecution of
God's prophets and ambassadors by an impenitent people, and
for Mark it would have to do not with *proving* anything from *OT*
texts but with the will of God expressed in Scripture. But for the
Evangelist it also has an element of *futurity*—not until the Son of
man has gone the whole way through suffering and death can the
essential paradox be revealed that God's victorious purpose is
achieved through lowliness and humiliation.

32-33. he said this plainly: a statement which underlines the crucial importance Mark attaches to the teaching of verse 31. **began to rebuke him:** no longer is Peter blind in regard to Jesus' metaphorical language. The word of the Son of man has been declared openly, and Peter indignantly refuses to accept that the way of rejection and death can possibly be God's way. **turning and seeing his disciples:** this comment is peculiar to Mark. It includes all the disciples and not only Peter in the reproof that follows, and might well have reminded Mark's readers that the community is not pure and perfect, but a company of frail people continually dependent on God's help. **get behind me, Satan . . . of men:** in Greek the expression **get behind me** probably means 'get out of my sight' rather than 'follow me' (i.e. 'occupy your rightful position as a follower and do not try to be the leader'). In the course of his ministry, Jesus' rebuke to Peter would probably have suggested that Peter had sought to *tempt* him to assume a political-messianic role. For Mark it possibly denotes only Peter's radical opposition to God's will for Jesus and his disciples. It is as one opposed to God's will that Peter 'acts for Satan' and regards things still from a human point of view ('you are not on the side of God, but of men'). What it means to regard things from God's point of view is elucidated by Mark in verses 34ff.

SACRIFICIAL 'FOLLOWING' THE PRELUDE TO VICTORY **8:34-9:1**

This section consists of a number of separate sayings of Jesus no doubt connected together in the tradition on a topical basis and possibly associated before Mark with the 'Son of man' saying of verse 31 (cf. Jn 12:24-26). Mark himself was presumably responsible for the linking words of verse 34*a* (cf. 2:4; 2:15; 3:13).

34. he called to him the multitude with his disciples: with this Marcan transition, the crucial significance for the Evangelist of the saying on the Son of man's suffering and rejection becomes quite clear. The good news that goes forth to all the world (**the multitude**) embodies the call to a discipleship that treads the Master's own way of sacrifice. **if any man . . . and follow me:** possibly the form of the saying here represents an expansion of the more ancient and shorter form of Mt. 10:38. The Greek word for **deny** in **deny himself** occurs also of Peter's 'denial' of Jesus in 14:72, where it denotes that he 'disowns' Jesus. To 'disown oneself' in the present context means forsaking one's selfish

pretensions and worldly securities for the sake of Jesus and his call
to obedience to God's will. We cannot be at all sure whether the
original saying would have included the summons to the disciple
to **take up his cross.** Though the idea of cross-bearing is not
found in the older rabbinic literature, the sight of a condemned
criminal carrying part of his cross to the place of execution by
crucifixion, according to Roman requirements, was presumably
familiar enough in Jesus' time, and so Jesus conceivably used this
image as a metaphor for self-denying obedience. On the other
hand this method of execution was normally reserved for *criminals*,
and Jesus would not necessarily have expected death by crucifixion
at the hands of the Romans. Consequently we may suspect that
the present formulation of the saying presupposes Jesus' own cross.
What is not in doubt is that the command to cross-bearing, i.e. in
a quite concrete sense to 'preparedness to die', would not have
been laid on the Marcan community as an impossible imposition,
but only in the light of the inspiring and empowering reality of
Jesus' self-sacrificial death and all that it implied.

35-37. For whoever would save ... will save it: again
there is some doubt about the original form of this saying (verse
35). Probably Jesus' utterance did not contain the words **for my
sake and the gospel's,** but in a straightforward parallelism expressed the truth that loyalty to God's rule (i.e. 'for the sake of
the kingdom'; cf. Lk. 18:29) of necessity involved a radical reversal of normal human values or standards. The words **for my
sake** occur in Mt. 16:25 but not in Lk. 17:33 or Jn 12:25, and
may have been added in the missionary context when the Church
wanted to explain to new converts that obedience was always
obedience *for Jesus' sake.* There is some textual warrant for the
omission of **for my sake** from Mark, but it should be allowed to
stand as the correct reading since it enshrines the typically Marcan
nexus between the way of Jesus Christ and the way of the disciple.
The words **and the gospel's** are peculiar to Mark. There is little
doubt that the phrase 'for the sake of the gospel' is Mark's own
addition and is of the highest significance for his own conception.
He thereby demonstrates the substantial unity of the gospel
preached by the Church and the good news brought by Jesus,
and suggests that the call to self-negating discipleship that accompanies Jesus' message continues with unabated force in the days
of the Church's missionary proclamation. Mark therefore specially
stresses the *ongoing* risk of belonging to the Christian faith in the

world (L. E. Keck, *NTS* 12 (1965–6), p. 357). To take the risk
of faith for the sake of Jesus and the gospel is to link oneself with
that obedience to God's will that emancipates men from all worldly
threats, even the threat of death itself (**will save his life**). To
protect life and hoard it for selfish ends as if one had no accountability to God or fellow-man (**whoever would save his life**) is
to deprive oneself of both the joy and hope that God intended
(**will lose it**). The Greek word for **life** in verse 35 (*psychē* =
Hebrew *nepeš*, cf. verses 36 and 37) means the animating principle
in both men and animals, and there is no question here of a distinction between 'life' and 'soul' or of an implied contrast between
the life of the body in the material world (which must be abandoned) and the life of the 'soul' or 'spirit'. Nor is the *reward* of
eternal life hereafter offered for those who are loyal in this life.
Rather the sole motivation is that everything is to be done here
and now in the world *for Jesus' sake and the gospel's*. **For what does
it profit . . . forfeit his life?** (verse 36): initially this saying was
most likely a general observation on the human condition. Men
strive endlessly for material success, but all in vain since death
must come soon or late to remove them from their worldly possessions (cf. Lk. 12:15–20). But in its Marcan context it drives
home the lesson that the *life* to which the gospel summons is one
of self-negation or renunciation in obedience to God's will, and
not to surrender to one's own earthly desires and aspirations.
what can a man give in return for his life? Nothing a man
can do will redeem a life that has followed the wrong norms and
been directed to the wrong goals. For the Christian community
this series of sayings would have had profound eschatological import. The time in which the summons to self-negating discipleship
to Christ goes forth is the 'last time' and the world and worldly
sanctions are passing away. This explains the addition to the
section of the saying on the Son of man's coming (verse 38), with
its orientation to the impending judgment.

38. The Q form of this saying appears to have been 'whoever
denies me before men, I will also deny before my Father who is
in heaven' (Mt. 10:33; cf. Lk. 12:9). Another form occurs in Lk.
9:26, 'For whoever is ashamed of me and of my words, of him will
the Son of man be ashamed when he comes in his glory and the
glory of the Father and of the holy angels.' In Mark the saying
reads **when he comes in the glory of** *his* **Father,** and this is
the only place where **Son of man** is allied with sonship to God.

Whatever the precise form of Jesus' original saying, it is accordingly unlikely that he was responsible for this combination. Again, **angels** are associated with the Son of man in *1 En.* 61:10; cf. Mt. 13:41; 25:31; Jn 1:51; with the heavenly Lord Jesus in 2 Th. 1:7; with God and Christ in 1 Tim. 3:13; with the Father and the coming Lord Jesus Christ in 1 Th. 3:13; and with the throne of God's glory in Rev. 4:5 (cf. Rev. 8:2). Apparently the saying as it stands in Mark has been overlaid with ideas popular in apocalyptic circles in the Church (cf. Lk. 9:26, and contrast the Q form in Mt. 10:33 and Lk. 12:9. See Taylor, p. 383; Schweizer, *GNM*, p. 178). We observed above (p. 209) that in sayings predicting the coming of the Son of man in judgment it is quite unlikely that Jesus was referring to a heavenly figure other than himself. But by the same token the statement in Mk 8:38 does not clearly or directly identify the earthly Jesus with the heavenly Son of man (**whoever is ashamed of** *me . . .* **of him will** *the Son of man also* **be ashamed, when he comes**). While the Evangelist could not have contemplated a differentiation between Jesus and the coming Son of man, he may have thought of the form of words here (**me** and **my** in reference to the earthly Jesus as speaker in the first part of the saying) as retaining the secret that Jesus' authority lies hidden in his lowliness. The saying concerns the man who is **ashamed** of Jesus and his **words** (or 'his own' = 'his followers', there being some textual evidence for the omission of 'words'), and for Mark what occasions shame with Jesus is not his lordliness but his friendship toward sinners and his lowly identification and solidarity with men (see 2:10; 3:31–35; 6:3). Significantly the words **this adulterous and sinful generation** are peculiar to Mark's version of 8:38. But they occur (albeit not quite verbatim) in the Q form of the saying concerning the demand for a sign (Mt. 12:39; cf. Lk. 11:29 'wicked generation'). We may suppose that here Mark has in mind that what causes offence in Jesus is that the one who faces men with life's ultimate decision is the one who makes no concession whatever to any demand for a spectacular sign, but goes the way of suffering and death. The supreme paradox is that this lowly one, who confronts men with the choice between the authentic life of discipleship and the inauthentic existence of self-concern, will occupy the place of power and glory with God in God's final judgment of the world (Leivestad, *NTS* 18 (1971–2), p. 266).

1. he said to them: this recurrent Marcan formula leads into an originally independent saying. The expectation of the kingdom of God and the expectation of the coming of the Son of man belong to separate layers of the Gospel tradition (although the two sets of ideas are by no means so incompatible as to justify the opinion that if the expectation of the kingdom of God was at the heart of Jesus' message, which is scarcely to be doubted, then he could not have spoken of himself as the Son of man (cf. P. Vielhauer, 'Gottesreich und Menschensohn in der Verkündigung Jesu', *FGD*, pp. 51–79). On the assumption that this is a genuine utterance of Jesus, the problem arises, in the light of the non-arrival of the kingdom, that in his prediction of its impending advent Jesus must apparently have been in error. Numerous interpretations that might take us out of the difficulty have been proposed. (a) The perfect participle of the verb 'having come' has been taken to indicate that Jesus here promises that men will shortly realise that the kingdom of God *had actually and fully come* in Jesus' earthly ministry. But the grammatical structure of the sentence and the notion embedded in other Gospel materials (e.g. the parables of the mustard seed and the leaven, etc.) that the kingdom is present in Jesus only as a 'hidden mystery' and in an anticipatory way, make this unconvincing. (b) The expression **taste death** has been thought to refer to a spiritual death from which the disciples are offered exemption. But the word **before** is then very difficult to explain, and **taste death** is most probably a Semitic idiom meaning 'to die' (cf. Heb. 2:9; 2 Esd. 6:26). (c) Suggestions that the saying refers to the elect community in which God's rule will be established (the Church?), the bestowal of the Spirit at Pentecost or the resurrection are hardly borne out by the most ancient gospel traditions. (d) The view that in speaking of the kingdom here Jesus is in fact pointing to the transfiguration is quite implausible (although *Mark himself* may have seen a connexion between the two). 'If Jesus solemnly affirmed that some at least of his hearers would survive his prediction by one week he was uttering ridiculous bathos' (Barrett, p. 85).

Accordingly, the interpretation that Jesus, if he spoke these words, was predicting in the most comprehensive way the final consummation of God's purpose in the *not too distant future* (some of his hearers would live to see it) should be allowed to stand. If that leaves no option but to think of Jesus as 'in error', his 'error' was that only of one who more even than all the prophets of Israel took with ultimate seriousness the intervention of God in human affairs and the impinging of the future God would bring on the present moment of men's existence.

But whether the saying in its Marcan form is in fact to be traced back to Jesus is questionable. Normally Jesus does not appear to have been concerned with the exact 'when' of the kingdom (cf. Mk 13:32–37; Mt. 25:1–13; Lk. 12:35–46; 17:20–22, 25–30), and the foreshortening of the eschatological perspective here may have arisen in a Church context where the aim was to stimulate hope of the impending end. The saying is a puzzling one, and the issue of its authenticity remains open. No doubt the Evangelist for his part regarded it as a confirmation of 8:38 and as stressing that the final divine judgment is imminent, so imminent that its force is experienced already in the obscure and repressed activity of the one destined for the cross. The *not yet* that figures prominently in 8:27–9:1 agrees with Mark's conception of the secret. The moment of final revelation has *not yet* come, not until Jesus' passion and death are accomplished. The disciples have *not yet* learned who Jesus is or wherein *life* consists, not until as true followers of his way they too have served their apprenticeship in cross-bearing. The future of God's rule in its fullness has *not yet* come, but it is near enough to transform the present. In the story of the transfiguration (9:2–8) the reader is permitted an anticipatory glimpse of God's future triumph in Christ, but the *not yet* reappears in the account of the descent from the mountain (9:9–13) and testifies once more that only in the suffering Son of man and those disciples who travel the same road reside the hope and the promise of that triumph.

THE GLORY OF THE SON OF GOD CONFIRMED 9:2–8

From the point of view of the history of the tradition, the story of the transfiguration presents serious difficulties. It is commonly held to have been originally a resurrection-story which was eventually read back, as here in Mark, into the earthly ministry of Jesus (see e.g. Bultmann, *HST*, pp. 259ff.). But against the theory is the fact that this report and its material content, the presence of Elijah and Moses, the cloud and the voice from heaven, Peter's curious words in 9:5, is quite unlike any other Easter appearance-story. Moreover, whereas in the Easter appearance-stories the word of the risen Jesus is paramount, here Jesus is silent. Others regard the narrative as entirely legendary or symbolic, a credal confession in story-form of the divinity of Jesus, or of the heavenly glory of the

Son of man in his parousia (e.g. Lohmeyer, p. 175). That the story contains symbolic features, as the presence of Elijah and Moses on the stage and numerous other data suggest, is undeniable. Nevertheless, it has been maintained that the story does have a historical basis in an objective manifestation of the divine *glory* in Jesus, or at least in a visionary experience of the disciples in Jesus' presence (Cranfield, p. 294; Taylor, pp. 386ff.). Those who take this line generally explain the event in terms of parallels from the 'luminous glory appearing to have transfigured the faces of the saints in ecstatic prayer' (Rawlinson, p. 119), or from the visions of the mystics. Attempts to authenticate the event by the study of the psychological phenomena involved in mystical visions no doubt have a certain appeal for the modern reader, but they scarcely illumine the way the Evangelist himself or those who told and passed on the story before him would have looked upon it. It is in fact no longer possible to reconstruct exactly what happened on the mountain. The narrative is permeated with Jewish apocalyptic elements, and while it may go back to a visionary experience of the disciples, it has been extensively overlaid by the Church with apocalyptic symbols designed to point to the coming eschatological status of Jesus. The principle meaning of the story for Mark is considerably less obscure. Jesus has taught openly the divine necessity of the Son of man's suffering and rejection (8:31). His disciples do not yet understand—Mk 9:6 is most probably a Marcan editorial comment on their continuing blindness. But in words reminiscent of the voice from heaven at the Baptism (cf. 1:11), *God* himself now confirms Jesus as his Son and so confirms also the open teaching of 8:31 (**listen to him,** 9:7). Beyond that, the story with its fleeting glimpse of the future eschatological dignity of Jesus is a graphic reminder that God's will and God's way of suffering, rejection, and death for Jesus and his own is the only way to ultimate victory (cf. 9:9–13).

2–3. after six days: nowhere else, except in the passion story (14:1), does Mark give such a precise chronological notice as this. Probably he derived it, already attached to the story, from the tradition and considered it a useful link with the preceding section, which from his own theological standpoint is to be closely associated with the account of the transfiguration. In the original form of the story, however, the **six days** may well have alluded to Exod. 24:16 which describes Moses as having to undergo a waiting period of six days before God can approach him, or may possibly have symbolised the six days of work for man preceding the sabbath rest. **Jesus took with him Peter and James and John:** as in 5:37, Jesus calls and the selected three disciples follow. Throughout the episode everything in the action is directed specifically toward them (**transfigured before them, appeared to them, a cloud overshadowed them, they no longer saw anyone with them**), and this suits well Mark's preoccupation with the *discipleship* theme in this section. The same three are allowed in on other peak moments of Jesus' ministry (cf. 13:3 where Andrew is present as well; 14:33), and appear to have been regarded by the Evangelist as a *representative inner circle* of the disciples. **a high mountain:** attempts to identify the mountain (Mount Tabor or Mount Hermon, closer to Caesarea Philippi?) are purely speculative and of little significance. What matters here for Mark is that the mountain is the place where God reveals himself, as usual in the biblical tradition (cf. e.g. Exod. 24 and 34; 1 Kg. 18:20; 19:8, 11; Mt. 4:8; 5:1; 28:16). **he was transfigured before them:** the word **transfigured** (a rendering stemming from the Vulgate *transfiguratus est* and common since the time of Wycliffe) represents the Greek *metemorphōthē*, meaning literally 'assumed a different form'. Matthew employs the word also but associates it with the idea of Jesus' face shining like the sun (17:2). Luke omits it (perhaps because of its connexion with pagan magical transformations? see Rawlinson, p. 119), and appears to think of Jesus' face becoming radiant in ecstatic prayer (9:29). Rather more explicitly than Mark's report, therefore, those of Matthew and Luke reveal the influence of Exod. 34:29–35 ('Moses did not know that the skin of his face shone because he had been talking with God', verse 29). The concept of transfiguration or transformation, however, has its strongest roots in Jewish apocalyptic, which in some instances expected that the Jewish righteous would take on a glorious new heavenly 'form' in the end-time (e.g. *Bar.* 51:3ff.; 2 Esd. 7:97; cf. the imagery of Dan. 12:3). Paul uses the verb 'transfigured' of the transformation of believers into the spiritual likeness of Christ (Rom. 12:2; 2 C. 3:18) and thinks of the glorious body believers will be empowered to share with the exalted Christ in his parousia (Phil. 3:21; cf. 1 C. 15:43, 49, 51–53). Against this apocalyptic landscape it would appear that in Mk 8:2 what is in view is in fact the revelation of Jesus' coming eschatological triumph and glory. This is confirmed by the apocalyptic symbolism of verse 3, **and his garments**

became glistening ... could bleach them: the notion of the clothing of the glorified righteous in pure white garments is a common feature of apocalyptic works (cf. *1 En.* 62:15–16; *2 En.* 22:8; Rev. 3:4; 4:4; 7:9 etc.). The homely additional touch in Mark **as no fuller on earth could bleach them,** merely corroborates for his readers the *supernatural* glory of Jesus' status. Thus as the Son of man now moves toward rejection and death (8:31), the veil is lifted suddenly and his coming victory is momentarily in sight.

4. And there appeared ... talking to Jesus: the Greek word for **appeared** (*ōphthē*) stands for rather more than a subjective visionary experience. It is used of the appearances of the risen Jesus in 1 C. 15:3–8, and suggests a *theophany*. For Mark (and even more emphatically for Luke; see 9:31) the fact that Elijah and Moses **were talking to Jesus** implies their actual presence (cf. Mt. 17:9, where the transfiguration is interpreted more as a *vision*). The priority accorded to Elijah, who is mentioned first, **Elijah with Moses,** adumbrates the prominent place given to him in Jewish eschatological expectation from the time of Mal. 4:5f. onward. Enoch and Elijah were sometimes associated as the two who were *translated* directly from earthly to heavenly life (on Elijah see 2 Kg. 2:11; cf. 2 Esd. 6:26). Evidence concerning Moses' role in the last things is slender, although there is limited rabbinic attestation of the view that he too 'went up into heaven' together with Enoch and Elijah, and presumably this legend may have arisen from the fact that according to Dt. 34:6 the place of Moses' burial was not known (cf. the late pseudepigraphical document *Assumption of Moses*). The appearance of Elijah and Moses on the stage may therefore point to Jesus as the eschatological prophet who was destined to be taken up into heaven and to return finally in the end-time. Certainly for Mark and his readers the presence of Elijah and Moses here with Jesus would testify to the decisiveness of Jesus' coming in relation to the end that God would bring.

5–6. By the beginning of the Christian era the Festival of Booths or Tabernacles had become one of the most joyous of all Jewish festivals (Zech. 14:16–19 predicts that in the new age the nations that have survived the judgment will come to Jerusalem to observe it). At the feast huts or booths were erected to commemorate Israel's wilderness wanderings (cf. Lev. 23:39–43). While this undoubtedly constitutes the background to Peter's remark to Jesus, what exactly is intended by his puzzling offer to **make three booths, one for you and one for Moses and one for Elijah,** is not altogether clear (since it was customary to build booths anyhow at the feast). What is clear enough is that in verse 6 Mark highlights his error and lack of understanding and the continuing bewilderment of the disciples. Is Mark here countering an erroneous form of belief prevalent in his own day and is Peter's mistake that, like some of the Evangelist's contemporaries, he puts Jesus on precisely the same level as Elijah or Moses, great prophet or law-giver (each one *equally* is to have a booth? (See M. E. Thrall, *NTS* 16 (1969-70), pp. 305-17.) On the other hand the words rendered by *RSV* as **it is well that we are here** are probably better translated 'How good it is to be here!' In that case the likelier view of Mark's conception here is this: Peter's fault is that even while the Son of man's way through suffering and death has not yet been fully accomplished, he wants prematurely to *settle down* and enjoy the blessings of the new age. The leading disciple wants to secure the glory and the victory before they have been won.

7-8. a cloud overshadowed them: the **cloud** recalls *OT* theophanies (e.g. Exod. 24:15-18; Ezek. 1:4) and resembles the cloud out of which the Son of man will be revealed (Mk 13:26; 14:62; cf. Ac. 1:9-11; 1 Th. 4:17). At the baptism the voice from heaven addresses Jesus alone (1:11). But here the divine voice expresses a revelation-word to men and confirms Jesus' status as Son of God *directly to the disciples*. They are commanded by God to **listen to him.** All emphasis is here placed on the word that Jesus brings, and in the present context that word is of the Son of man's coming suffering and death (8:31), the very word Peter does not yet understand (verse 6). It is commonly thought that Moses and Elijah figure in the story as the representatives of the Law and the Prophets respectively, and so suggest that Jesus is the fulfilment of both (see e.g. Taylor, p. 390; Nineham, p. 235). But in the Deuteronomic passage that is clearly echoed here it is not as law-giver but as *prophet* himself that Moses predicts the coming of the eschatological prophet (Dt. 18:15, 18-19). In terms of the Marcan story the fulfilment Jesus brings is in fact in striking contrast with everything that has gone before. The vision splendid fades and the great prophetic personages who belong to the heavenly world to which they had been translated disappear from view, and only Jesus and the word he brings remain (**they no**

longer saw anyone with them but Jesus only). Unlike Moses
and Elijah, Jesus has not been raptured to heaven from the mountain but moves back down again to his earthly road to rejection
and death (9:9–13). It is likely that Mark has placed the story of
the transfiguration where he has, not because he saw in it a partial
completion of the statement of 9:1, but because it furnishes him
with yet another opportunity to testify to the great paradox that
the way to ultimate triumph for Jesus and his disciples is not the
way to the mountain-top of apocalyptic expectation but the way
of suffering (see 9:9–13).

NO EASY GLORY: THE LESSON OF 'ELIJAH' **9:9–13**

The conversation on the descent from the mountain forms a short
but obviously composite section. There is a distinct break between
verses 9–10, where the topic is the resurrection, and verses 11–13,
where the theme is Elijah and his destiny and no mention of the
resurrection is made at all. Possibly Mark had access to source
materials in which 9:11–13 followed immediately on 9:1 (the
continuity being quite natural), himself inserted the transfiguration story and framed verses 9–10, with the charge to secrecy, as
a bridge between the story and verses 11–13. More probably he
introduced the question of Elijah at this point (having first made
clear his understanding of the event of the transfiguration in verses
9–10) either because of the mention of Elijah in 8:28 or because
of the tenor of Jesus' saying in 9:1, or indeed because of the appearance of Elijah in the transfiguration story. Even then, however, verses 11–13 themselves form a problematic and seemingly
confused segment, the unity of which appears to be broken by the
question: 'How is it written of the Son of man, that he should
suffer many things and be treated with contempt?' Several theories
of the dislocation of the text have consequently been brought forward, among them the proposal that verse 12*b* originally came
immediately after verse 10 (C. H. Turner, p. 61). Alternatively,
Wellhausen suggested that the logic of the question in verse 11
implies that if, as the scribes say, Elijah comes first to put everything in readiness, how is it that when the Son of man arrives
people are so little prepared for him that he is rejected and put
to death? Thereafter Jesus' reply in verse 12*a* has to be taken as
a rhetorical question, rejecting the scribal standpoint, 'Elijah come
first and restore all things, you say? But in that case how about the
prophecies of the passion? I tell you that in fact Elijah has already

come. . . ' It is possible, however, to take the *RSV* translation as it stands, in which case it is natural to suppose that Jesus in fact endorses the scribal viewpoint, based on Mal. 4:4, that Elijah must come first to put everything in order, only he then proceeds to add the altogether decisive thing that the Son of man on his appearance must **suffer many things and be treated with contempt.** Then verse 13 links the divinely willed fate of 'Elijah' in the person of John the Baptist with the divinely willed fate of the Son of man.

Despite its obscurities this short section (verses 11–13) assuredly owes a great deal, in its Marcan formulation, to the Evangelist's conception that the execution of the Baptist as the Elijah-fore-runner and the passion and death of Jesus are inextricably inter-twined in God's plan and purpose (see notes on Mk 1:14 and 6:16ff.). Whereas at an earlier stage of the tradition the citation formula **as it is written of him** might most naturally have re-ferred to 1 Kg. 19:2–10 and to the persecution of the *OT* prophet Elijah, it probably means no more for Mark here than that the interconnected tragic destinies of John the Baptist and Jesus are in conformity with the will of God in Scripture.

9–10. he charged them to tell no one what they had seen: it is unlikely that the injunction to secrecy is here designed to ex-plain how the transfiguration story was unknown prior to the resurrection. Rather Mark uses it here in the editorial verses 9–10 (Matthew omits 10 and Luke omits the whole section: see Mt. 17:9–13), to de-emphasise the apocalyptic vision of 9:2–8 and to point instead to the centrality of the good news which can arise only after Easter but of course presupposes the death of the cross, as the phrase **risen from the dead** implies. This is the only place in the Gospel where a definite limit is set beyond which the 'secret' may be promulgated. The 'not yet', the detainment of the full and final message of Jesus Christ can only be overtaken by the death and resurrection of Jesus. As earlier the 'secret' checked for Mark all merely propagandistic use of the miracle-stories, so now it checks the inclination of those who would follow Jesus to glory too soon in his heavenly glory. **questioning what the rising from the dead meant:** as Jews, the disciples would scarcely have been puzzled about the meaning of resurrection in general. What is in view here is specifically their lack of understanding in regard to Jesus and his way.

11–13. The sayings of Jesus reported in verse 12, **Elijah does**

come first to restore all things, would have served the Church
as a rejoinder to Jewish objections (on the basis of Mal. 4:4-5)
that Jesus could not be Messiah since Elijah had not yet come
back. The abruptly introduced question of verse 12*b*, **and how
is it written of the Son of man . . .** and the statement of verse
13 show that the 'restoring of all things' associated with Elijah's
return must of divine necessity be preceded by the suffering and
humiliation of Elijah in the person of John the Baptist (**Elijah
has come**) *and of the Son of man.*

In this brief section (9:9-13), problematic though it is in detail,
the Evangelist is none-the-less clearly enough placing the transcendent glory of the Christ under the aegis of the cross.

THE HEALING OF AN EPILEPTIC BOY: FAITH AND UNFAITH **9:14-29**

This section appears to combine two different versions of the one
story of the healing of an epileptic lad (Taylor, p. 396) rather than
two quite separate stories (Bultmann, *HST*, p. 211). The one
version as presented by Mark (verses 14-19 and 28f.) centres on
the disciples and their powerlessness to heal, and the other on the
boy's father and the paradox of 'unbelieving faith' (verses 20-27).
The boy's illness is described twice, once in verse 17 and again in
rather different terms in verses 21f. In verses 14 and 17 the crowd
are already gathered round: in verse 25 they are only in process
of assembling. Since no other mighty work is reported in this part
of the Gospel, the question of why Mark has located the twofold
account of a healing at this point is particularly acute. Suggestions that the amazement of the crowd in verse 15 is because
Jesus' face was still shining after the transfiguration or that the
Evangelist had in view the artistic contrast between the ecstasy of
the mountain-top experience and the anguish of men on the plain
below (as in Raphael's picture of the transfiguration) are not very
likely. Most probably Mark included this composite story here to
denote how the necessary qualification for discipleship to Jesus is
the faith that expresses itself as complete dependence upon God.

14-16. when they came to the disciples: these three verses
are characteristically Marcan in vocabulary and ideas, and it is
likely that the Evangelist has shaped them up as a brief transitional passage. The alternative reading, found in a number of
MSS, 'when *he* came, *he* saw', strengthens the impression that the
narrative was originally self-contained and unconnected with the
preceding story of the transfiguration, and in any case even if one

follows the reading, 'when *they* came, *they* saw', one might have
expected the connexion to be specified by the explicit mention of
'the other nine disciples'. **scribes arguing:** the narrative that
follows is by no means a dispute-story, and the presence of the
scribes indicates that the lessons on faith which follow were of
universal import to the Church in its struggles with opponents
(Schweizer, p. 187). **were greatly amazed:** did Mark have in
mind the stories of Moses' descent from Mount Sinai in Exod.
32–33 and of the lingering glory on his face that made the people
afraid (Exod. 34:30)? More probably the crowd's amazement
signifies for him the supreme authority of Jesus (infinitely greater
than that of the scribes) that manifests itself immediately and inescapably to all who encounter him.

17–19. The symptoms described are those of epilepsy (verses
17–18). The inability of the disciples to cure the boy, after they
had presumably tried everything, stands in marked contrast to
the sovereign authority exercised by Jesus before he has tried anything (verse 15). **he answered them, "O faithless generation
... bring him to me":** more than an indictment only of the
disciples for their failure to heal the lad because of their unbelief.
Rather this saying of Jesus (cf. Jer. 5:23; 1 Kg. 19:14; Num. 14:
27; Dt. 32:5, 20) sets Jesus apart as the one who brings God's
word of judgment to bear on all people.

20–23. Whereas the disciples had achieved nothing with the
boy, the power of Jesus is at work immediately with dramatic and
at first painful results. So far the focus in the story is on the unprecedented divine power and authority in this Jesus who knows
none-the-less that the cost of exercising it is to be death at the
hands of the faithless ones. In verses 21ff. attention is now turned
to the human condition of the father of the boy as a singularly
interesting representative of the faithless ones. The indications of
the long-standing nature of the lad's illness (verse 21) and of other
epileptic symptoms (verse 22) heighten the suspense and give rise
to the thought that if a cure is to be effected, the healer must be
great indeed. **if you can do anything:** the father's words, picked
up in Jesus' reply in verse 23, place him squarely among those
who lack faith. **all things are possible . . . believes:** the logic
of the passage up to this point would suggest that the faith here
referred to is that of Jesus himself as healer. But Mark for his part
elsewhere stresses Jesus' Sonship to God rather than his faith in
God, and also the father interprets Jesus' saying broadly as a

rebuke of his own unbelief (verse 24). Consequently Mark would
have understood the comment as an observation on the true nature
of faith, meaning not that the man who has faith can then by
himself achieve anything he desires but rather that God's power
is limitless for those who have the courage to expect the best from
him.

24. The father's cry is an eloquent expression of the anguish of
men in the face of the tribulations that put faith to the acid test.
I believe, help my unbelief: this passionate plea is a haunting
reminder that faith is not something a man *has* for ever as a secure
human possession, but is always gift of God that needs to be renewed again and again. The man of faith can never boast of his
faithfulness as a glorious accomplishment, but acknowledges it as
God's gracious response to his own emptiness and unfaith. This
story provides no point of departure (cf. 2:5) for the modern tendency to attribute Jesus' healings to the power of auto-suggestion
in the patient. Here nothing is said at all about the boy's state of
mind or heart, and it is the humility of the father's reply that
leads to his healing. In short the Marcan emphasis is not on a
specific case of healing but on the disciple-faith that depends completely upon God.

25-27. As most frequently in the healing and exorcism stories,
Jesus' word of command is in itself enough to overcome even this
most combative and shattering of demons (verses 25-26). The
unique authority of Jesus is further emphasised by his lifting up
of the boy left apparently dead by the demon's viciousness (verses
26*b*-27), and one may suppose that to the first Christian hearers
this part of the account would have suggested the power of the
risen Christ to awaken the dead.

28-29. These verses are often regarded as a post-Marcan addition to the story, reflecting the attitude of a Church seeking to lay
down rules for the practice of exorcism. That would no doubt
apply to the words *and fasting* which in many MSS are added after
prayer. But the location in **the house** and the expression
privately (verse 28) are typically Marcan, and it is quite possible that in the implied contrast between the disciples' failure of
faith (**Why could we not cast it out?**) and Jesus' own faithful
appeal to prayer, Mark saw not only a suitable conclusion to the
whole narrative of 9:14ff. but a reason for inserting it where he
has done after 9:2-13. Discipleship to Jesus is inevitably costly
(9:9-13) and such costly discipleship is possible only for those who

are completely open to God and wait in prayer upon his enabling grace.

ANOTHER INTIMATION OF THE SUFFERING OF THE SON OF MAN
9:30–32

The second prediction of the passion is not necessarily connected with surrounding events in the narrative. It is connected rather with the Marcan view that the destiny of the Son of man in which his followers are called to participate is extremely hard to understand and even harder to share.

30–31. passed through Galilee: this journey Mark probably understood as the beginning of Jesus' movement toward Jerusalem (not mentioned until 10:32). **And he would not have any one know it; for he was teaching . . .:** Mark would scarcely have thought of the desire to avoid arrest by officers of the Herodian government as the reason for Jesus' travelling *incognito*. In fact he explains the preservation of *secrecy* as due entirely to Jesus' desire to communicate to his still blind disciples the one essential truth that God's way for the Son of man is the way of his passion. The precise reference to Jesus' execution and resurrection **after three days** is most likely a later addition to what was originally a very general prediction of the passion, like **the Son of man will be delivered into the hands of men:** the shortest and most likely the oldest form of the prophecy of Jesus. The play on words **Son of man . . . men** suggests that far from recognising the true Man sent by God for their help, men in the terrible blindness of their unfaith want to do away with him. **will be delivered:** the present tense of the verb in Greek implies the inevitability of the Son of man's fate. The Greek word 'deliver' may mean 'to hand someone over' (normally for punishment) or 'to betray', and there is possibly an allusion here to the nefarious part played by the betrayer Judas in the arrest of Jesus. Even if that is so, however, the term **delivered** would also have had profound theological associations, and in the light of Pauline usage (cf. Rom. 4:25; 8:32, 'delivered for our transgressions') would have suggested that Jesus' passion was in conformity with the will of God.

32. The non-understanding and fear belong to those who can only see things from a *human* point of view and must therefore remain baffled by Jesus' word about the pathway *God* has set him on.

THE LOWLINESS OF THE TRUE DISCIPLE 9:33-37

From 9:33–9:50 different facets of the theme of *discipleship* are given prominence in the Gospel. The materials that make up the various relatively short pieces within this longer section are loosely strung together, mainly on the *catchword* principle, e.g. 'servant' in 9:35 recalls 'receiving little children' in 9:37; **in my name** in 9:37 recalls **in your name** in 9:38 (cf. the sayings grouped around the idea **to sin** in 9:42–47 and round the terms **fire** and **salt** in 9:48–50). No doubt most of these materials had already been linked up in this way to serve the catechetical interest of the Church before Mark's time. But in incorporating them here in the order and form in which he has done the Evangelist has by no means simply acted on a whim, for just as the first intimation of the passion (8:31) was followed by the account of the disciples' blindness and Jesus' own radical call to follow him in cross-bearing (8:33ff.), so now the second intimation of the passion is followed by the same blindness and attempted disclosures of what constitutes authentic *following*.

33–34. The characteristically Marcan setting of the episode **in the house** allows the Evangelist to place Jesus alone and apart with his disciples and to show how in Jesus God's Word is always resolutely seeking to overcome their obtuseness. To this end Jesus takes the initiative with them in the withering question **What were you discussing on the way?** Faced with the question posed by the one prepared to surrender himself to the lowliness and obscurity of the cross, they whose thoughts are all of their own status and prestige can have nothing to say. Over against Jesus' second announcement of his passion, the disciples' discussion about **who was the greatest** seems extremely puerile. It is probably only a somewhat contrived introduction to verse 35, although it is a fact that questions of rank and precedence in regard to the synagogue or tribunals or meals were not uncommon in Jesus' day, and the rabbis disputed who would be greatest in the new age.

35. It is unprofitable to speculate whether when **he sat down** here, Jesus was assuming the normal posture of the teacher or the judge, or was simply tired from his journey. Already in the house (verse 33) he would scarcely have required to call the Twelve at this juncture. Accordingly, the notice about his sitting down and calling the Twelve may be taken as the framework for the originally independent saying of verse 35 that Mark has inserted in the present context, perhaps a little artificially. That the saying was initially a 'floating' one is also borne out by its occurrence in different contexts and forms in the Gospels, cf. Mk 10:43f.; Mt. 20: 26f.; Lk. 22:26 and Mt. 23:11. The longer version of the saying, couched in typical Jewish parallelism in Mk 10:43f., probably comes closest to the original, and seems to be presented here in an abbreviated form. Jesus' words are not to be taken as a broad revolutionary plea for the abolition of all rank. Nor do they primarily hold out the threat of punishment and final overthrow for the ambitious and pretentious in God's judgment day. Standing in close proximity to the second passion prediction, this saying signifies for Mark that the God whose own Son submits, in accordance with his will, to rejection and death, does not measure or estimate men by men's own standards of status and success. The call of that God is rather to a faithful following of Jesus that puts service to others first and self last. The one who ranks first with God is the disciple-servant of all.

36-37. The logic of connexion between this verse with the action it depicts (only Mark reports that Jesus 'took the child in his arms') and the preceding saying (verse 35) and the following saying (verse 37) is difficult to trace. The notion of the true disciple's being 'servant of all' would link up quite naturally with that of the littleness, lowliness, or helplessness of the **child.** In fact the parallel version in Mt. 18:3f. focuses upon the child and his attitude as an example for the disciple to follow (cf. Mk 10:15; Lk. 14:11; 18:14). Here in this Marcan context, however, it appears to be not the attitude of the child himself that is involved in the saying of verse 37*b*, but *the attitude of others toward him.* Yet it is hardly in keeping with Mark's interest to depict Jesus only as one who, like the rabbis, commends generosity to orphans and waifs, or who seeks to safeguard the interests of a religious community by advocating concern for the children within it. We may suppose his attention is centred specifically on the theme of *authentic Christian discipleship.* According to 9:41f. he seems to have understood the *child* as a picture of the poor and needy disciple-believers. So possibly Jesus himself also, and certainly the early Christian communities, thought of the 'follower' as *child* (cf. Mt. 25:31-46). The phrase **in my name** in verse 37*a* also suggests a metaphorical usage of *child* since it refers apparently to those *little ones,* i.e. 'believers', who are closely connected with Jesus or with

whom he is identified. Consequently Mark's train of thought may
be as follows. As the saying of verse 35*b* indicates, God esteems
most highly, and so is to be found identified with, the disciple who
is the lowliest servant of all. Likewise Jesus identifies himself with
the *child*, with the poor and needy disciple who aspires to no status
whatever beyond this. To **receive** (that is, to respond to or obey)
such a disciple as this in his lowliness and littleness is at the same
time to respond to the gospel of the suffering Son of man, and to
respond to that gospel brought by the 'little envoys' of God in the
Church's mission is in turn to receive, respond to, and obey the
God in accordance with whose saving purpose for men the Son of
man has to suffer and die. In Mark's view, of course, there stands
in the way of such true discipleship the immense barrier of human
pride (verse 34) which no teaching or instruction by itself but only
God can overcome.

CAN ONE OUTSIDE THE CIRCLE BE A DISCIPLE? 9:38–40

Only here in the Gospel is the disciple John singled out to play a
leading part. This suggests that Mark took this item up from his
tradition where it was probably associated already with verses 33–
36 through the verbal link 'in the name' (see verses 37 and 38).
The openness Jesus here shows to the outsider in the person of the
strange exorcist is not inconsistent with what we know of his outlook on Gentiles and Samaritans elsewhere (e.g. Mt. 8:5–13; cf.
Lk. 7:1–9; 10:29–37). Nor is it inherently impossible that even
in the course of Jesus' public ministry his reputation was such that
magical use was made of his name by exorcists and healers. Nevertheless the story as it stands is most likely a product of the early
Church. The magical papyri from Egypt furnish evidence of pagan
magicians invoking sacred Jewish names, as well as the name of
Jesus, and in relating what happened to the seven sons of Sceva
the book of Acts roundly condemns the practice (19:13ff.). Here
by contrast tolerance of the non-Christian exorcist is called for on
the basis of a reported saying of Jesus, which if genuine would lead
us to wonder why the Church need ever have had any problem
with pagan exorcists or reached such different solutions. Probably
the nucleus of the story is the saying of verse 40, broad and general
in meaning and fairly current coin in the ancient world, and this
has then been given concrete application in the saying of Jesus
relating to the specific case in verse 39. The mode of expression
used by John in verse 38 strengthens the impression that we are

here dealing with an early-Church situation rather than a situation in the ministry of Jesus. The idea of **us** and **them,** of following the *disciples*, as if they were a closed circle (cf. 5:19) who could command allegiance aside from Jesus, scarcely belongs to the time of his ministry.

38–39. John appears here as an exemplar of the exclusivism and conformity in the Church that is inward-looking and concerns itself only with the members. The outsider is opposed simply on the ground that he is not 'one of us', and no thought is given to the perplexing question of what qualitative difference might exist between a work of healing performed by a member and one performed by a non-member. In verse 39 Jesus is represented as resisting this narrow institutional outlook and as eradicating the barrier between the insider and the outsider so long as the outsider operates *in his name* and is not an inveterate enemy. E. Schweizer is possibly right in regarding this reply as related to a question that has always vexed the Church. By what test is the ecstatic or charismatic person on the fringe to be accepted as member of the Church? (see Schweizer, *GNM*, p. 195, for a list of various responses given to this question in the early Church).

40. The general principle enunciated in this short proverbial saying in its present context is that the community of believers must leave room for late-comers and waverers. Accordingly, in the light of the saying Mark no doubt saw this little episode as a further appeal (cf. verses 33–37) for lowliness or humility on the part of the true Christian disciple.

WISE SAYINGS FOR DISCIPLES **9:41–50**

The saying of verse 41 was probably already linked with 33–37 and 38–40 through the catchword 'in the name of'. The group of miscellaneous sayings that follows in 42–50 Mark may have included here because he associated the **little ones who believe in me** in verse 42 with bearing **the name of Christ** in verse 41 or because he thought of the whole of 41–50 as bearing on the theme of *the oneness of Christ and his true disciples in sacrificial self-giving*. The sayings of 42–50 were no doubt collected before Mark's time, to meet the catechetical interests of the Church, on the catchword principle, which seems very artificial to us but was widespread in ancient writing as an aid to learning by rote (verses 43–48 are linked with 42 by the catchword **causes to sin,** verse 49 with 48 by **fire,** and verse 50 with 49 by **salt**). Since there is, therefore, no progression in meaning from one to the other, and even more since there is no indication of the circumstances in which they were originally uttered, the sayings severally are extremely difficult to interpret, especially those of 49 and 50. But in any case the important thing to ask is what they mean for the Evangelist in their present setting. In this section (verses 33–50) Mark wants to show that the crucial word of the Son of man's suffering cannot possibly become real to those who are still disputing among themselves about greatness (33–37), but only to those who identify with him and his cause in *following his way* of sacrifice and self-denial. The sayings of 41–50 then furnish graphic illustrations of what is involved in this *following*.

41. The saying seems to relate primarily to the subject of hospitality to Christian missionaries, and in fact Matthew has placed it at the close of the missionary discourse on the sending out of the Twelve (Mt. 10:42). However, there is considerable stress on the awkward Greek phrase 'in the name that you are Christ's' (*RSV* **because you bear the name of Christ:** the expression 'because you are Christ's' is Pauline, cf. Rom. 8:9; 1 C. 1:12; 3:23; 2 C. 10:7). Mark possibly thinks that the loyal Christian disciple must be completely satisfied with the most insignificant service, even as God himself is content with those who offer it.

42. The saying may have referred originally to the sympathetic treatment of children within the community of Jesus, and Matthew has so interpreted it (18:6; cf. 18:5). Luke, however, relates the **little ones** to humble Christian believers who will be subjected to the severest temptations in the last days (Lk. 17:1f.), and in Mark here, if one accepts the well-attested reading **who believe in me,** they are clearly defined as such. Probably for Mark verse 42 contains both a warning against succumbing to tempters and a reminder to lowly and humble disciples that they are always under the protective care of the God whose judgment inevitably falls on all who would lead them astray. **if a great millstone were hung round his neck . . .: a great millstone** is literally the millstone 'turned by a donkey' in contrast to the smaller hand mill served by a woman. The element of hyperbole in the expression reminds us that we are dealing only with a vivid metaphor designed to emphasise God's rigorously just concern for his little ones.

43-48. Aside from their Marcan context, these sayings would all have referred to the terrifying consequences of the moral corruption of the self. In Mt. 5:29-30 only the sayings about the *hand* and the *eye* are reported, no doubt because they specially suit a context in which the main subject is adultery. The three sayings in Mark relating to **hand, foot,** and **eye** may go back to an original single saying about *any member* of the body, and may have arisen through the Jewish tendency to associate the different members with different kinds of temptation (e.g. Job 31:1; Prov. 6: 17f.; 23:33; 27:20). The dangers of a literalistic understanding of these sayings are obvious. Self-mutilation is certainly not commended here as a work acquiring merit before God. Rather these verses, particularly for Mark, vividly portray how the true disciple has to deny himself and sacrifice what may be most important to him (even to the limit of martyrdom) for the sake of Christ and his kingdom. The life of the kingdom and self-sacrifice are inextricably bound together. Whoever will not give *all* (the three sayings cumulatively may suggest this) for the 'one pearl of great price' which endures for ever, links himself instead to what is ephemeral and destructible (the images of 'Gehenna', **fire,** and **worm** underline this) and so brings God's judgment on himself. We should not read into these sayings later speculations about the eternal punishment of the wicked in hell. **Hell** (*RSV*) is a rendering of the Greek 'Gehenna', which should be retained in translation because of the misleading connotations of the former word. The term 'Gehenna' referred originally to the Valley of the Son of Hinnom to the west of Jerusalem, where infants were once sacrificed to the pagan god Moloch (2 Kg. 23:10; Jer. 7:31; 19: 5f.; 32:35), and which after its desecration by Josiah became used as a refuse dump. Consequently the language of Isa. 66:24 could be applied to it, of worms fattening on offal and rubbish constantly smouldering, and it came to symbolise the future place of fiery torment for the damned. It is important to notice, therefore, that what occurs on the lips of Jesus here is not a developed doctrine of everlasting punishment, but an affirmation in quite conventional terminology that none could be more 'lost' than they who choose to renounce the life of the kingdom and cling to the life of this world and its fleeting powers.

49-50. The difficult saying of verse 49 has been very variously interpreted, and the problem is compounded by the fact that the MSS attest many divergent readings. Some MSS add the words 'and every sacrifice will be purified (salted) with salt'. Though this is no doubt a later gloss, it does point to one feasible explanation of

the saying. Just as salt cleanses the sacrificial offering so the fire
of persecution and suffering purifies (and preserves) the true
Christian disciple in the tribulations of the end-time. Perhaps the
best commentary on verse 50a is the recent appearance on the
market of a salt-substitute that looks and tastes like salt but does
not have the preservative or purifying quality of true salt. Probably the saying referred originally to the saline deposits of the
Dead Sea, from which the real salt could be leached out after a
time leaving only impure substances resembling salt in appearance. The words may have suggested to the Evangelist only the
urgent need for endurance and tenacity on the part of the Christian disciple. To respond to the high calling of Christian discipleship and then to forsake it in the day of crisis means an immeasurably great loss. **have salt in yourselves ...** (verse 50b): since
in 50a the disciples themselves are compared to **salt,** whereas here
salt is an inward quality of the disciples' lives, it is likely that 50a
and 50b were initially independent sayings. Numerous suggestions
have been made about the meaning of **salt** in 50b, e.g. sound
common sense (cf. Col. 4:6), charity toward the neighbour (cf.
Rom. 12:18; 2 C. 13:11; 1 Th. 5:13), knowledge of what God
requires in the last days, etc. If 50b is not the comment of a com-
piler who wished to round off thus a section that began with the
dispute about greatness (see Taylor, p. 414), then possibly, since
salt was used in the preparation of sacrifices, Mark had in mind
that when the followers of Christ were ready to sacrifice themselves for his sake and the kingdom's all arguments about status
would be silenced and the peace that stems from a genuine community of purpose would be assured.

GOD'S RIGOROUS DEMAND REGARDING MARRIAGE **10:1–12**

Chapter 10 is hardly a distinct section of the Gospel (cf. Johnson,
p. 168); it continues the theme of discipleship, signally important
for Mark. The arrangement of verses 1–31 is somewhat reminiscent
of the patterns of material gathered for catechetical purposes and
assembled as *Haustafeln* or 'house-regulations' addressed to different groups in the Church, wives, husbands, children, fathers,
slaves, and masters (e.g. 1 Tim. 2:8–3:13; 5:1–6:2; Tit. 1:5–9;
2:2–10; Eph. 5:22–6:9; 1 Pet. 2:13–18; 3:1–7; 5:1–5). Verses
1–31 deal with discipleship as it relates to married people, to
children, to the wealthy, and to leaders in the Church.

The setting in verse 1 for the episode of 10:1–12 is Marcan (see commentary below). Neither the **Pharisees** nor any Jew of the period would have put to Jesus the question of verse 2, since all alike believed that a man could legally divorce his wife. Accordingly, the question posed in verse 2 is a Christian formulation (contrast Mt. 19:3, when the reference is to an actual question debated by the Pharisees, namely, whether a man could divorce his wife *for any cause*). In that case the motive attributed to the Pharisees, **in order to test him,** is most probably also a reflection of the controversy between Church and Synagogue on such matters as marriage and divorce. Since therefore the hand of the Church and of the Evangelist is in evidence here it is difficult to ascertain with any precision how much of the teaching reproduced actually goes back to Jesus himself. Verse 10 is a typical Marcan transition and clearly conforms to his editorial practice of appending to public pronouncements of Jesus his private instruction to the disciples (cf. 4:10–20; 7:17–19; 9:28–29). The verses 11–12 that have been added here deal, as it happens, less with *marriage*, the subject of verses 6–9, than with legalities affecting the *re-marriage* of divorced persons.

1. went to the region of Judea and beyond Jordan: reverses the order envisaged by Mark elsewhere, whereby Jesus travels along the east bank of Jordan and *thence* into Judea. That even early copyists sensed the difficulty is clear from the variant MS readings. Is the notice simply a relic of an old tradition underlying Mark at this point? Or has Mark himself put Judea first here to emphasise Jesus' set intent, after the passion prediction of 9: 30–32, to advance on Jerusalem to his death? Whatever the origin of the notice, and however Mark may have pictured Jesus' journey, his primary interest lies less in the geography than in those favourite motifs of his, the magnetic attraction of Jesus (**crowds gathered to him again**) and of the good news he brings through his teaching activity.

2. Bent only on putting Jesus to the test or trapping him, the **Pharisees** appear here as representative of those who do not come to Jesus with genuine openness, but have their minds made up in advance before they hear him or give him a chance. A number of MSS, however, omit **Pharisees** and leave unspecified the subject of the verb **asked,** and possibly the original text did not name the questioners of Jesus here. In any case the question posed here could not have come from *any* group of Jews, since a man's legal right to divorce his wife was everywhere accepted on

the basis of Dt. 24: 1-3. What the rabbis did discuss extensively
was the *grounds* for such divorce (cf. Mt. 19:3)—the stricter school
of Shammai allowing it only in the case of the wife's unchastity
or infidelity, the more liberal school of Hillel in almost every case,
even where a wife had merely spoiled her husband's food or had
become less attractive to him than some other woman. The question put in verse 2 as to whether it is *ever* lawful for a man to
divorce his wife is therefore a Church or Marcan formulation,
leading up to Jesus' teaching in verses 6-9. The Greek word rendered, **'Is it lawful?'** (*RSV*) means literally, 'Is it allowable or
permissible?' and there is a contrast between Jesus' opponents
who seek loopholes in such regulations as exist and try to bend
them to their own advantage by asking only about what is permitted to them, and on the other hand Jesus' own emphasis on
the inescapable *commandment* of God in verses 3 and 5 (see
Schweizer, *GNM*, p. 203).

Mark's inclusion of Jesus' teaching on marriage and divorce at
this juncture in the Gospel has troubled some commentators who
regard it as much less obviously connected with the discipleship
theme of chapter 9 than the sections that follow in 10:13-16 and
10:17-31 (see Nineham, pp. 259f. for Lightfoot's implausible suggestion that Mark sees here an allusion to Israel as the bride of
God and to Christ as the bridegroom, and for other proposals).
But if 10:1-31 had already been composed on a similar pattern
to the household rules dealing with different groups in the Church,
it would be quite natural that the duties of husbands and wives
would come first, and its location here in Mark is readily accounted
for.

3-5. In verse 3 Jesus answers his opponents with a counter-
question which puts them on the spot by forcing them to reckon
with God's *will* for them as it is expressed in the **commandment**
of the Law. They reply, with reference to Dt. 24: 1-3, that **Moses
allowed** divorce provided that certain legal formalities designed
to protect the divorced woman were carried through. In the light
of verses 5ff., their reply together with the original form of their
question in verse 2 ('Is a man *allowed*?') shows that in fact they
reckon less with *God's will* for them than with their own rights
within the limits of what is permitted. When Jesus says **'For your
hardness of heart he wrote you this commandment'**, he is
neither here nor in what follows overthrowing Scripture, nor setting God's command against that of Moses. Rather he makes it

clear that in adopting Dt. 24:1 as their starting-point his interlocutors mistakenly suppose that first and foremost God approves divorce, whereas this commandment of the Law is no concession to human weakness but stands as a divine judgment on man's impenetrable stubbornness and obtuseness in regard to what is God's true will for them. In verses 6ff. Jesus appeals from Scripture to Scripture, to the only real starting-point, namely *what God has intended* **from the beginning.**

6–9. It is not necessary to take the words **from the beginning** as meaning 'at the beginning of his book' (i.e. 'of Genesis'), and then supplying 'Moses wrote', as though Jesus were diverting attention from what Moses wrote later to what he wrote earlier about God's will. His appeal is from how things *may be* from the human point of view in respect of the Law concerning divorce to how things *are* in the order of God's creation. Jesus' standpoint is itself solidly founded on Scripture, on Gen. 1:27, **God made them male and female:** in creating two sexes God declared his intention that *one* man is for *one* woman. **For this reason . . .:** in Gen. 2:24 the phrase 'for this reason' refers back to the creation of the woman out of Adam's rib, but here it is applied to the statement of Gen. 1:27 which is thus interpreted as a sign that the union between one man and one woman in marriage was ordained by God to transcend all other human ties and relationships. **the two shall become one:** the Greek reads literally 'become one flesh'. Whether 'flesh' here is synonymous with the Greek word for 'body' denoting the *whole person* (cf. 1 C. 6:16) or denotes rather *kindred* (cf. Gen. 29:14; Rom. 11:14), Jesus' argument is that in accordance with God's will marriage is the closest conceivable bond. The text of Gen. 1:27 which is here used by Jesus to uphold the indissolubility of marriage was apparently used in defence of monogamy at Qumran: 'The builders of the wall . . . are caught in fornication in two respects: by marrying two women in their lifetime, although the principle of creation is *Male and female he created them*, and they who were in the ark *two and two they went in to the ark*' (*Damascus Document* 7:1–3). **what therefore God has joined . . . asunder:** sums up the position stated by Jesus in the plainest possible way. Whatever a man may say or do, or whatever proceedings he may take, he remains inescapably under the absolute command, will, and authority of God in creation.

The extreme stringency of Jesus' stance on marriage and divorce has given rise to mitigating interpretations, e.g. (a) Jesus excludes cases of the wife's adultery altogether from the argument since they were dealt with already in Dt. 22:22, or divorce on the ground of the wife's unchastity or adultery was so widely accepted as to require no discussion (cf. Mt. 5:32; 19:9), or Jesus himself believed that an adulterous wife would already have broken the true marriage union; (b) Jesus' teaching here issues from his own conviction that in his ministry the kingdom of God is dawning and his sole concern is with the pure and final will of God in the new world of his kingdom (see further Nineham, p. 262). But Jesus' statement in verses 6–9 implies no exceptions and appears to be addressed quite realistically to the present moment of his hearers' existence. To be sure the early Church soon ventured on legal modifications of the principle affirmed by Jesus, see e.g. the exceptive clause in Mt. 5:32 and Paul's own concession in 1 C. 7:13. And it may always have been right and proper for the Church, as for the state ever since, to make provisions for divorce where any true marriage relationship was effectively destroyed anyhow and where divorce was the lesser evil. But at all events it is most important to remember that here in Mk 10:6–9 Jesus is not absolutely prohibiting divorce *by way of a binding legal enactment*, but is absolutely elevating marriage (as an indissoluble union) by way of leading men to understand it, not as a remote ideal, but as a gift of God's creation, to be received gladly and celebrated naturally and spontaneously. What is essentially a gift of God can never of course be forced on men by law, but only responded to in gratitude. It is important to remember also that this 'pure teaching' on marriage is embedded in a section of the Gospel where the salient theme is the need for the faithful disciple to share in the destiny of the suffering Son of man through sacrifice and self-renunciation. Here too Jesus' teaching may be construed as an invitation to accept God's gift and a call to the sacrifice for the sake of others that is necessary for its reception. Accordingly, from the Marcan viewpoint, the first responsibility on the Church is always to affirm that invitation and that call.

10–12. The setting of the scene **in the house** provides the customary Marcan transition from public pronouncement of Jesus to private communication. The disciples still do not understand, and the fact that further special instruction is offered to them indicates how strong is Jesus' desire to get across to them. No doubt Mark considered the saying(s) of verses 11–12 an endorsement of Jesus' 'pure teaching' on marriage (6–9). But these verses are so only indirectly and in fact relate less to divorce than to remarriage, which is condemned as a grievous sin for divorced persons. **whoever divorces his wife ... against her:** the normal Jewish view, according to rabbinic law, was that a man could be said to commit adultery against another married man, and a wife could be held to commit adultery against her husband, but a husband could not be held to commit adultery against his wife. According to Jewish law only the man had the right to divorce his wife, so whereas at this point the statement of verse 11 is thoroughly Jewish, it represents a dramatic departure from Jewish norms in claiming that the man who has put away his wife and remarried commits adultery against his wife. The saying of verse 11 has a parallel in Q, Mt. 5:32 = Lk. 16:18, where it may be preserved in its most ancient form. **if she divorces her husband ... adultery:** since at Jewish law the wife had no right to divorce her husband, the statement of verse 12 can hardly have a Jewish background. Roman law, however, gave the woman the right to divorce her husband, and so in verse 12 we may see the Hellenistic Church accommodating the older and more Jewish statement of verse 11 to new circumstances and new relationships. In so far as the saying of verses 11–12 appear to be legal in character, it is very doubtful whether in their present form (or even in the form of the less precise version of verse 11 in Q at Lk. 16:18), they can be traced back to Jesus. Certainly Jesus' 'pure teaching' on marriage (verses 6–9) is opposed to and transcends every kind of legal regulation.

THE CHILDLIKE DISPOSITION OF THE DISCIPLE 10:13–16

The picture conjured up by this brief and vivid report has been highly influential. However, its interpretation is more problematic than may appear at first glance. The saying of verse 15 is widely acknowledged as a genuine saying of Jesus. The notion of the coming kingdom as a gift of God to be received in faith now seems to be characteristic of his teaching. Initially the saying most probably circulated independently, since it occurs in a different context in Mt. 18:3 and probably lies behind Jn 3:5. Whether Mark began with verse 15 and clustered the materials of 13–14 and 16 around it, or began with the setting of 13–14 and 16, and inserted 15 into it, it is impossible to say. Placed where it is here, it creates a certain difficulty in that while the rest of the material describes

Jesus' attitude to children, verse 15 apparently holds up children
as a model to be copied.

13. The story is attached to what precedes by a simple **and,**
without further note of time or place. How little Mark is interested
in biographical details is illustrated also by the fact that we are
told nothing about who brought the **children,** who the children
were, why **the disciples rebuked them,** or why exactly Jesus
was so **indignant.** The Greek word for **children** may denote
anyone from infancy to twelve years of age, although Luke speaks
of 'infants' (18:15) and the Coptic *Gospel of Thomas* (*logion* 22)
refers the episode to infants being suckled. **that he might touch
them; and the disciples rebuked them:** if all the children's
escorts wanted was a blessing of Jesus on the little ones, it is hard
to understand the disciples' rebuke. Given the absence of biographical connexions from Mark, it is unlikely we should suppose
they merely wanted to protect Jesus in his weariness from the
crowd. Were the disciples annoyed then because the children were
members of families outside the circle of the committed (cf. 9:38),
or too immature to make any responsible decision about Jesus for
themselves, or because the adults mistakenly looked for a miraculous flow of power from Jesus in a magical way? We cannot be
sure. But at any rate we see Jesus once again at odds with his still
insensitive disciples, and this time his instruction to them takes
the form of an enacted parable (verse 16).

14. Only here in the Gospels is Jesus said to be **indignant.** No
doubt there is an echo here of 9:33–37 and Mark will have understood his indignation as that of one who stands on the God-ward
side over against those disciples who reckon in all too human
terms and seek to exercise their worldly powers and prerogatives
over against the powerlessness of the little ones (cf. Jesus' anger
with illness and unbelief in 1:41, 43; 3:5). The openness of Jesus'
invitation to the children is all the more highlighted by contrast
with the disciples' erecting of obstacles, and the contrast shows
also that Jesus possesses a unique, sovereign authority to offer the
blessings of God's coming kingdom here and now to whomsoever
he will. **to such belongs the kingdom of God:** a considerable
variety of opinion exists as to the scope of this **such.** Does it refer
to all actual children who have not yet attained the 'age of the
Law'? If so, then Jesus appears here as demolishing all legal prescriptions about the *who* and the *when* of entry into the inheritance
of the kingdom (cf. Mt. 21:15–16; 11:25). Or does it refer to those

who are not literal children, but share the child's characteristics, receptiveness, purity, humility? The danger here is that we might think of the cultivation of certain childlike qualities of personality as a merit that earns the right of entry to the kingdom (see Cranfield, p. 324), and this certainly runs counter to Jesus' teaching that the kingdom is not a human achievement but always and only God's gracious gift (as to Paul's teaching that justification is by faith alone). Perhaps the surest clue to an understanding of 10:14 lies in the truth that in the Gospels Jesus promises the kingdom to the underdogs, the poor, the dispossessed, the mourners, the outcasts, who have no standing whatever in the eyes of Jewish religious officials. So here the kingdom is promised to those who quite objectively are obscure, trivial, unimportant, weak (cf. 1 C. 1:26ff.), who come empty-handed like a beggar (Schweizer, *GNM*, p. 207). Jesus' statement in 10:14 comes therefore as a radical reversal of normal human standards of measurement. With him the kingdom of God is a 'realm of surprises' which those who like the disciples have disputed about human greatness are in no position to inherit.

15. The kingdom is now promised to *all* who are ready to receive it **like a child,** that is as something given to them in their helplessness or defencelessness, without any claim on their part that they have deserved or earned it. The saying of verse 15 is thus interpreted by Matthew and applied in fact to the child's humility ('except you turn and become like children . . . whoever humbles himself like this child', Mt. 18:3f.; cf. Jn 3:5). However it is just possible that Mark understood verse 15 differently. The Greek words **like a child** may be read as an accusative with the meaning 'whoever does not receive the kingdom *as one receives a little child*', in which case it is the nature of the kingdom that is likened to that of the child. On this understanding, verse 15 is an invitation (to all disciples) to welcome the kingdom as Jesus welcomes the child (verses 14 and 16), and this accords well with the fact that in this section of the Gospel Mark's theme is the close identity of the way and conduct of the Son of man with the way and conduct of the disciple. There is an old saying of Heraclitus, 'The course of the world is a child at play, moving figures on a board, back and forth; it is the kingdom of a child'. While there is no way of knowing whether Jesus or his near contemporaries were acquainted with this saying, **the kingdom of God** in its nature as a child in Jesus' teaching may describe it as neither

forced upon men nor forced by them, but as God's gracious gift
even as the child is his gift. It is the realm of spontaneity which
is simply to be participated in with joy, where the assuming of
roles is for ever ended, the realm of *play* (for an interesting discussion on the kingdom as the kingdom of *play*, see J. Moltmann,
Theology and Joy, London, 1973, pp. 38ff.).

16. The gestures of Jesus here are a living parable of the truth
enshrined in verses 14–15. Jesus and the kingdom of the child
which is the kingdom of God are seen to be inseparably connected.

The saying of 10:14 may have lain behind Jn 3:5 with its baptismal reference. Possibly also the words **do not hinder them**
gave rise to the liturgical question 'What hinders?' posed before
candidates were baptised (cf. Ac. 8:36). Certainly from an early
period the Church regarded this little episode as a justification for
infant baptism. Its instinct was no doubt quite proper. But of
course the story says not a word about community *praxis*, even
though the understanding of the kingdom it embodies may have
important light to shed on the symbolic meaning of infant baptism
(the promise of the kingdom for the weak and helpless ones).

THE CONFLICTING CLAIMS OF WORLDLY POSSESSIONS AND DISCIPLESHIP
10:17–31

There is no biographical connexion between this episode and the
preceding, as though the blind man had witnessed the episode of
the children and determined to find out how he might qualify for
the kingdom. The connexion is as usual with Mark theological.
The lesson that the kingdom of God belongs to the totally unpre-
tentious is now reinforced by the particular case of a man whose
captivity to the world and worldly prizes cuts him off from entry
to the kingdom. Verse 23 is a typically Marcan transition from an
individual case to general teaching of Jesus given to the disciples
by themselves, and the transition to sayings dealing broadly with
the perils of wealth is facilitated by the way in which the **man**
of verse 17 is described only in a sort of parenthetical comment
at the close of verse 22 as a 'rich man'—**for he had great possessions.** A number of MSS place verse 25 before verse 24, and in
that case there is a progression from the particular, the difficulty
of salvation for the rich, to the universal, the difficulty of salvation
for *all* men (the words added in some MSS, 'for those who trust in
riches', in 24*b* being a later gloss and rightly omitted by *RSV*),
and the increasing astonishment of the disciples is accounted for.

Alternatively, if we accept the text as it stands in verses 23–26, verses 24a and 26a may be regarded as editorial observations, emphasising the Marcan motif of the disciples' non-understanding. Whereas the sayings of verses 23–25 were probably brought together by the Church before Mark's time, verse 27a shows that Mark himself may have introduced the sayings of 27b at this point. The saying of 29–30 relating to the blessings (and hardships) of true discipleship would seem in this form to reflect the experience of a Church that had tasted persecution. It would follow verse 21 more naturally, and possibly the Evangelist himself has placed it after verse 27, introducing it with the declaration attributed to Peter, and finally adding the originally independent saying of verse 31, found in different contexts in Mt. 20:16 and Lk. 13:30.

17. The setting of the story in the context of a journey is consistent with Mark's desire to stress the onward *movement* of the good news with Jesus. The **man** in the story, neither named nor characterised at first in any way, is really 'everyman'. He is described as a 'youth' in Mt. 19:20 and a 'ruler' in Lk. 18:18. His action in kneeling and his mode of address to Jesus, **Good Teacher,** betoken a reverence that would not be accorded to a rabbi as such. **inherit eternal life:** virtually synonymous here with 'receive the kingdom of God' (see 9:43, 45; cf. Dan. 12:2). His question shows not that he is one who relies on earning salvation by further works, but that he senses inwardly that the vital thing is missing from his life, and this prepares for the crucial element in Jesus' response in verse 21, **'You lack one thing'.** The man's quest is not just for the happy life but for God's permanent blessing both now and then beyond death.

18. The obsequious and flattering gestures of the man toward Jesus coupled with the form of Jesus' reply here probably indicate to the story-teller that he has come to Jesus looking to him alone in his *earthly* presence and wisdom for a formula of salvation. Jesus immediately diverts attention away from himself to the **One** (probably a title in the Greek, with **God** an interpretative addition), namely God as the source of all good life. **Why do you call me good? No one is good but God alone:** authentic words of Jesus. A Church that had reached a growing conviction and concern about the sinlessness of Jesus (Jn 8:46; 2 C. 5:21; Heb. 7:26; 1 Pet. 2:22) could scarcely have been responsible for a statement that might have seemed to detract from Jesus' moral perfection and obviously occasioned serious problems at an early stage. Witness

Matthew's doctrinally innocuous modification, 'Why do you ask me about what is good? One there is who is good' (Mt. 19:17). Witness also the later suggestion of the Church fathers that Jesus sought to lead his questioner on beyond the recognition that he was merely the **Good Teacher** to the conclusion that he was God, an interpretation which must be considered a *tour de force*. However, the fact that Jesus' words were preserved at all means that for the early Church, and presumably for Mark himself, they were not thought to be incompatible with their notion of Jesus' sinlessness. They would have seen Jesus' rightful claims to Sonship as residing precisely in this that he pointed men from himself to the Father, claimed nothing for himself but everything for God and threw himself entirely upon the will and the mercy and the goodness of God, so that in his life as in his death men of faith could encounter God in him.

19-20. you know the commandments: Jesus appears here as one who by no means subverts the Law. He now points his Jewish enquirer to God in the most natural Jewish way, by referring him to the will of God as expressed in the second table of the Decalogue. **Do not kill . . . and mother:** The practical injunctions of the second table are cited by Jesus in random order, the fifth commandment being placed last and the words **do not defraud** (suitable in a situation where the danger of riches is uppermost) being substituted for the tenth commandment. Jesus is no prisoner to the strict *letter* of the Law, though he does respect it as a clear and simple call to the God-like life for *all* men (**you know . . .**). The man's answer in verse 20 does not imply boastfulness or self-righteousness on his part. He is conscious of his lack (verse 17) as Jesus is lovingly conscious of his diligence and seriousness (verse 21a, **Jesus . . . loved him**) in regard to obedience to the Law.

21-22. Jesus looking upon him loved him: the fixing of Jesus' eyes on the man suggests his firm intention to help him, and **loved him** may denote either that 'he openly showed his affection by putting his arms around him' or 'had the profoundest sympathy for him in his need'. **You lack . . . follow me:** not an additional prescription or regulation imposed on the man which he must fulfil as an indispensable prerequisite of becoming a disciple. Rather, a challenge and an invitation to perceive the one altogether decisive and all-embracing truth, that discipleship to Jesus and sacrificial renunciation inevitably go hand in hand. The life of the true disciple is linked to and empowered by nothing ephemeral like worldly possessions, but the grace and mercy of God that abides for ever (**you will have treasure in heaven**). Discipleship is ultimately a gift of God's enabling grace, and since this man is captive to what the world has offered him (only in verse 22 do we learn that he is wealthy) he is not free to receive God's offer, vexed though he is to say No to it (**his countenance fell and he went away sorrowful**). The account in the apocryphal *Gospel of the Nazarenes* shows how a story like this could be embellished. It tells of two rich men, the second of whom at this point 'scratches his head'. The Lord asks him how he could possibly have fulfilled the Law and the Prophets, and then adds, 'It is written in the Law, Thou shalt love thy neighbour as thyself; and behold many of thy brethren the sons of Abraham are covered with filth and dying of hunger, and thy house is full of good things, and nothing goes from it to them.'

23. Jesus' gesture, **he looked around,** and his address to the disciples in particular would suggest to Mark's readers that no one in the Church of Mark's time was exempt from the 'hard' instruction that follows. The saying of verse 23 universalises the lesson given in the specific case of the rich man in the story of verses 17-22.

24-27. The teaching of Jesus on riches is alien to the spirit of Judaism which, while not unaware of the dangers of wealth, nevertheless tended to regard it as a sign of God's favour toward the righteous. However, in the Marcan context the alarm of the disciples is not occasioned simply by the freshness of Jesus' teaching, but signifies the blindness of those who still look at things from a human point of view and reckon how man can *earn* the kingdom. The mode of address used by Jesus, **Children,** found elsewhere only in the Johannine literature, suggests his affection and pity for the blind ones and his compassionate longing to communicate to them the true nature of the kingdom and of discipleship. In verse 24 the majority of mss read, 'How hard it is *for those who trust in riches* to enter the kingdom of God!' But the extra phrase, which makes *riches* alone the whole subject of the section, is almost certainly a simplifying addition. *RSV* rightly omits the additional words, and the issue as we see it then is that riches are but one example of the worldly, the ephemeral, and the trivial, that preoccupies men to their neglect of the reality of God's kingdom. Different worldly interests (even among the poor) equally constitute a barrier between man and God. The saying of verse 25 is a humorous hyperbole, which as it stands here shows that entry to God's kingdom is impossible on the basis only of human enterprise or acquisitiveness. The later rabbis spoke about the impossibility of an elephant passing through the eye of a needle. The temptation to tone down the stringency of Jesus' saying should be resisted—'procrustean attempts to reduce the camel to a rope (reading *kamilon* for *kamēlon*), or to enlarge the needle's eye into a postern gate need not be taken seriously' (Cranfield, p. 332). The reaction of the disciples in wondering how *in the world* anyone can be saved (verse 26) admirably prepares the way for Jesus' statement (verse 27) that salvation (the word **saved** in verse 26 has a distinctly Pauline ring, but is synonymous here with 'entry into the kingdom of God') cannot be guaranteed by anyone or anything in the world, but is entirely in God's power to bestow. The reference to Jesus' 'looking at the disciples' in verse 27 draws attention to the central importance of his statement. It is to be remembered that the predominant theme in Mark after the second prediction of the passion (9:30-32) is discipleship and the sacrifice and suffering necessarily involved in it. Here now it is made abundantly clear that true discipleship does not lie within the realm of *human* possibilities at all. It ensues not from the fulfilment of any specific regulation or any particular act of renunciation, but only where God's gift and God's claim take precedence over everything else for men. All that men could never be, God alone makes possible.

28–31. Peter's remark in verse 28 Mark probably found in his tradition but has employed it here as a connecting link with the promise that follows. In his remark Peter puts the act of renunciation first (even exaggerating it, **we have left everything,** since his break with home ties was not complete, see 1:29; 3:9; 4:1, 36; cf. 1 C. 9:5), and discipleship second, thus implying from the Marcan viewpoint that he is still among the blind ones who put what man can do before what God can give. Jesus' promise in verses 29–30 reverses the priorities, focuses upon what the disciple *receives* from God, and shows that God's gift is unimaginably greater than anything men can do even by way of honest self-denial. The saying of Jesus in 29–30 has no doubt been coloured by the Church. Possibly with the substitution of Luke's 'for the sake of the kingdom of God' (Lk. 18:29), for the Marcan **for my sake and for the gospel,** the words down to **receive a hundred-**

fold are genuine words of Jesus. What follows is the interpretative comment of a Church that knew how to rejoice in the larger fellowship of the Christian community, experienced the goodness of God there and then, not only in that fellowship but in the midst of the sufferings it had to endure (**with persecutions**), and believed that death itself could not terminate such goodness (**and in the age to come eternal life**). **Many that are first will be last, and the last first:** an independent saying (cf. the different contexts in Mt. 20:16 and Lk. 13:30), which in its Marcan setting may refer to the final divine reversal of the fortunes of the rich and the poor or of the more prominent and the more obscure disciples. But probably from Mark's point of view, verse 31 comes as a reminder that far from being a fundamental prerequisite of discipleship (Peter's stance in verse 28), human achievement is an obstacle to that self-giving of God to men which alone makes authentic discipleship possible—so radically different is the divine ordering of things from man's.

The section 10:23-31 is not to be construed as a universal call to all would-be disciples to a life of voluntary poverty after the manner of a St Francis, nor yet as teaching that money or material possessions are inherently evil. Mark's message here is more searching. The disciple is not qualified as such by his own human endeavours, even by the abandonment of worldly goods and bonds. Rather, God's call and God's gift alone, when one is open to receive them, create the true disciple, leading him to put God first, hence to see the world and its prizes in their ultimate insignificance, and to attain to what by his own unaided effort would be impossible.

YET ANOTHER INTIMATION OF THE SUFFERING OF THE SON OF MAN
10:32-34

In the third prediction of the passion, replete with more graphic details, there is no reference back to the other two. The pattern of 10:32-52 is similar to that of 9:30-10:31: the coming passion, the blindness of the disciples, the true nature of discipleship and the miracle of God's grace that makes it possible. Mark's view that the gospel of the suffering Son of man includes also the call to a discipleship of suffering and sacrifice, is well served by his placing of this fuller form of passion prediction at the head of the section 10:35-52. The reference to Jesus' being delivered to the Gentiles (not paralleled in 8:31 or 9:31) and their treatment of him (33–34), suggests that this version of the prediction may have been formulated in a Palestinian(?) Jewish-Christian Church (Schweizer, *GNM*, p. 216). Possibly Mark himself was responsible for the bridging comments of verse 32.

32. Here for the first time in the Marcan narrative **Jerusalem** is expressly mentioned as the goal of Jesus' journey. Since the city is for Mark the seat and centre of bitterest hostility to Jesus (cf. 3:22), its mention symbolises the inevitability of Jesus' coming death, and the alarm and fear that occur here are at their sharpest. The fact that **he was walking ahead of them** indicates that he is out on his own in moving of deliberate intent towards his passion. All others can follow in their bewilderment only at a distance. The unspecified **them** in the phrase **of them** denotes the Twelve, who in their astonishment cannot comprehend that this road to Jerusalem must be God's way for Jesus. Those who followed and were afraid will then refer to the larger company of adherents who are also touched by a mysterious sense of impending terror. For Mark the taking aside of the Twelve once more (cf. 5:40; 9:2) shows up the continuing incomprehension of the disciples and at the same time God's longing to overcome their blindness through Jesus as the bearer of his word.

33–34. In view of his special interest in the close association of Jesus' destiny of suffering and death with the way of the disciple, the Evangelist may have seen a special significance in the first person plural, *we* **are going up to Jerusalem.** Much of the vocabulary in these verses is common in Mark and may reveal the Evangelist's hand. At any rate the various details enumerated appear to reflect the Church's knowledge of the event after Easter and the influence of *OT* passages like Isa. 50:6 and Ps. 22:7. The six stages of the cross are clearly referred to (although there is no specific mention of the crucifixion itself as in Mt. 20:19; cf. Mk 16:6; Ac. 2:36; 4:10), and the segment reads like a skeleton outline of the passion story and may owe something to the Church's liturgical interests.

RANK AND PRECEDENCE ERADICATED AMONG DISCIPLES **10:35–45**

Luke omits this story altogether, but does report the saying of Mk 10:42–44 in the context of the Last Supper (Lk. 22:25–27), significantly excluding the theologically profound statement of Mk 10: 45 and including a much simpler statement of Jesus: 'I am among you as one who serves.' Matthew attributes the request of the sons of Zebedee to their mother (20:20f.), no doubt to avoid discrediting the disciples themselves, but his dependence on Mark is shown by the fact that in his report the two brothers are by no means completely absolved either (Mt. 20:22-24). In Mark, the response of Jesus to the request of the sons of Zebedee in verses 38-39, where he invites them to share in his destiny, seems to be at variance with his repudiation of their request in verse 40. Consequently it is often held that verses 38-39 are a later Church addition, reflecting the Church's sacramental practice in Baptism and the Eucharist, the cost of participation in which was very likely to be martyrdom, or the Church's thoughts on the martyrdom of the two apostles, or controversies about leadership in the Church with regard to the position of James and John relative to others (cf. Mt. 16:18). However, it is not impossible that the sayings of 38-39 simply pick up *OT* metaphors and go back in something like their present form to Jesus himself. Certainly the saying of verse 40 would appear to be authentic, since the Church is unlikely to have played down the prerogative of Jesus in this way.

While the complex problems of the history of the various items of tradition in this story remain unsolved, the Evangelist's primary interest in and understanding of the section are clear enough. In 42a he has provided a typically Marcan connexion between the episode of 35-41 and the sayings of 42b-45. Moreover the sequence of 10:32-45 parallels that of 9:30-37, an intimation of the passion is followed first by a dispute about precedence and then by teaching on *true* discipleship. Above all, Mark's dominant theme is the disciples' lack of understanding in face of the truth that God's way of suffering and sacrifice for Jesus is identical with God's way for his disciples, and the **ransom** saying of verse 45 (whatever conclusions are reached about its background and authenticity), which rounds off the story, is of the highest importance for the Evangelist since it holds up the *One* who suffers for the many as a paradigm for all those followers who must suffer in their turn.

35-37. James and John are stamped out here as representative of those who cannot understand God's will and way. They still reckon by purely human norms and standards and are preoccupied with the question of who shall be first in rank and dignity rather than who shall be first in suffering and service. **grant us to sit ... at your left:** the place of highest honour was the seat on the right, and next to it that on the left, of the host or ruler. **in your glory:** Mark will have had in mind the glory of Christ, in his parousia (see 8:38; cf. Mt. 25:31). Matthew has 'in your kingdom' (20:21) and so makes it refer to the messianic kingdom expected by the disciples in the very near future. But the Marcan phrase is compatible either with the notion of thrones of judgment (cf. Mt. 19:28; Lk. 22:30) or of the chief seats at the messianic banquet (cf. Mk 14:25). The point for Mark is that their human desires and aspirations run counter to God's will for Jesus and his disciples.

38. You do not know what you are asking: underscores for Mark the disciples' blindness. They are as yet bound by traditional ideas and expectations out of the Jewish past and so are unprepared to comprehend the new and unexpected element in the strange good news of the Son of man's suffering. When Jesus asks **Are you able to drink the cup that I drink?** he is using an *OT* metaphor. In the *OT* **the cup** is a symbol either of joy or salvation (Ps. 16:5; 23:5; 116:13); or, on the other hand, of suffering and punishment (Ps. 11:6; 75:8; Isa. 51:17, 22; Jer. 25:15, 17, etc.). The words about **being baptized with the baptism with which I am baptized** are more problematic and their meaning much more debated. Again the imagery of 'being drowned in the flood' as a metaphor for 'being overwhelmed with calamity' occurs in the *OT* (e.g. Ps. 42:7; 69:2, 15; 124:4–5; Isa. 43:2), although the Greek *OT* does not use the word *baptizein* in this connexion. Paul testifies to the concept of baptism as incorporation with the Lord *in his death*, followed by rising to new life (Rom. 6:3–8). While the words of verses 38–39 would have reminded the Church of the 'cup' of the Lord's Supper and of the rite of Baptism, and of how the sacraments identified them with Christ in his destiny, we need not suppose they were first formulated in the light of the Church's sacramental practice or theology. Nor is it necessary to suppose that 38–39 represent the Church's reflection on the martyr deaths of the two brothers. The evidence that John was martyred hangs in fact on a very slender thread of tradition, and the other tradition that he died peacefully in old age at Ephesus has, if anything, a better claim. Possibly then Jesus himself took up *OT* imagery to refer in a general way to the extreme tribulations the brothers would have to undergo as followers of his. Whether in 38–39 he also entertained apocalyptic ideas of his suffering and death as a baptism anticipating the coming regeneration of the world (see Schweizer, *GNM*, p. 221) is very doubtful. At all events, for the Evangelist, verses 38–39 serve to illumine the Marcan theme that the way God has laid down for the suffering Son of man and the way of his disciples after him are integrally interrelated.

39–40. Jesus' question in verse 38 implies that he and he alone must first travel the Son of man's road to suffering and death. When the two disciples claim in reply, **We are able,** it does not mean their blindness is overcome and that they know there and then the secret of the Son of man's destiny, for they are no doubt thinking in glowing traditional terms of suffering as but a painful prelude to heavenly reward and blessing (as with the Maccabean martyred righteous), in accordance with their request in verse 37. Jesus now (in verse 39) promises them only that, on the basis of the completed way of the Son of man, the *future* lot of the disciple will be suffering and sacrifice, and as it stands in Mark, verse 40 shows that the focus is entirely there and all thought of reward or glory is relegated to the margin. They are to serve sacrificially as disciples and leave all else to God. The clause, **but it is for those for whom it has been prepared,** is highly condensed and consists of only three words in Greek, meaning most probably that 'rewards and places are not the disciple's concern but *only God's*'.

41–44. The action of Jesus in summoning the disciples, **called them to him,** is a typically Marcan connective and suggests the crucial significance for the Church of the instruction that follows. The words **supposed to rule over** imply not that men do not acknowledge their authority, but that their power is as nothing compared to God's sovereignty. **but it shall not be so among you:** a summary statement of how radically different from all worldly economies is the economy that must prevail (by reason of the divine sanction given in the Son of man's own service, verse 45) among the followers of Jesus. **whoever would be great . . . slave of all:** a brief but masterly description of the new economy of service and sacrifice for others in action (cf. 1 C. 9:19; 2 C. 4:5; Gal. 5:13).

45. The word **ransom** as used in the LXX has a variety of meanings, including money paid in compensation for a crime (Num. 35:31–32), or to redeem a life which would otherwise be forfeit (Exod. 21:30), or the fee handed over by the next of kin to purchase the freedom of a relative (Lev. 25:51–52), or the price paid as an equivalent for the sacrifice of the first-born (Num. 18:15). But the verb 'redeem' and the noun 'redemption', from the same root as the Greek word for 'ransom', are quite widely used also in the LXX and the *NT* in reference to God's deliverance of his people without any notion of a ransom-price paid, and in the light of this more general usage it is unwise to import back into the ransom-saying of Mk 10:45 later dogmatic theories of substitutionary atonement. The phrase **for many** (the preposition **for** (Greek *anti*) may mean simply 'for the sake of' or 'on behalf of', and not necessarily 'instead of') does not denote the majority as opposed to the minority (who are not 'ransomed'), but all others, the **many** over against 'the one' (see Isa. 53:11, 12; cf. 1 Tim. 2:6). There is no warrant here for the idea that Christ died only for the elect. Whether the ransom-saying is a genuine saying of Jesus has been long disputed. The view that it is, and that it has arisen on the basis of Jesus' application to himself and his mission of the Isaianic picture of the Suffering Servant who gives himself as an offering for sin (Isa. 53:10) through his obedience unto death (see e.g. Jeremias and Zimmerli; cf. Taylor, pp. 445f.), is no longer so secure as it once was. It appears that the influence of Isa. 53 on the synoptic tradition is merely peripheral. It is cited in only two passages (Mt. 8:17 and Lk. 22:37), in neither of which is it connected with the vicarious suffering and death of Jesus. In Mk 10:45 (as in 14:24) there is no direct literary allusion to Isa. 53, nor is the Greek word *doulos* (= 'slave' or 'servant') ever applied to Jesus in the Gospels. Elsewhere in the *NT*, when Isa. 53 is quoted, it is not associated with Jesus' death as an atonement, but as in Ac. 8:32f. with humiliation–exaltation, and as in 1 Pet. 2:24f. with his suffering as an example to be followed (Hooker, *JS*; *SMM*; Barrett, *JGT*, pp. 40, 51, 100; Schweizer, *GNM*, p. 219). If then the evidence of the *NT* scarcely bears out the contention that Jesus clearly interpreted his mission in terms of the Suffering Servant role, arguably the ransom-saying has a more immediate background in the notion of the Maccabean martyrs giving their lives as a ransom-price for Israel, and arguably in that light Jesus could have uttered it. On the other side, however, while there is no precise verbal parallel to the saying in Paul, the complex of ideas behind it seems to be typically Pauline (Gal. 3:13; Rom. 3:24; 1 C. 7:23, etc.). Even more significantly Luke (correctly from the historical angle?) places the sayings of Mk 10:42–44*a* in the context of a meal and attests that Jesus said only, 'But I am in the midst of you as a servant'. Since there is little if any evidence in the *NT* that Jesus thought of his death as a sacrificial offering for sin, we may infer that the ransom-saying is a later theologising expansion of Lk. 22:27. Whatever stance we occupy in regard to the historicity of Mk 10:45, there is no doubt that the Church which repeated the saying would have thought of Jesus not just as a heroic sufferer among others, but as the *One* who in his passion and death *had finally and uniquely fulfilled all suffering* and so had brought God's plan of redemption for men to ultimate fruition. Certainly also for the Evangelist the ransom-saying admirably rounds off the section 10:35–45. For him the truth enshrined in it is not merely something to be confessed or preached or even believed in, but the actual way laid down for all subsequent disciples and the divine justification for the new economy of sacrificial self-giving (described in 10:43–44) that must operate among them.

SIGHT BESTOWED AND DISCIPLESHIP MADE POSSIBLE 10:46–52

Healing miracles are *not* a feature of the section of the Gospel 8:27–10:52. The only other one is the cure of the epileptic lad in 9:14–29. We may therefore suppose that Mark has a quite special purpose in view in introducing the story of blind Barti-maeus' healing here at the close. Tradition clearly associated the story with a departure of Jesus from Jericho (**as he was leaving Jericho**) and in order to get Jesus *there*, Mark has provided the connecting link in 46a, **they came to Jericho.** The specific mention of the disciples in verse 46 is probably also a Marcan touch and a reminder to the reader that the dominant theme in 8:27–10:52 is in fact *discipleship*. Since the Aramaic *bar* means 'son', the name **Bartimaeus** means simply 'son of Timaeus', and the explanatory comment in the text **son of Timaeus** (quite un-necessary in the Jewish context) was most probably added when the story was taken up and repeated in the Greek-speaking Church. The concluding notice in verse 52, **followed him on the way,** plainly connects the report of the blind beggar's healing with the Marcan motif of discipleship.

47. Jesus, Son of David: nowhere else in Mark is Jesus called **Son of David;** it is here simply a messianic title. The *Psalms of Solomon* (17:23), from around the time of Jesus, testify to Jewish expectation of a Messiah of David's line, and the Qumran sec-tarians also awaited a Davidic or royal Messiah (as well as a Messiah of the house of Aaron and an eschatological Prophet). Mark may have seen a connexion between the designation Son of David here and the messianic fervour of the people on the entry into Jerusalem in 11:9–11.

48–51. The people's rebuke to the blind man, **many rebuked him, telling him to be silent,** acts as a foil on the one hand to the blind man's strong intention toward Jesus, **he cried out all the more** (48) and **throwing off his mantle he sprang up and came to Jesus** (50), and on the other hand to Jesus' initiative in calling him and his readiness to do for him what needs to be done. For Mark the emphasis in the story is not on the *healing* as such (no action or healing word of Jesus is mentioned) but on the response of faith to God's call in Jesus (the form of address, **Master,** *Rabbouni* is higher than *rabbi* and perhaps is indication also, of the blind man's reverence for Jesus), through which blind eyes are opened and true discipleship becomes possible.

52. At the close it becomes particularly clear that the story functions as an example of how the veil is removed from the blind eyes only through the miracle of faith, by which Jesus is both understood and trusted. The Greek word for **has made you well** refers not only to physical well-being but to salvation in the religious sense. But we are reminded that salvation is no static inward possession, but expresses itself in the concrete actions of discipleship **on the way.** These last three words are a singularly appropriate link with the report that follows of Jesus' fateful journey into Jerusalem, but they would imply also for Mark and his readers that the way of the Son of man in suffering is the way of discipleship laid down for all subsequent believers.

THE PASSION AND RESURRECTION 11:1–16:8

Although included here under the above general heading, chapters 11–13 really form only a prelude to the passion story proper, which begins at 14:1. However, like the passion story itself, chapters 11–13 are set in Jerusalem, which Mark regards as the centre of opposition to Jesus, and in the thought of the Evangelist the events and teaching of 11–13 are for the most part closely associated with what is related in 14:1ff. (see e.g. the relation of 14:1 to 11:18). One or two considerations weigh against biographical reconstruction on the basis of chapters 11–13. (a) Against the impression derived from Mark that Jesus made his first and only visit to the holy city at this point are the facts that he was apparently known to Simon the leper (Mk 14:3), that Mt. 23:37 (= Lk. 13:34), implies other visits, and that John's Gospel records two other visits; (b) the Marcan arrangement of the ministry in Jerusalem into three days (11:1, 12, 19f.) is somewhat artificial, the last day being particularly overcrowded and 14:49 recording that Jesus' taught 'day after day' in the Temple; (c) some at least of the teaching particularly in chapter 12 is not specifically related to the impending crisis, and may equally well have had its setting in the Capernaum ministry.

It may be that Mark wanted to schematise the pre-passion ministry in Jerusalem into three days to conform with the three days of the passion story itself, and that his arrangement owed something to the already existing liturgical practice of the Church in celebrating a 'holy week'. But much more probably his collection of materials and the connections he makes are theologically motivated, and our attention should be directed to the message he wants to convey by means of them.

THE ENTRY INTO JERUSALEM 11:1-11

This story in Mark is remarkably muted compared with the corresponding stories in the other Gospels (Mt. 21:1-17; Lk. 19:28-38; cf. Jn 12:12-19), where Jesus' messianic action and claim are fully exposed. Here there is no open intimation that Messiah has come. Nor is there any citation of or allusion to Zech. 9:9, although the phrase by which the colt is described, **on which no one has ever sat** (11:2) looks like an embellishment of the tradition at the pre-Marcan stage to bring it into line with Zech. 9:9. No doubt when the story was repeated in the process of its transmission in the Church, it became more and more exposed to the beam of the believers' conviction that Jesus entered Jerusalem as Messiah of set intent and in conformity with *OT* prophecy. But as it stands in Mark, it is impossible to say whether Jesus himself aimed at a demonstration that he was a Messiah not of the Davidic warrior type of popular expectation but rather like the peaceful king of Zech. 9:9. In fact, aside from the fleeting excitement of the crowd, there is little to indicate that the entry was a spectacular event. In the sequel the authorities do not proceed against Jesus because of it, and he himself makes no capital out of the plaudits of the crowd.

1. The geographical notice is strange, since **Bethphage** is mentioned first although it actually lies closer to Jerusalem than

Bethany. The MS tradition witnesses to a number of variants, and
either Bethphage or Bethany may be a scribal insertion (Mt. 21:1
reads only Bethphage). But the reading **Bethphage and Bethany**
is very well attested, and it is likely that the reverse order of the
villages is due to Mark's lack of first-hand knowledge of their
exact location. According to the prophecy of Zech. 14:4, **the
Mount of Olives** was to be the place where God would come in
final judgment of Israel's enemies, and Josephus (*Ant.* xx.8, 6)
associates it with the appearance of Messiah. The mention of **the
Mount** would have awakened in Mark's readers thoughts of the
kingdom of God coming in and with Jesus.

2–8. That Jesus here undertakes a symbolic act of messianic
fulfilment is nothing like so explicit as in Mt. 21:5 (cf. Jn 12:15),
and this is in accord with Mark's interest in the 'messianic
secret'. The focus in Mark is on the sovereign authority with which
Jesus acts so that his command is at once obeyed and things turn
out exactly as he says. The notion that Jesus had entered into a
pre-arrangement with someone in the city and knew that the **colt**
would be ready is quite foreign to the spirit of the story. Rather for
Mark Jesus appears as the one with the knowledge and power to
make things happen. The Greek word for **colt** usually means by
itself the 'colt of a horse'. Unlike Mark, Matthew specifies the
colt of a donkey and, although the villagers most likely did use
donkeys, he does so on the basis of Zech. 9:9. The comment **on
which no one has ever sat** probably entered the tradition before
Mark as an accommodation to Zech. 9:9. It describes the animal
as consecrated to a unique and holy use almost as if it were a
sacrificial animal (Dt. 21:3; Num. 19:2). According to verse 3
Jesus arms his disciples against difficulties in advance, by furnishing them with the word to speak. When Jesus says **The Lord
has need of it,** only here in Mark is **Lord** used as a title. By way
of protecting the substantial historicity of the story, some commentators resort to explaining it as meaning 'God' or 'the owner
of the donkey' who was with Jesus (Taylor, p. 455). But in a context in which the supreme authority of Jesus over all things is
highlighted, the later Church title 'Lord' with all that it implies
is particularly appropriate. **found a colt tied at the door out
in the open street:** the prophecy of Zech. 9:9 arises from the
blessing of Judah in Gen. 49:9–12, 'binding his foal to the vine
and his ass's colt to the choice vine'. It appears that certain Church
fathers like Justin and Clement read in their text of Mark 'tied to

the vine' (*epi tou ampelou*) for **tied . . . in the open street** (*epi tou amphodou*), but this is a further accommodation of the story to *O T* prediction. According to verses 5–6, precisely what Jesus had said would happen does happen. Since Jesus is riding and has a fair distance to cover, the spreading of **their garments on the road** is surprising. 2 Kg. 9–13 reports the laying of garments under the feet of King Jehu. **leafy branches . . . cut from the fields:** only Jn 12:13 speaks of '*palm* branches'. But palms were not native to the Jerusalem neighbourhood and **branches** here probably refers to other foliage or even to grasses. The description here and in verse 9 is reminiscent of the actions of pilgrims at the Jewish Feast of Tabernacles, and may imply that the entry to Jerusalem took place in the autumn. But it has been conjectured by F. C. Burkitt (*JTS* 17 (1916), pp. 139ff.; see Taylor, p. 456; Nineham, p. 293), that the Feast of Dedication accompanied by similar actions and celebrating the rededication of the Temple is in view, in which case the entry would have taken place in December.

9–10. The recitation of the *Hallel* (Pss. 113–118) was a feature of the Feast of Tabernacles, as of other Jewish feasts. The cry of the crowd here **Hosanna! Blessed be he who comes in the name of the Lord!** approximates very closely to the closing words of the *Hallel* (Ps. 118:25–26a). The Hebrew word **Hosanna** is a prayer to God and means 'Save now!'. But coupled with the blessing that follows, **blessed be he who comes in the name of the Lord!** it could be used as a greeting to any pilgrim coming to the feast (Ps. 118:25–26a). Accordingly, the first shout here does not make any overt reference to Jesus as Messiah, although no doubt for Mark and his readers the designation **he who comes** would have strong eschatological overtones. The final shout in verse 10 much more explicitly relates the coming of Jesus to the dawning of the kingdom. In Jewish sources **David** is not described as **our father.** The name is usually applied to the patriarchs, especially Abraham, Isaac, and Jacob. Verse 10 is wanting in Matthew and Luke, and in view of this and the strange expression **kingdom of our father David,** we may think of it as added by a Church that knew Jesus as Son of David, and wanted to express more openly what is implicit in the cry of verse 9. In the acclamation **Hosanna in the highest!** the term **Hosanna** has clearly lost its original force of 'Save now!' and has become simply a liturgical formula of praise meaning 'Praise to God in high heaven'.

11. This verse is without parallel in Matthew and Luke, where the cleansing of the Temple follows immediately upon the entry to Jerusalem. In Mark it appears to be a somewhat detached notice, and the mere mention of a 'tour of inspection' of the Temple by Jesus seems pointless. Possibly it is a piece of ancient and perhaps authentic tradition picked up by Mark. On the other hand various items are typically Marcan (e.g. the abrupt singling out of the Twelve), and it may be that since Mark chooses to insert his account of the cleansing of the Temple in the midst of the story of the fig tree, he has composed this verse to prepare the way for the Temple episode. Only at 11:15 does this apparently quite incidental visit take on significance.

In contrast with the messianic over exposure in the other Gospels' account of the entry into Jerusalem, the messianic reserve of the Marcan story is striking. Thus Mark preserves the paradox that in the lowly pathway of the Son of man to his passion and death, still not fully understood either by the disciples or the people, resides his divine authority.

THE FIG TREE, THE TEMPLE, AND ROOM FOR THE GENTILES
11:12-26

In accordance with the stylistic device he has adopted elsewhere also (3:22-30; 5:21-43), Mark here inserts the cleansing of the Temple (11:15-19), within the framework of the story of the cursing of the fig tree (11:12-24 and 20-25), so that the two help to interpret each other and together illumine the message he wishes to communicate. There are numerous objections to the historicity of the cursing and subsequent withering of the fig tree. It is the only miracle of destruction recorded of Jesus, and is out of character with the rest of what we know about him; it has traits in common with the legendary stories of the later apocryphal gospels; it is inherently irrational, for why should a tree be cursed for not bearing figs *out of season*! Nor does the Marcan story, which reads like a nature-miracle and is of a different order from the parabolic actions of the prophets in 2 Chr. 18:10; Jer. 13:1ff.; 19:1ff.; 27:2 and 28:10ff., yield readily to the explanation that Jesus originally undertook an *acted* parable symbolising God's judgment upon the fruitlessness of Jerusalem. Probably the actions attributed to Jesus in the story represent a legendary concretising (the suggestion that it arose from the existence of a conspicuous withered fig tree on the road between Bethany and Jerusalem is purely speculative) of the parable of Lk. 13:6–9, where the fig tree is an image for the house of Israel, and the fact also that in several *OT* passages (e.g. Jer. 8:13; Jl 1:7; Ezek. 17:24; Mic. 7:1–6; Hos. 9:10, 16f.) the fig tree refers to unfruitful or unrighteous Israel shows how the legend would have been told and transmitted from the first for its symbolic importance. The Church surely saw in it a symbol of God's final judgment upon faithless Israel. Later it was interpreted rather differently as a sign of the power of faith and prayer and the initially independent sayings of 11:22–26 were added to it to bring this out. Finally Mark incorporated the cleansing of the Temple with it in order to show that with the passing away of the old Israel under the judgment of God the new day of the turning of God's grace, in the gospel of the suffering Son of man, to *all* peoples had dawned.

By contrast, the account of the cleansing of the Temple has behind it an actual historical incident in the ministry of Jesus. But were his actions in the Temple a blow at the priestly Sadducean aristocracy with their vested interests in the Temple commerce, and through them at the Roman authorities to whom they were friendly disposed (Brandon, pp. 338ff.)? Or do the residual elements of violence in the story indicate that Jesus entered the heavily guarded Temple area by force at the head of an armed band of insurrectionists (Carmichael, pp. 111ff.)? Or failing such extreme views of Jesus' act as political or revolutionary in character, was he leading a movement of reform for the Temple, as verse 16 might suggest? So theologically orientated is the story and so much has each Evangelist given it his own particular interpretation that it provides no firm basis for historical reconstruction. Far from a major military or political or reform exploit having been 'denatured' in the story, it appears much more likely that what was originally a minor episode in a corner of the Temple court has been magnified in the tradition and developed according to the theological predilections of the Evangelists.

Some later prophecies of the *OT* (Mal. 3:1; Zech. 14:21; Hos. 9:15) predict the renewal of the Temple in the last days, and it is just possible that these have had an influence on the development of the report. However, it is the statement of Jesus in 11:17, citing Isa. 56:7 and alluding to Jer. 7:11, that forms the centrepiece of the whole passage for Mark. As the fig tree representing stubborn Israel comes under Jesus' curse and thereby under

God's ultimate judgment, so the Temple and what it stands for comes under the withering blast of his prophetic word. In introducing the statement of verse 17 with the formula **and he taught, and said to them,** Mark shows that for him Jesus appears in the Temple above all as the supremely authoritative Teacher whose word greatly agitates the Jewish authorities, and it is around this theme of word-conflict with the leading representatives of Judaism that 11:27-12:37 is organised (E. Trocmé, *NTS* 15 (1968-9), pp. 4ff.). The way of Jesus culminating in suffering and death is a dire threat to existing institutions and offends and alienates their upholders.

Whereas Mark fuses the cleansing of the Temple and the cursing of the fig tree together, and makes then the introduction to a series of controversies with Judaism and its leaders, Matthew makes the cleansing of the Temple the climax of the entry to Jerusalem, sees both as the revelation of the prophet-Messiah, and places the cursing of the fig tree later (Mt. 21:18ff.). All the Synoptic Gospels are at one, however, in locating the cleansing of the Temple at the close of Jesus' ministry, and their chronology is probably correct, since Jesus' activity in the Temple seems largely to have occasioned the final vehement opposition that led to his arrest, trial, and death (see e.g. Mk 11:18, 28; 14:58; 15: 29f.). When in his Gospel John places the cleansing of the Temple at the very beginning of Jesus' ministry, he does so probably because of his own literary and theological design by which he aims to stress that the split with Judaism was final and irremediable from the very first.

12-14. The notice that **he was hungry** is best explained as an attempt made during the transmission of the tradition to furnish a natural, if inadequate (since hunger is a lame reason for cursing a fruitless fig tree) explanation of what follows. Discussions among the commentators about the habits of fig trees in Palestine have not, like the tree in the story itself, proven fruitful. The explanatory comment **for it was not the season for figs,** almost certainly an editorial insertion, is correct enough since figs do not ripen before June, but it makes the curse upon the tree all the more irrational. (Why fault it for not bearing fruit before the time?) Whether the interpolated comment had to do with the dating of the event around Passover time or was intended to show that the story had only symbolic significance is difficult to say.

15. With the editorial phrase **and they came to Jerusalem,**

Mark introduces the Temple cleansing into the still unfinished story of the cursing of the fig tree. In his understanding, just as the cursing of the tree is a picture of God's judgment on hard-hearted Israel, so Jesus' expulsion of the merchants is a sign of the divine judgment on the Temple in particular. The scene of the cleansing was the outermost court of the Temple, the Court of the Gentiles. By the colonnades around it the scribes were fond of teaching their pupils (see Mk 1:22), and on the pavement the traders conducted their business of selling wine, salt, oil, and sacrificial animals, and at certain seasons the money-changers exchanged the Greek or Roman money of pilgrims into the Jewish or Tyrian currency that was required for the payment of the Temple tax. What was Jesus' intention in driving out the merchants and overthrowing the money-changers' tables? Did he set himself up as the champion of the poor pilgrims victimised by corrupt traders? Was he thus the instigator of a reform in the Temple, either through zeal for the purity of the Law or for the purity of God's house (cf. Jn 2:17), and did he wish to arrest the process of secularisation of the Temple system? Against this is the fact that although the system provided ample opportunities for abuse, no doubt often taken, there was nothing inherently illegal or evil in the commerce of the Court of the Gentiles. It was an accepted and indeed necessary part of the total life of the Temple. In fact the story in itself gives little if anything away about Jesus' own motives. Possibly his gesture against the merchants was a prophetic symbolic act accompanied by a warning about God's impending judgment on the Temple.

16. The injunction against carrying a vessel **through the Temple** and so making it a short-cut is peculiar to Mark. But it shows a thoroughly Jewish respect for the Temple and conforms in fact to a rule of the Mishnah against entering the Temple with staff, sandal, or wallet, or with dust on the feet (*Berak.* 9:5). Accordingly it most probably came to Mark as a piece of tradition from a Church that was eager to tone down Jesus' opposition to the Temple as expressed in the cleansing.

17–18. It is difficult to see how amid the disturbance created by his actions (verse 15) Jesus could have entered into a session of teaching. The words **taught and said to them** are a Marcan formula which shows the real importance for him of the Temple cleansing episode. Jesus' cleansing of the Temple is thus brought by Mark under the cover of his *teaching activity*—in Greek the verb

taught means 'taught continually (cf. 1:21-28). It would appear
that Mark understood the quotation of Isa. 56:7 and the allusion
to Jer. 7:11 on Jesus' lips as directed not against the merchants of
verse 15 but against the Jewish authorities in general (see verse 18)
and possibly the Temple authorities in particular. For Mark
verse 17 sets the scene for the controversies with the Jewish
authorities that follow in the section 11:27-12:37. The weapons
Jesus carries on the eve of his passion are certainly not those of the
freedom-fighter or revolutionary political agent, but those of the
uniquely authoritative teacher whose prophetic word terrifies the
leading representatives of Judaism. The phrase **for all the
nations,** omitted by Matthew and Luke, is clearly extremely
important for Mark. When this is coupled with the perfect tense
of the verb 'make' in the statement **you have made it a den of
robbers** (or better 'a cave of brigands') it will be seen that Mark
is presenting Jesus not as the reformer of an institution that remains viable, but as the one who declares the final word against
an inward-looking and enclosed institution whose day of exclusivism is now over and done with, since the grace of God offered in
the place of prayer must be available not just for a select group,
but for all peoples. In verse 18, in terms characteristic of him and
reminiscent of 3:6, the Evangelist shows how it is this **teaching,**
this prophetic word that overcomes all narrow institutionalism
and opens the way to God for *all* men, that bewilders the multitude,
alienates the Jewish leaders, and is inseparably connected with his
suffering and death (**sought a way to destroy him**).

19. It is hardly worth speculating about the motives for this
withdrawal, **they went out of the city.** Probably it is no more
than an accommodation to Mark's somewhat artificial time-
scheme and prepares for verse 20, although it may also symbolise
for Mark Jesus' separation from Jerusalem and its institutions
(Schweizer, p. 234).

20-21. The interrupted story of **the fig tree** is now resumed
and Peter's observation that it **has withered** as a result of Jesus'
curse draws attention dramatically to the finality of Jesus' prophetic word of judgment against the arid legalism and institutionalism of Jewish religious practices.

22-25. To the story of the fig tree symbolising God's judgment
on unfruitful Israel are now appended sayings on faith and prayer,
the connexion being made somewhat artificially on an understanding (by the Church) of the cursing of the fig tree as symbolic

not of God's judgment but of the miraculous power of Jesus' own *faith*. The sayings of verses 22–25 were originally independent but were no doubt brought together in the tradition before Mark for catechetical reasons around the catchwords **faith** (22) and **believes** or 'has faith' (23), **prayer** (24), and **praying** (25). Possibly the sayings were linked with the fig tree story also before Mark, since what appears to be the Q version of Mk 11:23 in Lk. 17:6 speaks of a 'mulberry tree' instead of a 'mountain', and this may have arisen through association with the account of the fig tree. In 11:22 Mark stresses the applicability to the Church at large of the instruction that follows by reporting that **Jesus answered them,** that is not only Peter but all the disciples. He then leads into the sayings of 23–25 with the general exhortation, **Have faith in God.** The saying about the **mountain** being **taken up and cast into the sea** might in its Marcan form at first seem to imply that lively faith is a human accomplishment— 'make the effort of faith and obstacles will be overcome'. Any such implication is avoided in what may be the original version of the saying in Mt. 17:20, 'If you have faith as a grain of mustard seed, you will say to this mountain, "Move hence to yonder place", and it will move', for here the call is certainly not to a greater or stronger faith but to 'a faith to which everything has been promised just because it expects everything from God and nothing from itself' (Schweizer, p. 234). But Mark's version of the saying states essentially the same thing (in what is obviously figurative and hyperbolic language). The Marcan expansion, **and does not doubt in his heart,** has ultimately the same effect as 'like a grain of mustard seed' in Mt. 17:20, since the Greek verb for **doubt** has the sense of 'waver' or 'hesitate'. So the message here also is that whoever does not dally with reliance on his own worldly resources but waits wholly upon God will not find God wanting. The saying of verse 24, **Therefore I tell you . . . you will,** makes a similar point once more in an exaggerated, if less picturesque way. Here again the stress is not on what man desires or the strength of his desire but on faith's openness before all else to what God is ready to give. Introduced here as belonging to the theme of prayer, the saying of verse 25 comes as a reminder that the great barrier to a fruitful relationship between man and God is one's alienation or estrangement from his fellow-men (cf. 1 C. 13:2). The custom of standing for prayer (**you stand praying**) was common among the Jews, although kneeling also was permissible. The last clause of verse 25 does not necessarily reflect a knowledge of the Lord's Prayer, but it does reveal the influence of Mt. 6:14, just as verse 26, omitted in most MSS and rightly excluded by *RSV*, appears to be a slightly revised form of Mt. 6:15.

THE QUESTION OF JESUS' AUTHORITY RENEWED IN JERUSALEM
11:27-33

In 11:12-22 Jesus is pictured above all as the bearer of the final prophetic word of judgment on Israel. The scene is thus set for a series of controversies (cf. 2:1-3:6) regarding the authority by which he brings this word, and the first of these is now reported. Even if Mark composed verse 27 himself to link up this controversy story with the Temple, the repeated phrase **these things** in verse 28 would to his mind refer not merely to Jesus' cleansing of the Temple but to his whole preaching and teaching activity (11:12-25). The suspicion that the setting of this story in the Temple is secondary (rather than historical) is increased by the thought that following on the incident of 11:15 Jesus would hardly have been able to walk unimpeded so shortly after in the Temple area. The counter-question posed by Jesus in verse 30 would normally have been the conclusion to this rabbinic-style of debate in which Jesus no doubt participated with his Jewish opponents. It suggests that Jesus' questioners were open to accepting John's credentials and implies that if, as they must, they acknowledge these to be **from heaven** they must also acknowledge the same of Jesus. In verses 31-33 a different situation is reflected, however, and a high Christian estimate of the Baptist's role appears to be set against Jewish rejection of him. We may therefore detect in these verses the influence of the early Church in its conflicts with Judaism, and if they are in fact secondary we do not need to ask whether *Jesus* perceived the Jewish authorities' dilemma on their faces or perhaps overheard their whispered conversation.

27-30. The three groups **the chief priests and the scribes and the elders,** are the divisions of which the Sanhedrin was composed, but what is in view here is that a representative delegation from the Sanhedrin came to Jesus. The **authority** at issue in the question put to Jesus (verse 28) is not of the legal or political or official religious order but has to do with the divine legitimation of his ministry, as the sequel shows. The **baptism of**

John mentioned by Jesus in verse 30 is a case of 'the part for the whole', and refers to the ministry of John in its entirety (cf. 1:4). The phrase **from heaven** is a periphrasis for 'from God', a reverential Jewish usage to avoid mentioning the divine name. The repeated **answer me** in Jesus' counter-question in verses 29-30 underlines the fact that he wants a *straight* reply.

31-33. The Jewish authorities might more naturally have been expected to reckon that if they held John's credentials to be **from heaven,** Jesus would have insisted his were also. Instead they suppose he would say **Why then did you not believe him?** and the notion of '*believing John*' sounds like a formulation of the early Church from its own faith standpoint. At any rate the Jewish leaders are here depicted as men who, even while they come to Jesus with their questions, are quite unprepared to come to a decision about him. This is further clarified by their final response, **we do not know:** they equivocate or sit on the fence, and the implication is that they are waiting for further corroborative evidence before making up their minds. The closing words of Jesus, **neither will I tell you by what authority I do these things,** are most important for Mark in that they summon his hearers to decision about him without any evidence beyond hs own presence and maintain the truth that God acts in 'hiddenness' on the pathway of Jesus.

THE PARABLE OF THE WICKED HUSBANDMEN **12:1-12**

The opening formula in 12:1 and the conclusion of the story in 12:12 are distinctively Marcan in style and vocabulary. By providing such a framework for the parable, the Evangelist accommodates it to a context in which the dominant theme is the conflict of Jesus as the authoritative Teacher (on the way to his passion) with the Jewish leaders. Of course in terms of its content the parable lends itself well to such accommodation, for like the story of the cursing of the fig tree, it calls Israel to judgment. Mark and his first readers must surely have come to this story in the light of their knowledge of the actual passion and death of Jesus and must have understood it as an allegory in which the **vineyard** stands for Israel, the **tenants** for the Jewish authorities, the **servants** for the *OT* prophets, and the **son** and **heir** for Jesus. In its present form the story seems in fact to presuppose such knowledge. Whereas it may not be categorically stated that Jesus himself always scrupulously avoided allegorical details in his stories, his customary method was undoubtedly to confront his hearers with only one principal point of comparison or analogy (e.g. 'the kingdom of God is like . . .'). The Church for its part did introduce allegorising interpretations into the parables of Jesus (see e.g. Mk 4:14–20; cf. 4:3–9), and the Church rather than Jesus himself has most likely been responsible for certain allegorical traits in this parable. Notably the specific mention of the 'only, beloved son', would appear to reflect the Church's confessional standpoint, its faith in Jesus as the Son of God. Moreover the destruction of **the tenants** and the handing over of **the vineyard to others** (verse 9) reflects a period of the Church's existence when the day of God's protective care for Israel alone is believed to have passed, and the day of God's turning to the Gentiles through the proclamation of the gospel has come.

Possibly, however, there stands behind the Marcan version of the parable a simpler and less embroidered story told originally by Jesus. Several features of the story are consistent with what we now know of the conditions prevailing in Palestine at the time of Jesus. Estates in Galilee belonging to foreign owners; the rebelliousness of tenant farmers, working under a share-cropping agreement, against their absentee landlords; the possibility of revolt against and violent treatment of a landlord's produce-collecting agents; even the possibility of the tenant farmers' believing that if they disposed of the landlord's own son, sent as a final recourse, they might take possession of the property. The Coptic *Gospel of Thomas* (65) in fact contains a brief tale along these lines, in which two servants are beaten and the son killed. In this more rudimentary form the parable would have been, like the cursing of the fig tree, a prophetic word of judgment against Israel.

Whatever the case may be concerning the origin of materials in the parable, there are certainly good grounds for regarding the 'stone-testimony' of verses 10–11 as a secondary addition to the story of verses 1–9. In this citation of Ps. 117:22–23 (LXX) the emphasis is not on 'rejection' but on the placement of the corner-stone or keystone, and it does not so much round off what is substantially a parable of judgment (1–9) as express the fullness of the Church's faith that the rejected 'son and heir', namely Jesus, has been vindicated by God and triumphed in the resurrection. It occurs in various *NT* passages sometimes in combination with other *OT* texts, usually as a testimony to Easter (Ac. 4:11; 1 Pet. 2:6–8; Rom. 9:33; Eph. 2:20).

1. **in parables:** Mt. 21:23 and Lk. 20:1 have 'parable', and of course only *one* is related here. But for Mark **in parables** means 'metaphorically' or 'figuratively', and describes Jesus' manner of speaking. **a man planted ... built a tower:** the vocabulary here is drawn from the LXX text of Isa. 5:1f., but with the statement **rented it out to tenants** this parable departs from Isa. 5:1f., where the subject is the tending of the vineyard, and concentrates on the behaviour of the tenants. As in Isaiah, however, the **vineyard** here represents Israel. The **hedge** set around the vineyard was probably a rough wall constructed of stones gathered from the soil, the pit a sunken trough into which the juice was filtered when the grapes were trodden, and the **tower** a hut of leaf-covered wood or possibly of stone which served both as a look-out on its high place and as a shelter for the vine-dressers at harvest time. The details of the description have no bearing on the development of the story and are not to be interpreted allegorically. The owner of the vineyard lives abroad, **went into another country.**

2-4. The usual arrangement was for the tenant farmer to meet his own expenses and return to the owner a quarter to a half of the produce (**sent a servant ... to get from them some of the fruit**). An atmosphere of sedition against foreign landlords with vested interests in Jewish territory would account for the brutal treatment of the owner's servants. The story affords a telling illustration of how violence breeds on violence.

5-8. The owner's repeated sending of **many others,** only for them to be cruelly handled also, is so exaggerated and incredible that it may be a later embellishment of the story designed to magnify the wickedness of the **tenants** (= Israel) and the inexhaustible patience of the **owner** (= God). The term **beloved,** which can mean 'only' (cf. 1:11), has messianic overtones and lends credence to the view that the Church has had a hand in shaping up the story allegorically in the light of its knowledge of Christ's passion and its faith in him as Son of God. The owner's feeling, **they will respect my son,** has the effect of underlining God's great expectations of his people Israel and of how terribly falsely stubborn Israel has played him in the end (see verses 7–8). The plot and crime of the tenants (the killing of the son, 7–8) is an act of folly, since the murder of the heir would plainly not have brought them the property so long as the owner was still alive. The irrationality of their conduct serves to stress once more how far gone they are in evil. Further the statement that they **cast him out of the vineyard** means that they did him the ultimate dishonour of leaving him unburied, an item in the parable which the Church has obviously not adapted to the story of the Lord's burial.

9. Jesus does not usually provide an answer himself to the questions with which his parables frequently close (in Mt. 21:41 it is the audience that answers). Here in Mark the response probably reveals the stance of a Church which knows already the great reversal that has taken place, the turning of God from an Israel who has brought his judgment upon herself and the offer of the blessings of the gospel to the Gentiles.

10-12. The quotation agrees verbatim with Ps. 117:22-23 in the Greek Bible. While it is not impossible that Jesus could have used these verses of the Hebrew Psalm to allude in a general way to his coming death and final vindication, in an attack on the Jewish hierarchy, their form here in Mark is no doubt due to a Greek-speaking Church. Possibly the Church was led to add this proof-text because it bore testimony to that other great reversal, the victory of the crucified Jesus in the resurrection, which made possible the reversal symbolised for the Church in verse 9. In the light of verses 10-11 the Evangelist himself would have thought that ultimate victory belongs with the rejected one, albeit in a manner only faith could understand. The parable both places the onus for Jesus' passion on the hard-heartedness and faithlessness of Israel, and summons men to decision in the face of the divinely willed pathway of suffering and death for the Son. The concluding statement of verse 12 is plainly Mark's own composition (the vocabulary and style are his), and in it he is careful to distinguish between the multitude, who while not yet understanding Jesus are not hostile to him, and the Jewish leaders who are well aware they have been put on the spot by Jesus' prophetic parable, but respond with a No to it. For Mark the parabolic teaching of Jesus admits of no evasion. In confrontation with it, it is a matter of Yes or No to the call of God concealed within it.

THE PHARISEES' QUESTION ABOUT THE TRIBUTE-MONEY **12:13-17**

This brief report is a pronouncement-story, in which everything is subordinate to the saying of Jesus in verse 17. The story begins with the impersonal plural **they sent** (in introducing it here Mark may have taken the **they** to refer to the Sanhedrin delegation of 11:27), and no notice is given of time or place. Accordingly not

knowing to what actual moment of Jesus' ministry the pronouncement of verse 17 originally belonged, we do not know clearly
either what he first intended by it, perhaps simply that the kingdom of God which demanded men's highest allegiance transcended
the political realm. At any rate there is no good reason to deny
the authenticity of the saying of verse 17, although the conflict-
story that leads up to it may owe something to debates between
the Church and Jewish circles.

13-14. The Herodians, the partisans of Herod Antipas, are
mentioned also in 3:6 as enemies of Jesus in league with the
Pharisees. Whether Mark considered them to symbolise a
nationalist group opposed to the payment of the tax is doubtful.
What is of the first importance for him is the radical insincerity
of their approach to Jesus. They do not come as honest and open
enquirers to listen to his word, but having closed their minds
against him already, **to entrap him in his talk.** Their strategy
is to force him into a position where whatever he says is bound to
outrage one group or another in Judaism (see also verse 15).
When they compliment him on being forthright, no respecter of
persons, and an esteemed guide to the way of life God wills for
men (verse 14), they are applying their strategy to get him to
declare himself on the thorny question they are about to pose. As
guide to the good life, Jesus should know whether the payment of
taxes to Caesar is part of it or not. Their question concerns the
payment of the poll tax, imposed on provincials in Judea, Samaria,
and Idumea and highly unpopular because it was a perennial
reminder of the Roman yoke and had to be paid in currency that
bore Caesar's name and image. This poll tax had provoked the
revolt of Judas of Galilee in AD 6, and according to Josephus
(*Ant.* XVIII.1:1 and 6) this brief and abortive exercise had something to do with the subsequent rise of the Zealot party, fanatical
in their hatred of Roman rule and active insurrectionists against it.

15-16. Jesus is pictured as detecting **their hypocrisy:** their
question is not a genuine one at all but merely a ruse to bring him
into trouble (**Why put me to the test?**) If he replied that the
tax should not be paid he would offend the Romans and their
fellow-travellers in Palestine. If he said it should, he would
alienate the nationalists. The **coin** was a silver denarius about the
weight of a Greek drachma. We ought not to read anything into
the fact that Jesus does not appear to have a coin himself. The
request, **bring me a coin,** shows that he is now taking over the

initiative from his enemies and is about to get the better of them. He does so not by denouncing their interest in such worldly things as money and taxes. Rather he himself accepts the facts of every-day life as facts, neither good nor bad, and constrains his questioners to do the same. The coinage they see and touch constantly is for their use, but as 'coin of the realm' it is a matter of fact ultimately the property of Caesar, and the **inscription** on the coin (Tiberius, Caesar, Son of the Divine Augustus, High Priest) itself bears silent witness to his right to rule. All this is just the ordinary course of affairs and Jesus does not appear here as one who is zealous to overthrow it.

17. Jesus' pronouncement has been endlessly discussed and very variously interpreted. The view that Jesus here counsels submission to the ruling political power and so defends the sovereign rights of the state is undoubtedly influenced by Rom. 13:1–7. But whereas the emphasis here with Jesus is on *God's call* to men *in the present*, in Rom. 13 the advice Paul gives about the appropriate Christian attitude to the state is given in the light of his expectation of the impending overthrow of the existing world order (see Rom. 13:11–14). Neither in this nor in his other sayings does Jesus give any indication that he considered the secular realm to have its own separate governing principles, so there is little to commend the view that he is here drawing a rigid line of division between the political and the religious spheres. Another view is that Jesus sets the higher law of God above the laws of the state and so by implication endorses political subversion. S. G. F. Brandon (pp. 345ff.) has taken this further in suggesting that the saying was in fact originally a political slogan. By subscribing to the prevailing Jewish conviction of his day that everything in the land of Israel was *God's* by right, Jesus, not unsympathetic to Zealot aspirations and ideals, was absolutely prohibiting the payment of any dues to Caesar. This political intention Mark eventually erased by incorporating the saying into a context which transforms it into a supine counsel to pay the tax. But from the slender clues afforded here, it is a mistake to attribute any particular political philosophy to Jesus. This is all the more so since in the form Jesus' saying takes the rendering **to Caesar** occupies a negligible place and all the weight of emphasis falls on rendering **to God the things that are God's**. In paying back the tax to Caesar in his own coinage men are *as a matter of course* simply giving him his own. But since men bear the image of God, they ought *as* *a matter of choice or decision* to surrender themselves always to the will of God. Caesar exists as a fact of everyday life. But his rule, like all ephemeral political forces, passes away. God's reign comes and remains and knows no end; and with its abiding reality Jesus challenges his hearers to come to terms. **And they were amazed at him:** at his cleverness in outsmarting his questioners? We do not really need to ask why, since by this conclusion the Evangelist himself simply draws attention to Jesus' supreme authority as teacher.

THE SADDUCEES' QUESTION ABOUT THE RESURRECTION 12:18–27

Representatives of another wing of Judaism, the **Sadducees,** now come to Jesus with a catch question. This story also culminates in sayings of Jesus, and these show how in controversial subjects the Church kept appealing to the word of Jesus. The conversation here is thoroughly Jewish and reflects the kind of debates in which different Jewish groups participated. It is quite possible that on occasion Jesus adopted some of the arguments presented in such debates. The saying of verse 25, for example, is echoed in the Talmud: 'In the world to come there is no eating or drinking or marrying or envying or hate; but the pious rest with crowns upon their heads, and are satisfied with the glory of God.' And the saying of verse 26 has the ring of a typical argument from the Pharisean tradition. But Christian teachers also were engaged in controversy with Jewish groups and no doubt gave a Christian twist to the interpretation of such sayings in applying them to the demands of their own situation (see commentary on 25–26). It is sometimes held that since the Sadducees in the hypothetical case they present in 12:19–23 really raise the characteristically Pharisean issue of the *manner* of the resurrection, the pronouncement of 12:25 which deals specifically with that must have formed the original conclusion of the story, and verses 26–27 are a later insertion. But the Sadducees, as we are immediately informed in verse 18, themselves denied the *fact* of the resurrection, and since the saying of verses 26–27 relates to the question of *fact*, it most probably also constituted an integral part of the original story.

18. The **Sadducees** are mentioned only here in Mark, and he tells his readers no more about them than what is necessary to understand the story, that they do not believe in the resurrection. The origins and history of the Sadducees, who scarcely formed a clearly defined and organised party, are obscure. They are gen-

erally believed to have derived their name from one Zadok,
possibly the high priest of David's time (2 Sam. 20:25). Conser-
vative in outlook, they came mainly from the priestly and aristo-
cratic class. From rabbinic sources we gather that they differed
from the Pharisees on certain points of interpretation of the Law.
Above all, whereas the Pharisees stood by the oral tradition as well
as the Law, Prophets, and Writings, the Sadducees considered
only the Pentateuch to be normative. In this regard it is interesting
that Jesus' response to them in 26–27 is based on Exodus. According to the *NT* their particular hallmark appears to be that they
did not believe in angels and spirits nor in the resurrection of the
dead, and this is confirmed also by Josephus (*Ant.* XVIII.1, 4). Their
non-belief in the **resurrection** is consistent with their reverence
for the Pentateuch alone. Neither the Pentateuch itself, nor for
that matter most of the remaining books of the *OT*, witness to
anything like a positive doctrine of life beyond death. The orthodox Hebrew notion was that the dead continued an existence that
was virtually non-existence as departed shades in Sheol. Only in
one or two passages in the later reaches of the *OT* literature are
there indications of a breakthrough to belief in the resurrection of
the dead (Isa. 26:19; Dan. 12:2). Not until after the martyrdoms
of the Maccabean wars did the doctrine of the resurrection of the
dead (in bodily form) begin to figure prominently in Judaism,
nourished to be sure by the conviction that Yahweh in his mighty
power would not allow death to come between him and his own
suffering righteous ones. The pseudepigraphical literature of the
intertestamental period testifies widely to the belief. By the time
of Jesus, therefore, the idea of the resurrection of the dead had
become fairly standard in Judaism, and it is unlikely that Sadducean disbelief in it constituted any real threat to him in his
ministry. However, at a time when the Church was seeking to
articulate its own new faith that the resurrection of Christ was the
divinely given pledge of the general resurrection of the dead
(see e.g. 1 C. 15:12ff.), it would have cherished a story like that
of Mk 12:18–27 as showing how the Lord himself had been involved in the question and had supported the belief from Scripture.

19–23. The introductory formula, **Moses wrote,** is particularly appropriate for the Sadducees because of their acknowledgement of the Pentateuch alone as binding. The words following
the formula in verse 19 are a free rendering of Dt. 25:5ff. and relate to the law of levirate marriage, which has very ancient

pre-biblical origins, but among the Hebrews was designed to ensure posterity for the deceased brother. The hypothetical case presented by the Sadducees in good rabbinic style (and the concluding question of verse 23) assumes the *Pharisees'* standpoint on the resurrection and is just such a case as the Pharisees discussed. The Sadducees' intention is to demonstrate that the law of levirate marriage laid down by Moses makes nonsense of Pharisean ideas of the resurrection. In such oriental stories the number **seven** is a common feature, as is the repetition, **died, leaving no children.**

24–25. In his reply, Jesus enters into no casuistical debate about the case of the seven brothers, but immediately raises the argument to a higher level with a counter-question. The mistake of the Sadducees is that they **know neither the scriptures nor the power of God:** by mentioning the **scriptures** and the **power of God** together Jesus shows that it is not the purpose of the scriptures to limit the horizons of men's thought to a law of human relationships *out of the past* but to bear testimony to the God whose power enables him to 'make all things new'. Not to know that God has surprises in store hereafter, beyond what is experienced in this everyday life, is the grievous fault. In the saying of verse 25 the life beyond death is at one and the same time unequivocally affirmed (**when they rise from the dead**) and portrayed as mysteriously transcending all that men can imagine here and now. This pronouncement could be construed as a rejoinder on Jesus' part to materialist hopes of an earthly, political kingdom of God which would be no more than a reformation of the *present* order of things. By the same token the Gentile Church would have found it useful as conveying to Gentile converts a transcendentalising of the Jewish climate of ideas, in which crass notions of the resurrection body were frequently entertained (cf. 1 C. 15:35ff.). The likening of the resurrected dead to celestial phenomena like **angels,** and the 'spiritualising' of the resurrection belief symbolised by it, are not of course peculiar to Jesus (see 'celestial bodies' in 1 C. 15:35ff.; 'angels' in *1 En.* 15:7; 104:4; *2 Bar.* 51:10.

26–27. Verses 24–25 are directed to the typically Pharisean question about the *mode* of the resurrection life, 26–27 to the Sadducean question about the *fact* of the resurrection. **in the passage about the bush:** the Greek reads literally 'at the bush'; cf. Rom. 11:2 where 'in Elijah' means 'in the passsage about Elijah'—a familiar style of abbreviated reference to a particular text. The argument adduced here from Exod. 3:6, not very convincing by modern standards, is a verbal one of the type common in contemporary rabbinic exegesis, and depends on the *present* **I am** in **I am the God of Abraham . . .:** in the context of Exod. 3:6 the declaration means that the God who once *was* with the patriarchs is not going to desert his people now in the wilderness under Moses, but promises to lead them to the land of Canaan. Here the idea is that since God says he *is* the God of the patriarchs, they cannot belong to the past but are alive with him in a life beyond death. Strange though the argument is and little as it actually mentions the *resurrection* of the dead, it expresses well the conviction that lies at the heart of the Church's resurrection faith that the God who fondly cares for his people here and now will not go back on his promise and forsake them in death. Stories like Mk 12:18–27 usually close with a notice about the people's reaction to Jesus' words (cf. Mt. 23:33; Lk. 20:40). But although the concluding statement in Mk 12:27, **you are quite wrong,** is somewhat unusual, it is not necessary to infer that verses 26–27 are a secondary interpolation, which has replaced a more usual ending. Certainly for Mark 'you are quite wrong' would have precisely the same effect as 'they were amazed at him' in the preceding story (12:17), of drawing attention to Jesus' unique authority as a teacher.

THE SCRIBE'S QUESTION ABOUT THE FIRST COMMANDMENT
12:28–34

This is not a conflict-story like the previous ones in the section. There is no condemnation of the scribe, overt or implied, but rather praise. The apparently parallel narrative in Q, preserved in Lk. 10:25–28 (which has possibly influenced Mt. 22:34–40), is a conflict-story in which the scribe seeks to put Jesus to the test, himself supplies the answer concerning the Law which is given by Jesus in Mark, and in turn raises the question of who the 'neighbour' is that leads into the parable of the Good Samaritan. If Lk. 10:25–28 is indeed a variant account of this incident (some think it is not, e.g. Manson, *Sayings*, pp. 259f.), Mark's version is probably the more original, since it is more likely that in its struggles with Judaism the Church would have transformed a peaceful dialogue of Jesus with a Jewish scribe into a conflict story than vice versa. The piling up of participles in verse 28 (there are three: 'having come', 'having heard', and 'having seen') is a Marcan stylistic trait, and it is likely that he has constructed the verse as a link with the preceding episode. However, his motive for including this story here is hardly to emphasise 'the essential orthodoxy of Jesus and his faithfulness to the Law' (Nineham, p. 323). It is true that in stating the first commandment Jesus only repeats what Israel had repeated for centuries (verse 29). But the way the commandment of 'love to the neighbour' is introduced and combined with the first (verse 31), and the striking reference to the scribe's 'nearness to the kingdom of God' (verse 34) suggest that Mark took a much more radical view of the passage and the subject of Jesus and the Law.

28. seeing that he answered them well: impressed by Jesus, the scribe offers him none of the fulsome compliments of the Pharisees and Herodians (12:13–14). Nor does he seek to trap Jesus. His question **Which commandment is the first of all?** is quite genuine. The rabbis searched for the weightiest commandment of the Law and came up with different answers. Hillel told a proselyte who asked to be instructed on the whole Law while standing on one leg: 'What thou hatest for thyself do not to thy neighbour: this is the whole Law, the rest is commentary; go and learn.' Rabbi Akiba said that Lev. 19:18 was the great principle of the Law.

29–31. The opening words of Jesus' reply to the scribe's question about the first commandment, **Hear, O Israel . . . the Lord is one,** are the beginning of the *Shema*ᶜ (Dt. 6:4–9; 11:13–21; Num. 15:37–41), the prayer which all pious Jews were expected to recite three times daily and which occupied a similar special position in late Judaism to the Lord's Prayer in Christianity. Only in Mark among the Synoptics (cf. Mt. 22:37; Lk. 10:27) are these words included. Though they are not strictly part of the commandment, they are of vital significance and must be presupposed, since it is only because God **is one** that he is worthy of all of man's devotion. That they were retained out of a need to defend monotheism in a Gentile *milieu* like Mark's is doubtful. The quotation from Dt. 6:5 in verse 30 corresponds fairly closely to the LXX but is not quite the same, nor does it fully match the Hebrew, and we may suppose that the Marcan form goes back to oral tradition passed on by a Church that did not any longer recite the *Shema*ᶜ. But here at least in his statement of the first commandment Jesus stands foursquare within the orbit of Jewish piety. **The second is this:** only Mark separates the two commandments so definitely as this (only of course to fuse them together again in a moment—**There is no other commandment greater than these**). Luke joins the two together by a simple 'and' (Lk. 10:27) and Matthew couples them with the comment 'and a second is like it' (Mt. 22:39). Now from the way Matthew and Luke run together the two commandments, there may just be the danger of our assuming that love to God and love to the neighbour are one and the same thing, in which case the divide between God and man would be violated and his insurpassable majesty lost. The way things are stated in Mark this danger is effectively overcome, for the absolute priority of love for God is established. The two commandments are directly interrelated but not identical, for recognition of the sovereignty of God and of the loving devotion that is his due is first, and the sole ground and sole dynamic of love to the neighbour. How original is Jesus' contribution here? His statement consists entirely of an almost word for word citation of two *OT* texts (Dt. 6:4–5 and Lev. 19:18), the former at the heart of Jewish piety and both much canvassed by the rabbis. Nor is it at all obvious that Jesus is here in creative fashion universalising the concept of 'neighbour' as in the parable of the good Samaritan (Lk. 10:29–37), where the 'neighbour' is the person next to us in need, of whatever race or condition, who claims our compassion and through whose person God calls to us. In any case there was a tendency in late Judaism to extend the meaning of the term 'neighbour', which in the *OT* refers only to the Jewish citizen, to include the resident alien, and even all men, as in Philo. It is not even certain that the welding together of the two commandments of love to God and love to the neighbour into an inseparable unity, impressive and innovative though it was, can be attributed solely to Jesus. There is evidence of the combination in Philo (*De Spec. Leg.* 2, 63), and in the *Testaments of the Twelve Patriarchs* (*Test. Dan.* 5:3; *Test. Issach.* 5:2; 7:6), although it is generally agreed that the *Testaments* have been subject to Christian influence and interpolation. We have to look at Jesus' word *and action* overall, according to Mark's presentation at least (cf. 1:21–3:6), to see what was really new and decisive with him. When the rabbis debated about the weightiest commandment of the Law and even when they singled out 'love to the neighbour', they were searching for a principle under which the whole Law could be subsumed, and the commandment was really subservient to the Law for the whole Law still had to be obeyed in all its parts and the web of casuistry of Jewish legalism remained intact. By contrast Jesus cuts right through the web of legalism. For him in the twofold commandment God is present and the fellow man is present, calling for an immediate and spontaneous response, and faced with this direct call no one can any longer hide behind the security of legal observance. The notion of man's love to God occurs remarkably rarely in the *NT* (cf. Lk. 11:42; also Rom. 8:28; 1 C. 2:9; 8:3; 16:22; Eph. 6:24). No doubt this is because the early Church placed an overwhelming weight of emphasis on God's prior love to man as manifested in Jesus (cf. e.g. Rom. 5:8; Jn 3:16; 4:9–11) and saw in it the only basis of man's loving obedience to God's will and love for the neighbour. In the command to **love your neighbour as yourself** there is no commendation of self-loving nor any trace of the Stoic idea of 'man's sacredness to himself'. The compelling thing is the complete realism with which it is accepted here that man instinctively desires to promote his own good. One needs only to think of the self's natural regard for the self to learn what is involved when this self-regard is directed to the neighbour instead. Kierkegaard states: 'If we are to love our neighbour *as ourselves*, then this commandment opens, as with a master-key, the lock to our self-love and snatches it away from us' (see Bornkamm, p. 113).

32-34. The scribe wholly endorses what Jesus has said and adds that faithfulness to the twofold commandment **is much more than all whole burnt offerings and sacrifices.** There is nothing very novel about his statement. The prophets of Israel too had denounced the tendency among their compatriots to parade their 'religion' and seek to please God by outward religious observance instead of by the spontaneous expression in action of love to God and man which alone is God's will (1 Sam. 15:22; Hos. 6:6; Isa. 1:11). Even the Pharisean rabbis could voice the same sentiment. Rabbi Johanan ben Zakkai, for example, said 'Grieve not, we have an atonement equal to the Temple, the doing of loving deeds, as it is said, "Desire love and not sacrifice".' Yet only here in the Gospel is a representative of Jewish religious officialdom found agreeing with Jesus. Presumably this signifies for Mark that the miracle of believing-response to Jesus' word can take place for any man just where he stands, even if he stands among those who are opponents of Jesus. Above all the miracle takes place when as here the scribe ceases to measure the quality of life by the criterion of how far he has kept the Law's prescriptions or to justify himself by his own works and achievements. Only so is he in a position of waiting and preparedness before the direct call of God and the neighbour, and only so can he receive the promise that he is **not far from the kingdom of God,** which has drawn near in and with Jesus. The concluding statement, **after that no one dared to ask him any question** (most probably Mark's own), once again stresses the sovereign authority of Jesus as teacher and denotes also that the outcome of genuine encounter with Jesus is not prolonged theoretical discussion but that kind of being and activity which the nearness of the kingdom of God brings forth. With Jesus on his way to his passion at this point in the Gospel story, there is in any case little time for theoretical question and answer.

JESUS' OWN QUESTION ABOUT DAVID'S SON 12:35-40

The materials of 12:35-44 may have been attached to the preceding series of stories (11:27-12:34) in the tradition before Mark on the catchword principle (**scribe** (32)—**scribes** (35)—**scribes** (38); **widows** (40)—**widow** (41). But there are also clear indications of Mark's own editorial activity in the section, the stress on Jesus' teaching activity in the renewed statement that he **taught in the temple** (cf. 11:27), the favourable response of the crowd (37b) and the further notice of his teaching (38). The Evangelist has therefore his particular interest in the connexions here. In the previous stories the unique authority of Jesus' teaching has been stressed and in 12:34 a final closure has been declared on all public questioning of him. Now Jesus takes the initiative and himself poses *the question* about who he is, about his Person. The inclusion here of the question about his Person is well suited to Mark's purpose, since he has sought to show in the Gospel that Jesus' teaching is altogether inseparable from his Person and work and cannot be detached as a separate body of interesting religious instruction that might have been spoken by anyone. Also the messianic reticence of Jesus' saying in 35b-37a is congenial to Mark who must have regarded it not as a spectacular claim to an exalted title on Jesus' part but as a challenging question prompting decision about himself. Striking too is the graphic contrast between the threat of judgment pronounced against those who are both exhibitionist and hypocritical in their outward religious observance (verse 40) and the promise of the kingdom of God given to the scribe who has no legal defence or ritual pretence before God. Jesus thus appears for Mark in 12:28–40 as the one who decides the destinies of men.

If the saying of verse 35*b*–37 is authentic, it is most natural to suppose that in debate with his opponents Jesus was defending the (non-Davidic) character of his Messiahship against the popular Jewish recognition that Messiah must be of David's line. But this is most unlikely, since the early Church, despite the problems created for it by the nationalist political associations of the Davidic Messiah idea in late Judaism (see e.g. *Ps. Sol.*, 17, where nationalist and more refined ideas of the kingdom of David's Son lie alongside each other), universally accepted the Davidic descent of Jesus (on the ground of its knowledge of the fact that his family was of Davidic lineage?) and had apparently no objection to 'Son of David' as a title for Jesus (Mt. 1:6, Lk. 2:4; 3:31; Rom. 1:3; 2 Tim. 2:8). The saying, which is rabbinical in form, probably arose then out of the christological discussions of the Palestinian church and was used to demonstrate possibly that Son of man was a more adequate category for Jesus than Son of David (cf. Mk. 8:31), or possibly the Hellenistic church saw in it the evidence that Jesus was not just Son of David but Son of God (cf. 15:39).

35. How can the scribes say that the Christ is the son of David? If we are right in thinking that the saying as it stands is a Church production, then the matter at issue is not whether Jesus is actually of Davidic lineage but whether from the standpoint of the Church's christology he is not something other or more than Son of David.

36–37. Ps. 110, like all the rest, is attributed in the *OT* to David, and Jesus like all his Jewish contemporaries would have accepted Davidic authorship of the Psalms without question. This Psalm may in fact come from the early period of the Hebrew monarchy, but most critics believe that it is late and belongs to the Maccabean period. The introductory formula, **inspired by the Holy Spirit** (the Greek reads 'David himself, in the Spirit . . .'), occurs only here in the Synoptics (cf. Heb. 3:7; 10:15; Ac. 1:16; 28:25; 2 Tim. 3:16): the rabbis associated the Spirit especially with prophecy and here the formula underscores both the prophetic nature of Ps. 110:1 and its accuracy and truthfulness. The quotation follows the LXX (Ps. 109:1) almost exactly. Whether Ps. 110 was used as a messianic proof-

text among the Jews of Jesus' day is very doubtful. It is not found
at Qumran nor among the rabbis until the third or fourth century AD, and it is speculative to suggest that a messianic interpretation may have existed earlier and then been shelved for a long
time in the face of Christian appropriation and usage of the text.
Certainly Ps. 110:1 is one of the most widely used *OT* testimonies
in the whole *NT*. The early Church related it to Jesus' victory and
exaltation after Easter (e.g. Heb. 5:6; Ac. 2:34f.; 1 C. 15:25),
his taking his seat at the right hand of God (Ac. 2:30; Heb. 1:3;
Col. 3:1), and no doubt Mark regarded 35*b*–37*a* as an indicator
of the heavenly Lordship of the Christ who on his way in lowliness
to his passion could not be explained in purely Davidic categories.
In the quotation of Ps. 110:1 **the Lord** is Yahweh and **my Lord**
is the monarch or sovereign (who as Yahweh's viceregent could
even carry the divine name itself) who is then taken to prefigure
Messiah when the Psalm is messianically interpreted. The point
of the argument in verse 37, **David himself calls him Lord . . .,**
depends on the first six words of the Psalm, and the meaning is
that if David as the author of the Psalm calls Messiah 'Lord', then
Messiah must be more or higher than Son of David. The title
'Lord' was used extensively of Jesus in the early Church, though
Mark's own preference is for 'Son of God' (see 1:1 and 15:39),
which is of course a cognate and not a rival designation. The comment that **the great throng heard him gladly** probably refers
to the teaching introduced in verses 38–40 and appears to be a
general statement of Mark's contrasting Jesus' popularity with the
crowd and the final cleavage between Jesus and official Judaism
represented in these sayings.

38–40. Verse 40 was probably an originally independent saying not necessarily referring to the scribes. It describes men of
avarice whereas verses 38–39 describe scribal hypocrisy, and in
the Greek **who devour** is not grammatically connected with what
goes before but represents a change of construction. The two
sayings might well have been separate but genuine utterances of
Jesus, the former alluding to particular scribes whose vanity and
ostentation were thoroughly reprehensible and the latter possibly
to some moneyed members of the priestly class. Condemnation of
such people as bad examples is to be found in Jewish literature
also (cf. Josephus, *Ant.* XVII.2, 4; see Abrahams, chapter 10). But
the way they have been brought together and introduced in Mark
(**Beware of the scribes . . .**), without any qualifications at all,

suggests that they are here regarded from the Christian perspective as an overall characterisation of the Judaism that had failed in true loyalty to God and had brought itself under his ultimate judgment. **Go about in long robes:** the alternative reading 'go about in porticoes' (involving the omission of only a single letter in Greek) is probably inferior. The **long robe** or outer garment (the *tallith*) reaching nearly to the feet was usually worn by the scribes during the performance of their religious duties, but here they are accused of wanting to make a public display of their status by wearing it all the while. Their desire for **salutations in the market place** indicates that they want members of the public to overhear the deference paid to them in their superior position. They coveted **the best seats in the synagogues,** where at that time special seats were beginning to be reserved for the most important members of the community, and **places of honour at feasts,** at which in the orient generally much store was set by rank and precedence (cf. Lk. 14:7-11). The picture in verse 40 is of greedy men who try to cover up their exactions from the needy by an outward show of devoutness in prayer.

Is this an account of an actual incident in Jesus' ministry? How then could he have known what amount the people were contributing or that the woman had given her all? There are parallels to the story in Indian and Buddhist literature, as well as in Jewish sources, one of which reports how a priest refused a handful of meal from a poor woman and was subsequently rebuked by God in a vision and told, 'Despise her not; it is as if she offered her life.' It seems likely therefore that a similar parable or illustration originally put out by Jesus has been transformed into a record of an event in his life. But the question of the historicity of the story is secondary to considerations of how appropriate it is, from the Marcan viewpoint, in its present context, to which it was probably attached even before Mark through the catchword 'widow' (verses 40 and 42). The poor widow who offers her whole living to God contrasts markedly with the hypocritical and avaricious leaders of Judaism, and affords a superb example of complete loyalty and devotion to God's call. According to the Evangelist, the saying of verses 43*b*-44 about the poor widow's sacrificial gift is an address specifically to the *disciples* (he introduces it with a familiar formula of his, **And he called his disciples . . .**). He thus implies that discipleship involves absolute surrender to and trust in the God to whose will and purpose Jesus is about to commit himself absolutely in his passion.

41–44. What is meant by the **treasury** here is uncertain, possibly one of the thirteen trumpet-shaped receptacles for offerings in the Court of the Women. The **large sums** contributed by the rich involve no real sacrifice on their part in proportion to their whole resources, and cannot compare with the widow's tiny gift which is a sacrifice of everything she has. The two copper coins she puts in (she could have withheld one) are two *lepta*, the smallest in circulation, explained by Mark as the equivalent of a *quadrans* (the Latin word is simply translitered in Mark's Greek), that is one sixty-fourth of a denarius, and a denarius was the daily wage of a labourer (cf. Mt. 20:2). The saying of verses 43*b*–44 brings out quite clearly that it is not the outward show but the depth of surrender to God's mercy and care that counts.

THE DRAMA OF THE LAST DAYS 13:1–27

With chapter 13 we appear to enter a different world of thought and expression from the rest of the Gospel. Elsewhere the stress is on the hiddenness of God's kingdom in Jesus' word and deed, discernible only to faith. Here the stress is apparently on the visible cosmic events of the last days leading up to the end. Here too and only here in the Gospel does Jesus' speech take the form of a long discourse, reminiscent of the form if not the content of the Johannine discourses (see especially Jn 14–17). Now the practice of closing a book or a section of a book with materials relating to the secrets of the end-time was common in early Christianity (see e.g. Mt. 25; Jn 14–17; Heb. 6:1f.; *Did.* 16). Moreover Jewish writings (and Greek also) of the time used the literary device of placing a lengthy discourse, as a kind of last will and testament, on the lips of a great man just before his death (cf. the *Assumption of Moses* and the *Testaments of the Twelve Patriarchs*, with their basic models in e.g. Gen. 41:21–49; Dt. 31:28ff. and 32; 1 Sam. 12). However, the frequency of such practices should not lead us to conclude that chapter 13 is only of incidental literary interest to Mark. Nor should we infer from the general difference in atmosphere and ideas between this chapter and the remainder of the Gospel that it can be excluded from an analysis of the Evangelist's overall witness to Jesus Christ (as with Bultmann, *HST*, pp. 338–

350). On the contrary, from the standpoint of the Marcan redaction, the inclusion of strange apocalyptic subject-matter at a point just before the story of the passion is particularly instructive.

Chapter 13 consists largely of pronouncements which echo passages from apocalyptic segments of the *OT* (verse 12: Mic. 7:6; verse 22: Dt. 13:1ff.). Further verses 7–8, 14–20, 24–27, also couched in the technical vocabulary of apocalyptic literature (verse 7: Dan. 2:28; verse 8: Isa. 19:2; verse 14: Dan. 7:27: 11:31; 12:11; verse 19: Dan. 12:1; verses 24f.: Isa. 13:10; 34:4; verse 26: Dan. 7:13; verse 27: Zech. 2:6), seem to read like a brief drama of the last days in three acts—signs of the end, the appearance of the Antichrist and the parousia of the Son of man. Many interpreters have thus subscribed to the long-standing 'Little Apocalypse' theory, that behind Mk 13 lies a Jewish or Jewish-Christian apocalyptic pamphlet which first circulated possibly when Pilate put up Roman ensigns in Jerusalem or possibly when Caligula in AD 40 threatened to place his image in the Temple (see commentary on verses 14–20). But the debate about its precise extent (does it go beyond verses 7–8, 14–20, 24–27?) has been inconclusive. One result of scholarly concentration on the matter of sources or on the analysis of apocalyptic details in the chapter has been a comparative neglect of the crucial question of what the Evangelist himself is seeking to say in the passage *as a whole*.

The chapter in fact contains several indications of Marcan editorial activity. The introduction in verse 1*a* to Jesus' prophecy of the destruction of the Temple and the resetting of the scene in verse 3 for the great discourse, dealing not with the destruction of the Temple but the much larger subject of the coming end of the world, are most probably due to Mark, as are the somewhat artificially introduced question of verse 4 (with **these things** referring to what follows) and the opening words of the discourse in verse 5. Whether or not Mark was first responsible for attaching the parables on 'watching' and 'waiting' of verses 28–37 to verses 3–27, he apparently prepares for the 'watching' and 'waiting' motif by such earlier editorial comments as **but the end is not yet** (7), the reiterated **take heed** (9 and 23) and 'the necessity of the universal proclamation of the gospel' (10—a typically Marcan theme). If we take account of this repeated editorial **not yet** and also of the great restraint expressed regarding the end in the sayings of 28–37, it appears that for his part Mark wants indeed not to encourage apocalyptic speculation and excitement but to suppress it. Again, the warning against **false prophets** in verse 6 and verses 21–22 is a traditional motif, but its twofold occurrence suggests its outstanding importance for Mark. So direct are these admonitions we may suppose that here more clearly than anywhere else in the Gospel are mirrored the conditions prevailing in the Church to which, in a situation of crisis and indeed of suffering and distress (see 9–13), Mark addressed his version of the good news of Jesus Christ. That Church is perplexed and confused by some in the midst who not only are filled with apocalyptic zeal in the conviction that the end is very close but also believe they are the chosen agents of God to bring it about. The Church is here directed away from such apocalyptic fervour to a patient but none-the-less active waiting that fills the critical interim with the constructive task of preaching the gospel (verse 10).

Mark's purpose in chapter 13 is both practical and pastoral, to set his Church before the living Word of her exalted Lord Jesus who has control over everything the Church has to face now (verse 11) and in the future (verses 24–27), who alone speaks with unimpeachable authority about the end and its secrets (verses 28–37), and who above all calls the Church to steadfastness under trial and to faithfulness to her task in the intermediate period between the anxious present and the future God has in store for all who endure to the end (verse 13). In short, the Evangelist's principal interest in this passage is not that it furnishes a manual of apocalyptic instruction or a detailed schedule of the events of the end-time, but that it issues an appeal to faith to recognise that concealed in the tribulations of the present lies the coming glory of God, to be manifested finally in the parousia of the Son of man (whose own triumph is hidden in Jesus' way of the cross). The fact is that many of the normal ingredients of apocalyptic are conspicuous by their absence from Mk 13, e.g. the sweeping survey that divides the time of the world into measurable epochs predetermined from the days of creation; the terrors of the bestial or demonic onslaught of Antichrist described in bizarre imagery; the replacing of all earthly empires for ever by the visible kingdom of God on earth (cf. Dan. 7:14; Rev. 11:15); the resurrection of all, just and unjust, for the last judgment; God's final vengeance on his enemies; the ecstasy of the visionary who sees and describes these cosmic phenomena (cf. Rev. 1:10–12). Accordingly, it may

be held that 'Marcan Apocalypse' is not really an appropriate
title for Mk 13 at all. It does scant justice to the Evangelist's
intention.

How far the materials employed by Mark here go back to Jesus
himself is a matter of controversy. The passage as a whole is not
necessarily incompatible with the *attitude* of Jesus, who might well
have affirmed this world and at the same time subordinated the
world and all that is in it to the future God would bring when he
would be all in all. But it is another thing to claim that the entire
chapter represents substantially the undoubted teaching of Jesus
(Beasley-Murray, *JF*). From what can be gathered elsewhere in
the Gospel tradition, it is not in character for Jesus to string
together *OT* quotations or to indulge in apocalyptic time-
tabling even as sketchily as here in Mk 13. His message of the
kingdom of God, which invites faith to perceive the *hidden* coming
of the kingdom in, with and around him, is truly reflected in the
'watch' and 'wait' parables of verses 28-37, and is not so much an
expression as a transmutation of the Jewish apocalyptic hope. It is
probably best therefore to think of Mk 13 as an amalgam of
authentic sayings of Jesus, like the prophecy of the Temple's ruin
(verse 2) or the denial of knowledge of the day or hour of the end
(verse 32), and the pronouncements of a Jewish or Christian
prophet or prophets, worked together and developed gradually
by the Church and given its final shape by the Evangelist himself.
By locating the passage immediately before the passion story, and
indeed, if Lightfoot (*GMM*, pp. 51f.) is correct, connecting it with
the passion (verse 9 = 14:53-15:15; verses 22-23 = 14:33-46,
50, 66-72; verses 32-33 = 14: 35, 37; verse 35 = 14:17, 43,
72; verse 26 = 14:52), Mark wishes to imply that just as the
future glory of the Son of man through whom God will finally
appear in triumph, is of necessity bound up with Jesus' suffering
and death, so the disciple Church's hope in God's ultimate
victory lives on and must live on through all present suffering and
sorrow.

1-4. Is the comment **as he came out of the temple** more for
Mark than simply a connective clause, possibly signifying the final
separation of Jesus and his followers from the Jewish Holy Place?
The legendary magnificence of Herod's Temple notwithstanding,
the disciple's exclamation, **What wonderful stones and . . .
buildings!** is in its naïveté a rather contrived way of leading into
Jesus' prediction. In prophesying the destruction of the Temple,

Jesus stands in line with the prophets of Israel (Mic. 3:12; Jer. 26:6, 18) and, in roughly the same period as Jesus, Rabbi Johanan ben Zakkai is said to have made a similar prophecy. The saying of verse 2 is found in varying forms in all four Gospels (according to Mk 14:57-59 *false* witnesses report that he had said he would himself destroy the Temple) and the genuineness of some such *logion* as we have in 13:2 is hardly in doubt. But whether Jesus foresaw that he would become himself an instrument of the Temple's ruin, or that the political intransigence of his people must culminate in Roman revenge and military action against Jerusalem, or whether he meant, like the prophets before him, merely to symbolise God's impending judgment upon disloyal Israel, it is no longer possible to determine. In the outcome, the prophecy was fulfilled, but only partially so, for in the sack of Jerusalem in AD 70 Roman soldiers actually *burned* the Temple, which was subsequently dismantled stone by stone. Obviously then the general saying of verse 2 has not been adapted to match precisely what happened *after the event* and can scarcely be taken to support a post-AD 70 date for Mark's Gospel. The scene for what follows is now set **on the Mount of Olives,** a particularly suitable place, with its sacred associations (Zech. 14:4) and overlooking the Temple, for Jesus' revelatory discourse. Why **Andrew** should be introduced last here (and not coupled with Peter his brother) together with the inner circle of the three, it is no longer possible to determine. **Andrew asked him privately:** the proceedings take place in secret session with the leading disciples, a customary feature in Mark (cf. 4:10; 7:17; 9:28; 10:10) and probably a means of stressing the high significance for the Church of the instruction given. For Mark the disciples' question in verse 4 links the prophecy of the destruction of the Temple to the ensuing discourse, but it does so somewhat awkwardly and artificially. When the disciples enquire **when will this be?** the **this** refers to the foregoing prophecy, whereas **all these things** that are **to be accomplished** appears to refer to the phenomena mentioned in the discourse. It is noticeable that the disciples do not ask for a mapping out of the events of the end-time but for a single **sign** in their own midst that God's purpose is about to be consummated.

5-8. The opening words of the discourse, **Take heed that no one leads you astray,** possibly Mark's own formulation (cf. 9a), reveal straight away Mark's paraenetic interest in the whole section. The 'when' of the disciples' question in verse 4 is by-passed and gives way instead to words of exhortation. The exhortation takes the form first of a warning to look out not for something that lies in the more distant future but for something that is already taking place in the Christian congregation of Mark's time. Apparently would-be leaders of the community were appearing under the banner of the slogan **'I am he!'** (in Greek, only two words = 'I am'). Although in the early age of the Church up to AD 132, the time of the revolt of the messianic pretender Bar Cochba, Palestinian Judaism produced a number of imposters who if not exactly 'messiahs' at least claimed to be wonder-workers, like the Judas and Theudas of Ac. 5: 36f. (cf. Ac. 21:38), it is quite unlikely that the people involved in Mk 13:6 were pseudo-messiahs. In the statement, **many will come in my name,** the phrase **in my name** is probably a Christian interpretation of the slogan 'I am', denoting that they believed that in one sense or another they were 'Christ-figures' wanting to exercise the sovereign authority of Christ returned to earth. That Mark's first readers could have been perplexed and agitated by such fanatics in the midst is distinctly possible, since early Christianity was in fact faced with the peril of fanaticism (see 2 Th. 2:1–12; cf. Ac. 20:29f.; 1 Jn 2:28). **Wars and rumours of war ... earthquakes ... famines,** considered to be marks of the divine judgment in the *OT* (see e.g. 1 Kg. 8:37; Jer. 4:11ff.), had become a familiar feature of apocalyptic calendars of the end-time (see e.g. 2 Esd. 9:3; 13:31; 15:14f.; *Sib. Or.* 3:633–647). Mark's earliest readers would have thought of the turmoil of recent history, of the alarms caused by Rome's foreign wars and by recurring natural disasters in many places. **This must take place** (verse 7): not a justification for a theory of the inevitability of war among men, but a reminiscence of Dan. 2:28 (LXX), where too the 'must' relates to *God's* sovereign rule and purpose, and so an appeal to hold fast to the faith that despite **wars and rumours of wars** God is still in control. That is how Mark's reader would have understood it, just as he would have understood the (Marcan?) observation that **the end is not yet** (cf. 2 Th. 2:2 and note the similarity in the tone generally beween the Pauline apocalypse in 2 Th. 2 and Mk 13) as a counsel to keep calm and not be swayed by current apocalyptic excitement. The summons to avoid frantic apocalypticism is reinforced in verse 8, where it is emphasised that even worldwide war or calamity **is but the beginning of the sufferings:** the Greek word for **sufferings** means literally 'birth pangs'.

It had become a technical term (relating to an idea rooted in the *OT*, e.g. Isa. 26:17; 66:8; Jer. 22:23; Hos. 13:13; Mic 4:9ff.) for the fearful tribulations out of which the new age would at last be born. The fact that the terrible disasters mentioned in verse 8 are but the prelude to the final 'birth pangs' serves to emphasise the need for faithful obedience on the Church's part in the meantime, while it awaits in hope God's eventual victory.

9-13. The injunction which opens this segment of the discourse, **take heed to yourselves,** stands by itself, and is not to be interpreted as a request to guard against any particular danger or avoid any particular weakness under trial (cf. Johnson, p. 214). It is a characteristic Marcan expression and draws attention to the fact that the warnings that follow are of the greatest seriousness and urgency for Mark's Christian reader and are directly addressed to him in his concrete circumstances. While it is possible that Jesus spoke of the sufferings his followers would have to undergo, most likely in the days of crisis before his death (cf. 8:34ff.), the exhortations of 9-13 clearly reflect the Church's retrospective view of the hard experiences it has already suffered in its first age. The vicissitudes spoken of in verse 9 recall especially the career of Paul (2 C. 11:23ff., etc.). The first part of verse 9, **for they will deliver . . . beaten in synagogues,** is Palestinian in background. The word translated **councils** in *RSV* is literally 'sanhedrins' and refers presumably to local Jewish governing bodies, consisting of thirty-three members each, in towns and cities. **beaten in synagogues:** the practice goes back to the law of Dt. 25:1-3 (cf. 2 C. 11:24). The hardships described here hark back to a time when the Church had still not broken away from the Jewish jurisdiction. The background of the second part of verse 9, **and you will stand . . . kings for my sake,** may also be Palestinian, since governors may refer to Roman procurators like Felix and Festus (Ac. 23:24; 24:27) and kings to such as Herod Agrippa (Ac. 12:1-3). But the frame of reference may also be much wider, certainly so in the minds of Mark's readers, for **governors** could refer to proconsuls like Gallio in Achaia (Ac. 18:12), and **kings** could include even the emperor. The phrase **to bear testimony before them,** in Greek simply 'for a testimony to them', normally relates to the witness given at a legal trial. But in the present context it has a much more profound *Christian* connotation, as verses 10-11 confirm. It denotes that in their appearances before governors and kings

Christians must and will by their words as by their very presence
witness to Christ, and the notion of the responsibility of martyrdom
(the Greek word for **testimony** is *martyrion*) for Jesus' sake is not
far away. Verses 9 and 11 were no doubt closely connected in the
tradition before Mark through the catchword **deliver,** and so
verse 10 is evidently a (Marcan) intrusion prompted by the idea
of 'witnessing to Christ' presented in verses 9 and 11. To interpret
the words **the gospel . . . preached to all nations** as implying
no more than a mission to *Jews* in the cities of the Diaspora is
inappropriate in the present context. Mark, it appears, is anxious
to extend 'witnessing to Christ' far beyond appearances in (Jewish)
courts to all the world. The universal proclamation of the gospel
is a typical Marcan motif (cf. 4:32, 11:17; 15:39), as it is also
a feature of the Pauline writings (Rom. 1:5, 8–17; 11:11ff.;
15:16, 19; Eph. 3:2–9; Col. 1:23). By **first** in the statement
the gospel must first be preached to all nations, Mark
means not first in importance, but rather that the necessity of the
worldwide proclamation ordained for the Church by God must be
fulfilled before the end can come. What we have here is of course
a radical early Christian reorientation of the traditions of Jewish
apocalyptic. **And when they bring you to trial . . . it is not
you who speak, but the Holy Spirit:** a very rare reference to
the Holy Spirit in Mark (cf. 1:12). The saying appears in
divergent forms in Lk. 12:11–12 and in Lk. 21:14–15, where the
Spirit is identified with the exalted Jesus. In both the *OT* and
NT the Spirit is frequently associated with inspired prophetic
utterance. The promise of the Spirit here is a strong consolation
to the Church, for in the intimidating surroundings of a Roman
court or tribunal the lowly Christian must often have felt 'stuck
for words'. The consolation is not that in the ordeal Christians
can expect a miracle (of divine speech) to secure their release,
but that they do not need to rely on their own poor resources,
since the Spirit will help them to match the hour with an un-
swervingly loyal witness to Christ.

    **And brother will deliver . . . hated by all for my name's
sake:** grievous splits within families as a result of conflicting
loyalties figured among the 'woes' preceding the end-time in
apocalyptic expectation (*1 En.* 99:5, *Jub.* 23:59; 2 Esd. 6:24,
etc.). But Mark's first readers would have known that such
divisions did occur within familes in early Christianity, and that
in the rising tide of persecution the disaffected members of a

convert's household could easily bring down the wrath of the Roman authorities upon him. **Hated by all for my name's sake:** not here a picture of the little Church against an alien and scornful world, but a reminder that the cost of faithfulness to the name of Christ may well be just this hatred from one's closest kin. **But he who endures to the end will be saved:** possibly handed down initially as an independent saying that promised the reward of the life hereafter to those loyal unto death (cf. Rev. 2:10). In the present apocalyptic context it might be expected to mean that those who held out until the *end-time* would enter the new age without passing through death (cf. 2 Esd. 6:25; 7:27). Whether Mark expected many of his readers to survive until the end-time is doubtful, however, and perhaps his understanding of the saying is that God's endless mercy is assured for all who go through the tribulations described in verses 9–12 without flinching (**to the end** thus taken adverbially = 'finally', 'without breaking down').

14–20. This section differs remarkably not only from the immediately preceding exhortations addressed specifically to Christians in their various harsh experiences, but from the descriptions of the universal and cosmic phenomena, which are part of the genuine stock-in-trade of apocalyptic, in verses 7–8 and 24–27. The present passage could be entitled 'Prophetic Oracle for Judea in a Time of Emergency'. It may emanate from a Palestinian Jewish or Christian prophet who tolls the warning bell in a situation of extreme danger when the war-clouds are looming close—**let those who are in Judea flee to the mountains.** Whether the situation envisaged is the outrage caused to the Jews by Caligula's nearly successful attempt to set up his statue in the Temple (**the desolating sacrilege set up where it ought not to be**) or the early days of the Jewish War culminating in the Roman siege of Jerusalem in AD 70 is not easy to say. Luke has plainly the siege of Jerusalem in mind and has presumably adapted the oracle to suit this fulfilment, after the event. But there is no such explicit reference in Mark.

Integrated as this extraordinary piece is with the whole eschatological discourse of Jesus, Mark intended his readers not only to regard it as a sign of the approaching end, but more importantly to understand by it that the Lord knew in advance the trials in store for his people and called them to preparedness against the day.

14. The phrase **desolating sacrilege** is from Daniel (9:27; 11:31; 12:11), where it originally designated the pagan altar erected in the Temple by Antiochus Epiphanes in 168 BC (cf. 1 Mac. 1:54ff.). The words **set up where it ought not to be** can only refer to a similar profanation of the Temple, and since the participle **set up** is masculine in Greek (whereas the noun **desolating sacrilege** is neuter) it seems that an individual person is in view here, a successor in the Antiochus–Caligula line of desecrators. But Mark's language is cryptic and it may be he understood the figure more symbolically. The parenthetical observation **let the reader understand,** if not on the one hand simply an indication that the original oracle was already in written form or on the other hand a post-Marcan scribal insertion, is possibly Mark's signal that a larger than life symbol is involved, namely the 'man of lawlessness' or the Antichrist (cf. 2 Th. 2:1–12) who would war with God at the end. The suggestion that **let the reader understand** means 'pay close attention', that therefore Mark actually wants everything here to be taken literally and is pleading with the Church in Jerusalem to flee to Galilee, there to await the parousia of Christ (Marxsen, *ME*, pp. 102ff.) is quite implausible. Nowhere, either in chapter 13 or the rest of the Gospel, does the Evangelist look like that kind of apocalyptic pamphleteer.

15–20. The flight before the advancing terror (it has not quite arrived as yet, as verse 18 shows: **Pray that it may not happen in winter,** when travel would be doubly arduous) is depicted in very vivid terms. There is not even time to proceed from the **housetop** inside the house, but hasty escape must be made by the outside stairway, nor time to pick up the **mantle** that was usually laid aside for work in the fields. Expectant and nursing mothers (verse 17) will suffer the greatest distress—a tender touch at the heart of such a strident oracle! Verse 19 is an almost exact replica of the great tribulation prophesied in Dan. 12:1 (cf. Jer. 30:7; Rev. 7:14), and has the effect of enlarging the relatively restricted Judean crisis portrayed in verses 14–18 into a great act in the apocalyptic drama of the end-time. The shortening of the days spoken of in verse 20 became a feature of apocalyptic (*2 Bar.* 20:1–2; 83:1; 2 Esd. 4:26; cf. 1 C. 7:29; *Epistle of Barnabas* 4:3)— in the apocalyptic calendar the duration of the great tribulation was fixed (at $3\frac{1}{2}$ years according to Dan. 12:7), but if it had lasted so long humanity in its weakness could not have survived.

Accordingly, **for the sake of the elect** (see e.g. Ps. 105:6; Isa. 42:1; 43:20; for the development of the idea of the elect in apocalyptic literature, see e.g. *1 En.* 1:1; 38:2-4), the righteous remnant whom God has chosen to be heirs of his kingdom (Mark's readers would have thought of the Church), God has actually **shortened the days.** At the oracle's close this declaration would have brought great comfort to Christians, conveying as it does the message that come what may even of unprecedented tribulations, God is still in charge and his mercy is assured to the faithful.

21-23. The warning of verses 5-6 is here reiterated by Mark through the addition of these verses. The saying of verse 22 probably went closely with verse 20 originally (the idea of the elect is common to both), and the saying of verse 21 is attested in a slightly variant form and different context in Q (Lk. 17:23 = Mt. 24:26). In connecting the warning about **false Christs and false prophets** with the great tribulations before the end-time, it is very likely that Mark understood it symbolically and took it to refer not to literal pseudo-messiahs but to the false teachers of the Church of his day (cf. 13:5-6; cf. also the use of the term 'Antichrist' in 1 Jn 2:18; 4:3), men of perfervid apocalyptic enthusiasm who claimed in some sense to be Jesus *redivivus* and who appealed to their wonder-working prowess (**show signs and wonders,** cf. 2 Th. 2:9) as a sign that they were God's special envoys in the last days. **Do not believe it** (verse 21): there is no **it** in Greek, only in an unqualified sense **Do not believe.** No real rival to Christ is possible for the Christians. The only one to be believed in, the only one whose word is sure and trustworthy is the one who speaks in the great discourse of chapter 13. So against those who are fanning the flames of apocalyptic excitement in the Christian congregation Mark sets the authoritative statements of the exalted Jesus ('the end is not yet'; 'the gospel must first be preached to all nations', 'of that day or that hour no one knows'). **But take heed:** yet another token of how Mark uses apocalyptic materials as a cover for admonition and encouragement to the Church. No encouragement could be more uplifting than the concluding declaration, **I have told you all things beforehand:** since Christ knows beforehand what his own have to face, he does not desert them in the hour of the ordeal, but is present (in the living words of Mk 13) to guide, support and strengthen them.

24-27. Cosmic signs in **sun, moon,** and **stars** are associated frequently in the *OT* with turbulent times on earth (e.g. with war in Isa. 13:2–10 and with earthquake in Am. 8:8f.) and with God's final intervention in world history. In the apocalyptic literature such supernatural portents, interpreted literally and actually expected, became a regular item in pictures of the last days (e.g. 2 Esd. 5:4; *1 En.* 80:4–7; *Sib. Or.* 3:796f.). Here the terrifying celestial phenomena are described entirely in *OT* language (cf. Isa. 13:10; 34:4). They signify the winding up of the universe, but this becomes but the backdrop to the all-important scene which follows, the appearance of the **Son of man** in **glory.**

24. In those days, after that great tribulation: in those days, a customary Marcan expression, might be expected to refer to the time of the events preliminary to the end (cf. 13:17 and 19), but the addition of the defining phrase **after that great tribulation** has the effect of pushing the phenomena described in 24–25 forward and making them part of the *end* itself (so stressing the 'not yet' with which Mark is here concerned). There is no linear connexion, therefore, between the cosmic portents of 24–25 and the historical oracle relating to 'the desolating sacrilege set up where it ought not to be' of verses 14ff.

26–27. Then they will see: the discourse is addressed to the disciples who are referred to throughout as *you.* The third person plural here, **they will see** is probably an impersonal plural equivalent to a passive, 'then will be seen', but it may perhaps point to those who will be alive to witness such things at the end, after the great tribulation. The **coming** of the **Son of man** at the end is described in the language of Dan. 7:13. Whatever exactly Son of man may have meant in Daniel or later Jewish apocalyptic literature (cf. *1 En.* 46:1ff.; 48:2ff.; 62:9ff.; 70:1, etc.; 2 Esd. 13:1–58), Mark's first readers would have identified the figure here with Jesus and would have thought of his parousia. **Coming in clouds:** the 'cloud' was thought to be, in later Jewish literature, supremely the dwelling-place of the presence of God. For the **angels** as agents of God's purpose in the last days, see *1 En.* 61 (cf. Mt. 13:41). The idea of the ingathering of the **elect** related in the *OT* to the bringing in of the Israel of the Dispersion to join the righteous remnant in Judea (cf. Isa. 11:11, 16; 27:12; 35:8ff.; Ezek. 39:27ff.; Zech. 10:6–11). The chosen ones of the Son of man, Jesus, namely faithful Christians, are in view here. There is no reference to the resurrection as in 1 Th. 4:16, and all emphasis is on the gathered and finally vindicated fellowship of the people of God, the Christian community (cf. 1 Th. 4:17). **From the ends of the earth to the ends of heaven:** an unusual expression (cf. *1 En.* 57:2), probably a fusion of Dt. 30:4 (LXX), 'from one end of the heaven to another', and Dt. 13:7, 'from one end of the earth to the other.'

SAYINGS CONCERNING WATCHING AND WAITING **13:28–37**

This section would appear to have been assembled for catechetical purposes through the presence of various catchwords in the different items, **these things** (verses 29–30), **pass away** (30–31), **watch** (33, 34, 35, 37), **at the very gates** or **doors** (29 and 34, **doorkeeper**). But the elements of which it is composed were originally disparate, and the connexions of the section both with what precedes and within it are awkward and difficult. The little parable of **the fig tree,** and its application in verses 28–29, hardly stands in its original context here. The phrase **these things** in the saying of 29 clearly relates to the *preliminaries* leading up to the end and not to the events of the end-time itself described in 24–27. Possibly as a genuine utterance of Jesus the parable initially referred his hearers to the signs of the coming kingdom of God in and with his ministry. The saying of verse 30 was also separate, since here **all these things** applies to the dramatic events of the end-time itself, including those portrayed in verses 24–27. The pronouncement of verse 31, originally independent as well, seems to be an adaptation of Jesus' own statement about the Law (Mt. 5:18). When in verse 32 knowledge of the actual time of the end is disclaimed on the part of the Son, the perspective is fundamentally different to that in the rest of the chapter (even in verses 30–31), where apocalyptic predictions are openly made. The parable of 34–35 gives every impression of being composite—it combines two motifs. The first is that of watchfulness, exemplified by the command to the **doorkeeper** which is introduced somewhat abruptly and strangely in Mk 13:34, but derives probably from the tradition underlying Lk. 12:35, where the householder goes away to a marriage banquet and expects his servants to be awake and ready to open the door for him on his return at a late hour. The other motif is the duty laid upon the servants to fulfil their respective tasks and responsibilities during the longer period of the master's absence abroad, and this is reminiscent of the parable of the talents (Mt. 25:14–30 = Lk. 19:11–27). It should be noted that the twin themes of waiting and of active duties to be accomplished are congenial to the Evangelist's intention to de-emphasise the *temporal* expectations of apocalyptic and to highlight the need of the Church to fill the period of waiting, longer or shorter, with the carrying through of constructive labours.

28-29. The point of the parable of **the fig tree** on Jesus' lips was presumably that just as the greening of the tree bears the promise of the near approach of summer, so enshrined in his own words and deeds lay the promise of the coming kingdom of God. Here, however, the parable is referred to the apocalyptic materials of chapter 13, that is to the end of the world. But *quite imprecisely*, since **these things** in 29 may apply to 13:5-23, but hardly to 13:24-27 and it is not stated who or what is **at the very gates** (the Greek may mean either 'he' or 'it' **is near**). It is enough for Mark that all signs of the end are subordinated or subjected to the sovereign authority of the one who speaks here, that Jesus who *in himself* brings and is the good news of the kingdom of God and who thus offers something much more decisive than an apocalyptic calendar (cf. verse 32).

30. Here **all these things** refers to the whole drama of the end-time, including the events pictured in verses 24-27. The words **this generation** scarcely mean the whole human race contemporary with Mark and his readers, but rather in view of Mk 9:1 the people around Jesus in his ministry and actually addressed by him. If, as some have held (e.g. E. Grässer, *Beih*, *ZNW*, 22, pp. 156ff.; 169), part of Mark's concern was to deal with the *delay* of the end, it is all the more interesting that this saying about the *imminence* of the parousia has been allowed to stand as we find it here. In fact the Jesus who encounters the hearer in this saying, especially in the present context, does not so much fix an exact terminal date for the end as fill the hearer's present moment with urgency and make it impossible for him to evade or postpone decision indefinitely (Dodd, p. 71; see also Nineham, p. 360; Schweizer, *GNM*, p. 282).

31. Here too the emphasis is not on the apocalyptic prediction that heaven and earth will pass away (cf. Isa. 51:6; 34:4; 40:8; 54:10; Ps. 102:25-27). Rather the saying is an eloquent reminder that in all difficulties and dangers the Church's comfort and help lies in the enduringly authoritative and valid words of the one who speaks in this discourse and, in the wider terms of reference of Mark's Gospel, is the bearer of the good news.

32. This statement, which freely confesses a limited knowledge on the part of the Son, raised an embarrassing theological problem for the Church later (witness the omission of **nor the Son** from Mt. 24:36 in the MS tradition). On the ground that the Church would not have created a saying which clearly attributed such limitation to **the Son,** it has been regarded (by Schmiedel and others) as one of the pillar passages for scientific reconstruction of the historical life of Jesus. However, aside from the legitimate doubt as to whether Jesus referred to himself absolutely as **the Son** (the title occurs only here in Mark), it is quite possible that these words could have been ascribed to him by a Church that had at its disposal no saying of Jesus defining the time of the end or wanted to offer an explanation for the delay of the parousia. Mark's own concern in locating the originally independent *logion* of verse 32 here is to show that if even the Son does not presume to possess every secret in the Father's keeping, far less should Christian believers seek to force God's hand by subjecting *his day* (the phrase **that day** goes back to the *OT* idea of the Day of the Lord, e.g. Am. 5:18ff.; Isa. 2:12, etc. cf. Lk. 21:34; 2 Th. 1:10, etc.) to their own fallible calendrical calculations. From the point of view of christology, it is noteworthy that Jesus is here mentioned alongside the **angels** but is at the same time distinguished from them and so placed above them, as in Heb. 1:4ff.; also that **the Son** is subordinated to **the Father**—'he it is who always turns the attention from himself to God and makes God a present reality' (Schweizer, *GNM*, p. 283).

33-37. In the opening of verse 33, **Take heed, watch,** Mark's paramount interest in exhortation appears once more. The concluding words of the discourse in verse 37, **And what I say to you I say to all: Watch,** bring out still more clearly that he is concerned not about apocalyptic instruction *for the few* but the demeanour of the *whole Church* that must await the future God will bring. In the first instance those who **do not know when the time will come** will have learned to allow God to be God by leaving the appointed hour in his control. Next the two-edged parable of 34-36 commits the future entirely to God, and also suggests in picturesque fashion that every present moment is transformed and renewed in the light of that future since it becomes the very moment in which God may surprise men by his coming (**you do not know when the master of the house will come, in the evening or at midnight, or at cockcrow, or in**

the morning—the four watches of the night according to the Roman reckoning). It is therefore incumbent upon the Church not *ever* to be found asleep, or in that attitude of passive waiting that always has plenty of time to spare before *doing* anything. The call is to an *active* watchfulness (**he puts his servants in charge, each with his work**) which makes ready for the coming Lord by filling the here and now with faithful service and high responsibility, in Mark's view particularly the responsibility of the worldwide promulgation of the gospel (cf. 13:10).

THE PLOT TO KILL JESUS **14:1–2**

The Passion Narrative

With 14:1 the passion story proper begins. Whereas the rest of the Gospel is made up almost entirely of small independent pieces rather loosely strung together, the account of the passion in chapters 14–15 is noticeably different in character and forms a continuous narrative with a coherent chronological sequence. It is sometimes maintained that the first draft of the Gospel consisted only of chapters 1–13. E. Trocmé (pp. 172ff.) has argued that the passion story is in fact a considerably later and indeed unnecessary addendum which actually annuls the original Marcan plan. (1) Why should a writer who in no sense intends a biography and who says nothing of the beginning of the earthly life of Jesus at the outset have felt it necessary to relate in detail his sufferings and death? (2) Chapters 14–15 recount a history instead of exhorting the readers to make history as is the case of 1–13. (3) Only the fact of the passion and resurrection interests Mark and constitutes the hidden centre of gravity throughout his work, and the fact is sufficiently attested already in the threefold passion prediction of 8:31; 9:31; 10:33–34 and in the transfiguration story of 9:2–8. (4) In 1–13 Jesus is almost invariably portrayed in the company of his disciples; in 14–15 he is isolated and goes to his death alone. Now it is certainly possible to exaggerate the importance of the passion narrative as such within the framework of the Gospel (see Introduction, p. 37). Nevertheless it *is* germane to the Evangelist's theological intention, for in so far as he focuses upon the paradox that the coming glory of the Son of man resides for faith in Jesus' suffering, the story of that suffering is a much more natural conclusion to what he has to say in 1–12 than are the pronouncements of the exalted one in chapter 13 (see Schweizer in Ellis and Wilcox, *NS* pp. 114ff.). Moreover the passion story does not distort the theme of discipleship which is so prominent in the Gospel, but is its necessary completion. The picture of Jesus, bereft of the companionship of his disciples, going to his lonely death dramatically establishes the uniqueness of his way to the cross and demonstrates that the disciple is never above or equal to his Master but can only follow him in 'cross-bearing' at a distance and on the ground of what the Master has done on his own beforehand. Accordingly the passion narrative is more, much more than a mere appendix.

The basic structure of the narrative is broadly the same in all four Gospels and has been much less subject to adaptation than the traditions relating to the earlier part of Jesus' ministry. Coupling this with the known fact of how preoccupied the first Christians were with the cross and its central redemptive significance (1 C. 2:2; Rom. 3:25; 5:8; Phil. 2:8; 1 Pet. 1:19, etc.), we may suppose that the main lines of the passion story were drawn together at a very early stage and that the Evangelists were subsequently dependent on some such ancient account (see e.g. Grant, *Gospels*, p. 79). However, neither the Evangelists nor their unknown predecessors told the story out of a purely biographical interest. Their motive was to uphold Jesus' innocence of the charges brought against him and above all to show that his death, contrary to all appearances, was in agreement with the will of God (hence the *OT* phraseology that permeates the story and the ever-increasing appeal to specific *OT* texts in the process of its expansion). Consequently, imprinted as it is with the faith and theology of the Church, the narrative serves the modern historian less well than he would like for detailed reconstruction of the last days of Jesus' life. However, the story or its main kernel is very ancient, lacks nothing in realism, often reflects accurately the prevailing circumstances of the time and relates numerous episodes that are meaningful only in their connectedness with the whole chain of unfolding events, and so its outlines are undoubtedly to be recognised as solidly factual—that Jesus was arrested and tried, brought before Pilate, and put to death by crucifixion.

It is difficult to know whether the passion complex arose in the context of the Church's liturgy and worship (possibly in relation to the Lord's Supper and then as a lectionary for Holy Week) or of its preaching. Probably the different blocks built into the narrative as it gradually developed reflect different situations of practical need in the Church, e.g., the report of the institution of the Lord's Supper in 14:22–25 its liturgical need and concern; the scene in Gethsemane (14:32ff.) the need for edification in preaching; the story of Peter's denial (14:66–72) the need for exhortation to faithful confession of Christ at all costs (see further Schweizer, *GNM*, pp. 285f.). Finally, how little the passion narrative is to be judged purely in terms of its historical reliability becomes even plainer when we recognise that, beyond the aims and interests of the Church reflected in the various portions included in the tradition in the process of its transmission before Mark, we have to reckon with salient motifs emphasised by the Evangelist himself, like the cry of dereliction on the cross and the centurion's confession (15:34 and 39).

1–2. It was now two days before the Passover and the feast of Unleavened Bread: the two festivals, originally distinct, had been combined by the time of Jesus (Josephus, *Ant.* XIV.2, 1; XVII.9, 3, cf. 2 Chr. 35:17). The week-long **feast of Unleavened Bread** began on the same day as **the Passover,** which opened with a solemn ritual meal after 6 p.m. on the 15th day of the month Nisan. According to the Jewish reckoning, the day of the 14th, on the afternoon of which the paschal lambs were slain in the Temple, ended at sunset. Since the crucifixion occurred on the Friday (Mk 15:42), the day of the evening on which the Passover meal was eaten (cf. Jn 19:14), Mark would here appear to be placing the plot to kill Jesus on the Wednesday and the meal in Simon's house (14:3–9) possibly on the Wednesday evening. But it has to be noted that this chronology does not fit well with the notice of Mk 14:12, where the Last Supper seems to be identified with the Passover meal on the *Thursday* evening (and not Friday)—possibly in 14:1, where the Greek reads literally: 'after two days it was the Passover', Mark is employing the inclusive Jewish mode of reckoning, in which case 'after two days' would mean 'on the next day after' and 14:1 would then be compatible with the Thursday implied in 14:12 (although the problem of Mark's identification of the Last Supper with the Passover meal would still remain; see below, on 14:12). The mention of **the chief priests and scribes** suggests an informal, *ad hoc* meeting (a formal meeting of the Sanhedrin would have included the elders, whom Matthew (26:3) couples with the chief priests without mention of the scribes). The deliberation of the Jewish authorities **not during the feast lest there be a**

tumult of the people conflicts with what actually happened, since according to Mark at least (14:12–16) Jesus *was* arrested **during the feast.** Is this then an indication that Jesus was executed before the Passover? Or can the Greek words for **during the feast** be taken to mean 'in the crowd gathered for the festival' (Jeremias, *EW*, pp. 71ff.)? Or are we to suppose that the Jewish authorities changed their plans for some reason? These questions should not be too rigorously pressed, since the words **not during the feast** may not strictly denote a firm decision on the authorities' part to take *no* kind of action against Jesus at the feast. Possibly for Mark verses 1*b*–2 simply set the scene in a general way for what follows, spotlighting the bitter hostility and trickery of the Jewish authorities (in contrast with the sympathy of the crowd) and their eagerness to get rid of Jesus *with all haste*, and perhaps implying that 'the very thing which men desire to prevent must be brought to pass by God' (Schweizer, *GNM*, p. 287).

THE ANOINTING AT BETHANY **14:3–9**

This story apparently circulated at first without any indication of the point at which it occurred in Jesus' ministry. Luke places what looks like a variant of the story in a totally different context (7:36–50), and locates the episode in the house of Simon the Pharisee. John puts it before Jesus' entry to Jerusalem, locates it in the house of Lazarus and has Mary, Lazarus' sister, figure prominently (12:1–8). Matthew follows Mark with only minor variations in one or two details (26:6–13). In the form in which the story came to Mark, it was probably already associated with Simon the *leper* and must have originated in an environment where he was well known since no attempt is made to identify him as one healed by Jesus or anything else. Originally the story most probably ended with the words of Jesus in verses 6–7, which have a strong claim to authenticity. Jesus teaches that good works such as almsgiving (verse 5; cf. 'fasting' in 2:19) are not so much ruled out (verse 7) as transcended by the new and higher loyalties unfolded in and with his ministry and message (of the kingdom of God). Verse 8 connects the woman's action with the passion of Jesus and introduces a quite different dimension to the story. It was added presumably by a Church that regarded the woman's action as an anticipatory compensation for the fact that no proper anointing of Jesus' body was possible after his death (cf. Mk 16:1), and Jesus' closing statement in verse 7 (**but you will not always have me**) certainly lent itself readily to such an interpretative addition. In verse 9 the observation that **what she has done will be told in memory of her** may very well go back to Jesus, but the theme of the universal proclamation of the gospel is typical of the Gentile Church and of Mark in particular. In its present form the saying of verse 9 could only have been added (possibly by Mark) through the connexion of the woman's action with Christ's passion (verse 8). It is not so strange, in view of the connexion with the passion, that it is the woman's *deed* if not her *name* that is to be perpetually remembered. By inserting this story here, Mark separates the plot to kill Jesus (verses 1-2) from the perfidy of Judas (10-11), and effectively shows how despite all hostile powers arrayed against him, the one who goes the way of the cross constrains the love of the unnamed faithful.

3-7. The Greek word *alabastron*, here translated **alabaster jar,** was just as likely a glass phial, which the woman broke by snapping off its neck (it would never be used for the purpose again). The **ointment of pure nard** it contained was an unguent oil made from the root of a rare Indian plant. Whereas in Lk. 7:38 and Jn 12:3 it is the feet of Jesus that are anointed, here she **poured it over his head** (cf. Mt. 26:7). The people who put the indignant question (4) are not named by Mark: in Mt. 26:8 it is the 'disciples' and in Jn 12:4 'Judas Iscariot'. Although the abrupt appearance of the **woman** at the meal in Bethany is somewhat surprising, the action of anointing with oil after a journey or in connexion with a meal was quite customary. What arouses indignation is not the act in itself but the sheer extravagance of the woman's gesture. The price of **three hundred denarii** represented roughly a year's wages. In his response, Jesus does not deny (see verse 7) the point made by the protesters that the proceeds from the sale of the ointment could have been **given to the poor** (5). Their fault is that they cannot see beyond the level of good works to the deeper implications for life and conduct of devotion to Jesus. Jesus alone sees the woman's act of devotion to him for what it is, **a beautiful thing.**

8-9. The introduction of the theme of **the gospel preached in the whole world** in close connexion with an act directly related to Jesus' passion (**anointed my body beforehand for**

burying) shows how important the passion is for the good news
according to Mark.

THE PERFIDY OF JUDAS 14:10–11

There is no good reason to deny the historicity of the story of the
betrayer. That one in the circle of the Twelve should play so
nefarious a role is quite unlikely to have been invented by the
Church. Little clear indication is given of the motives for Judas'
action. There is just a hint in Mk 14:11 that he took the step he
did for **money;** though in fact the money is not promised until
after he has made his report; Mt. 26:15a suggests avarice; Lk.
23:3 and Jn 13:2, 27 ascribe it to the work of Satan. The Greek
word used of Judas, **betray,** means literally 'hand over' or
'deliver up', and has theological overtones for Mark (cf. 1:14;
9:31; 10:33; 14:41), implying that though on the one hand
Judas acted of his own volition, on the other his terrible deed was
not outside the reach of God's control, a comforting lesson the
Church derived also from turning to *OT* prophecy (e.g. Ps. 41:9;
109:8; Zech. 11:12f.).

What exactly it was that Judas 'betrayed' about Jesus cannot
easily be gleaned from the Gospel stories—his movements or
whereabouts (cf. Jn 18:2)? his messianic intentions? simply his
identity (Mk 14:44f.)? We know little more for sure than that
Judas was *somehow* involved in bringing Jesus to his trial and death.

10–11. The **Judas** incident originally followed immediately
upon 14:1–2. The simple 'and' (*RSV then*) with which it is introduced gives nothing away about how or why Judas made contact
with the Jewish authorities. The name **Iscariot** has been variously
interpreted: (1) 'man (Hebrew *îsh*) of Kerioth', a village in
southern Judea; (2) 'dweller in Jericho', the name being a
corruption of *Ierichōtēs;* (3) a transposition of the Aramaic
sheqarya = 'deceiver', a description applied to Judas by the
Church in the light of his actions; (4) a transliteration of the
Latin *sicarius* = 'assassin'. The theory that Judas was an insurrectionist, a sympathiser with the Zealot movement (which
fits in with the fourth interpretation), that he was disillusioned
with Jesus' unreadiness to take political action and wanted to
force his hand, while not unreasonable, remains merely conjectural. **One of the twelve:** his presence among the Twelve is
attested in all the Gospels. The Greek reads here *the* **one of the**

twelve, possibly with reference to 3:16–19, or to distinguish him from some other Judas.

PREPARATION FOR THE PASSOVER **14:12–16**

Indications are that this brief section did not belong to the earliest narrative of the passion: (1) this report speaks of the **disciples,** 14:10 and 14:17 of the **Twelve,** and the opening words of the account of the Last Supper in 14:17, 'and when it was evening he came with the twelve', take no notice of the sending ahead of the **two disciples** into the city in 14:13, 16; (2) the time of the sacrifice of the Passover lamb was the afternoon on the 14th Nisan, as we noted earlier (see on 14:1). Accordingly, the assigning of the sacrifice to the first day of the feast of Unleavened Bread in 14:1 is inexact from the Jewish standpoint (for which the feast began on 15th Nisan), and is unlikely to belong to early tradition. Only in the Roman reckoning, by which, as with us, the day stretched from midnight to midnight, could the Passover and the beginning of Unleavened Bread be part of the same day; (3) this report has remarkably close affinities with the story of the triumphal entry in 11:1–7 and looks very like a secondary development from it. From these considerations it may be inferred, therefore, that verses 12–16 are a later piece of tradition included by a Christian community that aimed to identify the Last Supper with the Passover meal. Probably the Evangelist himself, witnessing emphatically as he does to the obsolescence of old Jewish ordinances (see e.g. 2:21–28), regarded the Lord's Supper as the replacement for the Passover ritual meal.

Only here in Mark (verses 12–16), however, is the Supper identified with the Passover meal (cf. Lk. 22:15). Was it actually so in fact? According to the Fourth Gospel, the crucifixion coincides with the sacrifice of the Passover lambs (Jn 18:28; 19:14, 31), in which case the Last Supper cannot have been a Passover meal. It is argued (see e.g. Jeremias, *EW*, pp. 41–62) that the Johannine chronology is theologically conditioned, inspired by the belief that Jesus was sacrificed on the cross as the paschal lamb (cf. 1 C. 5:7). But equally there is no guarantee that the Synoptic chronology was unaffected by theological motives. Whereas Mark apparently thinks of the Lord's Supper as replacing the Passover, there is nothing in the account of the Supper itself that demands it be understood as a Passover meal (14:17–25). Taken by itself, the account of 14:17–25 does not even expressly mention Jerusalem, where the Passover meal *had to be eaten*. Certain features *are* consistent with a Passover meal: the hymn at the end (14:26), which could have been one of the *Hallel* psalms associated with the Passover; the late hour of the night (14:17); the reclining posture of the guests (14:78); the use of wine (14:25) instead of the usual water at an ordinary meal. But these features, with the probable exception of the hymn-singing which in fact stands outside of the report of the Supper, are not inconsistent either with a specially solemn religious fellowship (*ḥaburah*) meal, which could take place any time. Moreover there is no mention of the *lamb* that figured very prominently in the Passover ritual, nor of the *bitter herbs* nor of the traditional lengthy *explanation of the meaning* of the bread and the lamb that preceded the serving of the meal in the Jewish context, nor of the first part of the *Hallel* (Pss. 113–114) that was always recited. Other important considerations weigh against the Synoptic view of the Last Supper as a Passover: (1) if the Last Supper had been known to be a Passover, we might have expected the Church to celebrate the Eucharist only annually instead of at least weekly; (2) on the Synoptic dating it is hard to imagine (though the possibility is not excluded) the wholesale desecration of a sabbatical feast-day involved in the arrest in Gethsemane, trial, and execution of Jesus.

Attempts have been made recently to reconcile the conflicting Johannine and Synoptic chronologies, mainly by recourse to the notion that different groups in Judaism observed different calendars. Mlle Jaubert (*RHR* 146 (1954), pp. 140–73, and *The Date of the Last Supper*) supposes a tradition that Jesus celebrated the Passover on the Tuesday night, the date fixed by the solar calendar employed among the Qumran community and some other groups, in which case the Synoptics have condensed into one night and morning events that were spread over several days (see on this view the hint of an earlier celebration in Mk 14:1–2; cf. Mt. 26:2). On the other hand the Johannine dating of the Passover (on the Thursday evening) presupposes the official Pharisaic calendar. But why then it may be asked, if the tradition of an earlier celebration of the Passover by Jesus were known to them, should the Synoptic writers actually follow the regular Jewish calendar and point to a time after 6 o'clock (15th Nisan) on the Friday (see Hill, p. 337)?

Whatever the correct solution to the vexed chronological

problem may be, we can recognise that the Eucharistic practice prevailing in the early Christian communities would inevitably have coloured accounts of the institution of the rite, and whether in the Johannine or Synoptic *milieu* the colouring included *some* association of the Last Supper with the Passover ritual.

12–16. By the way they put their question **Where will you have us go?** the disciples accede to the supreme authority of Jesus. As with the story of the triumphal entry (11:1–7), the form in which this story is told does not encourage speculation about whether or how Jesus could have made practical arrangements in advance with the **householder** (14). From the story-teller's point of view it is enough that Jesus knows beforehand what is afoot in the city, and that his word of command **go into the city . . .** not only sets everything in motion but brings to pass what he has promised (**found it as he had told them**). Nor from Mark's standpoint would one wish to press that the man was **carrying a jar of water** rather than the customary leather container, as a prearranged signal. It was quite usual for pilgrims to plan ahead for a room for the Passover (14–15). But the title **The Teacher** (cf. 5:35), correctly rendered as a proper name in *RSV*, and the somewhat unexpected possessive in the phrase **my guest room** suggest that the one involved here is far more than an ordinary pilgrim.

THE LAST SUPPER **14:17–25**

The story of Jesus' foretelling of the betrayal (verses 17–21) did not initially belong where it now stands. The statement that **he came with the** *twelve* takes no account of the sending ahead of the two disciples in verse 13. Nor do verses 22–25 presuppose 17–21, since verse 22 reports the beginning of a meal, which according to verse 18 is already under way. Luke in fact places the prediction of the betrayal after the Supper (22:21–23). It is of course easy to see how the story of 17–21 became a part of the passion narrative and was located in the context of the Supper, especially in view of verse 18*b*, 'one who is eating with me' and verse 20. Jesus may well actually have prophesied the betrayal, but the story as it stands is more theological than historical, witness the allusions to Scripture, the fact that the betrayer is not even named (but cf. Jn 13:26), and the strange behaviour of the disciples who take no step whatever to amend a desperate situation. Everything hinges on the truth that nothing can stop Jesus from proceeding with assurance on the way to death God has mapped out for him, and that the betrayal is part of that way.

18. The phrase **one who is eating with me** echoes Ps. 41:9 ('who ate of my bread, has lifted his heel against me'), which is expressly cited in Jn 13:18 (note the quite different wording, possibly closer to the original, in Lk. 22:21). The description of the betrayer in *OT* terms helps to underline the fact that his treachery is no surprise but is clearly foreseen by Jesus.

19-20. Only the withholding of the name of the betrayer in verse 18 makes possible this description of the disciples' extraordinary conduct. They still do not clearly comprehend how things stand either with Jesus or themselves. No doubt this element in the story, the question **Is it I?** served a paraenetic purpose also for the Church and challenged the hearer to search his own heart. The **dish** does not necessarily contain the sauce into which bitter herbs were dipped at Passover. The statement of verse 20 dramatically confirms that of verse 18 without identifying the betrayer. His treachery is revealed as all the more horrible because of his intimate fellowship with Jesus.

21. The Son of man goes as it is written of him: the Greek word for **goes** (*hupagei*) occurs only here outside of the Fourth Gospel where it is common (e.g. 8:14, 21f.; 13:3, 33; 14:4, 28), with the sense of 'going to his death under the will of God'. The formula **as it is written of him** makes no reference to a particular *OT* text, but denotes rather that the death of the Son of man is in conformity with the plan and purpose of God manifested in Scripture. Accordingly the betrayal does not fall outside the scope of the divine plan and purpose, but at the same time the betrayer is no puppet without responsibility or guilt in his crime (**woe to that man . . .**).

The Last Supper

The extreme economy (lack of circumstantial detail) in the various *NT* accounts of the Supper is remarkable. Only the barest essentials, the words and actions of Jesus, appear in the picture. The simplicity of the meal itself contrasts markedly with the quite elaborate preparations reported (Mk 14:12-16). The question of which of the four primary traditions of the Supper (Mk 14:22-25; Mt. 26:26-29; Lk. 22:15-20; 1 C. 11:23-25) is the most primitive has been long debated but not finally answered (see e.g. Jeremias, *EW*, pp. 96-105; Higgins, *LSNT*; Taylor, pp. 542f and 664ff.; Nineham, pp. 455ff.). Matthew's account follows Mark's closely but introduces a little more liturgical regularity by the addition of the word 'eat' to the Marcan **Take; this is my body,** and the change of the Marcan narrative clause **and they all drank of it** to a command 'drink of it, all of you' (Mt. 26:26f.). The shorter text of Luke 22:15–19a (read by some MSS) seems to be drawn from a tradition independent of Mark, whereas the longer text of 22:19b–20 (read by most MSS and by all Greek MSS except Codex D), adds a second cup and appears to blend in touches from both Paul's and Mark's reports (for arguments against this, see Ellis, pp. 252ff.). The most important variation is that 1 C. 11:24 and Lk. 22:20 include the command to repeat the rite, 'this do in remembrance of me' (a more developed liturgical formulation), and Mark does not (cf. Mt. 26:26–30). But neither this nor the fact that Mark's account contains one or two Semiticisms, e.g. **poured out for many,** necessarily means that it is more ancient than the Pauline version. Mark and his readers would have thought of 14:22–25, even without the command to repeat the rite, as quite clearly the record of the institution of the Church's eucharistic celebration.

The differences in the primary sources should not, however, be allowed to obscure the highly significant elements common to all four—the inauguration of a new covenantal relationship between men and God secured by Jesus' sacrificial death and renewed always and again in the Lord's Supper, and the joyous expectation of the sure coming of the kingdom of God pledged to all who participate and enter into this new relationship.

22. The immediately preceding prophecy of the betrayal in the Marcan narrative (17–21) casts the shadow of the cross over the meal. It is as the one absolutely convinced of his approaching end that Jesus celebrates the Supper with his disciples. This fact does not call in question but is indeed the ground of the hope of the kingdom held out in the eschatological words of verse 25. The fellowship-meal proper customarily began with the breaking of bread—**he took bread:** the Greek word for **bread** (*artos*) normally denotes a flat cake of leavened bread, but it may also be used of unleavened bread (cf. 2:6, where it means the 'show-bread'). **And blessed:** refers not to consecration of the bread but to the usual Jewish prayer of thanksgiving: 'Blessed art thou, O Lord our God, king of the world, who bringest forth bread from the earth.' The grace said over the wine opened with the same ascription of praise and ended: 'creator of the fruit of the vine'. Accordingly, the only altogether novel thing at the beginning of this fellowship-meal is the word of Jesus, **Take; this is my body:** although one would not suspect it from Mark's account, according to Jewish custom the meal intervened between the breaking of bread and the taking of the cup. Accordingly, with Jesus the bread-word and the cup-word would have been separate from each other, and **body** in verse 22 and **blood** in verse 24 may not simply have been correlative terms. Also if we could assume behind the Greek words for **my body** here (*to sōma mou*) not the Aramaic *bisrî* (= 'my flesh') but *guphî* (= myself), we may perhaps the more readily take **my body** to signify, as it can do in Greek, 'my person', 'my whole being' (see Cranfield, p. 426). The bread-word is then a solemn promise of the continuing nearness of Jesus himself whenever bread is broken within the disciple-community. The force of the **is** in **this is my body** has been discussed for centuries. But in Aramaic there would be no copula and no thought of the material identity of body and bread. If on the other hand as is often proposed, we insert 'represents' or 'symbolises' we tend to reduce the statement to a mere figure of speech. We may think of it this way: when we say 'knowledge is power' we are not asserting that 'power' is substantially the same thing as 'knowledge' but suggesting that knowledge is a means to participation in power. So the bread (broken) is a means of participating in the real if unseen presence of the living Lord himself. But in Mark the cup-word, **This is my blood of the covenant** (verse 24), stands, without any gap at all, very close to the bread-word, and so fills out all that is implied by **my body** (cf. 1 C. 11:24, 'This is my body, *which is for you*') and makes it quite clear that to participate in the presence of the living Lord is also to share in the saving benefits of his unique sacrificial death.

23. And he took a cup . . . and they all drank of it: there is no conclusive evidence here that the meal either was or was not a Passover. It can be argued on the one side that the use of a common cup was contrary to the Passover practice, and on the other that the drinking of wine was particularly associated with Passover. The solitary narrative detail that intrudes in the description of Jesus' actions and words, **they all drank of it,** could have been a reminder to the Church that all, however reprobate (even the betrayer?), were admitted to the fellowship of Jesus and were offered the mercy and love of God in and through him (for other views, see Taylor, p. 545). Schweizer (*GNM*, p. 304) rightly observes that since the disciples had all drunk of the cup before Jesus spoke the cup-word, 'there is no implication here that Jesus' saying altered the wine in any substantial or material way'.

24. **This is my blood of the covenant:** the reading 'my blood of the *new* covenant' found in some ancient authorities is an assimilation to 1 C. 11:24. The Marcan **my blood of the covenant,** in Greek literally = 'the blood of me of the covenant', is awkward and virtually untranslatable into Aramaic and may be an attempt to import the covenant idea from the Pauline form of the cup-word ('this cup is the new covenant in my blood', 1 C. 11:25) into the statement, **this is my blood** parallel to the Marcan bread-word **this is my body.** It is not certain, however, that even the Pauline form with its mention of the 'new covenant' represents the most ancient strand of tradition. The probably initially independent account of the Supper preserved in Lk. 22:15–19*a* (or 15–18 if 19*a* is a Lucan addition) and 25–30 definitely equates the Supper with the eating of the paschal lamb but makes no reference at all to the covenant. We may therefore think of the different texts as reflecting different liturgical traditions in the Church, and above all of the formative influence of the faith and experience of the worshipping community in retrospectively interpreting Christ's death as the redemptive act that established God's new covenantal relation with men. The Marcan cup-word has been shaped up under the influence of the record in Exod. 24:6–8 of the ratification of the old covenant through the sprinkling of sacrificial blood on the people, and that of Paul (1 C. 11:25) and Luke (the longer text 22:19*b*–20) by Jeremiah's prophecy (31:31–34) of the new covenant. But in each case the meaning is essentially the same. In partaking of the cup, or rather of the wine it contains, in the Lord's Supper, men are incorporated with the redeemed people of God's new covenant, inaugurated by Christ's sacrificial death. The words **poured out for many** have a Semitic flavour, the **many** in Semitic usage being inclusive and signifying 'all mankind'.

25. The **fruit of the vine** is a Jewish liturgical formula for 'wine'. The saying of verse 25 is rather loosely attached to the words of institution in Mark. Luke in fact places it first (22:16–18). But from what we know of Jesus' message of the kingdom and from the Semitic vocabulary and ideas (**fruit of the vine;**

truly = 'amen'; the notion of the messianic banquet in the new age, Isa. 25:6; *1 En.* 62:14; *2 Bar.* 29:5ff.; cf. Mt. 8:11; Rev. 19:9), we may be fairly sure these words take us back to Jesus' own farewell Supper with his disciples. The Lucan version of the saying, 'I tell you that *from now on* I shall not drink of the fruit of the vine until the kingdom of God comes' (22:18; cf. the Greek of Mt. 26:29), might seem to suggest a *vow* on Jesus' part of abstention from subsequent Passovers and at the same time an affirmation that he is one with his followers in the fasting time pending the consummation in the kingdom of God (cf. the Passover fast of the third-century Christian group, the Quartodecimans, which may go back to the first-century Palestinian Church, see Jeremias, *EW*, pp. 207–18; Ellis, pp. 252f.). But Mk 14:25 appears to distinguish between the destiny of Jesus and that of his disciples, and simply 'places Jesus' death in the light of the coming kingdom of God' (Bornkamm, p. 160). The word **until,** which appears in all forms of this saying and within a different frame in Paul ('until he comes', 1 C. 11:26) is indelibly inscribed on the banner that stands over every Lord's Supper. The promise it contains fills the celebration with joyous hope of the fulfilment in the kingdom of God and transforms the present moment with all its risks and challenges (such as the Son of man had himself to face on his way through Gethsemane to the cross) by placing it in the light of that future.

PROPHECY OF THE DISCIPLES' DEFECTION **14:26–31**

The seams of this little composition are not too well stitched together. Peter's words in verse 29 take no account of the prediction of Jesus in verse 28 or of the Scripture quotation in 27*b* but refer back only to Jesus' statement in 27*a*, **You will all fall away.** Moreover, the mention of the resurrection in Jesus' forecast that he would **go before you to Galilee** (28) plus the fact that the forecast is matched by Mk 16:7 prompt the conclusion that verse 28 is a Marcan insertion. With 27*b* and 28 bracketed off, we have a clear and unified account of Peter's denial. We may suppose that the citation of Zech. 13:7 circulated in isolation in the Church (cf. Jn 16:32), perhaps originally, in the light of the whole context in Zechariah (see 13:6 and cf. 12:10), as a proof-text for the sufferings of Jesus (Lindars, pp. 129ff.). But the change from the imperative of the Hebrew and Septuagint texts, 'strike the shepherd!' to the first person singular **I will strike** (cf.

Mt. 26:31) suggests that the passage was uplifted from its Zechariah context so that God is now the 'striker', Jesus the **shepherd,** and the fleeing disciples the scattered **sheep.** The verse on its own would then have found its way into the Gospel tradition as showing that the disciples' flight had already been predicted in Scripture as something foreseen in God's plan. However, in the Marcan context, in close proximity now to the prediction of Jesus in verse 28, the citation of Zech. 13:7 on Jesus' lips functions as a demonstration for Mark of Jesus' prophetic foreknowledge that not even the worst failure of the disciples could impede God's purpose or invalidate the promise of a new fellowship with him after Easter.

26–27. The singing of a **hymn** (part of the *Hallel*, Pss. 114–118) is consistent with the Jewish custom at the close of the Passover meal. It does not of course necessarily prove that the Last Supper *was* a Passover meal, since it may simply reflect the practice obtaining in the narrator's *Christian* community (cf. 1 C. 14:26; Col. 3:16; Eph. 5:19; see Schweizer, *GNM*, p. 307). The meaning of the Greek word for **fall away** is 'take offence at', 'be scandalised by and so alienated from'. As the one who utters the prediction of Zech. 13:7, Jesus is pictured as prepared in advance for the very worst that can happen and as facing his passion without flinching.

28. This verse is missing from the third-century Fayyum fragment in the Rainer papyri (probably because the scribe sensed its difficulty?). But there is little doubt that Mark inserted it here in anticipation of 16:7. The words **I will go before you,** ambiguous in English as in Greek, could mean either, 'I will march at your head' or 'I will go there earlier in time than you' (cf. 6:45, and see on 16:7). The possibility that Jesus himself foresaw and foretold not only his suffering and death but his coming vindication by God cannot be categorically excluded (see Barrett, *JGT*, pp. 68ff.). But in the light of Mk 16:7 and what appears to be the *Marcan* motif of a rendezvous of the risen Jesus with his disciples *in Galilee*, it is very questionable whether he did so in the terms represented in verse 28. From Mark's standpoint the prediction of verse 28 conveys the assurance that not even the tragic defection of the disciples which will leave him to face his final ordeal alone (but of which he is aware already, verse 27) can shatter the promise of God's impending victory in the resurrection or of a new and lasting fellowship with him after Easter.

29-31. The verb **deny** means 'to disown', and is almost a technical term in the Gospels (cf. Mt. 10:32f. = Lk. 12:8f.). The phrase **before the cock crows twice** is strange. It occurs only in Mark, and is omitted by some MSS, possibly through assimilation to Mt. 26:34 and Lk. 22:34. The expression 'cock-crow' was probably proverbial for 'the early hours of the morning', but the **twice** may have arisen from the fact that the Romans gave the name of 'cock-crow' to the watch that began at midnight and ended at 3 a.m. (the usual times of cock-crowing). Whereas verses 27-28 deal with the flight of the disciples and their re-assembling with the risen Lord, verse 29 rather abruptly introduces another theme, Peter's disowning of Jesus. May we infer that in Mark Peter's act of disavowal, which clearly had a greater impact on the tradition than the flight of the disciples, is given a greater prominence as much more reprehensible than 'flight'? The (typically Marcan) misunderstanding on the part of Peter as the leading spokesman and of the rest of the disciples here (**they all said the same**) is not that their protestations of loyalty result from a lack of honest intention, but rather that they are *premature* (cf. Jn 13:36, 'Where I am going you cannot follow me now; but you shall follow afterward'). No one can go the way Jesus has to go or face what he has to face on his own human strength. Not until God has done everything that needs to be done in and through the cross and resurrection (verses 27*b*-28) is the grace supplied that enables men to follow Jesus in cross-bearing discipleship.

JESUS' LONELY STRUGGLE IN GETHSEMANE 14:32-42

The Gethsemane scene scarcely belonged to the most ancient passion narrative. It is linked rather uneasily with the prophecy of the disciples' defection (14:26-31) and with what follows (14:43-52). However, that the story contains a historical nucleus is highly probable. The Church believed that Jesus had overcome triumphantly the crisis that is impending here and would not have *imagined* her exalted Lord engaged in a great prayer-struggle before it. Moreover Jesus' agony in Gethsemane is deeply embedded in various layers of the tradition, in the more condensed and probably independent account of Lk. 22:40-46, and *in nuce* in Jn 18:11 (cf. also 14:31 and 12:27f.) as well as in Heb. 5:7f. Even so there are numerous irregularities in the construction of the story as we have it in Mark (cf. Mt. 26:36-46). Verse 32 begins with a reference to all the disciples, and verse 33 then apparently makes another beginning with only the inner circle of the three who are not thereafter mentioned again. The prayer described in narrative form in verse 35 is given in direct speech in 36. Jesus goes away only twice (35 and 39), but comes back three times (37, 40, 41). The account, we may assume, has been built up, possibly out of two main strata containing initially separate prayers and sayings of Jesus. One, dealing with 'vigilance and temptation' and serving the Church's interest in paraenesis, consists probably of 33-34, 36-38 (with 39 being editorial). The other deals mainly with Jesus' *'hour'* and is christological or soteriological: it consists of 32, 35, 40, 41*b*, with 41*a*, **and he came the third time ... taking your rest?** inserted perhaps in an attempt to conform the story to the model of threefold prayer (2 C. 12:8; cf. Dan. 6:10, 13) or less likely of Peter's threefold denial (on the question of sources, see further K. G. Kuhn, *EvTh* 12 (1952-3), pp. 263ff.; cf. Schweizer, *GNM*, p. 310).

At any rate the interwoven materials present twin themes of crucial importance to Mark in his Gospel: the blindness of the disciples, here exemplified by their hopeless torpor, in stark contrast with Jesus' wakeful communion with God (in prayer), and the interplay of the divine 'must' that rules over Jesus' passion (and appears in fact at the close here in 41*b* and the link verse 42), and Jesus' own *willing* submission to God's will (36*b*).

32. Only here and in Mt. 26:36 is the scene of Jesus' struggle described as **a place which was called Gethsemane:** after a mention of the Mount of Olives, Luke speaks only of 'the place' (22:39f.), John of a 'garden' on the far side of Kidron (18:1f.). **Gethsemane** means an 'olive-press', and since **place** probably denotes a plot of ground, we may think of an olive-grove. With Jesus' request **sit here, while I pray** the story stresses at once his apartness from his disciples. His way is not their way, he goes to prayer alone. This verse has a more natural continuation in verse 35 (see above).

33-34. The reference to the taking aside of the three, **Peter and James and John** may come from Mark and not his source or tradition. Elsewhere in the Gospel (5:37; 9:2-8; 13:3) the selection of the three is associated with a special revelation of Jesus' unique status. Here they are admitted only to a sight of Jesus' *anguish*. Mark does not want his readers to suppose that, if the disciples had shown faith, they would have been granted a glorious revelation like that of the transfiguration (Nineham, p. 391). Rather he challenges them to respond in faith, as the disciples here fail to do, to the essential paradox of his Gospel, that the ultimate divine glory ordained for Jesus by God is nowhere more real than when it is surrendered to the depths of human suffering. Jesus' suffering is here described in the strongest possible terms. The Greek words for **greatly distressed and troubled** suggest the most awesome feelings of revulsion from the dread prospect ahead of him. This is stated again in Jesus' own words **my soul is very sorrowful,** reminiscent of the Psalmist's laments (e.g. Ps. 42:6; 43:5), and the added phrase **even to death** implies an agony that knows the threat of extinction. Jesus does not face sorrow or suffering **even to death,** like an 'immortal divine being', as if it were not there, nor with Stoic apathy, as if it did not matter. The threat death *is* for every man, it is here for Jesus. The call to the disciples to **watch** is not a request to act as sentinels against intruders, but a call to active participation in his destiny of suffering, the very point at which they are to fail him by **sleeping.**

35-36. Jesus prostrates himself, **he fell on the ground** (cf. Mt. 26:39) and prays that **the hour might pass from him:** the term **the hour** has an apocalyptic background. In Daniel (e.g. 8:17, 19; 11:35, 40, 45) it refers to the time of judgment and fulfilment of the divine plan. In the Christian context it denotes the time appointed by God for the completion of his *saving* purpose in Jesus (note the possible link with Mk 13:11, 32; cf. Jn 2:4; 5:25; 7:30; 12:23 and 27). In praying **that the hour might pass from him** Jesus is not of course setting himself against God's purpose (note, **if it were possible**), but expressing his dread of the necessity of suffering God's 'hour' lays upon him. The use of the Aramaic **Abba** as a form of address to God was, so far as we know, shunned by Judaism in Jesus' day, as too intimate and not reverential enough, but was regularly used by Jesus and implied his certainty of a special relationship with God. But the Church retained Jesus' usage, and in the Greek-speaking *milieu* added the word **Father** as here in explanation. Some commentators ask in any case how the disciples could have known what Jesus prayed in private and think of the prayer of verse 36 as a model prayer (with its echo of the Lord's Prayer in **but what thou wilt**) fashioned by the Church. Whatever the case may be, the significance of this prayer for Mark's whole version of the good news is clear enough. It opens with the affirmation of God's omnipotence **all things are possible to thee,** but the Jesus who is pictured here is no unwitting victim of a fate arbitrarily imposed by an omnipotent Deity but one who struggles in his own will toward God's will and so doing enters into all the ambiguity of human existence and endures its worst tension. In the abyss of this struggle the God who is the Father of Jesus and who will finally vindicate him (cf. 14:62) is not absent but only *hidden,* as he is hidden also in the cry of dereliction from the cross (15:34). Jesus' entreaty to God to **remove this cup** is a restatement in different imagery of the preceding prayer that **the hour might pass from him,** the **cup** in the *OT* being a metaphor for retributive punishment but here obviously implying suffering and death.

37–38. Peter is here singled out as the leading representative of the disciples, as in verses 29 and 31, and the question put to him **Could you not watch one hour?** sharpens the challenge to Mark's reader to that active involvement in the way of Jesus that is required of all disciples. Jesus is uniquely qualified to summon his disciples to **watch and pray that you may not enter into temptation:** in Gethsemane he has himself suffered the last agony of the **time of testing** in which, though it is ordained by God, Satan is also climactically involved, and Jesus knows the bitterness within of the conflict between the Supreme Good and Evil (see R. S. Barbour, *NTS* 16 (1969–70), pp. 245 ff.). Thoughts of the Son of God's own inner struggle would no doubt have greatly sustained a Church experiencing persecution and the closeness of martyrdom. **The spirit is willing, but the flesh is weak:** the **spirit** here is hardly the Spirit of God or the Holy Spirit given to men to fight against human frailty (Schweizer, *GNM,* pp. 313f.). Rather the word **temptation** or 'testing' relates to the *outward* cosmic dimension of the eschatological warfare between God and Satan, and the terms **spirit** and **flesh** to the corresponding *inward* tension within the structure of man's existence (cf. the doctrine of the 'two spirits' at Qumran, 1QS 3:24ff., and possibly the rabbinic notion of the good and evil inclinations in man). In short **temptation** is here a more theological, and **spirit** and **flesh** more anthropological terms.

39–42. Verse 39 is probably editorial and the phrase **saying the same words,** lacking from some MSS, may be a later gloss.

The repetitions of 39–41*a* serve principally to intensify Jesus' struggle in all its loneliness and to expose the contrasting uninvolvement of blind or sleepy disciples. The Greek word *apechei* (*RSV*, **It is enough**) is obscure and is variously explained: (1) 'Enough of this!' in regard to the disciples' **sleeping,** but there is little if any evidence for this meaning of the word; (2) 'The bill is paid', in a technical commercial sense, either of Judas receiving his bribe or metaphorically of the 'time being up'; (3) supplying the words 'the end', with some MSS, 'The end is far off (as you think)? No! **the hour has come';** (4) 'He (Judas) is getting hold of me now'. Fortunately a final decision on the matter is not essential to an understanding of the words that follow, **the hour has come; the Son of man is betrayed into the hands of sinners:** he who has gone through the agonising struggle of Gethsemane now resolutely embraces **the hour** decreed for him by God. What God has willed for him is now at last his own choice. So the glory of God manifest in the ultimate victory of the (sinless) Son of man is present already in concealment in Jesus' voluntary submission to suffering and death. The starkness with which this saying combines the notion of God's overarching design for Jesus with a foul act of betrayal into the hands of sinful men (with **sinners** here cf. 'men' in 9:31) is quite remarkable. Verse 42, which furnishes a connexion with the story of the arrest, depicts Jesus as the one who does not wait to be taken but advances with complete assurance to meet the fate being worked out for him through the betrayer. The Greek word for **let us be going** may be translated 'let us march forward to meet him!'

JESUS' ARREST 14:43–52

The words **And immediately, while he was still speaking** are typically Marcan and did not belong originally to the story of the arrest. The notice that **Judas** is **one of the twelve** is strange in view of earlier disclosures about him. This suggests that the account of the arrest was at first independent of what precedes. The earliest passion narrative may in fact have begun here (the Johannine passion story which earlier deviates runs closely parallel from this point on, and early Christian summaries do not go back beyond the arrest, e.g. Ac. 2:23; 7:52; 13:28; cf. possibly 1 C. 11:23 'on the night when he was betrayed'). The report of the arrest in 43–46 is made in a very matter-of-fact way and is a unity. On the other hand verses 47–51 consist of several

independent items rather loosely cemented together. It is very
unlikely that we should account for the contrast between 43–46
and 47–51 by holding that the traitor's kiss (see notes on 44–45)
would be indelibly stamped on the disciples' memory, whereas
'information about what followed immediately afterwards would
tend to be scrappy and disjointed' (Cranfield, p. 436). The
materials clustered in 47–51 are in fact mainly apologetic in
intent. The violent incident of verse 47, inserted at a different and
more suitable point in Lk. 22:49f. and Jn 18:10–11, has here
become the frontispiece to a detached saying which portrays
Jesus' detestation of violence or his pacific nature (48), and to
another which, among other things, upholds the integrity of his
teaching activity. Finally, the fulfilment-of-scripture motif is
awkwardly introduced in 49*b*, and *only after that* the notice of the
disciples' flight (in fulfilment of the prediction of 14:27?).

43–46. By connecting this story with the foregoing (32–42) in
the way he has done, **and immediately, while he was still
speaking,** the Evangelist himself demonstrates that, confronted
now with the betrayer and an array of enemies, Jesus through his
surrender to God's will is completely prepared in advance for the
fate about to overtake him. The picture of the **crowd with
swords and clubs** around Judas in verse 43 is hardly of the
Temple police or of Roman soldiers, as in Jn 18:3, but of a
hastily gathered mob incited by the official leaders of Judaism.
The tradition has preserved some relics of violence amid the
scenes of the last hours of Jesus' life (cf. 14:48; 15:7), but while
these no doubt accurately reflect the (potentially) explosive
political situation in Jerusalem at the time, they do not justify the
hypothesis that Jesus or the movement led by him shared
Zealotist aspirations, or that the pacific Christ who appears in the
question of verse 48 obscures the genuine political element in
Jesus' actual ministry. The question of what it was that Judas
actually betrayed has been mentioned earlier (cf. 14:17–21).
According to this story it was a matter of Judas' identifying
Jesus for the crowd come to seize him—**the one I shall kiss is
the man.** We must therefore suppose that the area was busy with
pilgrims and that in the darkness it would have been difficult for
the marauding band to pick Jesus out. But several commentators
have justly asked whether the Jewish authorities would have
required the aid of a hired traitor to identify one who had become
well known through his teaching in the Temple (cf. verse 49), or

whether the wily Judas would not have avoided implicating
himself so obviously by simply pointing to Jesus from a little
distance. At any rate for those who first heard or read this story
Judas' dramatically treacherous gesture in kissing Jesus would
have conveyed the notion of superhuman powers of evil at work
in him. The **kiss** was a familiar salutation of honour among the
rabbis and their pupils, note the address to Jesus as **Master!** or
Rabbi. The verb **kissed** in verse 45 is an intensive form of the
verb in 43, and this further underlines the enormity of Judas'
crime.

47–50. The incident of verse 47 appears to have no theological
implication at all and is almost certainly a historical reminiscence.
The one who cuts off the ear of the high priest's slave is here an
unnamed sympathiser. John has it as Peter and also names the
slave as Malchus (18:10–11). The action in Mark seems somewhat pointless after the arrest has taken place, and Luke (22:49f.)
and John both place it before the arrest. Whereas in Luke
(22:51) Jesus roundly condemns the sympathiser's violence (and
heals the slave's ear!), the episode makes way in Mark for a
condemnation of his captors' violence (48f.). Although the word
robber could denote an insurrectionist or revolutionary (of the
Zealot type), there is nothing in the narrative to suggest that the
gang who came to arrest Jesus did so in fact because they regarded him *as a political threat*. The phrase **day after day** suggests
a longer period or more frequent visits to Jerusalem than the
Marcan passion narrative allows, but the Greek may denote 'in
the day time'. In any case the saying of verse 49 did not belong at
first where it now stands. When Jesus says **I was with you in the
temple, and you did not seize me** the **you** scarcely refers to
his motley band of captors but to the leading representatives of
official Judaism (cf. 14:1). Is there perhaps a hint here that the
Jewish authorities *could* do nothing to silence the bearer of the
good news? Certainly the saying suggests that (in its authority and
integrity) Jesus' teaching in itself was not the rock of offence, but
only misrepresentations of his activity, it is implied (48). All the
more darkly irrational, therefore, are the decisions and actions
of the Jewish leaders that have finally led up to his arrest. But even
the irrational decisions and actions of men are encompassed within God's design or plan. That appears to be the meaning of the
awkwardly introduced formula **but let the scriptures be
fulfilled:** not a later scribal gloss but a Marcan touch. No

particular *OT* text is in mind (cf. 14:21) and in terms of the Marcan perspective we might well paraphrase thus: 'It has all happened, both the work of the Teacher and the works of guilty men, in conformity with the will and purpose of God.' And the fact that Jesus is the speaker here shows with what sovereign assurance he accepts that it is so. His assurance is shared by no one else. With the bare intimation of the disciples' flight that follows (in fulfilment of 14:27), Jesus is entirely on his own. His pathway through the cross and beyond is unique and must be completed before a new kind of discipleship becomes possible.

51–52. The extraordinary vignette appended here, but omitted by Matthew and Luke, has given rise to much speculation. The incident in itself has seemingly no christological or soteriological significance, and most likely rests on historical reminiscence. The **young man** in question was possibly later a Christian convert whose story became familiar in the Church and found its way into the tradition. It is sometimes held that the young man was no other than the author himself, the John Mark referred to in Ac. 12:12, 25; 15:37, 39, whose parents' home was close by (14:15), and who here paints a tiny picture of himself in a corner of the Gospel. But the author, whoever he was (an eye-witness might have been expected to tell verses 47–49 rather differently and more fully), would surely have given us a less cryptic auto-biographical note. Suggestions that the episode is based on Am. 2:16, or is the nucleus of the story of a young hero (cf. Gen. 39:12), who serves as a type of Jesus in his passion, or anticipates the young man or angel at the tomb (16:5), are implausible. There may be some significance in the aorist of the verb 'seize' in verse 46, 'they seized Jesus and it was over and done with, his fate was sealed', and the present tense (in Greek) in verse 51, 'they seek to lay hold of the young man, but he resists arrest and makes his getaway'. Could the incident have been added to draw the contrast between the escaping youth and Jesus who makes no attempt to run at all, but calmly accepts his destiny?

JESUS BEFORE THE SANHEDRIN AND PETER'S DENIAL 14:53–72

In Luke (22:54*b*–62) the story of Peter's denial is placed before the report of Jesus' *morning* appearance before the Sanhedrin (verses 66ff.) and is told as a unity. Mark on the other hand gives a brief introduction to the Peter story in 14:54, and only after an interpolated account of a *nocturnal* trial picks up that story again in 14:66ff. He is therefore interfusing the two stories and allowing them to play upon each other according to a favourite stylistic device of the Gospel (cf. 5:21–43). His concern is no doubt to stress the contrast between Peter's act of disloyalty under relatively gentle pressure and Jesus' patient submission, under the sternest possible test, to vengeful rejection by his enemies (61a) or to an abasement in which lies hidden the seed of God's omnipotence by which the coming vindication of the Son of man in glory is assured (62). Possibly in Mark's tradition verse 53 originally introduced the story of the trial, and verse 54 the story of Peter's denial. In interweaving the two stories the Evangelist may have pushed both verses back into the position of a preface to the whole section and then composed verses 66–67a himself as a new lead into the account of Peter's denial. Certainly verses 66–67a contain distinctive Marcan features (the Greek genitive absolute construction in the participial clause, **as Peter was below in the courtyard;** the aorist participles **seeing** and **looked,** and the narrative present tense of the verb **came).**

The records of the trial (or trials) of Jesus in all four Gospels reveal significant discrepancies and opinions still differ widely about their historicity. Mark, who is fairly closely followed by Matthew, reports three meetings, one of the Sanhedrin at night (14:55–65), a second in the morning (15:1), and a hearing before Pilate (15:2–15). At the night meeting the proceedings lead up to a charge of blasphemy and a general condemnation. After a further morning session (15:1), Jesus is handed over to Pilate and is finally delivered up for crucifixion on the charge of claiming to be **King of the Jews.** Luke (22:66–71) mentions only a morning meeting of the Sanhedrin at which Jesus is condemned for suggesting that he is the Son of God. He subsequently appears before both Pilate and Herod Antipas and is handed over for crucifixion. The account in the Fourth Gospel is apparently based on independent tradition. It has Jesus examined by Annas and Caiaphas at night, then taken to the Praetorium for a hearing before Pilate (Jn 18:28–19:16), and the dialogue it reports as taking place at both sessions differs greatly from the other reports. Whereas the Synoptics place the emphasis on the proceedings of the Jewish court, the focus in John's Gospel is clearly on Jesus' appearance before Pilate.

From the divergences in the various Gospel records we may reasonably infer that the early Church lacked *precise* information on what actually happened after Jesus' arrest. Moreover it is clear enough that theological considerations have affected the way the story is told in the Gospels. For one thing, the tendency to exculpate Pilate and the Romans and to place the responsibility for the condemnation and death of Jesus on the Jews (stemming from the primitive Church's struggles with the Synagogue) is present already in the Synoptics (see e.g. Mk 15:10, 13), and reaches its climax in the Fourth Gospel (Jn 18:31, 35, 38; 19:4, 6–7, 12, 15–16), where the Jews *as a whole* are blamed for their deliberate rejection of Christ.

The stories being what they are, therefore, the task of historical reconstruction is particularly complicated and precarious. The question of the reliability of the Marcan narrative hinges largely on the hotly disputed problem of the scope of the Sandhedrin's jurisdiction over capital cases in Jesus' time. Evidence comes mainly from a relatively much later period, from the Mishnah tractate *Sanhedrin*, and it is highly debatable whether such prescriptions as it lays down for the Sanhedrin's legal procedures in capital charges actually applied in Jesus' day or not. If they did, then Mark's account is in open conflict with the stated requirements that the Jewish court had to be held in the daytime, on two consecutive days, and with the hearing of the witnesses in private. It has been suggested that normal procedures were not followed in this case because in fact the Pharisees were not at all involved and the Sandhedrin that heard Jesus was not a religious but a *political* Sanhedrin with Caiaphas playing 'the role of a Quisling who proved ready to sell out Judea to the Romans for personal gain' (see S. Zeitlin, *Who Crucified Jesus?* New York and London, 1942, pp. 165ff.). But there is nothing in the texts to support the contention of such purely *political* motivations. On the other hand many commentators have held (e.g. Rawlinson, p. 219) that the hearing before the Sanhedrin was more in the nature of a preliminary informal investigation preparatory to the trial proper before Pilate. But against that stands the fact that Mark himself obviously regards the Sanhedrin trial as *official*, and that the record of Jesus' appearance before Pilate (Mk 15:1ff.) makes no allusion to any previous investigation at all, and in fact in regard to the charges brought against Jesus bears little if any relation to the earlier proceedings.

Just how ambivalent is the evidence of the Gospel records themselves, the tractate *Sanhedrin* and such other slender pieces as

remain to us (for a useful summary, see Johnson, p. 241), may be
gauged from the quite contradictory historical views that arise
therefrom. For instance, in his book *On the Trial of Jesus* (Berlin,
1961) the Jewish scholar Paul Winter argues that since the
Sanhedrin in Jesus' time *was competent* to try capital cases and so
had no need to have recourse to Pilate for the execution of Jesus,
and since in fact Jesus was executed in the Roman fashion, as
laid down by Roman law, the whole story of the hearing before
the Jewish high court is unhistorical. On the other side a classical
scholar like A. N. Sherwin-White maintains (*Roman Society and
Roman Law in the New Testament*, Oxford, 1963) that in Jesus' day
the Sanhedrin had *no* jurisdiction in capital cases (cf. Jn 18:31),
that the Sanhedrin session and the condemnation for blasphemy
are historical, and that the Jewish leaders thereafter turned to
Pilate and put pressure on him, if not on the political charge of
sedition against Jesus then on the religious charge.

Possibly about the most that can be affirmed with confidence
is that the Roman procurator condemned Jesus to death by
crucifixion (on a nebulously understood legal-political issue),
and that the Jewish religious leaders were *also somehow* involved,
so well attested in the Gospel tradition is the rising tide of their
hostility to Jesus and his message, and in Paul the Jewish persecution of Jesus' followers very shortly after his death (Gal. 1:18;
2:1). Beyond that there may be something to be said for the view
adumbrated in the Fourth Gospel (cf. Jn 18:3, 12. See M. Goguel,
Jesus and the Origins of Christianity, Vol. II: *The Life of Jesus*, trans.
Olive Wyon, New York and London, 1960, pp. 464ff.) that both
the Romans and the Jews were implicated and in collusion *from
the very outset* in the proceedings that culminated in Jesus' death.
From all that can be gathered from sources extraneous to the
Gospels about Pilate's stubbornness and inflexibility of character,
it is unlikely that, without previous fairly lengthy negotiations, he
would have been so quickly suborned by the Jewish leaders into
sentencing Jesus to death as the Synoptic narratives (see especially
Mark and Matthew) seem to suggest.

At all events while the Evangelist Mark himself appears to lay
the greater stress on the relative responsibility of the Jews for the
condemnation and death of Jesus he does also want to convey the
message that the leading representatives of the religious *and*
secular power are both alike involved *officially* in bringing Jesus to
the cross. Beside the hostile forces arrayed against him Jesus is

absolutely *on his own* and his obedience to the way God has willed for him is unique. Not only so but by incorporating the story of Peter's denial with the narrative of the trial before the Sanhedrin, Mark demonstrates that even the closest disciple cannot endure the pathway on which God is determined to disclose himself in and through this Jesus. Even those who like Peter imagine they are well equipped to be travelling companions of Jesus fall under the judgment of God no less than Jewish and Roman authorities. Not until the way of Jesus through the cross and the vindication of Easter is complete can the new hope of God's mercy dawn even for the once faithless and disloyal.

53-54. The **high priest** is not named at all in Mark. He is correctly designated as Caiaphas only in Mt. 26:3, 57. In Jn 18:13, 24 Jesus is taken first to Annas, father-in-law of Caiaphas, and then handed over to Caiaphas (cf. the erroneous 'Annas and Caiaphas' in Lk. 3:2 and see also Ac. 4:6). Does this perhaps suggest that the earliest tradition named only Pilate, clearly referred to in all layers, as the one who both passed sentence and carried it out? With the mention of **all the chief priests and the elders and the scribes** (the inveterate enemies of Jesus according to Mk 8:31, 14:43; cf. 14:1), Mark has in mind presumably a regularly constituted meeting of the Sanhedrin, which numbered seventy-one members, out of which twenty-three formed a quorum. But this raises serious difficulties. A trial involving a capital charge could not take place at night (as this one obviously does; cf. 15:1). Also, since there had to be a second session on the following day in order to obtain a conviction, no such court would have been convened on the day before a sabbath or feast-day, as the necessary second session would then have been impossible. Even if Mark has mistakenly presented as a formal trial what was no more than an informal enquiry, it is still quite improbable that any such preliminary informal investigation would have been held at night in the Passover season. The notice of Mk 15:1 (see below) is somewhat ambiguous and while on the face of it, it seems to refer to a second separate morning session, it may also denote the closure of the night-time's proceedings. If Mark thought only of one official nocturnal meeting, has he then mistakenly transposed to this trial by night the proceedings which Luke, following a tradition of greater historical accuracy, has assigned to the morning assembly of the Sanhedrin (Lk. 22:66-71)? It is impossible to be certain about such matters. Again, the

Marcan narrative implies that the Sanhedrin assembly was held
in the high priest's house (**right into the courtyard of the
high priest**), and this constitutes a further irregularity, since
Mishnaic regulation forbade meeting there. **Peter followed him
at a distance:** is it implied that Peter, though coming to face
the situation in which Jesus is involved, seeks the safety of the
'glad, safe rear' while Jesus is altogether exposed to the wrath of
his enemies? The **guards** with whom Peter **was sitting** would
be the high priest's entourage including perhaps some of the
Temple police.

55-59. The hearing of witnesses and the giving of evidence,
which proves to be inadmissible and leads to the high priest's own
attempt to state the charge against Jesus, is not in accordance
with statutory procedure in the midst of a Jewish trial. Normally
there was a bias in favour of the accused, and witnesses were
heard and evidence prepared in advance of the trial. We must
entertain the possibility that the early Church, in the light of
its tendency to emphasise Jewish responsibility for the death of
Jesus, has shaped up the account of the grounds on which it
believed Jesus was condemned so as to stress his complete innocence and at the same time the court's perversion of justice. Most
of all in Mark is the gross unfairness of the court's dealings with
Jesus underlined, witness the opening statement that they were
bent from the first on a verdict against him (**the whole council
sought testimony against Jesus to put him to death**), and
the repeated notices of their inability to find valid testimony
against him in verses 56, 57, and 59 (with perhaps an echo of
Ps. 27:12; 35:11f.; 109:2ff.).

It is not easy to determine why Mark represents the allegation
that Jesus had said he would destroy the Temple and build
another as false testimony. Reporting the saying in another form
in which Jesus claims only that he *is able* to destroy the Temple
and rebuild it, Matthew suggests in fact that the necessary twofold
witness was forthcoming on this very point (26:60). It may be
that Matthew reflects the historical truth that the saying about
Jesus was used against Jesus at his trial. Luke omits the statement
altogether (22:66-71) and indeed in his report of Jesus' appearance before Pilate alludes to the tribute-money saying (23:2).
John applies the saying allegorically to the death and resurrection
of Jesus (2:19, 21). Since the Evangelists are all at pains to deal
with this difficult pronouncement in one way or another, it seems

likely that it both held a very secure place in the tradition and went back in some form to Jesus himself. Possibly Jesus uttered some such general prediction about the coming destruction of the Temple (by others) as is recorded in Mk 13:2, 'there will not be left here one stone upon another, that will not be thrown down'. Whether he also prophesied the rebuilding of a new Temple is very doubtful (contrast the view of Schweizer, *GNM*, p. 329). The Marcan form of the saying which contrasts **this temple that is made with hands** with **another, not made with hands** reflects the perspective of the Hellenistic Church which understood itself as the promised new Temple (cf. 1 C. 3:17; 2 C. 6:16; Eph. 2:22), the community whose rich inward spiritual life through the power and presence of the risen Christ made quite obsolete the outward observances of the old Temple (cf. Ac. 7:48; 17:24; Heb. 9:11, 24; Eph. 2:11). The phrase **in three days** may denote in Greek 'after a short interval', but it is just as probably an accommodation of the saying, by the Church responsible for it in this particular form, to the resurrection of Christ. But why then is Mark so reserved toward this statement which he has almost certainly taken over from the tradition of the Greek-speaking Church? Does he pass it off as false witness out of the desire 'to make verse 62 the sole ground of Jesus' condemnation' (see Nineham, p. 406, cf. p. 405), or because of uneasiness among those Christians who continued to observe the Temple worship (Taylor, p. 566)? It may be that, in view of the indications in Mark of a strong polemic against the ordinances and observances of the Temple (cf. 11:12–25; 13:2), he simply wished to de-emphasise or deny altogether the significance of a statement, which in the shape he knew it, appeared to suggest a continuing existence for the Temple in some form.

60–65. Since the witness given had been false and invalid, there was no reason why Jesus should have replied to the high priest's question, **Have you no answer to make?** There was as yet no charge to answer. Accordingly, his silence here had no doubt the profoundest theological significance for the Church that told or heard this story. The one who has all along surrendered himself completely to the will of God has no need of words to justify himself. The verbosity of his accusers is as much a means of protecting themselves from guilt and shame before God as of accusing him. The silence of Jesus is reminiscent of Isa. 53:7 and Ps. 38:12–14. The question that the **high priest** now puts to

Jesus, **Are you the Christ, the Son of the Blessed?** is introduced somewhat abruptly in so far as it has no obvious connection
with the foregoing proceedings, certainly not with the alleged
prediction on Jesus' part of the destruction of the Temple.
Although the description **Son of the Blessed** is a typically
Jewish reverential circumlocution for 'Son of God', it is quite
improbable that a high priest of the Saducean party would have
used this language in collocation with the term 'Christ' or
'Messiah'. The semblance of verisimilitude barely disguises the
fact, therefore, that here the Church has put its own language on
the lips of the high priest. The question then in turn becomes a
challenge to Mark's readers as to whether they can recognise the
essential paradox of the Gospel that nowhere more truly than in
the moment when his enemies are on the point of encompassing
his death is Jesus the Son of God. In view of the prevalence of the
secret in Mark, the reply of Jesus **I am** is somewhat surprising.
The reading found in some MSS, 'you say that I am' (or 'these are
your words, not mine') is probably an assimilation to the more
reserved formulation of Mt. 26:64. But in fact the **I am** in Jesus'
response in Mark does not preclude the necessity of faith, for the
claim to be **the Christ, the Son of the Blessed,** is not supported
by any appeal to credentials out of the past or to glorious prerogatives of the moment, but instead the hearer is pointed forward to
the *future* God will grant, the coming vindication of the Son of
man, when the victory wrought by God in Jesus will at last be
secured and plain for all to see. For Mark, the speaker here, the
harried and persecuted one, is the very one inseparably connected
with God's ultimate triumph. According to Mishnaic prescription,
the judge was to tear his garments on hearing blasphemy, and in
verse 63 it is recorded that **the high priest tore his mantle**
and said **you have heard his blasphemy** (64). **Blasphemy,**
however, involved using the name of God and railing against
him. Jesus has not done so here. In his statement about **the Son
of man** he has even used the respectful circumlocution **Power**
(or *the* **Power** = God). Are we to suppose, therefore, that his
claim to be **the Christ, the Son of the Blessed** or to sit as the
Son of man at God's **right hand** were regarded as tantamount
to blasphemy? It is not easy to say. Probably Mark wanted his
readers only to recognise that the decisive charge of blasphemy
was no less trumped up than all the others and that the hostile
forces of the world set against Jesus would go to any length to

justify themselves procedurally in getting rid of him. It is not clear whether Mark regards the statement **and they all condemned him as deserving death** as a judicial opinion or verdict or as an official sentence. The form of statement certainly allows him to stress yet again that of all those present *no one* escapes guilt and responsibility for the death of Jesus. The mocking and maltreatment of Jesus described in verse 65 Luke attributes to Jesus' captors before his trial (22:63–65). It is hard to imagine that the members of the Jewish high court would have so grievously flaunted the regulations for its orderly conduct. Accordingly the notice of the taunting of Jesus was most likely an originally independent piece of tradition. Inserted here in Mark, it dramatises the extreme vengefulness of spirit that had characterised the whole proceedings of the court. The forces lined up against Jesus as God's agent (cf. Isa. 50:6 and 53:35) are almost demonic in their cruelty. According to Luke Jesus is blindfolded and told 'Prophesy! Who is it that struck you?' (22:63), i.e. 'use your gift of clairvoyance to tell the striker's name'. A number of MSS of Mark also include the question 'Who is it that struck you?' possibly by assimilation to Lk. 22:63 or Mt. 26:68. If then the *RSV* **'Prophesy!'** is the correct reading, we have to understand it as: 'Play the prophet now!' in which case the words **to cover his face,** wanting from Mt. 26:67 and omitted in a few MSS of Mark, may be a later scribal gloss. The *RSV* **received him with blows** is a literal rendering of the Greek. The expression hardly means 'took him into custody with blows', but is probably a Latinism = 'slapped him repeatedly on the face' (the word for 'blow' here is the same as that used in the LXX of Isa. 50:6).

66–72. As we noted above, verses 66–67a are Mark's own way of linking the story of Peter's denial with the trial of Jesus. The disciple is 'distanced' from his Master, **Peter was below in the courtyard,** and is no participant in his Master's ordeal. The historicity of this story is scarcely in doubt. The Church would have had no reason to invent a tale that so denigrated one of its great leaders. Moreover it is related in a very matter-of-fact way and is conspicuously devoid of theological or apologetic motifs. It does not even raise the question of Peter's *faith* or the lack of it. Rather is it a matter of a servant-girl's recognition of Peter's identity as a member of the band of Jesus' followers. He could in the first instance have said Yes to her without too great risk. But this very factor may have had its own profound significance for Mark. Little enough is at stake for Peter. Everything, indeed God's whole plan for salvation, is at stake with Jesus. The form of Peter's reply, with its apparent tautology, **I neither know nor understand what you mean,** and his retreat **into the gateway** are signs of his confusion and embarrassment ('I could so easily have told this maid the truth!'). Here, as so often one lie leads to another, this time in more compromising and difficult circumstances for Peter, before **bystanders,** who are quick to detect the Galilean accent of his regional dialect, **you are a Galilean** (cf. Mt. 26:73, 'your accent betrays you'). After the word **gateway** (68) a number of MSS add 'and the cock crowed'. It is more likely that this would be a later insertion to prepare the way for verse 72, **and immediately the cock crowed a second time,** than that such words would have been omitted if Mark had himself included them. Accordingly, we may think of Mark as responsible for conforming the conclusion of the story (verse 72; note the characteristic Marcan **and immediately**) to the prediction of Jesus reported by him in 14:30. For Mark the word of the one who is outrageously treated and rejected by men is utterly sure and reliable. Peter is overwhelmed with remorse because he has heeded the sure word of his Master all too little. The verb translated **broke down** by *RSV* is really of quite uncertain meaning. Among suggested alternative renderings are 'covering his head', 'putting on his cloak', 'dashing out', 'set to and wept' or 'burst into tears'. In any case it is the fact that **he wept** that shows he is not heartless like the members of the Jewish court.

JESUS BEFORE PILATE 15:1–15

Read as a continuous story, this section presents numerous incongruous features. There is no retrospective glance at all at the previous proceedings of the Jewish high court. Between the handing over of Jesus to Pilate and the procurator's pressing of the charge against Jesus implicit in the question **Are you the King of the Jews?** things appear to happen with incredible speed. We noticed earlier how improbable it is that the obstinate and hardheaded Pilate would have been so swiftly prevailed upon by the Jewish authorities to move against Jesus, without rather protracted preliminary consultations. There is no hint of such here. Again it is odd that the substance of the case against Jesus implied in the title **King of the Jews** is presented right at the outset and that *after* that should come the somewhat hazy mention of the *many* accusations levelled by the chief priests and Pilate's amazement at Jesus' silence. The **Barabbas** episode, as introduced in verse 6 and developed in verse 8, raises the most serious historical problems since there is no evidence whatever in either Roman or Jewish sources of a Roman *custom* of releasing a prisoner each year at the Feast. Also Pilate's dalliance with the mob (8–9, 12–15), and not least his offer to release the prisoner before even any proper investigation is held (9), is incompatible with what we know of the stringencies of the Roman administration of justice. And how in the midst of a hearing before the procurator could the chief priests have had opportunity to inflame the crowd (sympathetic according to Mark's earlier testimony) against Jesus? Finally, there is no reference to a formal sentencing of Jesus.

We are forced to the conclusion that what we have here is anything but a straight transcript of the trial before Pilate. It is rather a mosaic of different pieces of tradition designed to bring out the deeper theological implications of what really went on in the trial, and so to promote the following challenging questions within the Church. Is not Judaism a lost cause, by-passed by God in his plan of salvation for men? For was not the onus for Jesus' death squarely on the Jews? To this question the narrative is at great pains to prompt a positive answer. Even in the midst of the hearing before Pilate it is the chief priests who are found still accusing Jesus of many things, acting out of envy, according to the insight of the procurator (10), and inciting the crowd to opt for the release of Barabbas instead of Jesus (11). By contrast, the Roman official, contrary to what we learn of his corrupt and violent nature from Philo and Josephus, for example, appears here in rather a good light (only less so than in Mt. 27:19, 24f. and 19:1–16), a matter of great significance for Gentile churches living in a Roman environment. Again, the narrative poses further questions: Can men accept that this Jesus who is so harshly treated goes to his death as King of the Jews and Son of God? Can men respond in faith to his mysterious and awesome *silence* (which makes even Pilate wonder) in face of the world's rage and in obedience to the will of God? Is it not exceedingly hard to be receptive to the good news that comes in and with Jesus, for do not men spurn it and follow their own worldly choices and whims, even as the crowd in Jerusalem demand the

release of a condemned criminal like Barabbas and crucifixion
for the altogether innocent Jesus?

1. The notice of a **morning** meeting of the Sanhedrin is not
intended to make the whole story comply with Jewish regulations
affecting the court—for that it was necessary that a sunset or
another day should intervene before the second meeting. It is not
even entirely clear that Mark has a *second* meeting in mind, since
the Greek words for **as soon as it was morning** mean literally
'forthwith, at an early hour' or simply 'very early'. If we could
accept for the reading followed in *RSV* **held a consultation** the
alternative reading found in some MSS, 'prepared a decision',
then the notion would be of a continuation and conclusion of the
night-time proceedings. At any rate Mark's own hand is in
evidence in 15:1, the vague temporal phrase, 'immediately early'
(*RSV* **as soon as it was morning**) and the redundancy involved
in the addition of **and the whole council** when the constituency
thereof has just been described, being characteristic. Presumably
then by the notice of 15:1 the Evangelist chiefly intends to show
that the Jewish deliberations were very *official* indeed. The evil
designs of the Jewish leaders against Jesus are all the more evil
because they do not spring from momentary feelings of passion,
but are worked out through a protracted legal process. The
word **delivered** frequent in Mark particularly in the passion
narrative (cf. e.g. 15:15), implies a handing over to that destiny
which God has willed for his chosen agent. **Pilate** is introduced
without any explanatory comment no doubt because he and his
part in the passion story were already familiar to Mark's readers.
Pontius Pilatus was the fifth Roman procurator of Judea and
held office in AD 26–36. How little interested in historical details
for their own sake is the narrative is apparent from the lack of
any mention of the location of the hearing before the procurator.
He was normally resident in Caesarea but generally came to
Jerusalem to keep order at the time of the feast. There he may
have occupied the palace of Herod the Great, or sometimes the
Fortress of Antonia in the northwest corner of the Temple area.
Either place might have been the scene of Jesus' appearance
before Pilate. Mk 15:16 favours the palace, Mt. 27:27 the
Fortress of Antonia. If the setting were the palace, then Luke's
special tradition of an appearance of Jesus before Herod becomes
more readily understandable.

2. The title King of the Jews, found here for the first time in the Gospel, figures prominently from now on (15:9, 12, 18, 26, 32). In the Greek form of Pilate's question the pronoun **You** is emphatic, and we may suppose he would actually have said something like: '*So you* are the one they claim is King of the Jews?' The title **King of the Jews** is a Roman mode of designation, with perhaps some irony in the use of a nationalistic term like 'Jews' (contrast the description of 'King of Israel' in 15:32; cf. Jn 1:49; 12:13). It is just at this point we see how telescoped the record of the trials is in Mark. There is no reference to Pilate's questioning of witnesses or of the accused and the charge implied in his question is introduced very suddenly. We are left to suppose that the Jewish authorities must have persuaded Pilate that Jesus constituted a serious political threat, of a treasonable and revolutionary kind, to the Roman *imperium* in Palestine (for such would be the force of the title to the Roman mind). Probably, however, Mark himself did not contemplate such a nuance, but regarded the designation **King of the Jews** as the Roman equivalent of the high priest's 'the Christ, Son of the Blessed' (14:61). There is little doubt that Mark regarded Jesus' answer **You have said so** (interpreted by some commentators as an admission, by others as a denial) as virtually a silence in the face of Pilate's question ('It is *you* who are doing the talking').

3–5. It is surprising that mention of the **many things** of which the chief priests accused Jesus should come only after the real charge already placed by Pilate. It emphasises again Jewish responsibility and also prepares the way for the story's emphasis on the *silence* of Jesus (**made no further answer,** verse 5). The comment that **Pilate wondered** not only serves to whitewash Pilate, but may symbolise for Mark that Gentile sympathy toward the gospel, which prepared the way for its spread among them (cf. 15:39).

6–8. Outside of the Gospels of Matthew, Mark, and John (it is omitted in Luke), there is no evidence for any such Roman custom as is described here. Attempts to trace the custom to the Maccabean era or to find an analogy in Livy's account of the *lectisternium*, the festival of the gods at which prisoners were released from their chains, are rather desperate. It does not follow, however, that the **Barabbas** incident is pure invention. That one Barabbas (always introduced in the Gospel as '*the* Barabbas', i.e. 'the well-known Barabbas') played some part in a minor insurrection of the time is more than likely historical fact.

Nevertheless, the story as told here contains numerous improba-
bilities. Pilate most surely need not have been placed in the
quandary described here, as though, if he released one condemned man, he had to execute the other. It was within his
power to acquit Jesus and at the same time grant an amnesty to
Barabbas. On the other hand, if Barabbas had already been
sentenced to death as an insurrectionist, only the emperor could
reprieve him. Accordingly we have to think of the Barabbas
report (which may go back historically to a known isolated case of
Roman clemency; see Schweizer, *GNM*, p. 335), in the form in
which it is inserted here, as theological in intent. It absolves the
Roman judge from having to pass a formal sentence against
Jesus and implicates *all* of Judaism directly (note **the crowd** in
verse 8). It also clearly poses for faith the challenge as to whether
it can trust the God in whose world his own Son, the *silent* one
amid the mob's howling, is handed over to be crucified, while the
condemned criminal goes free.

9–15. There is no suggestion in Pilate's question **Do you want
me to release for you the King of the Jews?** that the crowd
had come to him and already expressed a preference. Rather the
question here (in a form of words Pilate would scarcely have used)
both demonstrates again his own relative innocence and how
horrendous any other choice than Jesus must be. Nowhere else in
the Gospel does Mark ascribe **envy** or jealousy to **the chief
priests** (10), and he is careful to attribute the insight to Pilate
here. So he is able to stress once more Pilate's respect for Jesus,
Jesus' own innocence, and the altogether wicked motives of the
Jewish authorities in victimising him. There is scarcely need to
speculate about whether the chief priests were jealous because of
Jesus' popularity with the crowd. Nor should the statement that
the chief priests stirred up the crowd (11) lead us to think
about any characterisation of the crowd's fickleness here, nor to
speculate about whether this crowd is a group of dissidents,
partisans of Barabbas, and not the people who heard Jesus
gladly according to Mk 12:37. The narrative at this point is
devoted to this one thing, to showing up the *Jewish leaders* as the
arch-agents of evil who provoke *all* the people into clamouring
for Jesus' death. The grammatically strange sentence of verse 10
closes with the subject **the chief priests** and the word is immediately repeated at the beginning of verse 11, so their sinister role is
doubly emphasised. Possessed himself of the power of pardon or

acquittal, Pilate had no need to ask the Jews **what shall I do with the man . . . King of the Jews?** The question appears to imply that even granted the release of Barabbas, the Jewish people still had options open to them with regard to Jesus. They did not *require* to demand his death. The cry of **Crucify him** is thus revealed as all the more monstrously cruel. The Greek word (*palin*) for **again** is probably simply a connective here, meaning 'at this juncture', and not 'a device to express the stubborn and repeated rejection of Jesus' (Schweizer, *GNM*, p. 338). The more Pilate seems to uphold the innocence of Jesus (**Why, what evil has he done?**), the more insensate becomes the rage of the people. While Jesus in his silence follows God's will for him, Pilate **wishing to satisfy the crowd** follows the crowd's dictate. At the close the narrative shows considerable reserve. There is no mention of the gruesome details of the scourging, which was often inflicted on a prisoner before execution in order to weaken him, with a leather whip inset with pieces of bone and metal. All this is passed over here in a participial phrase, **and having scourged Jesus.** Jesus' suffering is more, much more than merely physical.

MOCKERY OF THE KING OF THE JEWS **15:16–20a**

This brief section is probably a later insertion into the earliest passion narrative. Verse 20*b* is a natural continuation of verse 15. Also, it is hard to think of Pilate's soldiers mocking Jesus in this way after the scourging which normally immediately preceded crucifixion. In John (19:1–3) the mocking comes earlier and Pilate's handing over of Jesus is followed at once by his being led out to crucifixion (19:16–17). In Luke, perhaps more correctly, the mocking is attributed to Herod and his soldiers (23:11). The brief description of the maltreatment of Jesus in verse 19*a* looks like an interpolation into the mime of taunting and may have been transferred from the tradition reported by Mark in 14:65. Mocking scenes quite similar to this one are found in the extravagant ritual of the Roman feast of the *Saturnalia* and the Babylonian festival known as the *Sacaea*, and Philo (*In Flaccum* 6, 36–39) tells how the citizens of Alexandria staged a mime in mockery of King Agrippa when he passed through Egypt on his way back from Rome. They seized an imbecile Jew, by the name of Carabas, put a paper crown on his head, wrapped him in a mat for a royal robe, and placed a papyrus reed for a sceptre in his hand. Far from disproving the historicity of the episode in Mark, the existence of several parallels tends to show that the mocking of Jesus could quite conceivably have taken place. However, the crucial thing for the Evangelist is that the scene depicted here once again poses most poignantly the question for faith. Can men trust that this Jesus who is so taunted and humiliated in the moments before his death, is *in very truth* King of the Jews and Son of God?

16-20a. The words **inside the palace** clearly indicate that the proceedings before Pilate have taken place in public, in the open air. The Greek word for **palace** more usually denotes 'courtyard', but the explanatory comment **that is, the praetorium,** introduced in a grammatically awkward way, supports the rendering **palace** here. The *praetorium* was the procurator's official headquarters in Jerusalem when he came from Caesarea, and possibly in view of what is known of the habits of procurators from Philo and Josephus, the old palace of Herod on the west of the city (rather than the Fortress of Antonia) is indicated in Mark. **The whole battalion** probably means a detachment ('company' or 'platoon') from the cohort which numbered 600 at full strength. The **purple cloak** is perhaps the scarlet cloak worn by Roman soldiers, and the **crown of thorns** is not necessarily an instrument of torture, but a mock imperial crown, made of thorny twigs. The salutation **Hail, King of the Jews!** is a parody of *Ave Caesar, victor, imperator.* The physical maltreatment described in 19a, **they struck his head with a reed and spat upon him,** seems to be an intrusion into the mime of taunting. In Mt. 27:29 the reed is given to Jesus in the first instance as a mock staff or sceptre, a symbol of kingly power. **They knelt down in homage to him:** possibly in a mock act of Caesar worship. The words **and when they had mocked him** remind us of the passion prediction of 10:33-34 in which it is stated, 'they will deliver him to the Gentiles and they will mock him'.

THE CRUCIFIXION **15:20b-26**

Many commentators are agreed that verses 20b-24a (down to the words **and they crucified him**) contain at least a nucleus which belonged to the earliest passion narrative. It is no longer possible to determine to what extent the offering to Jesus of a drink of **wine mingled with myrrh** or the dividing of **his garments** and the **casting lots** represents an embellishment of an originally bare and factual report, in the light of more protracted reflection on the *OT* and in line with *OT* texts, Psalm 69 and Psalm 22, the latter of which particularly assumed great importance for the Church in its reflection on the meaning of Christ's passion. Verse 25 would appear to be a later addition. The Greek reads 'and it was the third hour, *and* they crucified him', and the closing words duplicate those of 24*a* and are now coupled a little awkwardly with a note of time in accordance with the somewhat artificial Marcan scheme of the passion (see below). Possibly verse 26 also belonged to the earliest account of the passion, for although the inscription **The King of the Jews** is intended mockingly, it has an authentic ring, containing as it does just those insinuations of a political sort that would have led the Romans on their side to condemn and execute Jesus.

21. There is no good reason to doubt the historicity of this incident. It is introduced almost casually with no attempt to draw out any theological significance. Some scholars infer that **Simon** was enlisted to carry the cross-beam or *patibulum* (the upright plank would already be in place) because Jesus was exhausted and could not comply with the customary imposition on the condemned prisoner, but there is *no* hint of this in Mark. Nor from the Marcan standpoint does Simon yet conform to the true type of Christian discipleship which necessarily involved a free decision to follow Jesus in cross-bearing (cf. 8:34). In Luke there is an attempted development in this direction, when it is stated that 'they laid on him the cross, to carry it *behind Jesus*' (23:26). The episode is omitted altogether in John, perhaps because of the claim of the Gnostics that Simon became a substitute for Jesus and died in his stead. Presumably, in the first stages of its transmission, the tradition mentioned Simon by name to demonstrate that individuals existed who, by reason of their own involvement, could corroborate the actuality of those events on which the Church set such high store. **Simon of Cyrene,** otherwise unknown, may have been a pilgrim up from Cyrene in N. Africa for the feast. From the bare mention of his sons without any explanatory detail, **Alexander and Rufus,** common names in the early Church and therefore not easily identifiable with any known *NT* individuals (e.g. the Rufus of Rom. 16:13), we may assume they had become Christians and were well known in the Marcan community. If the statement that **he was coming in from the country** (= 'field' in Greek) indicates that 'he had just left off working in the fields', then this would militate against dating the crucifixion on the first day of Passover. But it is unwise to base any hypothesis on such a fugitive note as this, which most probably portrays Simon simply as a sojourner from outside the city who chanced upon the scene. Besides, we cannot even be sure that he *was* a Jew.

22. The name **Golgotha** is a transliteration of the Aramaic *gulgoltah* = 'skull'. The connexion of the spot with the burial place of Adam's skull is a later legend, and the suggestion that it was a skull-shaped rock just outside the city, and the tradition that it was located within the site of the present Church of the Holy Sepulchre are both quite uncertain. It need not have been a hill, but only a prominent place where the execution would serve as a dire warning to passers-by.

23-24. Wine mingled with myrrh: such a mixture would have been merely refreshing rather than pain-killing. Matthew has gall instead of **myrrh** (27:34) and so brings the account more into line with Ps. 69:21 (LXX): 'they gave me gall for food and for my thirst they gave me vinegar to drink' (cf. other echoes of this frequently used Psalm in Jn 2:17; 15:25; 19:28; Ac. 1:20; Rom. 15:3). We know that, in accordance with the injunction of Prov. 31:6, women of Jerusalem often administered an opiate to condemned criminals to alleviate their suffering, but we gather from the Talmud that it was a grain of incense as a narcotic that was put in the wine. But no doubt, although he speaks of **myrrh,** Mark has a sedative or analgesic potion in mind, and both he and his readers would have understood from the statement **but he did not take it** that Jesus allowed nothing to interfere with his full voluntary submission to the death God willed for him. **And they crucified him:** the verb is in the vivid narrative present tense in Greek, but the extreme reserve of the account at this point is striking. Nothing whatever is said of the physical agony involved in crucifixion, the contorted position of the body, the excessive strain on the heart, exposure to heat and insects, the longish time naked in this terrible posture in front of railing spectators before death finally supervened. Clearly the Church avoided dwelling on the physical details because it found in Jesus' passion a far profounder truth revealed of God's way with the world and men, and for his part Mark has had in view all along the *rejection* of Jesus as the bearer of God's word (cf. 3:6). **They divided his garments ... casting lots ... take:** an

exact fulfilment of Ps. 22:18. Although ownership of the prisoner's
clothes normally passed to the executioner, evidence is wanting
of any Roman practice of **casting lots** for them, and it is
reasonable to suppose that this detail in the narrative owes a great
deal to the *OT* text and the Church's reflection on it.

25-26. And it was the third hour: i.e. nine oclock in the
morning. The three-hourly intervals that are a feature of the
Marcan passion schema (reflecting the catechetical interests or
liturgical practices of the Church?) present difficulties (cf.
14:72; 15:1, 25, 33, 34, 42), particularly when we have to think
of all that is reported in 15:1-24 as taking place within a three-
hour period. In fact John fixes the moment when Jesus was condemned to die at twelve noon (19:14). The marking out of the
hours has to be sure its own theological significance. This is
God's time and throughout it his plan and purpose are steadily
worked out (see Schweizer, *GNM*, p. 346). **And the inscription
... Jews:** it was customary for the criminal condemned to
execution to carry in front of him or round his neck a tablet
(*titulus*) defining the charge against him, and then for it to be
exhibited on the cross. The charge in Jesus' case, ironic and
insulting to Jews and Jewish expectations (**The King of the
Jews**), is more likely authentic than not. It implies the kind of
treasonable or seditious activity on Jesus' part on the ground of
which the Romans would have executed him. In any case for
Mark it asks faith once again whether it can accept as the ultimate
truth what his enemies placard about Jesus only with biting
sarcasm, namely, that he is 'The King of the Jews'.

THE TAUNTING OF THE CRUCIFIED 15:27-32

It is highly improbable that the Church would have invented a
tradition that identified Jesus in his death with two notorious
criminals (verse 27). We may therefore take it for historical fact
that Jesus was crucified alongside **two robbers.** The fact is
reported quite straightforwardly in Mark. But the later Church
sought to overcome the scandal of the fact in different ways.
Verse 28, 'And the scripture was fulfilled which says, "He was
reckoned with the transgressors" ' (omitted by *RSV*), is found in
many MSS and versions, but a number of leading ancient authorities
leave it out and it is probably an addition from Lk 22:37. It
shows how the Church came up with an explanation for what
happened from *OT* prophecy, from Isa. 53:12. Another line of

development appears in Luke where the presence of the two criminals provides opportunity for a ministry of mercy on Jesus' part and the penitent thief evokes from him the promise of future blessing (Lk. 22:39-43). In John the **two robbers** have become simply 'two others' (19:18), who serve subsequently only to show how totally different is Jesus in his death (19:31-37).

The statement of verse 27 comes awkwardly where it stands in Mark. It would follow verse 25 more naturally as indeed verse 29 would follow verse 26. Possibly Mark took the report of the three acts of taunting in verse 29-32 (brought together out of catechetical interest?) from his tradition and used verse 27 as a preface to them and to prepare for verse 32b. The narrative of verses 29-32 appears to have been built up not out of independent historical tradition but out of the charges brought forward at the trial before the Jewish high court (14:58 and 61) and of *OT* allusions (cf. Ps. 22:6ff.; Wis. 2:17ff. and Ps. 69:9). The taunt of the **chief priests** and **scribes** in 31-32 is almost a doublet of the taunt of the passers-by in 29-30, and has the effect of emphasising once again the bitter hostility of the Jewish authorities to Jesus. It is most unlikely that chief priests and scribes would have been present at a crucifixion at the time of Passover. Accordingly we are dealing here with an idealised scene, and we have to pay close attention to its *theological* significance.

27-30. The words **one on his right and one on his left** are not a trivial detail. Jesus occupies *the* central position. That passers-by should have **derided** (literally 'blasphemed', the very charge levelled against Jesus himself) Jesus is quite plausible historically. **Wagging their heads:** a gesture of contempt in the orient (cf. Isa. 37:22; Jer. 18:16). The recurrence of the words about the destruction of the **temple** in the taunt is further indication of what a deep imprint they had made on the mind of the Church, but their force here is simply to suggest that if Jesus was possessed of the supernatural powers implied by his claim about the Temple he could surely save himself. The chief priests are hardly likely to have said in so many words **he saved others:** it looks like a statement of the Church placed on their lips. Even if they had said something like 'he sought to help others', they would have intended it sarcastically. In contrast with the Roman inscription 'King of the Jews', the designation **the king of Israel** (used ironically also of course by the chief priests here) is a Jewish title of *religious* honour and dignity.

The railing words **Let the Christ . . . that we may see and believe** represent for Mark the ultimate repudiation of the good news as he understands it. In asking for visible or tangible proof of the divine presence and power in Jesus, the chief priests align themselves with 'this (wicked) generation' which seeks from Jesus a sign from heaven, and which he *absolutely rejects* (Mk 8:11–12). Moreover, to yield to their request would have been for Jesus to abandon the abiding principle previously enunciated by him, 'whoever would save his life will lose it, and whoever loses his life . . . will save it' (Mk 8:35). Men's refusal to believe except on the ground of what is demonstrated by God in a worldly way before their very eyes, is of the essence of unfaith. According to Mark, the God of Jesus does not break in with a majestic or miraculous display of power to rescue his own Son from the cross. Jesus has to endure the cross to the end. Nor does he intervene miraculously to rescue the righteous or the martyrs in history from their sufferings or from death. The God of Jesus challenges men to trust him in the darkness, when no miracle takes place, when the worst that could happen does happen, and to trust him above all just then. According to Mark, the God of Jesus is nowhere more truly present to faith than in the very moment when his own Son is most utterly alone, forsaken by all the world, and even **reviled** (cf. Ps. 69:9) by the criminals crucified beside him. Just here in the Gospel, therefore, we are confronted with a central theme of Mark's whole message, and not least with an important clue to his own attitude to the miracles of Jesus.

THE DEATH OF JESUS AND THE GENTILE'S BELIEVING RESPONSE
15:33–39

The story of the crucifixion is told with remarkable restraint. There is no appeal to the reader's emotions nor any stress on the physical aspect of Jesus' suffering. His agony is God-related and is intensified by the mocking *unbelief* of those around him (verse 36). It is difficult to decide, however, how much of the story belongs to history or at least to the earliest passion narrative. Possibly the initially sympathetic gesture of a soldier in offering Jesus a drink has been transformed into a further act of taunting (verse 36) which not only serves to heighten the spiritual anguish of Jesus but presents a striking contrast with verse 39; one mocks, another believes, both having witnessed the same event. The last loud mysterious cry of Jesus, mentioned in verse 37 but not explained in any way, was probably transmitted accurately to the Church. Verse 34 may represent an attempt by the Church, in its predilection for Ps. 22 as furnishing materials for an understanding of the passion, to articulate Jesus' last cry on the basis of Ps. 22:1. In view of the importance Mark attaches to the term **Son of God,** he may have been responsible himself for the addition of the centurion's confession in verse 39, which now contrasts so vividly with the railing unfaith described in verse 36. Verses 33 and 38 are legendary or symbolic accretions by which the Church has sought to explicate the significance of Jesus' death for all the world. We should accordingly approach this report less with an eye to exact historical reconstruction than to its major contribution to the theological meaning for the Church of the event of the cross.

33. The naming of the hours, **the sixth hour** and **the ninth hour,** is a reminder once more that God is in control of this whole time, particularly here since the **darkness over the whole land,** beginning at **the sixth hour** (= noon) is a fulfilment of the prophecy of Am. 8:9: 'And on that day, says the Lord God, I will make the sun go down at noon, and darken the earth in broad daylight.' It is rather beside the point to ask whether the darkness might have been caused by a *sirocco* duststorm (Luke appears to have thought of an eclipse, 23:45), or to adduce parallels from pagan records of portents accompanying great events in the lives of outstanding figures of history like Julius Caesar. The Evangelist and his readers would have envisaged a supernatural darkness symbolising the advent of the divine judgment (cf. Isa. 13:9ff.; 50:2f.; Jer. 15:6ff.) with the death of Christ on the cross, which the Church also, significantly enough, believed to be the supreme act of God's mercy and love.

34. The Marcan form of Jesus' cry, given first in Aramaic and then Greek, occasioned difficulty for the Church later, and both Luke and John have omitted it, the former substituting: 'Father, into thy hands I commit my spirit' (Lk. 23:46) and the latter: 'It is finished' (Jn 19:30). Among modern commentators, also very sensitive to the difficulty, it is usual to understand the cry not as a cry of utter dereliction but as the prayer of a righteous sufferer who, in quoting the first words of Ps. 22, really has the whole Psalm in mind and the whole Psalm tells of the sufferer's assurance of God's continual protection and final vindication.

But so to interpret the words of the cry is to lose a great deal of its amazing profundity. We may rather think of the Church that records this cry (especially significant for Mark who reports only this one word from the cross) as sustaining by it its conviction, that in his death Christ has penetrated into the abyss of all men's lostness, when all worldly props or supports have failed them and God himself seems to have gone. And yet in Christ's case, he will not let God go, but dares to cling to him and to name him still **My God, my God.** The cry of dereliction thus both plumbs the depths of all men's doubts and scales the height of faith, and through it Christ becomes a rallying-point for men in the last extremities of life. There may even be materials here for a constructive understanding of the notion of Christ's descent into hell, and part of a little poem by Edwin Muir, 'The Good Man in Hell', is not inapposite:

> If a good man were ever housed in hell,
> Would he at last, grown faithful in his station,
> Kindle a little hope in hopeless hell,
> Sow among the damned doubts of damnation,
> Since here someone could live, and could live well?

35-36. Behold, he is calling Elijah: this somewhat weird misunderstanding might well have arisen of necessity among Jews, on the basis of the Hebrew version of Ps. 22:1 as we have it in Matthew, *Eli, Eli* (27:46), but hardly on the basis of the Aramaic **Eloi, Eloi** in Mark. Again the **drink** offered to Jesus (36) is generally understood to be the executioners' *posca*, a mixture of water, egg, and vinegar favoured by Roman soldiers. The **one** who **ran,** therefore, would appear to be a Roman soldier (cf. Lk. 23:36f.), but it is as unlikely that a soldier would refer to **Elijah** as that any *Jew* would approach the cross with a refreshment. Probably verses 35-36 represent a fusion of two initially separate traditions. The one, possibly historical, related a gesture of sympathy on the part of a soldier. The other (later) tradition, perhaps arising out of the historical datum of an unexplained and inarticulate last cry (verse 37), told of the mistake, **he is calling Elijah.** The *OT* witness to the fact that Elijah did not die but was translated directly to heaven (2 Kg. 2:9-12) gave rise to the later Jewish legend that he would return to the aid of the godly in time of need. The fusion of the two traditions, has resulted in the transformation of the whole episode into an act of mocking, which

now in a rather strange way shows up the malice of both Jews and
Romans, and at the same time demonstrates that in the last
moments of his passion Jesus has no solace whatever.

37. The Church obviously felt able to produce different
versions of Jesus' **cry.** In Lk. 23:46 it is a resignation to the will
and protection of God, in Jn 19:30 the victor's shout of triumph.
In view of 15:33, Mark may have thought of it as calling down
the judgment of God upon the world (cf. *1 En.* 62:2; 2 Esd. 13:4,
10). It is worth noting that the Evangelists appear to avoid the
more normal verbs for dying, and the word Mark uses for
breathed his last conveys the notion of a violent end.

38. And the curtain ... top to bottom: not a historical
reminiscence but a symbolic declaration of the meaning of
Jesus' death. It may have signified the divine judgment visited
upon the Temple and so upon the whole Jewish nation for its
sin (cf. the notice of the earthquake as a symbol of God's judgment
in Mt. 27:51). But probably the Evangelist interpreted the sign
in a more specifically *Christian* sense, the rending of the inner
curtain that stood before the Holy of Holies (cf. Exod. 26:31ff.;
40:21) symbolising for him the eradication of the Temple cultus.
Without the need to fulfil any prior ethnic, cultic, or religious
conditions, all men just where they are have now through Jesus'
death free and direct access to the gracious God. Further legendary developments of the tradition of verse 38 appear in Matthew
(see 27:51*b*-53) and in such later apocryphal gospels as the
Gospel of the Nazarenes and the *Gospel of Peter*, the former speaking
of 'the lintel of the Temple, of wonderful size, falling down in
fragments'.

39. As the words **saw that he thus breathed his last**
clearly indicate, the centurion's believing confession is a response
to Jesus' *death*. But by placing it at the close Mark has given it
special prominence and has no doubt understood it as an outstanding example of the truth enshrined in the statement of verse
38. In Jesus, and in the very moment of his death, God has unexpectedly turned in his mercy toward all men just where they
stand, even if it be entirely outside the pale of Jewish religious
ordinances. Though it is not definitely stated, the **centurion**
here is obviously a *Gentile*, and his expression of faith shows how
much the barrier between man and God is now eradicated
(cf. Heb. 9:1-12, 24-28; 10:19-25; cf. Eph. 2:14-15). **Truly
this man was a son of God:** the *RSV* rendering *a* **son of God**

is faithful enough to the Greek. In recognition of their extraordinary or indeed 'divine' powers, leaders of mankind such as emperors or rulers or philosophers like Pythagoras, Plato, or later Apollonius of Tyana, could also be hailed as 'son of God' or 'saviour'. But it is barely conceivable that Mark has in mind here anything else than a full and authentic Christian acknowledgement of Jesus as '*the* Son of God' (cf. Mk 1:1). Toward this climactic disclosure, hinted at from the beginning but in reality hidden from a blind world, Mark's whole Gospel has been moving inexorably. It is crucial for Mark's theology that the centurion's believing response arises not out of any overt claim made by Jesus nor out of any preconceived notion on his own part about who Jesus is, but only on the basis of what is accomplished in Jesus' death. Precisely there, in the obscurity, lowliness, and humiliation of the cross, and not in any miraculous display of power such as an unbelieving world demands in *proof* of God's presence, the God of Jesus confronts men. Only in and through his death on the cross can it become known who Jesus really is, the one in whom God seeks out men to fulfil his saving purpose with them. Then and only then too can true discipleship to this Jesus become possible.

WOMEN BY THE CROSS 15:40–41

This short report anticipates and paves the way for 15:47 and especially 16:1–8. But it may contain a genuine historical reminiscence of the presence of women near the cross. In view of the prevailing Jewish denigration of the validity of female witness, this tradition is hardly likely to have arisen as a means of providing reliable first-hand testimony to the crucifixion.

40–41. Women looking on from afar: up to this point in the Gospel **women** have played a minor part. Their introduction here is sudden, but necessitated by 15:47 and 16:1–8. The statement that they looked on **from afar** may support the historicity of the statement, since they would scarcely in fact have been allowed to stand in closest proximity to the cross (contrast Jn 19:25–27). **Mary Magdalene:** not mentioned previously by Mark, but Lk. 8:3 provides some information about her. She came from Magdala on the west side of the Sea of Galilee, and is an important witness of the Easter event in Jn 20:1–18 (cf. Mk 16:1–8). **Mary the mother of ... Joses:** the Greek of 15:47 would be more naturally taken to mean 'the *daughter* of

Joses', and that of 16:1 'the *daughter* of James', and the Greek of
the present verse could indeed be translated as 'Mary the daughter
of James the younger and the mother of Joses'. But it seems that the
intention here (by way of correction of the two variants?) is to
designate this Mary as the mother of the two men (as in *RSV*).
The description of **James** as **the younger** (literally = 'the small')
is to distinguish him in either stature or age from some other
James. The **James** and **Joses** mentioned here are introduced
without explanatory comment, and must have been well known
in the Marcan community, like the Alexander and Rufus of
15:21. Since Mary the mother of Jesus would hardly have been
described in this fashion, James and Joses are obviously not the
brothers of Jesus referred to in 6:3. **Salome:** described by
Matthew as 'the mother of the sons of Zebedee' (27:56). Since
the group of the Twelve, or now the Eleven, called by Jesus have
vanished from the scene, presumably having fled back to Galilee,
the tradition of the women's presence near the cross allows Mark
once more to place his typical emphasis on the theme of discipleship or following, and the mention of **Galilee** prepares for the
intimation of the new discipleship that will become possible
there in the light of Easter (16:7). Would Mark also have intended
the statement of verse 41 as an encouragement to faithful discipleship among the women of his own community?

THE BURIAL OF JESUS 15:42-47

The comment of J. A. Bengel is instructive—*sepultura mortem
ratam fecit*, 'the burial officially confirmed the death (of Jesus)'.
The story of the burial would have served the early Church as a
retort to the anti-Christian polemic against the Easter message
that insisted that Jesus only *appeared* to have died on the cross
(see especially verses 44–45). Possibly also *OT* passages like Isa.
22:16 and 33:16 (LXX) wielded some influence on the description of the tomb in verse 46. But the claim of this report to be
considered substantially historical is not thereby too seriously
impaired. It reflects the (actual) defection of the disciples, and
it is not easy to conceive of the Church inventing an account
which accorded to a *pious Jew* the privilege of providing an
honourable burial for Jesus. Moreover the discrepancy between
the way the second Mary is named in 15:47 and in 15:40 and 16:1
suggests, as E. Schweizer notes (*GNM*, p. 361), that this story was
originally an independent unit, scarcely designed to prove that

the women who saw the empty tomb could not have been mistaken about its location since the very same women had witnessed the entombment.

42. Here for the first time we learn that Jesus was crucified on Friday, **the day of Preparation,** correctly explained by Mark as **the day before the sabbath.** The Friday is consistent with Jn 19:42. However, Jn 18:28 suggests that the Passover fell on the sabbath or Saturday, whereas according to the Marcan chronology **the day of Preparation** on that year coincided with the Passover. Now since the present account says nothing about the coming **sabbath** being Passover, it does not support Jn 18:28 nor indeed does it give us any help in reconciling the Marcan and Johannine chronologies. Within the Marcan chronological scheme the difficulties are compounded by the fact that if **'the day of Preparation'** were the Passover, the actions attributed to Joseph in verse 46 would be pretty well impossible then also. Probably it is best to think of 15:42–47 as an originally independent report which handed on (correctly?) Friday as the day of the crucifixion, in which case the haste implied in the story about preparations for the burial is well accounted for (see further, Nineham, p. 433). In order to be consistent with **the day of Preparation, evening** in verse 42 has to be taken to mean, as it could mean, 'in the afternoon before sundown', since with sundown the sabbath would already have begun.

43. Joseph of Arimathea: unknown aside from this story. **Arimathea** is most likely the Ramathaim (northwest of Lydda) of 1 Mac. 11:34. It is not certain whether **member of the council** depicts Joseph as a member of the Great Council or the Sanhedrin in Jerusalem (cf. Lk. 23:51) or of some local council, probably the latter. The adjective rendered **respected** in *RSV* means 'of good social status' or in popular usage 'rich' (cf. Mt. 27:57). In Matthew (27:57) Joseph is drawn within the orbit of faith *in Jesus*, being described as 'discipled to Jesus'. The later *Gospel of Peter* portrays Joseph as 'the friend of Pilate and of the Lord'. The description in Mark, however, is consistent with the attitude of a loyal Pharisee who in **looking for the kingdom of God** was simply sharing the messianic expectations of his people. Such an one would also have shared the usual Jewish scruples about the dead, especially the dead bodies of criminals who were regarded as unclean, and would have been sensitive to the law of Dt. 21:22f., a criminal's 'body shall not remain all night upon the tree' (cf. Ac. 13:29). The fact that Joseph **took courage** (or 'ventured boldly') in going to Pilate implies that he was aware of asking for a favour and that the granting of it would be something of an exception.

44-45. The sequence of the narrative in which verse 46 would follow very smoothly on 43 is interrupted by verses 44-45. These are probably a later addition arising out of the Church's Easter apologetic and designed to show that Jesus was not removed from the cross *before death* (cf. Mt. 27:64). From the Marcan standpoint there could be no more reliable witness of the actuality of Jesus' death than **the centurion,** who has already been described as one 'who stood facing him' (39). The harsh reality of the death is underlined also by the use of the Greek word *ptōma* = 'corpse' (*RSV* **body**).

46. While the actions of Joseph depicted here may echo such passages as Isa. 22:16 and 33:16 (LXX), they are none the less quite compatible with known Jewish custom. The dead were usually buried not in cemeteries but in tombs hewn out of the rocks or in natural caves outside the city wall. Bodies were laid in recesses or on slabs of stone and the entrance was sealed with a large rectangular or rounded stone, which could be moved but not without some effort.

47. The statement about the women being *throughout* witnesses of the crucifixion (the Greek verb for **saw** is in the imperfect) is often thought to be a later addition (see e.g. Taylor, p. 602), again part of the Church's Easter apologetic aimed at showing that the women who discovered the empty tomb could not possibly have been mistaken about where Jesus was buried. But the women are listed differently here from Mk 16:1, and the notice may in fact have belonged to the initially independent story of the burial. At all events the important role ascribed to these women in early Christianity is all the more remarkable in view of prevailing Jewish and Greek denigration of women's status.

THE STARTLING NEWS THAT JESUS IS STILL ON THE MOVE 16:1-8

The so-called Longer Ending of 16:9-20 is found in most of the extant MSS of the Gospel, and the Shorter Ending of 16:9-10 in a considerable number, sometimes in place of and sometimes as a preface to the Longer Ending. But it is now almost universally agreed that these Endings are spurious and should be consigned

to the margin as in *RSV*. Accordingly to the best of our knowledge
the earliest form of Mark that can be traced ended at 16:8, and
the fact that neither Matthew nor Luke appears to show any
acquaintance with anything in Mark beyond that verse suggests
also that the form they used closed there. However, as a conclusion
to the Gospel, 16:1–8 presents a whole series of problems which
have for long been much debated. Could Mark possibly have left
his readers in the lurch by failing to report any appearance of the
risen Jesus to his own, and so in effect failing to report God's
vindication of Jesus through a triumphant reversal of the seeming
disaster of the cross? The principal objections to regarding 16:1–8
as the original ending of the Gospel are as follows:

(1) Everywhere else in the Gospels, as in 1 C. 15:3–8, the
    reality of the resurrection depends not upon the empty
    tomb but upon the *appearances* of the risen Jesus. This is not
    so in Mark!

(2) Since the resurrection is intimated in the passion predictions
    of 8:31; 9:9, 31; 10:34, we might expect an announcement
    of the fulfilment at the close of the Gospel.

(3) So starkly has the story of Peter's denial been told and so
    deeply embedded in the tradition is information about the
    appearance of the risen Jesus to Peter (1 C. 15:5; Lk. 24:34;
    Jn 21:15–19), that we might have looked to Mark also to
    mention Peter's restitution through an encounter with the
    resurrected one.

(4) Verse 8 ends abruptly enough in English, but even more
    abruptly in Greek with the enclitic particle *gar* = **for**
    after the verb **they were afraid.** It is unusual for this
    word to end a sentence, far less a book.

(5) To assume that Mark expected his readers to grasp the
    reality of the resurrection through these puzzling and
    highly allusive eight verses is to accord to him a degree of
    literary sophistication he could scarcely have possessed.

Defenders of the case against Mk 16:1–8 generally suppose
that the Evangelist intended to add something after verse 8,
probably an appearance to Peter and the Twelve, but either he
was prevented by some accident from doing so or a portion of his
manuscript was lost, as could happen with papyrus leaves or
scrolls (see e.g. Schweizer, *GNM*, p. 367). Of course there is no

evidence for such conjectures, and in fact some telling arguments can be adduced for considering 16:1–8 to be the genuine ending:

(1) It is hardly correct to infer that the Evangelist regards the *empty tomb* (without the appearances of the risen one) as a sufficient proof of the resurrection (see e.g. Johnson, p. 263). Indeed the angelic messenger at the tomb points away from the tomb itself to a new rendezvous of the risen Jesus with his disciples in Galilee. Here too then, as in the other Gospels, the empty tomb becomes a signpost to what really matters, the new encounter of the living Jesus with his own (cf. 1 C. 15:3–8).

(2) Throughout his Gospel Mark resists and restrains every tendency to think of God as disclosing himself in open manifestations of power in the world for all to see ('the messianic secret'). The hidden presence of God in the ministry of Jesus as the lowly bearer of his word is the constant challenge presented to faith. And it is as the bearer of God's word that Jesus three times (8:31; 9:31; 10:34) prophesies the coming vindication in the resurrection. Since for Mark Jesus' word in itself is altogether pure and trustworthy (see 13:23), conceivably he preserved its integrity every bit as much by not recording its fulfilment *in the form of a concrete appearance-story.*

(3) The singling out of Peter in 16:7, '**and** particularly **Peter**' Mark may well have regarded as sufficient indication of the retrieving of the desperate situation occasioned by his denial. The focus in Mark is on the *divine* promise (set forth in the angel's message), and the divine promise is adequate guarantee of the coming reality.

(4) Recent investigation has tended to confirm that the Greek particle *gar* = **for** could on occasion end a sentence or even a paragraph, if not a book. But Mark is fond of using the word *gar* in short, sharp parenthetical comments, as in the somewhat inelegant **for it was very large** in 16:4, and his inelegance of style could possibly have allowed him to end even a book with *gar*, especially since the subject of the verb **they were afraid** is so clearly visible in what has gone before and there was no need for him to add *hai gynaikes* = **the women** after *gar*.

(5) Are verses 1–8 really so allusive that only a literary sophisti-

cate could have produced them? Do they not rather in a few strokes say everything needful from the Marcan standpoint—the angelic message that Jesus is no longer in the realm of the dead and the promise of a new companion-ship with Jesus for the disciples? Again the *silent* dread with which the record closes can be taken as a sign of the awe and reverence of those for whom the old world has run its course and the new day of God is actualised through the living Jesus who is on the move toward encountering men.

Even if, like the present writer, one favours the view that Mark's procedures and attitudes throughout the Gospel are consonant with his intention to conclude with 16:1–8, perplexing questions of interpretation within these verses still remain.

1. From the words **when the sabbath was past** we have to assume that the women bought spices after sunset on the Saturday evening for use early the next morning, that is the Sunday, the first day of the *Jewish* week. The manner in which the women are listed here agrees rather better with 15:40 than with 15:47, and this shows, as does the repetition of names in 15:47 and 16:1, that the story of the burial was originally quite independent of 16:1–8, and no attempt has been made to harmonise them. Mark's account presupposes that the body of Jesus was never in fact anointed (contrast Jn 19:40). It was customary for relatives to visit a grave for three days after the burial. But that Palestinian women should think of entering a grave (even aside from the difficulty implied in verse 3) to anoint a body a day and two nights after death, **that they might go and anoint him,** is extremely doubtful. For all its strangeness, from the Marcan standpoint this notice serves to show that motivated as they were by ordinary desires, they had not the slightest expectation from the human side of the amazing divine sequel.

2. The phrase **very early** might normally be taken to suggest a time around 4 a.m. before daybreak. There is no need to suppose, however, that the clause **when the sun had risen** is a piece of Marcan typology that cannot refer to time at all, but to the 'Sun of righteousness' of Mal. 4:2 (LXX) who now has risen to over-come the darkness (see A. G. Hebert, *SJT* 15 (1962), pp. 66ff.). J. Jeremias has shown in fact that with Mark where two notes of time are recorded and the second seems to be merely pleonastic, it is intended to interpret the first (cf. 1:35; 14:2; 15:42. See Jeremias, *EW*, p. 3). So here 'after sunrise' defines the vaguer 'very early', perhaps with a view to confirming clearly the *third* day as the day of resurrection.

3-4. The women, who had witnessed the burial, might have been expected to raise the question **Who will roll away the stone ...?** before this present juncture. Matthew reports the sealing and guarding of the tomb in 27:62–66, and does not attribute to the women any intention of entering it (28:1; contrast Mk 16:1 **that they might go and anoint him**). Placed here in Mark, the question indicates that they are still looking only for *human* support or help. The added parenthetical comment **for it was very large** would have more naturally accompanied the question of verse 3, but it is typical of the Evangelist's style, and set down where it is by him, it is the first hint in the story of a mysterious *divine* intervention.

5-6. Mark's reserve toward the supernatural is evident from the way he introduces quite simply **a young man,** who is none-the-less clearly an 'angel', **a white robe** being the traditional garb of heavenly beings (cf. 2 Mac. 3:26, 33; Rev. 7:9, 13f.). The mention of *two* angels in Luke's account (24:4) attests Luke's fondness for stressing the importance of double witness. The presence of an angel or angels at the tomb in the Gospel reports should not be taken as an invitation to speculation about the actual existence of heavenly beings. Rather it signalises for the Evangelists and the early Church generally that the really crucial thing is not the physical emptiness of the tomb in itself but the incomprehensible action of God which faith alone knows is taking place here. That we are here most of all in touch with the Church's believing grasp of the *divine* reality involved is apparent also from the fact that the first part of the angel's message **Do not be amazed ... crucified** is couched in Marcan language, and the second part **he has risen ... laid him** sounds like a con-fessional formula of the early Church (cf. Ac. 4:10). The angel's first words **Do not be amazed** are a vivid reminder that it is God himself who is drawing near in this moment. Consequently the women require to be calmed in their anxiety in face of the numinous. **You seek Jesus of Nazareth, who was crucified:** Luke's 'Why do you seek the living among the dead? (24:5) brings out the implications of this statement. In looking for Jesus, the women are still moving in the realm where death is sovereign. Not out of their sad thoughts, or even any imaginings or expectations they might entertain, but only from the side of God, could come any assurance that Jesus was in truth in the realm of the living. The additional explanatory note **who was crucified** was hardly necessary for women who had just watched everything with their own eyes. But placed in the closest proximity to the words **he has risen,** this note confirms that the risen one is no distant, unknown heavenly figure but in direct continuity with the Jesus who died on the cross.

The remainder of the angel's message **He has risen, he is not here ... laid him** is astonishing in its brevity, economy and restraint. As in the other Gospel reports, there is here no description of Jesus' rising again. The mystery of the resurrection, **he has risen,** is simply intimated first in a single word in the Greek (*ēgerthē*), the very form of which suggests the rendering, '*God* has raised him'. Only in the *second* instance is there a reference to the empty tomb **he is not here; see the place ... :** the tomb is but a sign or token of the great reality, God's decisive act in raising Jesus from the dead. Consequently, Mark does not regard the empty tomb as a necessary guarantee or proof of the factuality of the resurrection. In this he is in line with other *NT* witnesses (cf. 1 C. 15:3–5. Note also how the women's account of the empty tomb is disbelieved by the apostles in Lk. 24:11, how Peter and the other disciple are not yet convinced by their own discovery in Jn 20:9, and how Matthew senses the 'neutrality' of the empty tomb tradition, since viable alternative explanations are possible, Mt. 28:13). But even though the resurrection does not depend on the empty tomb, and the stories of the empty tomb and of the appearances do not seem to have been combined at an early stage of the tradition (see the variations in the way they have been brought together in the Gospels), it does not follow that the empty tomb report itself must have been a late development designed to corroborate the truth of increasingly 'concrete' appearance-stories. On the other side it may be claimed that in the Jewish context the idea of a 'bodily' resurrection must inevitably from the very outset have implied an empty tomb. Moreover, if the story were a late creation, it is most surprising that it does not name a host of witnesses. Instead in Jn 20:1 Mary Magdalene is the only witness (as a woman, a very poor one according to contemporary standards), and she figures prominently in all other accounts (e.g. Mk 16:1). Nevertheless, even if we accept the historicity of the empty tomb tradition, the fact remains that in the Easter testimony of the *NT* it is secondary to what is the real heart of Easter, the encounter of the crucified and now living Jesus with men.

7. A number of interpreters have argued on the basis of this verse that in his conclusion Mark has in mind not a resurrection appearance at all but the parousia which is to take place in Galilee as the land of eschatological fulfilment (see e.g. E. Lohmeyer, *Galiläa und Jerusalem*, Göttingen, 1936, and *Das Evangelium des Markus*, Göttingen, 1937, pp. 355f.). Lohmeyer in particular holds that in the Gospels and Acts the form **you will see** is not used for witnessing resurrection appearances of Jesus, and so must refer here to seeing Jesus in the glorious triumph of his parousia appearance. But this whole view rests on nothing surer than the prominence of Galilee in the Marcan record. Also John does employ the Greek verb for **see** in the active voice to denote 'seeing the risen Lord' (Jn 20:18, 25, 29; cf. 1 C. 9:1), and it is also significant that after the transfiguration, in Mk 9:9–13 there is no mention of the parousia, but the limit prescribed by Mark for the disciples' silence about Jesus' glory is the resurrection. Accordingly it is unlikely that **he is going before you to Galilee** (note the present tense indicating that he is on the move already) means 'he is going at the head of his band of disciples to lead them to Galilee for the final consummation'. Rather, what is in view is an encounter with the resurrected one in Galilee. It is highly important for Mark that as God's representative the angel brings *God's own word*, which here confirms the word of Jesus, **there you will see him, as he told you** (cf. 14:28). With the Evangelist this is sufficient indication that whereas a hostile world could not understand or endure the word of Jesus, God now endorses it and so vindicates his Son in the triumph of Easter. The singling out of Peter (**and Peter:** which should perhaps be translated 'and Peter in particular') recalls his denial. For Peter who denied his Master and for all the disciples who forsook him, it is not the end. The new day of God's mercy and forgiveness through the restoration of companionship with Jesus is now at hand.

8. At the dawning of this new day the women's flight, **trembling and astonishment** are understandable and their silence a foil to the resounding news *'he has risen'*. The *silent* fear with which Mark's record closes need not be taken as an editorial insertion on Mark's part (**they said nothing to anyone**) to account for the lateness of the empty tomb tradition, nor yet as an implicit condemnation of the women's craven-heartedness or blindness. Rather their fearful silence eloquently enough proclaims the truth that the first word and the last word of the good news is not anything men or women can think or say or do, but *God's own witness to his Son* (verse 7). If Mark's ending was at 16:8, abrupt though it is, he could hardly have declared more effectively that God's Word is mightier than man's words, or that it is first and foremost the God who speaks in Jesus and for Jesus who brings to pass the promise of Easter and confers the gift of Easter faith.

A LONGER ENDING SUPPLIED LATER 16:9–20

Some of the best MSS of Mark end at 16:8. Many others include these verses. But in vocabulary, style, and content they are unquestionably non-Marcan, and have a distinct flavour of the second century. Tatian's *Diatessaron* (around AD 140) shows knowledge of this passage and Irenaeus (around AD 180) accepts it as part of Mark's Gospel. A very dubious tradition from a MS of the tenth century names the presbyter Aristion (around AD 100) as its author. We may assume only that it was initially an independent report (see on 16:9) and was latterly attached to Mark's Gospel by some person or group who felt that the Gospel was incomplete without an appearance-story or stories, and wanted to align it with the other Gospels. The passage reads like a manual of instruction, designed to answer questions about the Easter event and its theological meaning, and consists mainly of Easter traditions drawn from the later Gospels and Acts. From this we may judge that it comes from the earlier part of the second century.

9–11. The opening verse shows that 16:9–20 originally circulated as an independent report. It begins *de novo* with the statement **when he rose early on the first day of the week,** which takes no account of Mk 16:1 or 16:6, and also **Mary Magdalene** is introduced as if for the first time, and appears here as a primary witness as in Jn 20:11–18. The words **from whom he had cast out seven demons** echo Lk. 8:2. Here too, as in Jn 20:18, Mary **went and told those who had been with him,** but unlike the author of 16:11 John includes no statement that **they would not believe it.** Presumably this author either valued woman's

witness lightly, or more likely in view of his further stress on
non-believing in verses 13–14 he wanted to strike at Easter disbelief in his community.

12–13. The Greek verb for **appeared** here is not that used of a
resurrection appearance in the primitive kerygmatic formula of
1 C. 15:3–5 or 1 C. 15:6–8, but it does occur in Jn 21:1, 14.
Verse 12 clearly echoes the Emmaus story of Lk. 24:13–35 and
seems to presuppose in the reader an acquaintance with the details of that story. **in another form** recalls that in the Emmaus
report the two disciples did not at first recognise Jesus. In verse 13
the narrator deviates from the Lucan record, which knows of no
rebuff of the word brought by the two disciples (Lk. 24:33f.),
and this only shows how much he wants to emphasise the theme
of unbelief, possibly because of troublesome questions and
doubts in his own congregation.

14. The reference to an appearance **to the eleven themselves
as they sat at table** is a secondary derivation from Lk. 24:36–43.
It is by no means certain that the narrator's stress on **their unbelief and hardness of heart,** which is here related specifically
to the testimony to the Easter event, reflects an understanding
of the prominent *Marcan* motif of the disciples' blindness (see
Schweizer, *GNM*, p. 375). He probably picked up the idea from
Lk. 24:38 ('Why are you troubled and why do questionings rise
in your hearts?') and used it as the basis for a rebuke to sceptics
in his own congregation.

After verse 14, Codex W, a Greek MS from the fifth century,
includes a short passage commonly known as the *Freer Logion,* after
the name of the manuscript's original owner. Elsewhere it is
quoted only by Jerome in Latin and his citation provides a little
help in reconstituting the rather corrupt Greek text: 'And they
replied saying, This age of lawlessness and unbelief is subject to
Satan who, by the agency of the evil spirits, does not allow the
true power of God to be understood; therefore reveal thy righteousness now, they said to Christ. And Christ said to them: The limit
of the years of Satan's authority has been reached, but other
terrible things are drawing near, even for the sinners on whose
behalf I was delivered up to death, that they might turn to the
truth and sin no longer, in order that they might inherit the
spiritual and incorruptible glory of righteousness which is in
heaven.' This late (second- or even third-century?) interpretation
is obviously the work of a writer who wanted to enter his own

apology for the apparently impenetrable hardness of heart of the disciples in verse 14. He does so in an apocalyptic-sounding oracle, penned in a day of crisis and distress probably, which starkly depicts the fearsome unbelief of the times as due to Satan's rage. It then puts forth the assurance that Satan's dominion is ended, but at the same time holds out the prospect of a further period of travail through which only the truly contrite can have a hope of the final heavenly inheritance. So does the interpolator furnish an explanation of the unbelief of verse 14, and also an answer of sorts to the faithlessness of his day (see further Nineham, p. 453; Schweizer, *GNM*, p. 376).

15-16. The commission of verse 15 **Go into all the world . . .** is founded on Mt. 28:19 (cf. Mk 13:10; Lk. 24:47; Ac. 1:8), and greatly stresses the universality of the Gentile mission. The missionary injunction in the Longer Ending comes very abruptly after the stern rebuke to the disciples for their unbelief in verse 14, but the narrator in his wisdom knows that the way to overcome unbelief is not by argumentation but by a proclamation of the risen Lord himself that challenges men to an immediate response in missionary action. In Mt. 28:19 baptism figures also in the injunction of the exalted Lord. Here, however (verse 16), in contrast with Mt. 28:19 and also with Ac. 2:38, 'baptism' and 'belief' (at least on the positive side of the declaration) are incorporated in a narrower and more restrictive formula which reflects a growing exclusivism on the part of the Church that employs it.

17-18. The term for **signs** is not used by Mark of Jesus' mighty works, but is frequent in John (e.g. 2:11, etc.). The promise of charismatic gifts held out here to **those who believe** indicates clearly enough that the narrator belonged to a community which held that speaking in tongues, exorcism, and healing were not confined to the Church's most primitive age but were the *ongoing* marks of authentic Christian faith. All the signs mentioned can be paralleled elsewhere in the New Testament (Mk 9:38ff.; 1 C. 14; Ac. 2:4ff.; 10:46; 28:3ff.; 1 C. 12:9, 28; Ac. 5:12; 9:12; Jas 5:14f.), with the exception of drinking poison, **drink any deadly thing,** without harmful effect. Eusebius (*HE* 3.39.9) records, however, that Papias told a story of a certain Justus Barsabbas who did not die after drinking poison. It is interesting that the spectacular miraculous powers described in 17-18 are not accompanied by any mention of the

Spirit or the Spirit's inspiration, but simply are effected **in my name.**

19–20. The narrator seems to envisage the exaltation of Jesus to the heavenly session **at the right hand of God,** a favourite theme of the early Church under the influence of Ps. 110:1, as taking place immediately on Easter Day in accordance with Lk. 24:51 rather than with the forty days' interval of Ac. 1:3. But he shares the conception of Acts that Christ's ascension made possible and in fact initiated the missionary preaching of the gospel to all the world, and that far from remaining the 'distance of heaven' from them the Lord stayed close to his followers to empower them for their missionary service.

A SHORTER ENDING SUPPLIED LATER **16:9–10**

In the MSS and versions in which it occurs this short addition is sometimes an alternative to, sometimes a preface to the Longer Ending. Unlike the latter, it was obviously written with the express purpose of providing the necessary conclusion to what its author took to be an otherwise incomplete Gospel. Consistently with 16:7 it singles out Peter (cf. 1 C. 15:5). It shares the view of the Longer Ending that Easter inaugurated the missionary preaching. The language is most certainly non-Marcan, and the phrase **from east to west** implies a time when the Gentile mission was already very far extended in the Roman world, just as the words the **sacred and imperishable proclamation of eternal salvation** suggest advanced Hellenistic thinking.

These Endings can hardly be regarded as canonical. Yet they do have their own intrinsic significance. They show us how the Church continued to think of Easter as central and decisive, as the hinge of its history and belief and above all of its missionary proclamation and service. The Longer Ending represents one of the earliest attempts we know to construct a harmony of Easter events out of the varied data of the Gospels and Acts. The ancient harmony has its modern counterpart in the (unprofitable) endeavours of some modern critical scholars to piece together out of the many items of 1 C. 15:3–7, the Gospels and Acts a con-tinuous narrative of all that happened. Over against that, from the variety of Easter reports in the *NT* and from the rather tentative way in which several different reports are brought together in Matthew, Luke, and John respectively, it seems cer-tain that in the Church's first age single Easter stories at first circulated independently (contrast the earliest consecutive passion narrative) and each would have been sufficient in itself to promulgate the glad news 'He is risen'. The truth of Easter as the Church experienced it was manifold. It meant the bestowal of God's mercy and forgiveness, as even to Peter the denier, through renewed companionship with Jesus; it meant the coming of the peace that makes men whole (Jn 20:19–21) and the reinforcement of the Spirit's power (Jn 19:22); it meant the forging of a new and indissoluble community (Ac. 1:12–14); it meant the God-given impulse to missionary preaching and service to all the world (Mt. 28:16–20). The manifold truth of Easter has never been dependent on men's ability to agree on a uniform *mode* of Jesus' rising again or to reconstruct precisely what happened. The all-important thing is the fulfilment of the promise already enshrined in Mk 16:7, 'You will encounter him.'

GENERAL INDEX

INDEX OF AUTHORS